THE OTHER BOSTONIANS

Harvard Studies in Urban History
Series Editors: Stephan Thernstrom and Charles Tilly

Published in cooperation with the Joint Center for Urban Studies of the Massachusetts Institute of Technology and Harvard University

STEPHAN THERNSTROM

The Other Bostonians POVERTY AND PROGRESS IN THE AMERICAN METROPOLIS 1880–1970

Harvard University Press, Cambridge, Massachusetts, 1973

Library of Congress Catalog Card Number 73-77469
SBN 674-64495-6
Printed in the United States of America

TO ABIGAIL

acknowledgments

In the several years that this study has been in preparation, I fear that I have incurred more debts than a single book can possibly repay. Generous research support has come from several quarters: the American Council of Learned Societies; the John S. Guggenheim Memorial Foundation; the Mathematical Social Science Board; the American Philosophical Society; the Joint Center for Urban Studies of the Massachusetts Institute of Technology and Harvard University; the Institute of Government and Public Affairs, University of California, Los Angeles; and the Committee on Research of the Faculty Senate, University of California, Los Angeles Division.

With these funds I was able to retain a group of undergraduate and graduate assistants who ransacked the musty archives of Boston in search of evidence about the 7965 representative citizens whose life histories are treated here, and painstakingly coded this massive body of material for computer analysis. Once Norman Abrams, Donald Acklund, Margaret Beal, Michael Foley, David Handlin, Suzanne Keaney, and Glenn Padnick had done their work, Peter Allaman and Mary Hyde supplied the programming skill necessary to process the data through the computing facilities of Harvard University and the Massachusetts Institute of Technology. Further assistance with the research came from Marlou Belyea, Suzanne Bloom, Nancy Falik, Jack Larkin, and Ellen Mandel.

For suggestive comments on portions of the manuscript circulated earlier in various forms I am indebted to Sune Akerman, Donald G. Bogue, Samuel S. Bowles, Stanley Coben, Robert W. Fogel, Herbert G. Gutman, P. M. G. Harris, Emmet Larkin, Juan Linz, Arthur Mann, David Riesman, Leo Schnore, Joan W. Scott, Richard Sennett, William H. Sewell, Jr., Sam B. Warner, Jr., and Paul Worthman. Incisive and immensely helpful readings of the full manuscript were provided by Clyde and Sally Griffen, Oscar Handlin, Tamara Hareven, Michael B. Katz, Abigail Thernstrom, Charles Tilly, and Harrison C. White. The editorial suggestions of Joseph Elder and Ann Orlov of the Harvard University Press have greatly improved the final product. I am grateful to Patrick Blessing for his work on the index. Special thanks are owed too to Edward O. Laumann, who ran special tabulations from his 1962 survey of Cambridge and Belmont for my use here.

I have also been fortunate in having two helpful collaborators in developing some of the ideas advanced in this book. A section of Chapter 2 was originally written with the assistance of Peter R. Knights. The language of the chapter is my own, but the substance of the analysis of population change in Boston in the 1880's that appears there is a joint product. The first half of Chapter 8 was initially prepared with the aid of Elizabeth H. Pleck as a paper for the 1970 meetings of the Organization of American Historians. In this case too I was responsible for the actual writing, but Ms. Pleck participated in the collection of evidence and the shaping of the ideas.

Earlier versions of some of the material here have been published elsewhere in three instances. Part of Chapter 2 first appeared as a paper (with Peter Knights as junior author), "Men in Motion: Some Data and Speculations on Urban Population Turnover in Nineteenth-Century America," *Journal of Interdisciplinary History*, 1 (Autumn 1970), 7–35. Chapter 6 draws from my article "Immigrants and WASPs: Ethnic Differences in Occupational Mobility in Boston, 1880–1940," in Stephan Thernstrom and Richard Sennett, ed., *Nineteenth-Century Cities: Essays in the New Urban History* (New Haven, Conn.: Yale University Press, 1969), pp. 125–164, but the original paper has been so thoroughly revised that I now consider the initial version outmoded. Chapter 7 has appeared in substantially similar form in William Aydelotte, Allan Bogue, and Robert W. Fogel, eds., *The Dimensions of Quantitative Research in History* (Princeton: N.J.: Princeton University Press, 1972), pp. 124–158. I am grateful to the Massachusetts Institute of Technology Press, the Yale University Press, and the Princeton University Press for permission to use this material in the present book.

Los Angeles S. T.
November 1972

contents

tables

THE OTHER BOSTONIANS

We love to read the lives of the great, yet what a broken history of mankind they give, unless supplemented by the lives of the humble. But while the great can speak for themselves, or by the tongues of their admirers, the humble are apt to live inarticulate and die unheard. It is well that now and then one is born among the simple with a taste for self-revelation.[1]

MARY ANTIN

chapter one INTRODUCTION

Such was Mary Antin's justification for writing *The Promised Land,* her well-known account of immigrant life in the slums of Boston at the opening of this century. But few indeed of "the simple," alas, ever satisfy their "taste for self-revelation" in ways that leave an imprint upon the historical record. Not, at least, an imprint upon the kinds of records with which historians are most familiar—books and pamphlets, newspapers, government reports, sermons, speeches, and other products of the most visible and articulate elements of the community.[2] As a result we know far more about "the proper Bostonians" than about the common Bostonians.

There is, however, a body of rarely exploited historical evidence about certain key aspects of the past social experience of the masses of anonymous Americans. Such sources as manuscript schedules of the United States Census, city directories, marriage-license applications, local tax records, and other similar listings offer the opportunity to examine some dimensions of the past that have been hitherto neglected, and thus to write a less "broken" history of mankind. This study of the common people of Boston from 1880 to the present is one attempt.

I do not, however, pretend to offer anything like a comprehensive treatment of Boston society over the past nine decades. Instead I have focused upon certain critical questions about social structure and social processes in the community. What were the demographic sources of the city's growth? Who came to Boston, and who remained there and settled in? Was the occupational structure a relatively fluid one, or was an individual who began his career as an unskilled day laborer likely to remain a laborer for the rest of his life? Were the children of mere laborers likely, too, to remain permanently trapped in a "culture of poverty"? Did the immigrants who flocked to the New World cluster in ghetto neighborhoods from which escape was rarely possible? Was there a common pattern of immigrant social mobility, or did particular groups of varying national and religious backgrounds have radically different experiences? Did black migrants from the rural South fare much the same as other newcomers, or was the black experience in the Northern city different in kind? Did patterns of migration and social mobility change drastically in the course of urbanization and industrialization? Finally, and perhaps most important, were there radical differences between the social structures of Boston and other American communities, or was there a national pattern that manifested itself in much the same way throughout the entire society?

These are by no means the only worthwhile questions that might be asked about American society in the past, I need hardly say, but I think they are of fundamental importance and have not been given the attention they deserve. Until now they have languished in a no-man's land between two disciplines, at once too sociological for most historians and too historical for most sociologists.

Historians, by and large, have not viewed these issues as central, and those who have addressed them generally have been averse to using what seem to me the appropriate sources and methods. There are, to be sure, valuable insights into such questions as the assimilation of immigrants scattered throughout the historical literature, but systematic comparative studies based upon data pertaining to the masses of ordinary people have been rare. Likewise, there have been perceptive historical studies of the development of particular cities, but these have tended to focus upon formal institutions and the doings of the articulate, and have neglected underlying social processes and mass behavior.

Scholars from the other social-science disciplines, sociology in particular, have done something to fill the void, but their attention has been concentrated almost exclusively upon the present and the very recent past. In some cases this narrow present-mindedness has been the result of a misguided belief that the time dimension is irrelevant in social analysis. Perhaps more often, however, the lack of historical depth in their work has been attributable to excessive reliance upon a particular method of data collection—survey research—that happens to be ill adapted to historical inquiry. Reliable evidence, it has too often been assumed, must come from an interview schedule. Since dead men are not accessible to the poll taker, the historical reach of survey research is confined to the present and to that fraction of the past that can be remembered reliably by living respondents.[3]

Consequently, the sociological literature, however refined and sophisticated, has offered a dangerously truncated historical perspective on these issues. Thus a major thesis of some of the key studies conducted in the 1930's was that the American class structure was becoming increasingly rigid and that rates of social mobility were declining from their traditional high levels.[4] What was taken to be the "traditional" level of mobility in the American past, however, was based purely on conjecture. A proposition about long-term historical change was advanced on the basis of measurements made only at the end of the hypothesized change. Since World War II a more optimistic view of the American class system has prevailed in the literature, and the majority opinion has been that "the rate of mobility in American society is at least as high today as it has been at any time in the last fifty to one hundred years, if not higher."[5] But all that the studies cited in support of this conclusion really show is that mobility rates have not declined *since the Great Depression*.[6] Again a conclusion about long-term change was drawn from investigations that lacked the historical depth necessary to resolve the issue. Rates of social mobility in the United States might have declined precipitously between the late nineteenth century and 1929; alternatively, they might have been much lower in the nineteenth century than has ever been suspected and have remained unchanged since then. Historical analysis of social phenomena is thus not a luxury for those interested in the past for its own sake. A study of the present that neglects the processes of change by which the present was created is necessarily superficial.

I first wrestled with some of the issues dealt with in this study in an earlier book, *Poverty and Progress: Social Mobility in a Nine-*

teenth-Century City.[7] That volume treated hundreds of ordinary laborers living in a small Massachusetts industrial city, Newburyport, in the years 1850–1880, and yielded rather pessimistic conclusions about social mobility in nineteenth-century America.

The evidence suggested that relatively few of these laborers or their children enacted the success story envisioned by their contemporary, Horatio Alger, though many made small social gains that must have seemed significant to them—moving a notch or two upward within the working class by finding a better-paid job or accumulating the funds to purchase a small home. These minor gains, I argued, were sufficient to integrate these men into the prevailing social order, but there was a serious question whether the "traditional" level of opportunity in the American past was at all high, if the experience of the laborers of Newburyport was at all representative.

I suggested in a concluding chapter that there were indeed grounds for believing that the Newburyport findings might be generalized more widely, but my argument was highly speculative, given the paucity of comparable studies by other investigators. Questions about the broader meaning of the Newburyport data remained open. The community, after all, was quite small, with a peak population of less than 15,000 in the period; might not things have been very different in larger cities with a more complex economic base? Newburyport, furthermore, experienced little population growth or economic expansion in these three decades; did not its relative stagnation by comparison with more dynamic urban centers make it a special case? The study examined unskilled laborers; quite possibly other strata of the working class found much greater opportunities for advancement. What is more, a substantial majority of these men were Irish Catholic immigrants newly arrived on American shores. Possibly the findings told more about Irish workers, or perhaps Catholic workers, than about workers in general. The time period dealt with was relatively short, so that little could be said about either long-term trends or cyclical fluctuations in mobility rates.

Thus I resolved to attempt a broader and more ambitious study, which would treat all of the major social elements of a great metropolitan center over a span of nearly a century. This would supply much the fullest series of observations ever made of patterns of migration and social mobility in a changing American community. The difficulty of generalizing to the society as a whole would remain; no single place is America in microcosm, and yet the nature of the available sources is such as to make the study of even a single city extraordinarily time-consuming (see Appendix A). A major metroplis, however, is considerably more significant in its own right than a small and relatively isolated community like Newburyport. A further reassuring consideration was that a number of similar studies were then being planned, which might provide the basis for a systematic comparative analysis of mobility patterns in a broad spectrum of American cities. I decided, therefore, to begin work on Boston.

Why Boston? The choice may seem an odd one, given my interest in mobility, for the city has often been viewed as a deviant, stagnant, caste-ridden community, inhabited chiefly by Cabots, Lodges, George Apleys, and countless uncouth but colorful Irish ward heelers. I was highly skeptical of this stereotype, however, and I believe that the results of this study show my skepticism to have been well founded. There was indeed a trace of aristocracy in the Boston social mix, once the Brahmin group had closed its doors to the new men of wealth who appeared in Boston in the latter half of the nineteenth century. But precisely how distinctive the Boston Brahmins were as compared with their counterparts in Philadelphia, say, has yet to be established. More important, the Brahmins were at best a tiny element of the social structure of the city as a whole, and it is surely unwise to assume that the existence of a castelike group of a few hundred families puts the stamp of village India upon the social life of an American metropolis with a population numbered not in the hundreds or thousands but in the hundreds of thousands. In 1880, Boston had more than a third of a million inhabitants within its boundaries, and another third of a million in the surrounding suburbs, and it ranked as the country's fourth-largest urban center. Although in subsequent decades it failed to keep pace with a few of its rivals to the West—Detroit, San Francisco, Los Angeles—by 1970 the population of the Boston metropolitan area had risen to two and three-quarter million, which gave it seventh place in the national rankings. Not only in sheer size, but in ethnic diversity, economic importance, cultural contributions, and a variety of other ways, Boston was and is one of the great American cities. There were no convincing grounds, it seemed to me, for assuming a priori that the patterns of migration and social mobility that might be found there were necessarily deviant and peculiar to Boston alone.

One of the wisest and most observant of the Boston Brahmins long ago offered a different, and to me more congenial, perspective on the supposed uniqueness of Boston. When asked to contribute to the chapter on "Medicine in Boston" in Justin Winsor's 1880 *Memorial History,* Dr. Oliver Wendell Holmes observed that for him to write of medicine in Boston as if that were a self-contained, intellectually defensible subject would be comparable to an oceanographer's writing on the subject of the tides of Boston harbor. Boston, said Dr. Holmes, "is a fraction of the civilized world, as its harbor is part of the ocean. In both we expect to find general laws and phenomena, modified more or less in their aspects by local influences." [8] The presence of the Brahmin aristocracy in Boston was one distinctive "local influence," but what has been most striking to me, as argued at length in the concluding chapter, is how much the social patterns and processes that I have examined in this study of Boston were the products of "general laws" that operated throughout American society.

Even in 1880 Boston was far too large for me to attempt to deal with each of its inhabitants. It was necessary to select samples of representative citizens, from which generalizations about the entire population of the community could be made with a known degree of reliability. A number of random samples were drawn from local records for 1880, 1910, 1930, and 1958, and each sample member was traced through Boston city directories and tax records as long as he remained living in the city. (I have not burdened the text with an intricate discussion of the nature of these samples. The reader with questions about them is urged to consult Appendix A for a full explanation.) This yielded information about 7965 males, who represented, in microcosm, the population of the entire metropolis.

To be more precise, they represented the *male* population of Boston. Female residents of the city were not included in the samples, for both theoretical and practical reasons. As to the former, it is customarily assumed in the literature of social stratification that males are "the major breadwinners and carriers of the family's hopes and life chances." [9] This is perhaps less true today than it was in the past, but it was certainly the case for most of the period indicated in this study. There were, in addition, compelling practical reasons for restricting the samples to men. The difficulties of following women's careers over time through historical sources are formidable, both because females change their surnames at marriage and because their occupations are often unreported in the city directories. These difficulties, plus the absence of studies of female social mobility with which to compare my findings, were sufficient to deter me from making the attempt. But I recognize that women have played a role in the world of work that deserves far more study than it has yet received from historians. We need, for example, to know more about the extent to which the supplementary earnings of females within low-income families have provided the margin that financed education for the children, home purchases, and the like. That I have been unable to explore the matter here is a limitation of the study, one that I hope future investigators will soon remedy.[10]

Once the task of tracing these thousands of obscure men through the surviving records was completed, all of the information that could be gleaned about each was put on an IBM card, and the cards were fed into a computer. After receiving proper instructions, the machine spewed forth piles of tables that statistically summarized the patterns contained in the data. The core of this book is made up of the most important of these tables and my interpretation of what they mean.

This, then, is a largely quantitative study. There was a time when this admission might have demanded elaborate justification, for historians tended to be highly suspicious of statistical analysis. A heated and largely fruitless debate was under way between a few zealots who acclaimed computerized history as the wave of the future and the only way to Truth and a conservative majority that apparently believed that "all important historical questions are important precisely because they are not susceptible to quantitative answers." [11] There is still some polarization over this issue in the historical profession, but few sophisticated scholars today take either extreme position. More and more of my colleagues, I think, would agree both that there are important realms of historical inquiry to which the computer has nothing to contribute, and also that there are important historical issues that may be illumined by quantitative analysis. The grand question—to count or not to count—is too abstract. The real issue is whether the nature of the questions posed and the evidence available call for one analytical strategy or another, and that is best discussed case by case. I, of course, think that my approach is appropriate to the subject at hand. If some readers disagree, I hope that the debate can focus on that practical question rather than upon the cosmic issues that have inspired too many polemics in the past.

I must, however, concede that there is some force in one familiar complaint often raised about quantitative history—that it can be a painful chore to read. I have written this book with the most lucid and lively prose that I can muster, but there can be no doubt that a monograph that bristles with several dozen statistical tables is not good bedside reading. I assume no knowledge whatsoever of statistics on the part of the reader, and I comment in the text upon all of the features of the tables that seem significant, so that those who find the statistical detail too forbidding may move along quickly. But this is intended to be a scholarly rather than a popular book, in the sense that it presents not only substantive conclusions about the nature of American urban society but also thorough discussions of the evidence, the analytical procedures, and the chains of inference that led me to those conclusions. I think that there is a certain excitement in learning about how an investigator hacked his way through the forest as well as in seeing what he discovered on the other side. I hope my readers will agree.

chapter two POPULATION GROWTH, MIGRATION, AND TURNOVER

A little more than a third of a million people lived within the boundaries of the city of Boston in 1880, and approximately as many more resided in the suburban communities of the surrounding area. In 1970 the census taker found nearly two-thirds of a million persons in Boston proper, and two and three-quarter million in the entire metropolitan area. Nothing is more vital to an understanding of the social history of modern Boston than a grasp of the character and timing of this process of population concentration.

Conventional methods of measuring urban population growth and its causes will first be employed here. They point to the conclusion that in the late nineteenth and early twentieth centuries Boston was attracting newcomers in only modest numbers and was growing sluggishly as a result. After World War I, it will appear furthermore, complete population stagnation set in. The city proper had a considerably larger population in 1920 than in 1970; the entire Boston metropolitan area continued to grow, but at an extremely low rate. Net migration estimates for the post-1920 period make it seem that Boston was going the way of Appalachia or Mississippi, losing large numbers of migrants to more dynamic areas and gaining no newcomers from outside.

It will be shown, however, that these conventional methods of demographic analysis convey a partial and highly misleading impression of the true state of affairs. Some novel sources of data and estimating procedures that permit the measurement of annual population flows into and out of Boston will reveal that the city's demographic stagnation was more apparent than real. The turnover of the Boston population, the total number of people moving into or out of the city, was dramatically higher than net-migration estimates would lead us to believe. The population turnover rate in Boston has diminished modestly in the past 40 years or so, but this was a shift not from low turnover to no turnover, but rather from astonishing fluidity to a somewhat more stable but far from static population. Nineteenth-century folklore identified spatial mobility with the West, contrasting the open frontier with the closed city, and later research by disciples of Frederick Jackson Turner reinforced this stereotype. The migratory habits of the Boston population, however, challenge this view, and suggest the possibility that American city dwellers in general have lived in a far more fluid social context than has traditionally been thought.

GROWTH RATES AND THE CONTRIBUTION OF NET MIGRATION

In the closing years of the nineteenth century and the first decades of the twentieth, the population of Boston was increasing by 20 to 25 percent per decade (Table 2.1). This was below the growth rate for the urban population of the United States as a whole, reflecting the fact that Boston had already gone through its phase of most dramatic growth and that the most dynamic growth was taking place in the newer cities of the Midwest and West. Boston's expansion in those years was impressive only by comparison with the post-1920 pattern, which brought growth rates of only 4 percent in two of the subsequent decades, and actual losses in the 1930's, 1950's, and 1960's. The 1970 population of Boston proper was 18 percent below that of 1930.

This is somewhat misleading, to be sure, for part of the explanation was that Boston, like other American cities, was undergoing what demographers term decentralization, with more and more of the residents of the larger metropolitan area around the city clustering in the outlying communities of the surrounding suburban ring.[1] The distinction between the city as legally defined and the entire

TABLE 2.1. Population change and rates of change, Boston and Boston Metropolitan Area, 1880–1970[1]

	Boston City		*Boston S.M.S.A.*		
Year	*Population*	*Percent change*	*Population*	*Percent change*	*Boston as percent of S.M.S.A.*
1880	362,839	—	797,610	—	46
1890	448,477	+24	1,029,453	+29	44
1900	560,892	+25	1,312,784	+28	43
1910	670,585	+20	1,602,023	+22	42
1920	748,060	+12	1,868,859	+17	40
1930	781,188	+ 4	2,168,566	+16	36
1940	770,816	− 1	2,209,608	+ 2	35
1950	801,444	+ 4	2,410,572	+10	33
1960	697,197	−13	2,589,301	+ 7	27
1970	641,071	− 8	2,730,228	+ 5	24

[1] 1880–1960 U. S. Census data, as given by Leo F. Schnore and Peter R. Knights, "Residence and Social Structure: Boston in the Ante-Bellum Period," in Stephan Thernstrom and Richard Sennett, ed., *Nineteenth-Century Cities: Essays in the New Urban History* (New Haven, Conn.: Yale University Press, 1969), p. 249. The 1960 boundaries of the Boston Standard Metropolitan Statistical Area were retrojected back, so that the figures apply to a constant area. There were no major boundary changes for the city of Boston during the period, only the 1912 annexation of Hyde Park (1910 population = 15,507). This factor has produced misleading growth rates in many cities, as Schnore demonstrates in his book *The Urban Scene: Human Ecology and Demography* (New York: Free Press, 1965), pp. 114–134. The city figure for 1970 is from the advance report on final population counts for Massachusetts; the S.M.S.A. figure is from the preliminary report and may be slightly inaccurate.

metropolitan community is especially important to recall in the case of Boston, for the city proper has long been relatively small compared with the suburban ring; even in 1880 less than half of the population of the metropolis was located within the legal limits of the city, and by 1970 the fraction had fallen to less than a quarter. Population-growth figures for the entire metropolitan area suggest that some of the central city's losses in recent decades merely reflect the surge of population toward the suburbs; the Boston Standard Metropolitan Statistical Area has been outpacing the city proper for the past 90 years. Even so, it is plain that the entire Boston metropolitan community has been gaining population at a much lower rate than was the case prior to World War I, a pattern common to virtually all of the major urban centers of the Northeast.[2]

What accounts for these changes? A multitude of circumstances can affect the rate at which the population of a given community changes—transportation improvements that give access to new markets, the discovery of mineral resources nearby, political decisions that bring government contracts to local entrepreneurs, and so forth. But there are only two basic demographic processes by which growth can actually take place. In the absence of boundary changes that swell a city's population artificially (and this has not occurred in Boston since 1880), all growth must be the result either of natural increase, an excess of local births over local deaths, or of net in-migration, a surplus of people arriving and settling over those departing the community for other destinations.

The shifting importance of these two components of growth in Boston may be seen from Table 2.2, which contrasts the pattern of the 1880's with that of the 1940's. Between 1880 and 1890 the population of Boston increased by 85,638, or nearly 24 percent. Only about a fourth of this gain was attributable to reproductive change; there were 20,459 more births than deaths in the city during the decade. It follows that the number of newcomers who settled in the community in the 1880's must have exceeded the number of 1880 residents who moved elsewhere by 65,179.[3] By 1890, natural increase had swelled the 1880 population by 6 percent; net migration was far more important, adding numbers amounting to 18 percent of the 1880 population.

Contrast this with the pattern for 1940–1950. (The data here include Lawrence and Lowell as well as Boston, but it seems unlikely that figures for Boston alone would differ materially.) The total population increased in this interval by only 14,946, or slightly more than 1 percent. Reproductive change, however, was of about the same magnitude as in the earlier period. Births exceeded deaths by 65,358, which would have increased the population by 7 percent in the absence of changes due to migration. The reason the total population of the city grew hardly at all in the decade was that net migration was negative instead of positive. Whereas in the 1880's Boston gained 65,179 migrants, in the World War II decade it lost 56,375. This large loss attributable to net out-migration nearly canceled the gain from natural increase, leaving the population only a shade larger by the end of the decade.

Comparable figures for 1950–1960 indicate an accentuation of

TABLE 2.2. Components of growth of the Boston population, 1880–1890 and 1940–1950[1]

1880–1890		*1940–1950*	
1. 1880 population	362,839	1. 1940 population	964,282
2. 1890 population	448,477	2. 1950 population	979,228
3. Total change	+85,638	3. Total change	+14,946
4. Percent change	+24	4. Percent change	+1
5. Natural increase	+20,459	5. Natural increase	+65,358
6. Net migration	+65,179	6. Net migration	−56,375
7. Natural increase as percent of 1880 population	+6	7. Natural increase as percent of 1940 population	+7
8. Net migration as percent of 1880 population	+18	8. Net migration as percent of 1940 population	−6

[1] Natural increase was calculated from the Boston City Registry Department's annual reports of births and deaths in the city. The 1880–1890 section of this table and the main outlines of my subsequent analysis of the Boston population in the 1880's were developed in collaboration with Peter R. Knights; see Thernstrom and Knights, "Men in Motion: Some Data and Speculations about Urban Population Mobility in Nineteenth-Century America," *Journal of Interdisciplinary History,* 1 (Autumn 1970), 7–35, reprinted with minor corrections in Tamara K. Hareven, ed., *Anonymous Americans: Explorations in Nineteenth-Century Social History* (Englewood Cliffs, N.J.: Prentice-Hall, 17–47. Data for 1940–1950 are from Donald J. Bogue, *Components of Population Change, 1940–1950: Estimates of Net Migration and Natural Increase for Each Standard Metropolitan Area and State Economic Area* (Oxford, Ohio: Scripps Foundation for Research in Population Problems, 1957), p. 61. They apply to the central cities of Lowell and Lawrence, Massachusetts, as well as to Boston. It may be wondered why the surplus of natural increase over net migration, 8983, is not equal to the total change in population, given as 14,946. The remaining 5963 persons added to the population between 1940 and 1950 were military personnel, who are treated separately in Bogue's analysis.

this pattern, with a net out-migration loss to the city of nearly 154,000 persons and a natural increase of about 50,000, resulting in a population decline of approximately 104,000.[4] Once the prime source of population expansion, migration had become the prime obstacle to growth.

It would be an unduly laborious task to calculate the components of population change in Boston for each of the intervening decades, but some sense of the timing of this dramatic shift of pattern may be gained from published data on the growth of the population of the state of Massachusetts as a whole. Table 2.3 indicates the decadal growth rate of the state from 1880 to 1950 and specifies the respective contributions of natural increase by state residents and of migration from outside the state. As with the population figures for Boston and for the entire Boston metropolitan area in Table 2.1, a decline in growth rates appears around World War I. A sharp diminution in the amount of growth attributable to net migration was beginning to occur at the same time. Migration was the prime source of Massachusetts' population expansion prior to 1910; net in-migration, though still significant, was smaller than natural increase during the World War I decade; in the 1920's it added little to the population of the state; and after 1930 there was a net drain,

TABLE 2.3. Components of growth of the Massachusetts population, 1880–1950[1]

Year	*Population (thousands)*	*Percent change*	*Percent change due to net migration*
1880	1783	—	—
1890	2239	+20	+73
1900	2805	+20	+68
1910	3363	+17	+62
1920	3849	+13	+46
1930	4245	+ 9	+10
1940	4313	+ 2	−17
1950	4666	+ 8	− 7

[1] Drawn from Hope T. Eldridge and Dorothy Swaine Thomas, *Demographic Analyses and Interrelations* [vol. III of Simon Kuznets *et al., Population Redistribution and Economic Growth in the United States, 1870–1950* (3 vols; Philadelphia: American Philosophical Society, 1947–1964)], pp. 240–243.

though it was more than offset by the large excess of births over deaths in the state. These figures pertain to the entire state, and thus migration is defined differently, in terms of net movement across state rather than city boundaries, but there is little doubt that calculations for Boston alone would disclose a similar pattern.

The standard kinds of demographic evidence, therefore, seem fully consistent with the common stereotype of Boston as a sluggish, middle-aged community, the antithesis of a truly dynamic metropolis like Los Angeles or Chicago. Even in the 1880–1910 period the Boston population increased at a rather modest rate; after 1920 the city proper actually lost population, while the metropolitan area as a whole gained at an average rate of a mere 1 percent per annum. What is more, it appears that a dramatic decline in the attractiveness of the community to prospective migrants occurred somewhere around World War I. Partly because of restrictive national legislation that cut off immigration, the city ceased to draw in new blood from outside and became increasingly inbred. It began, as well, to lose its native sons to other places; local births exceeded deaths each year, but the surplus slipped away.

THE TWO MIGRATION STREAMS: A CLOSER LOOK AT THE 1880's

All this is true, so far as it goes. The city of Boston, and to a somewhat lesser extent the entire Boston metropolitan area, have become stagnant with respect to total population growth, largely because they no longer derive large net increments from outside. But this tells us much less than we might think, because the most convenient demographic measurements—population growth rates and estimates of net migration flows—are extremely crude and misleading indexes of the composition of a city's population. To say that the size of a population remained unchanged over a given interval is not to say that the same people comprised the population at the initial and terminal dates. All of the original inhabitants might, in principle, have departed in the interim, and their places have been filled by an equal number of newcomers. Net migration figures are similarly inadequate as a gauge of whether or not migration into and out of the community is taking place on a large scale, for they measure not the total flow of newcomers and departers but rather the *difference* between the in-migrating and the out-migrating population streams. The distinction may seem trivial and technical, but it is of enormous importance. Net migration is but the tip of the iceberg projecting above the surface; as with an iceberg, the mass hidden from the eye is several times larger. The role of migration in shaping the character of the modern metropolis simply cannot be understood without careful analysis of the two components which together determine the level of net migration, namely, in-migration and out-migration.

Let us reexamine population changes in Boston during the 1880's with this in mind. The total population of the city grew from 362,839 in 1880 to 448,477 in 1890, a modest growth of 24 percent. The net migration of an estimated 65,179 persons into the city accounted for about three-fourths of the gain.[5] It is tempting to take this as evidence that a total of 65,179 persons moved into Boston in these 10 years. Recent migrants, it could be incautiously concluded from these residual net figures, comprised a mere 15 percent of the Boston population in 1890, suggesting that even in an era of heavy European immigration the city had an overwhelming preponderance of relatively settled, long-term residents.

A radically different impression, however, may be gained from data that permit an estimation of total migration flows into and out of Boston each year of the decade. Such an analysis reveals that the proportion of the city's residents in 1890 who had moved into Boston since 1880 was not 15 percent but fully one-third; that the number of newcomers entering the city was several times larger than the net-migration calculations suggest; and that the actual number of separate families who lived in Boston at *some* point between 1880 and 1890 was a staggering 296,388, more than three times the total number residing there at any one time in this 10-year period!

These startling, indeed hardly credible, conclusions are based upon evidence drawn from the annual Boston city directories. Until 1921 (but not, alas, thereafter) the Boston city directories annually included a table indicating the number of listings dropped from the preceding year's directory in making up the current one and the number of listings in the current directory that had not been in the previous one.[6] These tabulations of listings added and listings dropped, if handled with due caution, can supply satisfactory estimates of the volume of migration into and out of Boston each year.[7]

The population of Boston increased from 362,839 to 448,477 between 1880 and 1890, and the number of listings in the Boston city directories increased correspondingly from 143,140 to 195,149, a gain of 52,009. (There were fewer listings than persons in the city because the directories excluded children and dependent women.) By summing the annual listings-added figures from the directories of the decade, as in Table 2.4, we learn that it took the addition of no fewer than 398,995 new listings to produce the net increase of approximately 52,000, because a stunning number of listings, more than 350,000, were dropped from the directories in the decade!

In their raw form, however, the listings-added and listings-dropped totals are imperfect measures of the in- and out-migration streams. One difficulty is that some changes in directory listings reflected not migration into or out of the Boston metropolitan area,

TABLE 2.4. Gross migration, net migration, and population turnover in Boston, 1881–1890

	1881–1885	*1886–1890*	*Decade total*
1. New listings added to directories	187,946	211,049	398,995
2. Listings dropped	161,755	189,774	351,529
3. Listings/family ratio [1]	2.029	2.131	—
4. Families added (1÷3)	92,698	99,015	191,713
5. Families dropped (2÷3)	79,780	89,033	168,813
6. Males reaching 21[2]	16,388	17,509	33,897
7. Deaths of household heads[3]	14,126	16,115	30,241
8. Families in-migrating (4−6)	76,310	81,506	157,816
9. Families out-migrating (5−7)	65,654	72,918	138,572
10. Population turnover, families (8+9)[4]	141,964	154,424	296,388

[1] Derived from comparison of directory listings for 1880, 1885, and 1890 with federal and state census counts of total families in Boston in those years.

[2] Estimated from census data on the age composition of the Boston population in 1880, 1885, and 1890.

[3] This figure is the total of adult male deaths in the city during the decade, plus one-sixth of adult female deaths to allow for female-headed households.

[4] Population turnover is the sum of in- and out-migration.

but short-distance moves between the inner city and the suburbs. The Boston directories did enumerate many suburban residents as well as persons living in Boston proper (see Appendix A for further discussion of this), but their coverage of the suburbs, particularly those on the outer fringes of the metropolitan area, was imperfect. Much of the migration revealed in Table 2.4 was movement across the boundaries of the metropolitan area, but by no means all of it was. It would take extensive further research in a variety of other sources to determine how much of the mobility revealed here was intermetropolitan rather than intrametropolitan, a task that cannot be attempted here. All that can be said is that both kinds of movement show up in the figures below, and that future investigations into the relative importance of each are very much needed.

A second problem, more readily dealt with, is that there were listings in local directories not only for individual household heads but also for business firms. Corporations were mixed in with individuals in the figures, and individuals in business for themselves were double-counted, once at their residence and once at their place of business. Entry into business thus becomes indistinguishable from entry into the city, and business mortality from migration out of the community. An entirely satisfactory solution to this problem would require replicating the herculean tabulation task originally performed by the directory staff, this time treating individuals and business listings separately, and that proved impossible here. But a partial correction for this distorting influence could be made. Published census figures indicated the total number of families in the city during the decade, and from these the ratio of families to total listings was calculated, a figure slightly more than 2. Dividing the listings-added and listings-dropped totals by this ratio provides an estimate of actual families added to and dropped from the directories.[8] Applying these ratios to the 1880–1890 figures indicates that some 191,713 families were newly listed in a Boston directory at some point in the decade, and that a total of 168,813 were dropped from a directory in those years.

Two further necessary corrections were simple to make. Some of the new directory listings were caused not by the arrival of newcomers from outside the city but by young residents of the city reaching the age at which they were eligible for listing—21. Likewise, some of the names dropped disappeared from the directories because of death. The magnitude of these two influences can be estimated from data from the Census and the City Registrar's report and their effect removed, and we are left with the final in- and out-migration estimates in Table 2.4.

During the 1880's, 157,816 families moved into Boston, more than twice the total number of families living there as of 1880! Precisely how many individual in-migrants this represented is uncertain. If incoming households were of the same average size as those already in the city—namely, 5 persons—this would mean that an amazing total of nearly 800,000 (157,816 × 5 = 789,080) individuals moved into Boston in this brief period. This is only the roughest of guesses, however, and I will not stake too much on its accuracy, for it is quite possible that single persons and men with unusually small families were overrepresented in the migration streams. It is by no means certain that this was the case; a careful study of a mid-nineteenth-century Canadian city revealed no significant differences in the household size of transient and settled members of the community.[9] In the absence of more complete evidence of the kind employed in the Canadian study, all that can be said now is that the 157,816 families that moved into Boston during the 1880's included anywhere from a minimum of 157,816 to a maximum of nearly 800,000 separate individuals, depending upon their mean size.[10]

Had not this flood of newcomers been offset by other demographic processes, the total population of the city would have swelled by far more than the modest 24 percent by which it actually increased. Indeed, it would have tripled if the average in-migrating family contained 5 persons. But in fact there was a potent countervailing force at work, because no fewer than 138,572 households were simultaneously leaving the city. Enormous though the stream of in-migrants was, it exceeded the volume of out-migration from the community by only 14 percent. The great majority of newcomers were thus only filling places vacated by out-migrants.

The residual method of estimating net migration employed earlier yielded results that could carelessly be taken to mean that less than 15 percent of Boston's 1890 population was composed of recent migrants into the community. Net-migration calculations, however, provide no sound basis for judging the proportion of newcomers in a population. It would be possible to have zero net migration over an interval and yet to find many newcomers at its end, so long as they filled places left vacant by out-migrants. Two different and more satisfactory methods of estimating the proportion of recent migrants living in Boston in 1890 show the actual value to have been at least one-third.

The first of these methods derives from an effort to trace in the 1890 city directory the adult members of a sample of Boston males drawn from the 1880 U. S. Census (N = 1982), which disclosed that 64 percent of them were still in the city in 1890; applying this persistence rate to the entire population would yield 232,217 people for 1890. In addition, there were children born in the city during the decade who were present to swell the population total in 1890. Through a calculation that utilized the total number of births in Boston during the decade, the number of deaths of children under 10, and an estimated out-migration rate for young children, it was estimated that 47,059 of the 115,974 infants born in Boston in the 1880's were there to be counted by the census taker in 1890.[11] Adding these children to the 232,217 persisters reveals that 279,276 of the 448,477 residents of Boston in 1890 had either been living in the city since 1880 or been born there during the decade; the remainder, 169,201, were migrants who had arrived in the 1880's and stayed. That would mean that 38 percent of the 1890 population of Boston was composed of recent migrants.

Some confirmation of this estimate may be obtained from the Massachusetts State Census of 1895, which inquired into length of residence in the state, though not in particular cities within it. These data were tabulated for Boston separately, and they indicated that 24 percent of the city's population aged 10 or more in 1895 had moved into the state since 1885.[12] What we want to know, however, is how many had moved into *Boston* during that interval, since residence in the state is not equivalent to residence in the city; a good many newcomers to Boston, after all, came from other parts of Massachusetts. To the 24 percent of migrants from outside the state we would have to add some allowance for such intrastate migrants. No solid basis for an estimate of this migratory stream exists, but some clue may be gained from the datum that 8 percent of the 1895 population of the city had been born in Massachusetts but outside of Boston. This figure is for the entire population, including young children who had had very little chance to migrate into the city; the proportion of intrastate migrants in the Boston population aged 10 or more was doubtless significantly higher. There must, in addition, have been migrants born in other states or abroad who had moved into Massachusetts by 1885, but had only come to the city itself between 1886 and 1895. On the other hand, the 8-percent figure pertains to individuals who moved to Boston at any time after their birth, and many must have done so more than 10 years earlier. It is hard to believe, however, that this last consideration was as potent as the influences biasing the estimate in the other direction, so that I would judge from this source that an absolute minimum of 32 percent (24 percent + 8 percent) and probably more like 35 to 40 percent of the 1895 residents of Boston had moved into the community during the preceding decade, which fits nicely with the preceding estimate for 1880–1890. A more precise figure cannot be obtained, but it seems indisputable that about a third, and probably a little more, of the people living in Boston in 1890 had migrated into the community during the preceding decade.

Boston experienced only a modest population increase of 24 percent between 1880 and 1890, and the net-migration calculations upon which students of population change customarily rely make it seem that the volume of migration into the community was similarly modest. Little more than 65,000 newcomers came into the city, and they comprised no more than 15 percent of its population at the end of the decade. But these undramatic conclusions are utterly erroneous. At least a third of the 1890 residents of Boston had come to the city within the past few years. The precise number of individual migrants who had entered the community at some point in the decade is unknown, but it was a minimum of 157,000 and possibly as many as 800,000. Net population change in the city between 1880 and 1890 was on a modest scale, but only because two very powerful migratory currents flowing through the community nearly canceled each other out, leaving only the small rivulet registered by the net figures.

THE TWO MIGRATION STREAMS SINCE 1890

This closer look at the determinants of population change in Boston in the 1880's should suffice to establish a point of broad significance: net figures may convey a grossly misleading impression of the process of migration and the dynamics of urban growth. Neither overall growth rates like those given in Table 2.1 nor simple analysis of the net components of growth as in Tables 2.2 and 2.3 offer us more than a hint of the quite astonishing population fluidity that prevailed in late-nineteenth-century Boston.

One of the implications of this discovery, of course, is that the seeming demographic stagnation of Boston in recent decades may possibly be more apparent than real. Overall growth rates both for the city proper and for the entire metropolitan area began to decline around the time of World War I, at about the same time that net-migration rates into the community fell abruptly. But it does not necessarily follow from this that the population of Boston was becoming notably more settled than before, with fewer and fewer of the city's inhabitants newcomers from outside. From 1930 on, Boston suffered modest losses from net out-migration, but whether this means that new migrants stopped coming into the city altogether and that modest numbers left it, or that in-migration continued to be heavy but that out-migration was even heavier, cannot be discerned from the net figures.

No definitive answer to this question, let it be said quickly, can be given here. Estimating net migration from published sources is a fairly simple matter, which is doubtless why demographers have customarily been content to work with net figures. Data with which to assess the magnitude of the opposing migration streams that together determine net migration are far more difficult to obtain. We have seen that in the 1880's the Boston city directories provided information which, with a number of adjustments, could be utilized for this purpose. Regrettably, the practice of tabulating listings added to and dropped from the directories each year was discontinued in 1922, just at the point when the city's overall growth rates and the contribution of net migration to population change were beginning to alter fundamentally. Given the likelihood that any major shifts in the pattern we have discerned in the 1880's would have taken place, if at all, after 1920, it did not seem worth while to analyze the directory migration material for 1890–1920 in detail, taking pains to separate out the effects of business turnover, deaths of household heads, and the coming of age of young men. But the raw figures for listings added and listings dropped do provide a rough sense of the overall level of migration into and out of the community in this period, and these figures are given in Table 2.5.

There seems little doubt that down to at least 1920 enormous numbers of newcomers continued to flow into Boston, while vast numbers of people left the community for other destinations. The number of new listings added to the city directories in each of the four decades from 1880 to 1920 was greater than the total Boston population at the start of the decade! The number of listings dropped, however, was also enormous. The "effectiveness" of migration—the ratio of population change accomplished through migration to the total volume of migration—was extraordinarily low.[13] Only 6 percent of the hundreds of thousands of moves into or out of Boston in the 1880's served to change the total population; in the World War I decade the figure was a mere 4 percent. The level of migration remained dizzyingly high, but the overwhelming preponderance of in-migrants were simply replacing departing out-migrants.

About the period since 1920 it is harder to speak with assurance, but some tentative conclusions may be ventured. It seems fairly clear that there was some diminution in the volume of new migrants entering the Boston area. One indication of this change, and

TABLE 2.5. City-directory listings added and dropped per decade, and the effectiveness of migration, Boston, 1881–1920

	1881–1890	*1891–1900*	*1901–1910*	*1911–1920*
1. Population at start of decade	362,839	448,477	560,892	670,585
2. Total listings added in decade[1]	398,995	501,288	611,872	701,062
3. Total listings dropped in decade	351,529	444,942	551,965	645,515
4. Turnover of listings	750,524	946,230	1,163,837	1,346,577
5. Net change in listings	+47,466	+56,346	+59,907	+55,547
6. Estimated effectiveness of migration[2]	0.06	0.06	0.05	0.04

[1] Both listings-added and listings-dropped figures for 1901–1910 and 1911–1920 are subject to minor error, in that the 1910 and 1920 city directories proved unobtainable. The mean listings-added and listings-dropped figures for the preceding 3 years were used as estimates for the missing years in those cases.

[2] The migration-effectiveness index is net migration, disregarding sign, as a percentage of total turnover. It indicates the ratio of population change accomplished by migration to the total number of persons who moved to produce that change, and thus measures the extent to which the two migratory streams canceled each other out. Using uncorrected directory listings-added and listings-dropped figures, of course, makes the figures quite rough; they are not, for instance, precisely comparable with the migration-effectiveness indexes given in Table 2.7. But they are sufficiently accurate for our purposes here. It seems highly unlikely that rates of either business turnover or reproductive change, which are left uncontrolled here, fluctuated so much in the period as to produce the observed decline in the migration-effectiveness index. Failure to correct for these influences depresses the index somewhat, doubtless, but this distortion should have affected all four decadal figures in much the same manner.

a principal cause of it, may be seen in figures on the shifting percentage of immigrants from abroad living in the Boston community (Table 2.6). In the late nineteenth and early twentieth centuries about a third of the city's residents at each census—32, 35, 35, 36, and 32 percent in 1880, 1890, 1900, 1910, and 1920 respectively—were born outside the United States, and, since young adults are overrepresented in most long-distance migration streams, the fraction of immigrants in the labor force was even higher. The foreign-born, for instance, accounted for almost 45 percent of the males 21 or over in the city in 1910. The restrictive legislation of 1921 and 1924 slowed the flood of immigration to a trickle and checked this source of population dynamism. By 1940 the fraction of the Boston population composed of migrants from abroad had fallen to 23 percent; by 1960 it was a mere 12 percent, and most of that small group consisted of aged men who had moved into the community several decades earlier.

TABLE 2.6. Percentage of Boston population born in Massachusetts, elsewhere in the United States, and abroad, 1880–1960 [1]

	Place of birth		
Year	*Massachusetts*	*Other U. S.*	*Foreign*
1880	54	14	32
1890	50	15	35
1900	51	14	35
1910	52	12	36
1920	56	12	32
1930	59	11	30
1940	n.a.	n.a.	23
1950	n.a.	n.a.	16
1960	70	18	12

[1] Drawn from the respective *Population* volumes of the U. S. Census. The figures for 1880–1940 refer to the city of Boston, those for 1950 and 1960 to the entire Boston metropolitan area. No separate tabulations of the Massachusetts-born were made in 1940 and 1950.

It would, of course, be possible for the vacuum left by the stemming of mass immigration to be filled entirely by heightened internal migration. This happened to some degree in cities like Detroit and Chicago, which have been major ports of entry into urban civilization for Southern blacks and poor whites. But Boston has not been a principal receiving center for these groups. A rough but useful indicator of the contribution of internal migration to a city's population is available in the form of data on how many of its inhabitants were born within the state in which the city is located. This underestimates internal migration somewhat, of course, for it fails to count moves into the city by persons born in other communities within the same state. Persons born in Massachusetts but outside of Boston must, however, have been a minority of the Massachusetts-born population of the city. The only dates for which precise evidence is available are 1885 and 1895, when the state census classified individuals by city as well as state of birth; in 1885 three-quarters of the Massachusetts-born residents of Boston had been born in Boston itself, and in 1895, 83 percent. No comparable figures are available for the twentieth century, but this suggests that for our purposes state of birth is not a bad proxy for city of birth. It is revealing, therefore, that in 1880 54 percent of the Boston population was Massachusetts-born, 14 percent came from other states, and 32 percent from outside the country, whereas in 1960 70 percent of the city's residents were born in the state, 18 percent in another state, and 12 percent abroad. The proportion of migrants from outside the United States living in Boston had fallen by 20 points; three-quarters of the decline was balanced by the rise in the number of Massachusetts-born persons and only a quarter of it by an increase in the number of migrants from other states. This is not direct and unimpeachable evidence of a notable decrease in the proportion of the Boston population that was born outside the city and migrated into it, for the entire rise in the number of Massachusetts-born residents could conceivably have been due to an influx of persons born in the state but outside the city, but this seems highly improbable. The proportion of newcomers migrating into the city and settling long enough to be counted by the census taker must have been lower than it was in the late nineteenth and early twentieth centuries.

The change, however, was not as abrupt and drastic as might be thought. In recent decades Bostonians do not appear to have become more securely rooted in their city and more immobile than in the past. Some 64 percent of the adult male residents of the city in 1880 were still to be found there in 1890. Comparable persistence figures are 41 percent for 1910–1920; 59 percent for 1930–1940; and 46 percent for 1958–1968. Methodological complications in the way in which these persistence estimates were derived make it unwise to conclude that there was a genuine long-term increase in out-migration rates over the period.[14] However imperfect, though, this evidence certainly indicates that there was no pronounced settling of the Boston population in the twentieth century.

That substantial numbers of people migrated out of Boston in these years was, of course, already apparent from the rather heavy net-migration losses the community incurred, but these persistence calculations suggest that the out-migrant stream was much larger than could have been guessed from the net figures. For the community to sustain out-migration on this scale without experiencing a radical decline in total population would have been impossible had not some in-migration been taking place. There must have been continuing migration into the community after 1930, despite the negative tilt of the net-migration scale, and the total number of people involved in the migration process must have been, as earlier, considerably higher than the net figures.

How much higher is not altogether clear, in the absence of conveniently tabulated information on listings added to and dropped from the city directories, but there are some clues in published census material. In both 1940 and 1960 the U. S. Census asked Americans where they had resided 5 years earlier. The information this yields on patterns of in- and out-migration is not perfectly comparable with the evidence from the annual city directories, because the choice of the 5-year interval leaves out all of the migrants who came and left within it—those who arrived after 1935 and departed before 1940, or after 1955 and before 1960. Since very recent arrivals to a community are also far more likely to leave it in the near future than longer-term residents,[15] the census figures minimize the mobility of the Boston population in these years.

Even so, as Table 2.7 reveals, the census data disclose a substantial amount of migration into Boston as well as migration away from it. More than 44,000 persons were lost to the city through net migration in the later years of the Great Depression, but in fact twice that many people who had lived in Boston in 1935 had departed for other communities by 1940; half of these out-migrants had their places filled by newcomers arriving in those years. Likewise the entire Boston metropolitan area lost 56,364 residents from net migration between 1955 and 1960, but more than four times that many individuals, 233,522, had actually left, with most of the vacancies they created absorbed by the 177,158 outsiders who entered the community meanwhile. The effectiveness of migration was apparently rather greater than in the past (though differences in the way the data were collected were in part responsible for this), but what seems most striking is that even in the 1935–1940 period 67 percent of the total flow of persons into and out of Boston effected no change in the size of the population, and for 1955–1960 the figure was fully 86 percent.

TABLE 2.7. Migration flows into and out of Boston, 1935–1940 and 1955–1960 [1]

	1935–1940	*1955–1960*
1. Total population (at terminal date)	721,110	2,317,570
2. In-migrants	43,855	177,158
3. Out-migrants	88,117	233,522
4. Turnover (2+3)	131,972	410,680
5. Net migration	−44,262	−56,364
6. Migration-effectiveness index	0.33	0.14

[1] U. S. Bureau of the Census, 1940, *Population: Internal Migration 1935 to 1940,* 20; 1960, Final Report PC (2)-2C, *Mobility for Metropolitan Areas,* Tables 4 and 5. The 1935–1940 figures pertain to the city of Boston, those for 1955–1960 to the Boston S.M.S.A. The base population given for the terminal date is the total population minus children born during the interval, that is, those under 5 in 1940 or 1960.

The general conclusion that stands out most clearly is that the population of the modern American metropolis, if Boston is any guide, has been far more fluid than could have been guessed on the basis of the evidence customarily employed in discussions of the issue. Measures of net changes in population size over time, and of the relative contribution of net migration and natural increase, give only the barest hint of the true situation, for the process of migration entailed enormous slippage, movement that canceled out in the ledgers that are normally used.[16] Seeming demographic stagnation may prevail in a community whose population is in fact being reshuffled at a rapid rate.

It does appear, however, that in recent decades the Boston population has become somewhat more settled and stable. The evidence is regrettably incomplete, but the rise in the number of Massachusetts-born residents (Table 2.6) suggests this, and the total turnover figures for 1935–1940 and 1955–1960 given in Table 2.7 were notably lower than those for the 1880's; with all due allowance for the short-term migrants whose movements were missed because of the nature of the census question, this is persuasive evidence of change. Though the Boston population remained much more fluid than appears from the net figures, the migratory currents sweeping through the community were running less strongly after about 1920. The blocking of mass immigration from Europe, first by World War I and then by the restrictive legislation that followed it, the shrinking pool of potential migrants from the rural New England countryside, and the explosive growth of urban centers outside the Atlantic seaboard all contributed to this end.

The Boston population had become less volatile, though by no means stagnant. To grasp the significance of this demographic change we must next discover whether there was any corresponding shift in the kinds of newcomers entering the city and of people leaving it during these years, a shift that might have altered the socioeconomic composition of the city's population and reshaped the local opportunity structure.

chapter three DIFFERENTIAL MIGRATION AND ECONOMIC OPPORTUNITY

The growth of the population of Boston since 1880 has been sluggish, but beneath the seeming stability suggested by the net figures was astonishing fluidity. Tens of thousands of newcomers poured into the city each year; tens of thousands of others left Boston for other destinations. If the population as a whole, however, was strikingly volatile, some of the city's inhabitants were much more prone to move than others. Most of this book is devoted to the analysis of the career patterns of individuals and families during their residence in Boston. It is necessary first, however, to set the stage by determining what kinds of people were moving into the community in these years and what kinds of people were moving away from it. Boston was not an island with a self-contained social system that can be analyzed in isolation; it was rather both a major importer and a major exporter of human raw material, and the shape of its social structure was heavily influenced by the shifting character of these two flows.

First we must assess the social and economic characteristics of newcomers to Boston over the past century and determine the level at which they initially established themselves on the occupational ladder. Popular folklore is rich with stereotypes about the connection between migration and worldly success—about struggling immigrant lads pulling themselves up by their bootstraps, about men on the move and on the make—and there is a substantial sociological literature that treats migration and economic opportunity in recent decades. But folklore is a poor guide to social reality, and the sociological literature, though useful, is contradictory and overgeneralized. There were, as we shall see, important historical shifts in the character of cityward migration over the past century that have not been properly recognized, and significant differences between particular migrating groups. Sweeping generalizations about "migrants" leave us ill prepared for the diversity of experience from group to group and from one historical epoch to another.

The other key issue to be explored here concerns the shifting composition of the stream of people migrating away from Boston during the period. This side of the migration process has been almost entirely neglected in the literature; the drama of the initial move from country to city has attracted all the attention, and it has been forgotten that the migratory impulse was not necessarily stifled by the initial arrival. That there was a continuous and massive stream of people leaving Boston over the entire period has already been made clear; here it will be shown that the social composition of the out-migration stream changed dramatically between the late nineteenth and mid-twentieth centuries, a change that critically affected the range of opportunities available within the city.

THE OCCUPATIONAL RANK OF NEWCOMERS TO THE CITY

Two competing models that describe the placement of new migrants in the urban class system have been advanced by social scientists. One of these might be termed the urban-escalator model. According to this view, migrants to the city typically enter the labor market at or near the bottom, providing a cheap and fluid labor supply which stimulates economic growth and creates new job opportunities higher up for men more accustomed to urban industrial ways.[1] Most of the studies supporting this notion dealt with migrants from rural America; much the same assumption, however, underlies the vast body of historical and sociological writing that deals with the assimilation of European immigrants in the American city. Newcomers from outside the community, the argument goes, are initially drawn in to take jobs on the lower rungs of the occupational ladder. As the years pass, however, they adjust to the demands of the urban setting and begin to edge their way into better posts, as other newcomers pour in to occupy the ill-paid menial jobs they leave vacant.

Recently this model of migration and assimilation has been advanced as an explanation of the dismal economic position of most black city dwellers. Negroes today are "the last of the immigrants," it is suggested, and their low levels of economic achievement are largely attributable to the heavy continuing influx into the ghetto of uneducated, unskilled migrants from backward rural areas.[2] Once the stock of ill-prepared black rural migrants is exhausted, Negro urbanites will presumably be drawn upward by the escalator in the same way as their predecessors.

The urban-escalator model, of course, entails propositions not only about the initial placement of new migrants on the urban occupational ladder but also about the social mobility experienced subsequently in the city by migrants and their offspring. Extensive analysis of this question will be offered later, in chapters assessing the mobility of European immigrant groups, religious differences in mobility patterns, and the economic position of black men in Boston. Here we are concerned only with the level at which migrants to the city initially entered the local labor market.

A quite different image of the typical urban migrant and of the relation between migration status and occupational rank emerges from a number of contemporary studies which suggest that migrants to the city today "tend to rank higher in education and occupation than the population already in the city." [3] In their massive and authoritative study, *The American Occupational Structure,* Peter M. Blau and Otis Dudley Duncan emphasize the advantages of migrants, though confessing uncertainty whether the explanation lies in the fact that the most talented and ambitious persons are least likely to remain at home, or whether it is the stimulating experience of encountering different environments that itself develops traits conducive to success. Whatever the cause, they assert, the pattern is clear. Instead of entering the city at the bottom and opening up room at the top for long-term urban residents, migrants today tend to move directly into the better positions themselves.

These contrasting views are not necessarily irreconcilable; each may be correct for a particular historical phase of the urbanization process. The older emphasis upon the low initial status of migrants to the city may have been appropriate when the cities were recruiting the bulk of their population from rural America and European peasant villages. The superior ranking of migrants to urban centers today reported in some studies may stem from the simple fact that most migrants now come from *other cities,* and do not bring with them the background handicaps that have classically been associated with country life.[4] The data for the present study extend from 1880, when barely a quarter of the population of the United States lived in communities with more than 2500 inhabitants and the migration of European peasants to these shores was taking place on a massive scale, to 1960, and thus provide a means of checking the historical limits of conflicting generalizations drawn from contemporary social research.

Table 3.1 indicates how the occupations of Boston males at four points in time—1880, 1910, 1930, and 1960—were related to their migration status. The occupational categories employed are broad, but they are adequate for these purposes. Professionals and the proprietors or managers of substantial businesses are ranked "high white-collar"; clerks, salesmen, and petty proprietors comprise the "low white-collar" stratum below them; skilled workers are a third stratum; and unskilled, semiskilled, and service workers are ranked on the bottom—a division that reflected reasonably well the distribution of income, security, prestige, and power in the community. (See Appendix B for supporting evidence.)

The index of migration status is crude except for 1960, when the Bureau of the Census tabulated separately the occupations of Bostonians who had lived in the city previous to 1955 and those who had moved into it within the past 5 years. The earlier figures, for 1880, 1910, and 1930, apply to random samples of the population drawn by the investigator from various local sources. (Sampling procedures and tests of statistical significance are detailed in Appendix A; all of the patterns singled out for discussion in the text here and subsequently were statistically significant unless otherwise indicated.) The only clue to migration status in the sources sampled—an individual's state or country of birth—was, alas, imperfect. Men born in the state of Massachusetts were considered nonmigrants,

TABLE 3.1. Occupational distribution (percent) by migration status, 1880, 1910, 1930, and 1960

		Occupational level				
Date	*Migration status*	*High white-collar*	*Low white-collar*	*Skilled*	*Low manual*	*Number*
1880	Nonmigrants[1]	12	35	24	29	834
	Native migrants	20[3]	24[3]	28	28	270
	Immigrants	5[3]	16[3]	31[3]	47[3]	776
1910	Nonmigrants[1]	8	39	21	32	301
	Native migrants	9	42	26	23	137
	Immigrants	3[3]	17[3]	30[3]	51[3]	626
1930	Nonmigrants[1]	7	32	26	36	306
	Native migrants	16[3]	29	23	33	114
	Immigrants	6	17[3]	34[3]	44[3]	334
1960[2]	Nonmigrants	15	30	19	35	554,629
	Migrants (since 1955)	35[3]	31[3]	12[3]	22[3]	45,007
	Immigrants	6[3]	23[3]	28[3]	42[3]	98,915

[1] Nonmigrants in the 1880, 1910, and 1930 samples are men born in Massachusetts. Some of these had migrated to Boston from other places in the state, but this is the closest available approximation for men born in the city of Boston itself, as indicated previously. Percentages here and elsewhere do not always add to 100, owing to rounding.

[2] This is from published census data referring to the entire employed male population of the Boston Standard Metropolitan Statistical Area; U. S. Bureau of the Census, 1960, Final Report PC (2)-2C, *Mobility for Metropolitan Areas* (Washington, D.C.: U. S. Government Printing Office, 1962), Table 4. The migrants isolated here are not precisely comparable with those elsewhere in the table; they are persons who were living outside of Boston in 1955 and had moved into it by 1960, all other persons being classified as nonmigrants. The occupational distribution of the foreign-born in 1960 was not tabulated by the Census Bureau; the figures given here are for 1950, but should be a fair approximation of the situation of immigrants a decade later; U. S. Census, 1950, *Population,* IV, Part 3, Table 22. The number of workers in the high white-collar category is underestimated in all the 1960 data; the data did not report occupations in sufficient detail to isolate major businessmen from petty proprietors, and the figures, accordingly, are for professionals only.

[3] The occupational distribution of the group was sufficiently different from that of nonmigrants to be statistically significant, as measured by a two-tail test, $P=0.10$; that is, the odds against the difference being a product of sampling error were 9 to 1 or more. Tests of significance were applied throughout; to avoid cluttering the text unduly, however, they are indicated only when an important point is at issue. For further discussion of this matter, and for justification of the choice of the rather weak significance level of 0.90, see Appendix A. All differences in the 1960 figures were significant, because the data are not from a sample but from a total enumeration.

though in fact some had doubtless been born in other communities in the state and subsequently moved to Boston. Men born outside of Massachusetts were indubitably migrants, but there is the difficulty that the sources do not indicate *when* they moved to Boston, whether as an infant with their parents or on their own as adults, a distinction of importance in both the urban-escalator and the migrant-superiority theory. Despite these limitations, however, some interesting conclusions suggest themselves.

Immigrants from abroad did indeed cluster on the lower rungs of the occupational ladder, as the urban-escalator theory would lead us to expect, and they continued to do so to much the same degree long after the restrictive legislation of the 1920's slowed the stream of entering immigrants. In 1880, 1910, and 1930, when about a third of the Boston population was foreign-born, 8 in 10 of the city's immigrants were manual workers, and only 1 in 20 was a professional or a substantial businessman. By 1960 the fraction of foreign-born residents in Boston had fallen to 12 percent, but the group was nearly as heavily proletarian as before, with 7 in 10 holding blue-collar laboring jobs and only 6 percent employed as professionals. There were some differences in the occupational distribution of particular nationalities, and important variations in the rate at which they subsequently advanced economically, matters to be explored at length in Chapter 6. But the relevant generalization to make at present is that men who were born abroad and later moved into Boston typically entered the occupational structure at the bottom in accord with the urban-escalator model of the migration process, and that this pattern remained very much in evidence as late as 1960.

Among native Americans, however, there was a quite different pattern. Men born in other states were not disadvantaged with respect to native sons of Massachusetts; they seem, on the contrary, to have fared rather better in the occupational competition, making a stronger showing in the upper white-collar category in every instance and avoiding low-manual jobs more successfully (except in 1880, when they were just a shade more concentrated in menial blue-collar jobs than native nonmigrants). The 1960 information is more precise, since very recent newcomers can be distinguished from men who had lived in the community for more than 5 years, and the advantages of newcomers show up especially sharply there.

More than a third of these recent migrants held professional jobs in 1960, but only 15 percent of nonmigrants; less than a quarter were low-skilled laborers, but more than a third of the settled population.

Not only did native migrants fare better than native nonmigrants. There was some tendency, as well, for men who moved relatively long distances to outrank those from near-by places. Tabulations that distinguish newcomers from outside the New England region (not given here) reveal that they ranked higher occupationally than migrants from the other New England states. The process of migration for the American-born population, it appears, approximated the migrant-superiority rather than the urban-escalator model as long ago as 1880.

This could mean that native rural migrants to Boston did not come with the background handicaps that have been described in the sociological literature. Alternatively, however, it might mean only that even in the late nineteenth century Boston was drawing the bulk of its native migrants from other urban centers. The evidence is too scanty to permit a resolution of this critical issue, because a migrant's state of birth is such an inadequate indicator of whether he was of rural or of urban origins. But a suggestive hint as to the answer may be obtained by isolating from the 1880 sample men who had been born in Maine or Vermont. By the twentieth century even these states were sufficiently urbanized to render suspect inferences about whether migrants from them were of farm backgrounds. But in 1880 Maine and Vermont were overwhelmingly rural. Only 18 percent of their populations lived in communities as large as 2500, as compared with 75 percent for Massachusetts. Barely 6 percent resided in cities of 15,000 or more, and by far the largest urban center in the two states—Portland, Maine—was less than a tenth the size of Boston. Since these migrants to Boston had left Maine or Vermont some time before 1880, decades before in some instances, these figures overstate the urban character of the two states at the time these men pulled up stakes and moved to Boston. Just how many of these migrants were actually Yankee farm boys, and how many were from families living in rural villages and engaged in nonagricultural occupations, cannot be determined, regrettably, but there must have been substantial numbers of the former in the group. How these lads from Maine and Vermont fared in occupational competition in Boston is indicated in Table 3.2.

The results suggest that the sweeping generalizations about the handicaps of rural migrants that have often appeared in the social-science literature need careful delimitation. The young men who left the declining areas of rural New England in the nineteenth century were probably no more familiar with urban ways than the Southern black migrants and the European immigrants who were coming to Boston at the same time, but their experience in the city was radically different. Yankee rural migrants were no more heavily concentrated on the lowest rungs of the occupational ladder than the settled native population, and far less so than immigrants or Negroes.[5] They were actually a little more likely to enter professional or major business positions than native nonmigrants, and far outranked immigrants and blacks in those areas too. They did not find their way into clerical, sales, and petty proprietary jobs as often as settled natives, but showed greater tendency to gravitate into skilled trades.

TABLE 3.2. Occupational rank (percent) of nonmigrants and various migrant groups, 1880[1]

	Occupational level				
Migration status	*High white-collar*	*Low white-collar*	*Skilled*	*Low manual*	*Number*
Nonmigrants	12	35	24	29	834
Migrants from—					
Rural New England	15	18[2]	37[2]	29	138
Europe	5[2]	16[2]	31[2]	47[2]	776
Southern U. S. (blacks)	2[2]	5[2]	9[2]	84[2]	1895

[1] The data on Southern-born black migrants to Boston, to be analyzed further in Chapter 8, were drawn by Elizabeth H. Pleck of Brandeis University from the manuscript schedules of the U. S. Census of 1880 for Thernstrom and Pleck, "The Last of the Immigrants? A Comparative Analysis of Immigrant and Black Social Mobility in Late-Nineteenth-Century Boston," unpublished paper for the 1970 annual meetings of the Organization of American Historians.

[2] See Table 3.1, note 3.

Unfortunately, it is not possible to isolate rural migrants to Boston in the 1910 and 1930 samples, but there is another shred of evidence pointing in the same direction in the 1960 Census material on persons who had moved into the city since 1955. No separate tabulation was made for migrants who had come from rural areas, but at least a distinction was drawn between migrants from other major metropolitan areas and those from outside one of the 212 S.M.S.A.'s.[6] That breakdown revealed that migrants from other cities fared better than those from outside urban areas, but that even the migrants from nonmetropolitan areas were of considerably higher occupational rank than the settled population of the city; 32 percent were professionals in 1960, more than double the proportion of nonmigrants in that category, and only a quarter were in low manual callings, as opposed to 36 percent of nonmigrants. Black migrants from nonmetropolitan areas, however, were an exception; 78 percent of them held low-skilled blue-collar jobs, as compared with 65 percent of black nonmigrants; 12 percent were white-collar workers, against 21 percent of the settled black population. Native white migrants from rural areas, to the extent to which classification in terms of movement from nonmetropolitan areas identifies men of rural origins adequately, do not seem to have labored under grave disadvantages in the occupational competition; their situation was different in kind from that of immigrants and blacks from rural backgrounds.

The two models of the migration process, then, both capture part of the truth. European immigrants and black migrants did enter the urban labor market at the lowest levels. Native white migrants, however, even those from heavily rural states, found a much wider range of jobs open to them. There were both "push" and "pull" factors influencing all migrants, circumstances impelling them to leave their point of origin and circumstances drawing them to one destination and not to another. But in the case of native white men on the move, the pull of perceived opportunity in Boston seems to have been especially strong, and that perception was correct. For them there was indeed room at the top and middle of the occupational structure as well as at the bottom. For European immigrants and black migrants, the alternatives were narrower. The pull of Boston lay not in the availability of employment in the skilled trades or the white-collar world; to find a job at all, however lowly, was apparently attraction enough. This was as true in 1880 as it is today; there is no evidence of basic change in the composition of either the native white or the immigrant and black groups of arrivals.

What did change over the period was the balance between the two groups, and thus the overall composition of the in-migrating stream. The flow of immigrants from abroad was largely halted in the 1920's, and the heightened influx of blacks into the community was not of sufficient magnitude to fill the void. A rising percentage of the newcomers to the community, therefore, were moving directly into jobs in the upper reaches of the occupational structure.

From some points of view—that of a local employer, for example—it might seem highly desirable that increasing numbers of new arrivals possess the requisite abilities to fill positions above the low manual level, but a different perspective on the matter might have been held by men already on the scene who aspired to move upward into these better jobs themselves. In the absence of other offsetting influences, the greater the importation of talent from outside, the smaller the prospects for upward social mobility by the local talent. The assistant professor hungry for promotion does not welcome the news that his department has decided to import a new associate professor from another university—unless, of course, new vacancies on the next rung of the academic ladder are simultaneously being created by countervailing forces, such as the resignation and departure of another associate professor. To see whether such a countervailing force operated in Boston, we turn to the question of what kinds of people were leaving the city for other destinations.

CHANGING PATTERNS OF OUT-MIGRATION FROM BOSTON

Boston was not only a busy receiving center for new migrants; it was also a dispatching point from which enormous numbers of migrants were directed to other destinations. This crucial and little-understood fact about the city poses serious difficulties for a study like the present one, in that any generalizations that can be advanced about the movement of individuals through the Boston social structure are limited to that element of the population that remained on the scene to be observed. The proportion of the city's Irish laborers who moved up into better jobs between 1880 and 1890 may be computed, but it must be recalled that over half of these men had disappeared from Boston altogether by 1890 and that their experiences in other communities may have been entirely different. The nature of the available sources makes the systematic tracking down of out-migrants in their new abodes so difficult that it could not be attempted.[7]

This is a severe limitation, and one that must be kept constantly in mind in evaluating any conclusions offered subsequently. A substantial fraction of the Boston population did not remain patiently under the investigator's microscope long enough to leave an impression; what happened to them elsewhere is imponderable. One can, however, gain considerable insight into the process of out-migration and its significance for the community by analyzing how out-migrants differed from the settled population at various points in time.

In the late nineteenth and early twentieth centuries, when Boston was drawing into it enormous numbers of newcomers, most of them of the kind described by the urban-escalator model, it was simultaneously exporting unusually large numbers of persons of similarly low status. There was substantial out-migration within every occupational group, but it was the middle class, as Table 3.3 makes plain, and especially upper-middle-class professionals and businessmen, that provided continuity in the community then. The lower an individual ranked on the occupational ladder, the smaller the likelihood that he would still be found in Boston by the next census taker a decade later; nearly half of the low-manual laborers living in the city in 1880 had left it by 1890; nearly two-thirds of the laborers of 1910 had departed by 1920.

Two interesting implications of these figures should be underscored. First, they conflict sharply with a familiar and well-entrenched stereotype about the American city of this era—the myth of the closed ghetto. According to the ghetto conception, poor city dwellers typically huddled together with others of their race or national origins in slum neighborhoods, neighborhoods in which many were permanently trapped.[8] One acute observer of the nineteenth-century city declared in 1876 that the inhabitants of "the more squalid sections of any city . . . do not migrate; they abide in their lot; sinking lower in helplessness, hopelessness and squalor." [9] What was thought to be the paralyzing, immobilizing character of life in New York's Hell's kitchen inspired a vivid metaphor: "The district is like a spider's web. Of those who come to it very few . . . ever leave it." [10]

In the light of this image of lower-class life, it is striking that in

TABLE 3.3. Occupational differentials in persistence in Boston for selected decades: percent of group residing in city at end of decade[1]

Decade	*Occupational level*	*Percent*	*Number*
1880–1890	High white-collar	80	903
	Low white-collar	71	
	Skilled	63	
	Low manual	56	
1910–1920	High white-collar	58	1053
	Low white-collar	50	
	Skilled	36	
	Low manual	35	
1930–1940	High white-collar	56	824
	Low white-collar	68	
	Skilled	66	
	Low manual	51	
1958–1968	High white-collar	40	981
	Low white-collar	39	
	Skilled	59	
	Low manual	51	

[1] It was not possible to make the age distribution of the four samples precisely comparable. Since young men are more migratory than their elders, this skewed the results somewhat. The figures for 1880–1890 pertain to men aged 20 to 39 in 1880; half were in their 20's and half in their 30's. The 1910 sample was of men married in Boston that year; 1 percent were under 20, 72 percent 20–29, 22 percent 30–39, and 5 percent 40 or older. In the 1930 sample, of men whose wives gave birth to sons in Boston that year, the age distribution was: under 20, 0.2 percent; 20–29, 40 percent; 30–39, 44 percent; 40 or over, 15 percent. No information was available as to the age of the 1958 sample, drawn from the Boston city directory of that year, but it must have been more heavily weighted toward the middle-aged than any of the others. The relatively low persistence of all occupational groups between 1910 and 1920 is probably attributable in part to the exceptional youthfulness of the sample, and perhaps to the disruptions accompanying World War I. The low rates for 1958–1968, however, might have been even lower had it been possible to confine the sample to men under 40. On the other hand, the incompleteness of the city directory's coverage of suburban dwellers may have biased the 1958–1968 figures downward; see Appendix A for further consideration of this. None of these possible biases should have distorted occupational differentials in persistence in any event.

Another source of bias in these figures is class differentials in mortality. Men on the lower rungs of the class ladder tend to late-nineteenth- and early-twentieth-century Boston blue-collar workers, and especially unskilled or semiskilled laborers, were so highly transient. Few of them served life sentences in particular slums; a substantial fraction of them failed even to remain within the boundaries of the entire city for as long as 10 years.

There were slight differences in the propensities of particular ethnic groups to persist in the community, but no element of the working-class population was rooted in the city in the manner suggested by the ghetto hypothesis; large numbers of every group left Boston altogether within a relatively short period, and many of those who did remain soon moved from the inner-city neighborhoods in which they first concentrated toward outlying areas of the city.

There were indeed ghettos in Boston, if by that one merely means neighborhoods with strong clusterings of poor people from ethnic minorities. But the presence of such clusterings does not mean, as has often been assumed, that the *individuals* who lived there at one point in time were doomed to remain there forever. Far from it. A crucial characteristic of American city life in the classic era of heavy immigration was precisely that city dwellers in general and poor people in particular were highly transient, leaving a single faint imprint on the census schedule or the city-directory files and then vanishing completely. The city was a Darwinian jungle, in which those on the upper rungs of the class ladder were most likely to survive to be counted in the future.

A second implication of the late-nineteenth- and early-twentieth-century pattern of differential out-migration from the city is that it raises questions about the historical validity of current assumptions about the relation between migration and economic success. The prevailing view of migration today emphasizes that the spatial mobility of labor yields higher returns, but the studies supporting that

---

die younger than men of higher status, and it might be that the patterns for 1880–1890 and 1910–1920 stem from that rather than from actual differences in out-migration. However, trial calculations that take this influence into account, using the estimated class differentials in mortality supplied in Aaron Antonovsky, "Social Class, Life Expectancy and Overall Mortality, *Milbank Memorial Fund Quarterly,* 45 (April 1967), 31–73, and cohort survival rates from Paul H. Jacobson, "Cohort Survival for Generations Since 1840," *ibid.*, 42 (July 1965), 36–53, narrow but do not eliminate the differentials that appear in these figures.

assumption have largely been conducted in an era in which socioeconomic status and the propensity to migrate are directly rather than inversely related.[11] We cannot be sure, for migrants from Boston are lost to the study once they leave the city, but one wonders whether the exceptional earlier volatility of the American working class, and especially of its least-skilled members, does not point to the existence of a permanent floating proletariat made up of men ever on the move spatially but rarely winning economic gains as a result of spatial mobility.[12] Did these droves of laborers, factory workers, and service employees leave Boston in the 1880's for the same reason that engineers and lawyers leave it today, namely, because they have been offered a better job in Denver? Or was their movement more often drifting than purposeful, initiated by the loss of a job rather than by the offer of a better one? The question is moot, in the absence of hard evidence about the fate of out-migrants after they left the city, but at least we may note that backward extrapolations from investigations made in a quite different historical era seem entirely unjustified.

It was not until 1930 that the migration differentials that prevail in contemporary America made an appearance in Boston. The older pattern was reversed in both the 1930 and the 1958 samples. Not that the working class became notably more settled than earlier. Persistence rates for blue-collar workers were much the same in the 1930's as they were in the 1880's, and a little lower for 1958–1968. Rapid population turnover continued to undercut tendencies toward the formation of class ghettos, as before. What changed was that the middle class became far less rooted than earlier. A flight of professionals and major businessmen began in the 1930's, and by 1958–1968 clerks, salesmen, and small proprietors too were on the move.

That a new pattern of selectivity in out-migration from the community prevailed after 1930 may be further substantiated with data less susceptible to error than those derived by tracing samples through city directories to identify persisters and out-migrants. The 1960 Census supplied information with which to compare the occupational rank of individuals who moved away from Boston between 1955 and 1960 with that of the settled population (Table 3.4). Fully a third of those who departed from the community in this period were professionals, but only 15 percent of nonmigrants were. Other white-collar workers and skilled craftsmen were also somewhat overrepresented in the out-migration stream, and men in menial blue-collar jobs were grossly underrepresented; only 18 percent of the out-migrants fell in the latter category, but 36 percent of the settled population did. Large numbers of people from every walk of life were leaving Boston, but now it was the middle class, and especially the upper middle class, that was taking the lead.

TABLE 3.4. Occupational distribution (percent) of nonmigrants and of out-migrants from Boston, 1955–1960[1]

	Occupational level				
Migration status	*Professional*	*Other white-collar*	*Skilled*	*Low manual*	*Number*
Nonmigrants	15	30	19	36	554,629
Out-migrants	35	32	16	18	57,962

[1] Calculated from U. S. Bureau of the Census, *Mobility for Metropolitan Areas,* Table 5. Occupations are those held as of 1960, so that the figures given for out-migrants from Boston indicate their occupational level in the community to which they moved rather than in Boston at the time of their departure. This is only a rough measure of their occupational distribution at the time they left Boston, for some out-migrants doubtless moved up occupationally as a result of migration. It is unlikely, however, that enough did so to call into question the point argued in the text—that out-migrants from Boston, as well as new migrants to it, were of much higher occupational rank than the settled population. It is unfortunate that the Census Bureau did not tabulate the occupations of out-migrants at both ends of their journey, so that this issue might be explored.

There was, then, a shift in the composition of the stream of migrants leaving Boston which corresponded neatly to the shift in the composition of the in-migrant stream that occurred in the second and third decades of the twentieth century. Just as the supply of newcomers of the type envisioned in the urban-escalator model began to be exhausted, and newly arrived migrants to the community tended increasingly to be the kinds of people who traditionally had moved directly into jobs on the upper rungs of the occupational ladder—native-born whites, that is—there was a reversal of traditional differentials in out-migration rates, a reversal that created an increased number of vacancies for in-migrants of this type. Had this development not taken place, the level of opportunities available to the settled population would presumably have been declining in recent decades. The competition for better positions would have become increasingly severe as a growing proportion of the in-migrating population came equipped to enter them, and ever fewer newcomers were immigrants ready to accept menial jobs. The post-1930 pattern of selective out-migration from the community, however, was an equilibrating influence that tended to offset the shift in the character of in-migration.[13] The data are much too rough to determine whether these two changes in migration patterns canceled each other out completely, but it appears that the net impact of changing migration patterns upon the level of opportunities within Boston was quite slight.

chapter four OCCUPATIONAL CAREER PATTERNS

The population of Boston was strikingly fluid. It does not necessarily follow, however, that the social system of the community was similarly fluid. Spatial mobility into and out of the city was very common; whether mobility up and down the local social hierarchy by men who remained in Boston for any length of time was common too is another question altogether. Newcomers who settled in Boston and their offspring may characteristically have risen on the social scale in accord with the urban-escalator model; they might, on the contrary, have found that class lines within the community were virtually impassable. Despite the dizzying demographic flux of the 1880's, some contemporary observers were fearful that the latter was the case. "We are rapidly developing classes in society as well as in the industrial world," declared Boston labor leader Frank Foster in 1883, "and . . . these classes are becoming more and more fixed." [1] The Reverend Newman Smyth, a local minister, offered a similar analysis in more vivid language:

> The man at the bottom of the ladder leading up to the social heavens may yet dream there is a ladder let down to him; but the angels are not seen very often ascending and descending; one after

another, it would seem, some unseen yet hostile powers are breaking out the middle rungs of the ladder.[2]

The meaning of social inequality, these remarks recognize, and the viability of a class system in which some citizens enjoy prestige, power, and affluence while others are poor and powerless, depends in considerable measure on the extent to which inequality is structured and permanent. Whether classes are "fixed" or open, whether there are "middle rungs" on the social ladder that are accessible to men on the bottom, are crucial questions about any system of social stratification.

This is the first of several chapters that wrestle with aspects of that broad issue. Here I am concerned with the occupational career patterns of representative citizens of Boston between 1880 and 1968. To know that John Jones is a banker, a bartender, or a bootblack is to know a good deal about him. It not only tells us what he does to earn a living, but enables us, with varying degrees of accuracy, to make inferences about how good a living he earns, how much education he had before leaving school, what kind of dwelling and what kind of neighborhood he lives in, at some times and places even his ethnic background, religious affiliation, and political preferences. Occupation is highly correlated with other social variables in any modern industrial society. It is for this reason that social scientists commonly view occupation as the most important determinant of social position, and the most useful criterion by which to place someone in a social category.

Too often, however, occupation is treated as a static rather than a dynamic variable. Occupational labels seem reassuringly solid and stable—once a lawyer always a lawyer, we assume, once a laborer always a laborer. But in fact the former is not always the case, and the latter is not very often the case. There are certain callings that require relatively rare talents and training and are sufficiently well rewarded to keep people who enter them in them for a lifetime. The odds are heavy that today's psychiatrists and tool-and-die makers will be doing the same kind of work 20 years from now. But is this the exception or the rule? In this Chapter I assess the extent to which residents of Boston were able to move from one occupational level to another in the course of their careers, and attempt to ascertain whether this period of nearly 90 years witnessed any fundamental changes in rates and patterns of career occupational mobility. Subsequent chapters will present a similar assessment of another variety of social mobility, mobility from generation to generation rather than within an individual career; examine the influence of nationality, religion, and race upon mobility patterns; and explore similarities and differences between Boston and other communities.

THE PROBLEM OF OCCUPATIONAL CLASSIFICATION

Only about half of the men who worked in Boston in 1880 and who were still employed there 10 years later used precisely the same occupational label to describe their jobs at the two points. The other half were doing something sufficiently different to employ a different job title. By this measure the Boston occupational structure was strikingly fluid. The measure, however, is obviously inadequate, for many of these job changes may not have entailed any significant change in social position. The clerk who becomes a salesman, the menial hospital employee who becomes a short-order cook, the longshoreman who becomes a truck driver—these are men who have not discernibly gained (or lost) in the process of changing jobs. They may have been drawn into the new post by slightly higher wages, or slightly more attractive working conditions; alternatively, they may simply have been fired from their former job, and have been forced to accept somewhat inferior wages or working conditions in order to find work at all. In either case, the student of social structure would classify their movement as horizontal, not vertical. There is a bewildering variety of occupational titles in any complex economy; the U. S. Labor Department's *Dictionary of Occupational Titles* has no fewer than 20,000 separate entries. A considerable proportion of the occupational changes that take place in the American economy are moves between closely related jobs of essentially similar status, and many moves between jobs that are not closely related nonetheless mean no vertical movement up or down the social ladder.

The measurement of occupational mobility, therefore, is not as straightforward a task as simply counting the number of people who change their occupational titles in a given period. To determine the rate of vertical occupational movement requires a specification of the broad occupational categories that may be considered socially distinct, and a definition of which jobs fit in which category. Social investigators have been making attempts to do this for a century or more without arriving at any consensus, and a dazzling new solution to this knotty problem will not be presented here. The approach, rather, will be flexible and eclectic. The question of which distinctions make a difference and which may safely be ignored depends upon the specific question being posed. The number of categories employed in the analysis that follows, and thus the fineness of the distinctions being drawn, will vary according to the issue under consideration.

The occupational information originally drawn from the Census and other sources was coded in 99 fairly specific categories, so that carpenters could be distinguished from machinists, physicians from attorneys, office clerks from store clerks. These categories, however, were too finely calibrated to be of use except at a few points. Employing this scheme to cross-tabulate the occupations of sample members at two different points yields a mobility matrix with 9801 cells (99×99), enough to paralyze the most indefatigable of analysts! I therefore grouped the data into broad occupational strata and even broader occupational classes. Five strata were distinguished—high white-collar, low white-collar, skilled, semiskilled, and unskilled. Job shifts across the boundaries of one of the five are termed *interstratum* mobility. (Occasionally the five strata or levels have been reduced to four, by classifying unskilled and semiskilled jobs together as "low-manual.") For some purposes an even greater simplification proved useful, and attention was directed at only those changes of occupation that entailed a shift from blue-collar to white-collar or from white- collar to blue-collar work; these moves I refer to as *interclass* mobility. (For a detailed listing of the occupations in the five strata and the two classes, and evidence of the validity of the classification scheme, see Appendix B.) Measurement of jobs shifts between strata and between classes will reveal those cases of occupational mobility that represented a significant change in social status.

THE CHANGING OCCUPATIONAL STRUCTURE AND THE LEVEL OF "MINIMUM" MOBILITY

Before we ask how much career occupational mobility there was in Boston between 1880 and 1968, it will be useful to inquire how much mobility there *had* to be. There are circumstances in which a good deal of shifting from job to job has to take place because of certain structural imperatives. These are of two kinds.

First, there can be an imbalance between the volume and character of the migration streams that bring some people to a community and remove others, an imbalance that creates a "migration vacuum."[3] If, for instance, out-migrants in a given period are drawn heavily from high-ranked occupations and the in-migrants that replace them are largely unskilled peasants, local persons on the lower rungs of the occupational ladder are likely to be drawn upward into the better positions left vacant. This need not necessarily take place—employers sometimes have the alternative of restructuring the work process to eliminate the vacant positions—but if it does not, the occupational structure of the community has to shift correspondingly. Similarly, there could be a migration vacuum that heightened competition for high-status jobs and limited upward-mobility opportunities for local residents, if out-migrants were predominantly of low status and new arrivals were equipped to enter the occupational structure at the upper levels. As far as can be determined from the rough data at hand, however, neither circumstance prevailed in Boston during these years. There was instead a certain symmetry in the two migration streams. When most newcomers entered on the lower rungs of the class ladder, places for them were being vacated by out-migrants of similar rank; when the in-migrant stream began to include larger numbers of professionals and white-collar workers, there was a corresponding shift in the character of the typical out-migrant. Little or no occupational mobility within the community was necessary to balance the books on this count.[4]

There is another structural imperative that requires a certain amount of occupational mobility in some instances, namely, changes in the occupational structure of the community that necessitate the redistribution of the labor force from one job category to another. A community in which the proportion of white-collar workers in the labor force increased from 30 percent to 60 percent over the course of a decade would be one in which a great deal of upward mobility from blue-collar to white-collar jobs would be necessary, in the absence of differential migration flows which filled that vacuum. The latter movement did not take place in Boston; it is time to see how much "minimum" mobility there had to be in the community as a result of changes in the local occupational structure.

Over the past century there has been a dramatic growth in the fraction of the American labor force holding white-collar jobs, particularly in professional and technical occupations, and a sharp decline in the relative size of the unskilled-labor group.[5] This would lead us to expect that a substantial fraction of Boston's workers moved upward on the occupational scale as a result of structural change in the local economy.

A close look at the Boston occupational structure over the period,

TABLE 4.1. Occupational distribution (percent) of the male labor force of Boston, 1880–1970[1]

Occupation	*1880*	*1890*	*1900*	*1910*	*1920*	*1930*	*1940*	*1950*	*1960*	*1970*
White-collar	32	33	38	35	32	36	39	42	46	51
Professions	3	3	6	5	5	8	8	11	15	21
Other white-collar	29	30	32	30	27	28	31	31	31	30
Blue-collar	68	67	62	65	68	64	61	58	54	49
Skilled manual	36	30	32	22	27	21	19	21	21	19
Semiskilled and service	17	24	18	32	31	30	34	29	27	25
Unskilled labor	15	13	12	11	10	13	8	8	6	5

[1] Calculated from the respective *Population* volumes of the U. S. Census. The data could not be made precisely comparable from decade to decade, but are sufficient to establish broad trends. The 1940–1970 figures were combined from the broad occupational groupings used in those censuses: "professional," "clerical," "sales," and so forth. The earlier ones were developed from census tabulations of the number of men working by detailed occupational category. The farther back in time they extend, the less satisfactory these categories become. There is the further difficulty that the data for 1880–1900 refer not to the entire male labor force but to men working in selected "major" occupations—60 of them in 1880, 50 in 1890, 129 in 1900. The seeming expansion of white-collar and skilled employment between 1880 and 1890 and the apparent reversal of this trend in the next decade is probably a result of the incompleteness of the earlier data, and likely does not indicate genuine shifts in the occupational structure. The figures from 1950 on pertain to the entire Boston metropolitan area rather than to Boston proper; the inclusion of suburban dwellers accounts for some of the post-1940 growth in the professions, but not all of it. The "other white-collar" category, it should be noted, is not identical with the "low white-collar" designation used throughout the present study. It is impossible from the published census tabulations to distinguish the proprietors and managers of major enterprises from other managers, proprietors, and officials to create "high white-collar" and "low white-collar" classes like those used with the sample data.

however, only partially sustains this expectation. Table 4.1 shows that there was indeed an expansion of the white-collar labor force, and especially of the fraction of professional and technical workers employed locally: 32 percent of Boston's males held white-collar jobs of some kind in 1880, 51 percent in 1970; the proportion of professionals, a mere 3 percent in 1880, increased sevenfold during the period, while unskilled-labor jobs shrank from 15 percent of the total to 5 percent. These were meaningful changes, but the significant thing about them is that they occurred so slowly and irregularly. The fraction of white-collar workers in the city was no greater in 1920 than it had been 40 years earlier; the only substantial changes were that both the top and the bottom strata of the working class were shrinking and the intermediate semiskilled and service stratum was expanding by precisely as much, which could not be considered net upgrading. After 1920 some structural upgrading of the labor force took place, but even then it was not very rapid or dramatic when measured on the scale by which occupational mobility is measured in this study. Much of the analysis that follows concerns occupational shifts over a decade; even that portion of it concerned with changes between first known and last known occupation concerns individuals whose career patterns could be traced for only two or three decades in most instances. Table 4.2 conveniently summarizes the net shifts in Boston occupational struc-

TABLE 4.2. Net redistribution (percent) of the male labor force in Boston, 1880–1970[1]

Occupation	*1880–1890*	*1890–1900*	*1900–1910*	*1910–1920*	*1920–1930*	*1930–1940*	*1940–1950*	*1950–1960*	*1960–1970*
White-collar	+1	+5	−3	−3	+4	+3	+3	+4	+5
Professions	0	+3	−1	0	+3	0	+3	+4	+6
Other white-collar	+1	+2	−2	−3	+1	+3	0	0	−1
Blue-collar	−1	−5	+3	+3	−4	−3	−3	−4	−4
Skilled manual	−6	+2	−10	+5	−6	−2	+2	0	−2
Semiskilled and service	+7	−6	+14	−1	−1	+4	−5	−2	−2
Unskilled labor	−2	−1	−1	−1	+3	−5	0	−5	−1

[1] As indicated in the note to Table 4.1, the somewhat puzzling changes in the earlier decades are probably attributable to inadequacies in the data and are not to be taken too seriously.

ture that occurred each decade between 1880 and 1970, and it shows that the amount of shifting that could be called minimum structural mobility was quite small in any decade. In no decade did more than 1 in 20 members of the labor force move upward into a white-collar position as a result of structural change; the mean decadal rate of shifting between manual and nonmanual jobs required by this structural imperative was a mere 3.4 percent. The amount of minimum mobility required by the shifting occupational structure was, of course, somewhat greater over longer intervals, but even in the 30-year period that saw the most rapid upgrading of the labor force (1940–1970), only 1 man in 8 moved upward for this reason.

There was, then, no overwhelmingly strong structural imperative that forced a considerable amount of shifting from job to job on the part of the Boston labor force. The migratory currents flowing into and out of the community did not create a sizable vacuum either at the top or at the bottom of the occupational structure, and the structure itself changed slowly enough to require relatively little job displacement in the short run. If there was significant career occupational mobility in Boston in this period, it was in excess of the minimum structural mobility that had to take place.

CAREER MOBILITY IN SELECTED DECADES

Even over the relatively short span of a decade, representative Bostonians appear to have shifted from one occupational stratum to another with some frequency. This may be seen from Table 4.3, which indicates the extent to which members of four samples of Boston men of roughly comparable age remained employed at the same occupational level over a 10-year period. Three conclusions may be drawn from it.

First, a quarter or more of the men in each of these four samples made a significant occupational change within 10 years of the time at which they were first observed. Only 74 percent of the members of the samples of males employed in the city in 1880 and 1930 who still held a job there a decade later, and 73 percent of the sample drawn in 1958, had neither gained nor lost occupational status. The World War I decade saw even more movement, though this was largely attributable to the predominance of young men in the sample employed; a little more than two-thirds of them remained at the

TABLE 4.3. Career continuity: percent of sample holding job in same stratum at start and end of first decade observed

Occupation	*1880–1890*	*1910–1920*	*1930–1940*	*1958–1968*
Entire sample	74	69[1]	74	73
High white-collar	88	90	94	97
Low white-collar	70	79	71	67
Skilled	82	66	71	68
Semiskilled	62	65	79	73
Unskilled	68	39	67	47
Number in sample	543	413	467	399

[1] As cautioned earlier (Table 3.3), there were some age differences between these samples that produced spurious variations in the patterns displayed, for young men are more mobile, both occupationally and geographically, than older ones. The 1880–1890 figures here are for men aged 20–39, with men in their 20's and in their 30's represented in nearly equal numbers. The apparently lower degree of occupational continuity between 1910 and 1920 was not quite of a magnitude to be statistically significant, and it probably reflects the special youthfulness of members of the sample, nearly three-quarters of whom were under 30 in 1910. Separate tabulations for men under 30 in the 1880, 1910, and 1930 samples yield nearly identical patterns. No information was available as to the age of the 1958 sample, drawn from the city directory. It was probably more middle-aged than the three preceding ones, which suggests that if an age-controlled comparison had been possible this decade would have seen more occupational shifting than any of the earlier ones.

same occupational level by the decade's end, while 31 percent moved either up or down.

A second point to note is that there was much greater occupational continuity in the highest stratum, composed of professionals and prosperous businessmen, than in any of the others. The only direction in which individuals in the high white-collar stratum could move, of course, was down, and it is noteworthy that few did so—a maximum of one-eighth in the case of the 1880 group, and a mere 3 percent of the 1958 sample.

None of the other strata were nearly so closed. It might be thought that skilled craftsmen, tested by long apprenticeships, typically remained in their craft for a lifetime. But this was by no means the case. In only one of the four samples did the skilled workers of Boston display greater occupational stability than the mean for all employed men.[6] More refined tabulations reveal that some particular crafts—printing and tool-and-die making, for instance—were notably more stable than others, but the striking thing is that skilled callings as a class were far from being closed compartments.

Similarly, it might be thought that unskilled men at the very bottom of the manual category, presumably lacking anything but a strong back, had little chance of escaping and moving up. This expectation, too, finds no support in the data here. The unskilled remained within their own stratum less than the mean for the entire sample in every case; in the World War I decade, in fact, fewer than 4 in 10 of them were still unskilled by 1920. The overall impression that emerges is that even over as short a period as 10 years there was a significant possibility that Bostonians of every occupational level except the highest would experience vertical occupational mobility.

A final observation about Table 4.3 is that it surprisingly suggests that the Boston occupational structure became neither notably more nor notably less fluid over a period of nearly 90 years. There was some variation in the continuity rates of particular strata, but a remarkable similarity in the figures for the groups as a whole. The decade 1910–1920 saw the least continuity but not enough less to be statistically significant, despite the special youthfulness of that sample; 1958–1968 would probably have shown less continuity had it been possible to control for age in that sample. But what seems most impressive is the broad uniformity of pattern between 1880 and 1968. It was not feasible to draw comparable new samples of men for each decade since 1880, which would be necessary to establish the point in a fully convincing way, but the figures for each of the four trial borings given here seem strikingly similar. The economy, ethnic complexion, demographic structure, educational system, and many other facets of Boston were substantially altered over the very long span of years between the presidencies of James A. Garfield and of Richard M. Nixon, but the rate of circulation between occupational strata, at least by this measure, has remained relatively constant, and at a significantly higher level than the minimum mobility required by change in the occupational structure.

A substantial minority of Bostonians moved from one occupational level to another in a typical decade. *How far* and *in what direction* did they move?

The beginnings of an answer appear in Table 4.4, which indicates how many men in these four groups remained on the same side of the blue-collar–white-collar line at the end of a decade. The degree of continuity registered here is naturally much higher, for many shifts of occupational level—from unskilled to semiskilled, or from low white-collar to high white-collar, for example—do not entail a change of broad occupational class. Taking movement across the manual-nonmanual line, rather than movement between the five occupational strata, as a measure cuts the volume of vertical mobility approximately in half. Roughly 2 out of 7 men changed strata in each of these decades; approximately 1 in 7 (between 12 and 17 percent), Table 4.4 reveals, moved to a job that was on the other side of the manual-nonmanual line. The World War I decade again appears to have seen more occupational shifting, but again this was attributable to the age composition of the sample. When that is taken into account, the uniformity of the process was impressive.

There was, however, some variation in the balance between upward and downward movement between middle-class and working-class occupations. In the earliest decade, 1880–1890, the two types

TABLE 4.4. Career mobility (percent) across class boundaries during selected decades

Occupation at end of decade	*1880–1890*	*1910–1920*	*1930–1940*	*1958–1968*
In same class	88	83	87	87
In different class	12	17[1]	13	13
White-collar to blue-collar	12	10	16[2]	9
Blue-collar to white-collar	12	22[1]	11	17
Ratio of upward to downward mobility	1.0	2.2[3]	0.7	1.9
Number in sample	543	413	467	399

[1] Significantly higher than all other samples.
[2] Significantly higher than 1910–1920 and 1958–1968.
[3] Although the higher rate of shifting across class boundaries for the 1910–1920 sample resulted from its exceptionally youthful age distribution, the high ratio of upward to downward mobility did not. In the other samples the ratio of upward to downward mobility for men under 30 was little different than it was for older men; for instance, it was 1.1 for young men in the 1880–1890 decade, compared with 1.0 for the total sample of men aged 20–39.

of mobility were in equilibrium; 12 percent of the white-collar workers in the city skidded to a manual job by 1890, while 12 percent of the blue-collar employees found their way into a white-collar job. This balance, however, was susceptible to considerable change, despite the relative constancy of the overall rate of movement across the manual-nonmanual line. In the boom period around World War I, more than twice (2.2 times) as many moved up as down; in the sluggish 1930's, only 11 percent climbed while 16 percent dropped, a ratio of upward to downward movement of 0.7. The Great Depression did not freeze the occupational structure of the city and sharply diminish the volume of mobility from class to class. What happened rather was that fewer workers moved upward, and increased numbers of white-collar employees found themselves unable to retain their positions. The decade 1958–1968 was another boom period for Boston men, with the proportion of climbers nearly double (1.9 times) the proportion of skidders. There was impressive similarity from decade to decade in the overall rate of interclass mobility of Boston men, but a good deal of variation in the relative number of passengers on the up and down escalators.

There was no clear trend toward diminished upward mobility; contemporary social critics who believe that the opportunity structure today is far less favorable to the poor than that of the nineteenth and early twentieth centuries, and who assert, without benefit of hard evidence, that poverty is increasingly a "permanent way of life," will find little support in these figures.[7] The decade 1958–1968 saw more upward movement from blue-collar to white-collar jobs than the 1880's, and it is likely that the figure would have been even higher had it been possible to confine the recent sample to men in their 20's and 30's, as was the case with the earlier ones. But neither was there a clear trend toward an increasingly open social structure, contrary to the opinion of some optimistic observers. Instead there seems to have been a rather stable pattern, with a fairly constant overall rate of interclass circulation and with cyclical fluctuations in the ratio of upward to downward movement, fluctuations obviously connected with changing local economic circumstances.

Generalizations about white-collar workers or blue-collar workers as a group are necessarily crude. A finer-grained portrait of the career patterns of Boston men in these years, such as is provided in

Table 4.5, reveals some of the important differences that existed within these broad groupings. The first conclusion to be drawn from more detailed inspection of the experiences of particular occupational strata is that virtually all of the downward movement from middle-class to working-class callings in Boston was movement by men in the lower-status white-collar positions to begin with. The proportions of low white-collar workers dropping into manual jobs was anywhere from nearly two and a half to nearly seven times as large as the proportion of high nonmanual men skidding. The sharp increase in downward mobility from the middle class during

TABLE 4.5. Interstratum and interclass career mobility (percent), first decade observed

		Stratum at end of decade					
Stratum at start of decade	*Decade*	*High white-collar*	*Low white-collar*	*Skilled*	*Semi-skilled*	*Unskilled*	*Number*
High white-collar	1880–90	88	6	4	0	2	52
	1910–20	90	7	0	3	0	31
	1930–40	94	3	0	3	0	35
	1958–68	97	3	0	0	0	71
Low white-collar	1880–90	15	70	8	5	1	157
	1910–20	10	79	2	7	3	134
	1930–40	9	71	3	14	3	131
	1958–68	19	67	4	9	1	122
Skilled	1880–90	4	6	82	4	4	164
	1910–20	2	21	66	10	1	103
	1930–40	2	12	71	8	7	156
	1958–68	0	18	68	10	4	100
Semiskilled	1880–90	1	18	10	62	8	95
	1910–20	3	20	5	65	8	106
	1930–40	2	8	5	79	7	118
	1958–68	3	15	6	73	4	91
Unskilled	1880–90	1	5	1	24	68	75
	1910–20	0	18	8	36	39	39
	1930–40	0	4	7	22	67	27
	1958–68	0	7	0	47	47	15

the Great Depression revealed in Table 4.4 was entirely accounted for by the rise in the rate of skidding by the clerks, salesmen, and petty proprietors or managers of the low nonmanual stratum; a mere 3 percent of the high nonmanuals were reduced to working with their hands by the economic catastrophe. Not many Boston bankers, it appears, were really forced to sell apples on the street corner!

Although workers in the lower echelons of the white-collar class were less secure in their jobs than professionals and important proprietors or managers, significant numbers moved not down but up into better posts: 15 percent climbed to a niche in the upper white-collar stratum in the 1880's, and 10, 9, and 19 percent in the later samples; only a tiny fraction of upwardly mobile blue-collar workers, by comparison, were able to rise to that level. About as many lower white-collar employees rose to the upper white-collar stratum as fell to the working class in the 1880's and in the 1910–1920 period. During the Depression twice as many skidded as climbed further, but for 1958–1968 the scales were tilted in the opposite direction, with 19 percent rising to the top stratum and 14 percent skidding.

There was a clear hierarchy within the white-collar world. Men in the low white-collar jobs were in a more vulnerable position than those in the upper stratum, and were far more likely to skid. Within the world of the working class, however, there was not such a clear mobility hierarchy. Unskilled workers enjoyed fewest opportunities for upward mobility, but there was surprisingly little difference between semiskilled and skilled workmen.

The unskilled were least successful in penetrating into the white-collar category, as expected. Hardly any made the dramatic leap into the upper nonmanual stratum, of course—only 1 out of a total of 156 unskilled laborers in the four samples. And only about 1 in 20 became a clerk, salesman, or petty proprietor, except in the World War I boom period, when 18 percent did so. More surprising is the fact that relatively few found their way into better-paid manual jobs in the skilled trades; skilled posts were even less accessible to them than white-collar jobs in three of the four decades. To the extent to which the unskilled were upwardly mobile, it was primarily via entry into the occupational stratum closest to their own, the semiskilled and service stratum. This was highly accessible to them—from a fifth to nearly half made this shift in the various cohorts—but it was but a modest improvement in their lot by such criteria as wages and regularity of employment.

The career prospects of the intermediate manual stratum—semiskilled and service workers—were considerably better. Few of these workers moved up into the skilled trades; in none of the four decades did the crafts absorb large numbers of recruits previously employed in lower-status manual occupations. But a large minority—from 18 to 23 percent—found white-collar openings, except in the Great Depression, when only 1 in 10 did so. Except during that bleak decade, the semiskilled were as successful as or more successful than skilled workers at leaving the manual laboring class altogether.

SETTLING DOWN: THE SECOND DECADE

The samples employed here, except that for 1958, contained disproportionate numbers of relatively young men, whom we would expect to change occupations with greater frequency than their elders. It would be incorrect, therefore, to extrapolate their occupational trajectories over a period longer than 10 years on the basis of their mobility in one decade. As men age, they tend to settle down to some degree, and it could also be that prolonged residence in one community has itself a settling and stabilizing effect in addition to the age factor. Table 4.6 indicates the extent of occupational continuity and occupational change, both by stratum and by broad class, experienced by members of three of the samples during their second decade in Boston. (The 1968–1978 record of the 1958 sample, of course, cannot be discerned as yet.)

In their second decade working in the city, Bostonians typically made somewhat fewer shifts between occupational levels. Less than three-quarters remained in the same stratum over the first decade; roughly four-fifths did so in the second 10-year period. (The low figure of 77 percent for 1940–1954 was probably affected by the necessity, for technical reasons, of taking a 14- rather than a 10-year trace interval.) A detailed breakdown of these figures, not given here, indicates that the main change accounting for heightened intrastratum continuity was the abrupt settling down of the skilled and the lower white-collar workers. The high nonmanuals were highly stable in each sample; the unskilled and semiskilled shifted around a good deal in each sample. For the clerk or the carpenter,

TABLE 4.6. Career continuity and mobility (percent) during second decade under observation

Occupation at end of decade	*1890–1900*	*1920–1930*	*1940–1954*
In same stratum	82	79	77
In same class	93	90	91
White-collar to blue-collar	4	11[1]	4
Blue-collar to white-collar	10	10	12
Ratio of upward to downward mobility	2.5	0.9	3.0
Number in sample	366	278	276

[1] Significantly higher than the other samples.

success or failure came relatively early; dramatic change of occupation was rare in the second decade. The unskilled and semiskilled settled down much less, though it should be added that their movement was largely between the two bottom levels. In the second decade 80 percent remained in a job somewhere in the two bottom strata, as compared with 85 percent of skilled men remaining skilled and 84 percent of low white-collar workers remaining at the same level.

The rate of crossing the blue-collar–white-collar line also slowed somewhat after the first 10 years had elapsed. Continuity within the two broad occupational classes was 93, 90, and 91 percent in the three cohorts. It is noteworthy, though, that men continued to climb out of the working class into the white-collar world at much the same rate. The overall slowing of interclass mobility was due largely to a diminution in downward movement out of the middle class. In each of the four groups represented in Table 4.4 at least 10 percent of the white-collar workers fell into a manual job in the first decade; in one instance the fraction was over 15 percent. In the second decade the rate of descent was only 4 percent in two of three instances, and the highest figure—11 percent for 1920–1930—probably reflects the impact of the economic collapse that began in 1929. The ratio of upward to downward mobility was highly favorable except in that instance, and even there the slight slippage that took place between 1920 and 1930 did not erase the gains of the preceding decade. After the passage of 20 years, as Table 4.7 shows, each sample had edged its way some distance up the class ladder. A third of the 1880 group held white-collar jobs in 1880; 47 percent did so 2 decades later. The corresponding figures for the 1910 sample were 31 percent in 1910 and 50 percent in 1930. The fraction holding high white-collar posts rose from 7 to 22 percent for the 1880 group, and from 5 to 14 percent for the 1910 group. Only the 1930 sample, consisting of men in an early stage of their careers during the Great Depression, had a much poorer record; its representation in white-collar jobs increased much less, from 31 to 38 percent. This suggests the possibility that the depression left scars on men of this age group that continued to handicap them long after, a question to be considered further at a later point in this chapter. In general we may say that there was some slowing of mobility during the second decade, but that the slowing affected the down more than the up escalator, so that the direction of net movement was upward.

FROM FIRST JOB TO LAST JOB

Another way of exploring patterns of career mobility in Boston is to inquire into the relation between the first job and the last job held

TABLE 4.7. Changes in occupational distribution (percent) of three samples after 20 years

		Occupational level				
Sample	*Year*	*High white-collar*	*Low white-collar*	*Skilled*	*Low manual*[1]	*Number*
1880	1880	7	27	30	35	987
	1900	22[2]	27	26	26[2]	366
1910	1910	5	26	27	42	1067
	1930	14[2]	36[2]	22[2]	28[2]	278
1930	1930	7	27	29	39	849
	1954	12[2]	26	26	36	276

[1] For a variety of reasons it was useful, at this and some later points, to combine the unskilled and semiskilled categories under the "low manual" rubric. The combining was done from more refined tabulations and is employed only when it does not obscure important patterns evident in the detailed tabulations.

[2] Significantly different from initial distribution.

by sample members. This can provide a better sense of the overall shape of an individual's career, and it has the further advantage of controlling better for variations in the age distributions of the different samples, in that in each case our initial point of reference is a job held at a relatively young age.

The evidence available, unfortunately, does not indicate the occupational level at which sample members worked at the moment they first entered the labor market or at the moment of retirement or death. The Census and other sources used did not include questions about first and last job, and it is necessary to work with rough approximations. "First job" has been arbitrarily defined as the first job known to have been held by a sample member prior to age 30. In many instances an individual first appeared in the sample in his late teens, while he was working at his actual first job. But in some cases men were already in their 20's at the time of the sample, and may well have already done some shifting since their first job. The concept really means a job held while still a relatively young man. Persons aged 30 or over when they entered the sample were excluded from this portion of the analysis, since they were already well launched on their careers. Likewise, "last job" means the last job known to have been held in Boston past the age of 30; youths who worked in the city in their teens or 20's but who disappeared before age 30 are similarly excluded on the grounds that too much of their careers lay still in the future. The choice of 30 as the watershed was dictated not by the assumptions of today's rebels in the war between the generations but by the data of the study itself, which disclose a marked slowing of occupational mobility after age 30.[8] Thus we have one observation at an age of maximal occupational flexibility, as early as possible but in all cases prior to 30, and a second observation, as late as possible but in all cases at least after the settling down that takes place around 30. (In each case, it should be added, the observations are a minimum of 10 years apart, and many are 20, 30, and even 40 years apart.) [9]

Table 4.8 indicates the proportion of Bostonians in four different age cohorts, born between 1850 and 1909, who ended their careers in the same occupational stratum they began them in. The first two groups, born 1850–1859 and 1860–1879 respectively, come from the sample taken from the 1880 Census; the third comes from 1910 marriage records, and consists of men who had been born in the 1880's;

the fourth, from 1930 birth records, is composed of men born between 1900 and 1909 whose wives gave birth to sons in Boston in 1930. (At some points later in this and subsequent chapters reference will be made to a fifth group, the sons of these men. Too many of these youths were away from the city, either at college or in the service, to allow a meaningful breakdown of their continuity rates by occupational stratum in Table 4.8. The sample from the 1958 city directory could not be employed here, because sample members were of unknown age and were traced for only a 10-year period.)

TABLE 4.8. Career continuity by occupational stratum, from first to last known job (percent of cohort remaining in stratum of first job at time of last job)

Stratum	*1850–1859*	*1860–1879*	*1880–1889*	*1900–1909*
Entire cohort	60	61	55	67[1]
High white-collar	92	96	88	86
Low white-collar	61	63	63	68
Skilled	60	60	57	58
Semiskilled	48	51	47	79[1]
Unskilled	44	30	30	40
Number in sample	310	663	443	247

[1] Significantly higher than all other cohorts.

In each generation roughly 4 out of 10 of these men ended their careers in an occupational stratum different from that in which they first worked. Fully 45 percent of the group born in the 1880's shifted from one occupational level to another in the course of their careers; 40 and 39 percent of the two earlier groups did likewise. Only for the generation in mid-career when the Great Depression struck was the rate of change lower, namely, 33 percent.

As in earlier tabulations of mobility for decade intervals, the high white-collar class was far more stable than others; 9 out of 10 men whose first job was there were still in the high nonmanual category in their last job. Workers in both the lower white-collar and the skilled callings experienced much greater mobility; their rate of job shifting closely corresponded to that for the sample as a whole, which is to say that it was high.

The lifetime career mobility of men in the two lower manual strata was distinctly above the average for the samples as a whole. In two of the cohorts less than a third of those who started work as unskilled laborers were unskilled still at the time of their last job, and in the other two the fraction was still well under half. Much of the mobility of the unskilled was movement only one notch up the occupational ladder, to be sure; from 27 to 40 percent of them rose only one notch to the semiskilled level (see Table 4.10 below). But the frequency of their ascent was nonetheless impressive.

Semiskilled and service workers displayed extremely low intrastratum continuity rates as well. With one exception, fewer than half of the young men who first worked as factory operatives, bus drivers, or something similar were still in the semiskilled stratum by the end of their working life. The one sharp deviation from the pattern of less than 50-percent continuity was in the last group, men younger than 30 who had just become fathers when the depression struck. Those in this age bracket who started their careers in the white-collar world, or who had attained a skilled position by 1930, doubtless suffered from the economic collapse in various ways, but the depression did not leave an indelible imprint on their career patterns as measured here. But for those young men who worked in less demanding and well-rewarded semiskilled jobs, there was a dramatic shrinking of the opportunity to climb the occupational ladder, and this, it should be noted, was not a mere interruption but a permanent effect, still visible at the end of their careers. The depression was short-lived, but by the time it ended it appears to have been too late for these men ever to catch up. More than three-quarters of them, Table 4.8 reveals, remained semiskilled at the time of their final job, as opposed to less than half in earlier cohorts. Only 11 percent, as Table 4.10 indicates, later found their way into a white-collar spot, a half to a third as many as in previous periods. (It may be that the depression had a similarly calamitous impact upon the unskilled as well. This cannot be determined from the evidence at hand, because so few unskilled workers from the 1900–1909 cohort subsequently remained in Boston that the number of cases on which the unskilled distribution is based is a mere ten, too small to provide significant results. But it is a reasonable surmise.)

To discover how many of those who changed occupational strata between their first and last jobs made the big leap across the blue-collar–white-collar dividing line we may turn to Table 4.9. (A fifth group was added to Table 4.9: sons born in Boston in 1930. Only a small fraction of these youths were employed in the city in 1954, when they were first traced in the city directory, so that the findings concerning them are highly susceptible to chance variation and have little statistical weight. There is the further difficulty that these youths were still an early point in their careers at the time they were last traced—1963—and could be expected to experience

TABLE 4.9. Career mobility (percent) across class boundaries from first to last job

	Birth cohort				
Occupation at last job	*1850–1859*	*1860–1879*	*1880–1889*	*1900–1909*	*1930*
In same class	80	81	76	82	74
In different class	20	19	24	18	26
White-collar to blue-collar	12	17	16	16	16
Blue-collar to white-collar	27	23	28	18[1]	31
Ratio of upward to downward mobility	2.3	1.4	1.8	1.1	1.9
Number in sample	310	663	443	247	84

[1] Significantly lower than for 1850–59, 1880–89, and 1930 cohorts.

further mobility in the future. Still, the figures have an illustrative value if treated with proper caution.) Roughly 60 percent of the men employed in Boston typically ended their careers in the stratum in which they began them; roughly 80 percent ended their careers on the same side of the manual-nonmanual line on which they began. Of those who moved to another stratum, about half entered a stratum within the broad class they started in; the other half changed class as well as stratum.

Given the fact that the careers of these men span a period of several decades, and given all of the economic and social changes that occurred in Boston (and in American society as a whole) in those years, the pronounced similarity in the class continuity rates of these five groups is impressive. Again we see evidence of a stable process of social circulation that was relatively impervious to change. The continuity rates for three of the groups were virtually identical—80, 81, and 82 percent—and the other two—76 and 74 percent—were not sufficiently lower to be statistically significant at the 0.90 level.

Despite this similarity in overall rates of continuity and mobility, the ratio of upward to downward movement was not identical for all groups; some—those born in the 1850's and 1880's and in 1930—had a more favorable balance than others. But it is interesting that the fluctuation was due almost entirely to changes in upward-mobility rates, which ranged from a high of 31 percent to a low of 18 percent for the depression generation. The fraction of men who began their careers wearing white collars and ended them in blue-collar jobs was strikingly constant: an identical 16 percent in three of the groups, a single point higher than that in a fourth, not quite enough lower to be significant even in the fifth. The depression of the 1930's, it was shown earlier, forced unusually large numbers of white-collar workers down into manual jobs as of 1940. It is evident from this consideration of career patterns between first and last jobs that, unlike men in the two lowest manual strata, these individuals eventually recovered from the depression and regained their middle-class posts to the same extent that was normal in the city in earlier periods.

Further insight into both of these matters—the striking stability of the process of occupational circulation and the vulnerability of unskilled and semiskilled workmen to hard times—may be gained from a more detailed tabulation of movement from stratum to stratum between first and last jobs (Table 4.10). (The fifth group—youths born in 1930—is not included here because the sample size was too small to permit a detailed breakdown.)

It is evident that the rather small group of men who began work in the highest category—professionals and prosperous businessmen—had very similar career lines after their first job in every period. Not one skidded to a working-class post in three of the groups, and the 8-percent figure for the group born in the 1880's—4 percent dropping to skilled and 4 percent to semiskilled jobs—represents only two individuals and is not statistically significant. There is

TABLE 4.10. Interstratum and interclass career mobility (percent) between first and last known occupations

		Stratum of last job					
Stratum of first job	*Birth cohort*	*High white-collar*	*Low white-collar*	*Skilled*	*Semi-skilled*	*Unskilled*	*Number*
High white-collar	1850–59	92	8	0	0	0	26
	1860–79	96	4	0	0	0	49
	1880–89	88	4	4	4	0	24
	1900–09	86	14	0	0	0	14
Low white-collar	1850–59	25	61	9	6	0	109
	1860–79	17	63	8	9	2	313
	1880–89	20	63	4	10	3	135
	1900–09	13	68	6	11	3	69
Skilled	1850–59	4	22	60	9	6	82
	1860–79	6	20	60	12	2	137
	1880–89	6	22	57	13	2	117
	1900–09	8	18	58	15	1	79
Semiskilled	1850–59	5	25	17	48	5	59
	1860–79	4	18	18	51	11	114
	1880–89	4	27	10	47	11	117
	1900–09	5	7	5	79	4	75
Unskilled	1850–59	3	21	6	27	44	34
	1860–79	2	14	20	34	30	50
	1880–89	2	18	12	38	30	50
	1900–09	0	10	10	40	40	10

some hint that the depression of the 1930's displaced somewhat larger numbers of them a notch downward into lower white-collar jobs—14 percent, as opposed to 8, 4, and 4 percent for earlier groups—but again the numbers on which the percentages are based are too small for us to be sure whether this reflects a genuine change or merely chance variation. Young men who were at the top of the occupational structure in 1930 weathered the depression quite well, it seems safe to say.

Young Bostonians who first worked as clerks, salesmen, or small businessmen likewise followed quite similar career patterns in all four groups. Somewhat more than 6 in 10 remained working at the occupational level at which they began; the small fluctuation in continuity from group to group was not large enough to be statistically significant. There was only a slight tendency for men of the depression generation to fall permanently into blue-collar callings more often; 20 percent did so, as opposed to 15, 19, and 17 percent in the earlier groups, not a significant difference. In this sense these men recovered from the depression quite successfully. The economic collapse of the 1930's, however, did put a damper on the upward movement of this group into upper white-collar posts; their rate of ascent within the nonmanual category was only half what it had been for men born in the pre-Civil War decade, and two-thirds that for the 1880–1889 birth cohort, both significant differences.[10] For young men who had been able to get a foothold in the white-collar world by 1930, the threat that the depression would render many of them permanently *déclassé* never materialized. But the thirties left another scar, in the modest but distinct increase in the number of men whose hopes of becoming something more than a petty clerk, salesman, or proprietor were doomed to disappointment.

The career patterns of the skilled workmen of Boston seem to have been remarkably unaffected by the depression or by any other force making for change. In each cohort 57 to 60 percent of them were still working at a skilled task at the time of their last job. Of the approximately 40 percent who were mobile, slightly more than a quarter climbed to a nonmanual position in each cohort, generally becoming salesmen or proprietors of small stores. The remaining 15 percent or so moved downward, chiefly into semiskilled posts. Thus, 85 percent either maintained or bettered their positions over the course of their careers.

Upward mobility into middle-class occupations by men originating in the two lower manual strata fluctuated more than for the skilled, but was generally on the order of 25–30 percent for the semiskilled and 20–25 percent for the unskilled. Men born in 1930 were not included in the table because of the small size of the sample, but there were 48 young men in that group who started work in unskilled or semiskilled jobs, and 33 percent of them later climbed to white-collar posts. Access to jobs in the white-collar world was by no means confined to men at the top of the blue-collar hierarchy. Nor does the evidence here indicate any long-term trend toward a more rigid occupational structure; the level of opportunities seems to have been remarkably constant.

Two exceptions should be noted. Youths born between 1860 and 1879 who started working as ordinary unskilled laborers had less than the normal chance of attaining white-collar status later. Unusually large numbers of them entered skilled trades, however, so that the fraction of them climbing to a job in either the highest blue-collar category or the white-collar class was not lower than customary.

The other, and more glaring, exception to the generalization that 25-30 percent of the semiskilled and 20-25 percent of the unskilled escaped the working class before the end of their working days is the record of the depression generation. In this cohort only about 1 in 10 of the young men first working in either of the two lower manual strata finished their careers wearing a white collar, a highly significant drop. There was some decline, too, in their rate of entry into skilled jobs. These were youths in their 20's, burdened with family responsibilities (all were fathers of male infants born in 1930), lacking either special skills or outstanding educational qualifications. In ordinary times, young men like these had excellent prospects of climbing some way up the occupational ladder in the course of their careers. In the three earlier groups, 47, 40, and 41 percent of the men with semiskilled first jobs later rose to either skilled or white-collar jobs; for the depression generation the figure was a dismal 17 percent. In this ill-fated group 8 in 10 remained semiskilled blue-collar workers for life, and 1 in 20 dropped to an unskilled laboring job. The unskilled men of this generation were probably hit equally hard by the depression—the 1930–1940 data in Table 4.5 suggest that—but the number of cases in which both first and last jobs were known for these men was too small (ten) to sustain a firm conclusion.

The impact of the Great Depression on the later lives of men at an early point in their careers in 1930 depended on the occupational levels they had reached by the time calamity struck. Skilled craftsmen and white-collar workers suffered unemployment and loss of income in many cases, but their long-term prospects of finding a better job were little affected. A few more workers in the upper white-collar stratum slipped into a lower-status nonmanual post than had been true in the past, and the normal flow of lower white-collar employees into high white-collar jobs was somewhat slowed. But the only men whose later careers took a fundamentally different shape than could have been predicted from the experience of previous groups were the unskilled and semiskilled laborers. Prosperity returned to the city within a decade, and the economic growth of the Boston area in the post-World War II era was particularly impressive.[11] Neither Boston society nor American society as a whole had been transformed into a closed caste system, in which those on the lowest rungs of the class ladder were permanently trapped there. The mobility patterns of youths born in the depression decade show that this assumption is unfounded, as does the 1958–1968 record of the sample drawn from the 1958 Boston city directory (Tables 4.3, 4.4, and 4.5). But the recovery and boom that followed the depression did not affect all age groups and occupational categories equally. Men old enough to be at work in 1930 but too young and insufficiently educated or skilled to be settled into a stable career pattern were in a uniquely vulnerable position, and the damage done to them was not temporary but permanent. "The occupational pattern of a specific group of men . . . at any one point in time is, in large measure, a function of their past occupational experiences."[12] The early "occupational experiences" of Boston's low-skilled workers of the depression generation were traumatic, and by the time prosperity returned it was too late for these men to recover the ground they had lost. Comfortably situated middle-class observers of post-World War II America sometimes complained that workingmen suffered from a "depression psychology," and were unduly apprehensive about the recurrence of another collapse. The data in Table 4.10 provide some insight into the harsh experiences that underlay that "depression psychology."

CONCLUSIONS AND IMPLICATIONS

The occupational experiences of the thousands of representative Bostonians captured in the web of one of the samples have been plotted over time intervals of varying lengths, in both relatively broad and relatively refined categories. A review of the general conclusions and implications that may be drawn from this exercise is in order now.

There was throughout the entire period a great deal of upward career mobility for men situated on the lower rungs of the class ladder. There are, to be sure, no absolute standards that can be invoked to establish how much is "a great deal." Whether a glass of water may best be termed half full or half empty depends on the observer; it is not only beauty that is in the eye of the beholder. Likewise, whether a particular rate of shifting from occupation to occupation seems surprisingly high or surprisingly low depends upon what the analyst expected to find. If one approaches the evidence offered here with expectations derived from some enthusiastic prophets of the American dream of success, anything less than the discovery that every poor man in the study became a millionaire by the age of 40 will seem disappointing. If, on the other hand, one begins with the suspicion that the class structure was rigid and opportunities for social ascent were open only to a tiny minority of exceptionally talented (or lucky) individuals, even a very modest amount of occupational shifting will seem impressive.

Different observers may thus react to what has been disclosed here about the career patterns of Boston men in somewhat different ways. What seems indisputable, however, is the following. None of the three blue-collar strata were closed compartments from which escape was impossible. Even over a span as short as a decade, substantial minorities of manual workers—a mean of more than a third of them—moved to a job at a different occupational level (Table 4.3); over the longer interval between first and last job the figure was approximately half (Table 4.8). Much of this movement, of course, was movement within the working-class world, but a good deal of it was not. Roughly 1 in 4 of all the sample members who started their careers on the lower side of what many observers have taken to be a nearly impassable social gulf eventually found themselves in white-collar callings; equally surprising, mobility into nonmanual jobs was no more difficult for semiskilled than for skilled workers, and only a little more difficult for unskilled laborers (Table 4.10). Except in the case of the ill-fated depression generation, 40 percent or more of the semiskilled laborers of Boston and about a third of the entirely unskilled later became either skilled craftsmen or white-collar workers. Men who began their careers in the skilled category were more successful still. In none of the samples did as many as 1 in 6 of them later skid to a lower-ranked blue-collar job; fully 85 percent either remained at the skilled level or climbed into a nonmanual post. This is not, of course, to say that the social order was a perfectly just one, against which no one had legitimate complaints; more about that complex issue later. It is to say that the lower levels of the community occupational structure were strikingly fluid, and that most of the workers who did move moved upward. The level of upward mobility was far in excess of the minimum upgrading demanded by changes in the Boston occupational structure.

A second conclusion is that, somewhat paradoxically, the excellent upward-mobility opportunities open to Boston workers were not obtained at the expense of their social superiors. It is tempting to think of the competition for occupational status as a zero-sum game, in which one party's gains are necessarily matched by another party's losses. In the case at hand this would mean that every upwardly mobile worker displaced someone already holding a white-collar job, forcing him downward into a blue-collar post or into the ranks of the unemployed. A highly mobile society of this type could be an extremely unstable one, harboring large numbers of aggrieved *déclassé* individuals. The process did not work in this fashion in Boston, however. In most of the samples, the proportion of white-collar employees skidding into working-class jobs was only about half that of manual workers climbing to white-collar posts (Table 4.9), and the discrepancy in absolute numbers was even larger (because the white-collar class was smaller). With respect to mobility, the community seems to have had the best of all possible worlds, with lots of the desirable kind (upward) and a much lower volume of the undesirable kind (downward).

Third, it is clear that there was a remarkable underlying uniformity in the way the process of social circulation operated in Boston over this entire 90-year period. Given all of the dramatic changes, both in the city and in American society as a whole, that took place in these years, it is startling to find that the extent of occupational shifting varied so little over time. There was a variation of only 5 percent in the tendency of members of the four samples to remain employed in the same stratum over a decade (Table 4.3), and of 12 percent in the likelihood of their remaining in the stratum of their first job at the time of their last job (Table 4.8). Similarly, the tendency of high-status men to remain at the same occupational level and of lower-status workers to shift from stratum to stratum appeared in every sample, from that composed of men born before the Civil War to that consisting of men working in Boston in 1968.

To find so little evidence of change may seem uninteresting, at first glance, but in fact it is as revealing as Sherlock Holmes's dog that did not bark in the night. Observers of American society have long debated whether or not the class structure was becoming more rigid, from the Boston minister who argued in the 1880's "that some unseen yet hostile powers" were then "breaking out the middle rungs" of the social ladder to the social critics of the 1960's who insisted that there was a new kind of poverty abroad in the land, a poverty from which escape through social mobility was impossible. Part of the controversy over whether arteriosclerosis was setting in and traditional channels of social circulation being closed off concerns mobility from generation to generation, a matter treated in the next chapter. But the data already presented, which constitute the longest and fullest series of mobility measurements ever made in an American community, certainly bear on the broad issue, and they suggest that over the past nine decades no long-term change took place in whatever mechanisms governed the flow of persons between positions at different levels of the occupational hierarchy during the course of their careers.

A final observation is that, for all the fluidity of the Boston occupational structure, the community nonetheless was one in which prior social advantages or disadvantages counted heavily. Men who started their careers in a high-status position were very likely to retain them; those who started at a lower level had good chances of moving upward a notch or two, but not of moving to the highest level. The common move was not from rags to riches but from rags to respectability, and there was much less complementary movement from respectability back to rags. Not a single professional or substantial businessman from the samples ever skidded to an unskilled job, and only two moved downward into any blue-collar position.[13] Only about 2 percent of the unskilled workers and 4–5 percent of the semiskilled ever made their way into the upper white-collar stratum.

What is more, the burdens that fell upon citizens of the community in economically unfavorable periods were distributed very unequally. Two of the groups traced here—the 1860–1879 cohort to some extent, and more notably the 1900–1909 cohort—were at a vulnerable point in their careers when hard times struck, the depressions of the 1890's and 1930's respectively. These economic calamities, however, do not seem to have disturbed the careers of upper white-collar workers in the slightest. They somewhat retarded the rate of climb of lower-status nonmanual employees and dispatched slightly larger numbers of these men down into the blue-collar world. The movement of skilled workers into white-collar jobs was distinctly slowed in hard times (Table 4.5), but the effect was temporary; by the time of their last jobs these men had arrived at precisely the position of the other cohorts, with from 26 to 28 percent of them in nonmanual posts and 57–60 percent of them still in skilled jobs (Table 4.10). By far the greatest losers in hard times were the unskilled and semiskilled workers, whose access both to skilled and to white-collar jobs was sharply reduced, not merely for a decade but permanetly. Though no long-term trend toward a more rigid and closed occupational structure could be discerned, there were important short-term fluctuations of this sort, and it is noteworthy that the impact of these fluctuations was by no means random. The ordinary unskilled and semiskilled workers of Boston during most of this period had greater opportunities to advance themselves occupationally than many observers have assumed, but they were vulnerable to economic catastrophe. A serious depression could mean not only lengthy unemployment, but also a blighted career. From the point of view of the community social system as a whole one can call this a "short-term" fluctuation, but this was slight consolation to the individuals involved, whose only chance for higher income, greater personal security, and more attractive working conditions had been forever lost.

The occupational structure of Boston, in sum, was remarkably fluid in one sense of the term, offering significant opportunities for self-advancement to a very substantial proportion of the men who started work in menial manual jobs. But it was far from a perfectly open structure, if by that we mean one in which initial advantages count for nothing. Blue-collar workers rarely rose above the lower white-collar level, and men fortunate enough to start their careers in the upper white-collar stratum rarely fell later, and only very rarely indeed into the working class. Men in the lower strata were far more subject to the vicissitudes of the vast impersonal economic forces that determined the health of the economy than were their social superiors. Neither those who boasted that America was a land of endless opportunity nor their critics who insisted that the deck was stacked against the poor man were entirely correct; the two groups, it seems, had seen different facets of the same complex social reality.

chapter five SOCIAL-CLASS ORIGINS AND OCCUPATIONAL ACHIEVEMENT

A close look at patterns of occupational career mobility in Boston between 1880 and 1968 has disclosed a strikingly stable process of occupational circulation, in which approximately 40 percent of the labor force shifted out of the occupational stratum of their first jobs before the end of their careers, and about 20 percent moved from a blue-collar to a white-collar or from a white-collar to a blue-collar job. Manual workingmen typically moved more often than white-collar workers, so that the net shift in the distribution of each sample was upward.

This is sufficient to challenge a number of familiar stereotypes about the Boston social structure and about the fate of men on the lower rungs of the class ladder in an increasingly complex technological society. Despite automation, rising educational requirements for many jobs, the emergence of giant corporate bureaucracies, and other massive changes in American society that might have limited the opportunities for social ascent from the bottom, no clear trend toward a more rigid and constricted social structure was visible. On the other hand, I have emphasized, the community social system was far from perfectly fluid. There was a ledge at the lower white-collar level above which workers rarely rose and below which men from the upper middle class rarely fell.

Career mobility, however, is only one variety of mobility. Full understanding of the process of occupational circulation requires another type of analysis as well. In the preceding chapter I discussed the career patterns of representative Bostonians without any reference to one influence that may have been of decisive importance—the social position of the families in which they grew up. Thus the millowner's son and the ditchdigger's son who both began their working lives as mill hands, the former to learn the business from the bottom up, the latter because it was the best job open to him, appeared as equals. If in 10 years the millowner's son became sales manager, this was registered as career mobility from the middle stratum of the blue-collar class to the top level of the white-collar class. If the ditchdigger's son succeeded in acquiring enough training to become a machinist during the same interval, this counted as much less impressive career mobility, movement only one notch up the ladder, from the semiskilled to the skilled stratum. But the ditchdigger's son had, of course, risen two levels above his father, whereas the millowner's son had only reached his father's level, and had not been upwardly mobile at all with respect to his family origins.

This illustrates the necessity of examining mobility not only from point to point within a career but from generation to generation as well. A more vivid, if somewhat farfetched, illustration of the same principle is the following. It could be that none of the upward and downward career mobility revealed in the preceding chapter was actual upward or downward movement from an intergenerational perspective, for all of the upwardly mobile blue-collar workers might have been sons of middle-class fathers, sons who had been slumming, as it were, in their early jobs and who later reverted to the status they had inherited from their parents. Likewise, the white-collar workers who later skidded to a working-class calling might all have come from laboring homes, so that their later downward mobility, too, was a reversion to the status level of their origins. A seemingly open community characterized by high levels of career mobility might at the same time be a quite closed one in this sense, one in which the social status at which individuals typically arrived after a period of early experimentation was very closely related to the status of the families from which they came.

It is equally possible, of course, that measuring mobility intergenerationally will give a heightened sense of the fluidity of a particular social structure. Someone who is a clerk in both his first and his last jobs has experienced no career mobility, but he has made a substantial upward move intergenerationally if his father was a mere unskilled laborer.

The importance of assessing the influence of family origins upon occupational achievement is thus obvious. Some of the representative Bostonians who appear under our microscope grew up in spacious, middle-class homes, others in crowded tenements. Some were consistently well clothed and well fed; others lived close to the margin of subsistence. Some were encouraged to study and to plan for the future, and could do so with the assurance that their family would supply the requisite financial backing and connections; others confronted circumstances that dampened their expectations, such as the pressure to leave school as early as legally possible in order to add their earnings to a slender family budget. There was, in short, great diversity and inequality in the early environments to which they were exposed.

The question, however, is precisely how much of an imprint these differences in environment left upon individuals in later life, and specifically upon the occupational trajectories they subsequently followed. A cherished American tradition holds that the social-class position an individual inherits at birth is not itself a prime determinant of his subsequent personal achievement; the contest for wealth and power is thought to be open to all men, regardless of their social origins. Exponents of this view have often stressed the importance of coming from a "good" family and receiving a "proper" upbringing, but it was thought that poor but honest parents could prepare their children for the world just as well as those who had attained economic success.

Some observers of the American scene, however, have been less sanguine. The system is not truly open, they have insisted; social-class background exerts a profound influence upon life chances. Thus the editor of the Boston Irish newspaper, *The Pilot,* declared in 1883: "The race is not run with an equal chance; the poor man's son carries double weight." [1] The distinguished Boston economist and statistician, Francis A. Walker, was even more pessimistic, declaring that "there is a strong constraint, made up of both moral and physical forces, which keeps the vast majority of children not only within the vast industrial group into which they were born, but even within the very trades which their fathers individually pursue." [2] To assess the validity of these conflicting views about the nature of social stratification in the United States is the aim of this chapter.

SOME PRELIMINARY DIFCULTIES

The historical evidence is far from ideal for these purposes. The chief available index of an individual's social origins is his father's occupational rank, supplemented by some scanty evidence about family property holdings. There is information too about national origins and religious and racial identity; these are dealt with separately in subsequent chapters. Nothing, however, is known about the educational attainments of the parents of members of the samples, not to mention such elusive matters as parental aspirations and values. The proposition that early and prolonged exposure to the gospel of thrift and hard work was the key to success thus cannot be tested with the historical evidence at hand.

If the influence of parental values must remain elusive, however, it is possible to assess directly the significance of social-class background. Did young men in Boston typically follow career lines laid down by their fathers? Did the "poor man's son" indeed carry "double weight" in the contest for success, or was occupational achievement unrelated to parental status? Although a variety of explanations can be offered for any observed pattern of intergenerational mobility—class biases in the labor market, differential access to education, class differences in values conducive to achievement, perhaps even class differences in innate ability—it is nonetheless revealing to discover precisely what the pattern in fact was.

The samples employed here were those utilized in the preceding chapter, with one important addition. To provide supplementary information about levels of intergenerational mobility in the post-World War II period, I made use of Edward Laumann's 1962 sample of 405 male residents of the Boston suburbs Cambridge and Belmont.[3] The age range of this sample was rather wide, which limited the accuracy of the comparisons that could be made with the other samples, and there was the further difficulty that Cambridge and Belmont are communities of a somewhat more middle-class composition than Boston proper. The Laumann sample thus provides, in all likelihood, only a rough approximation of the general Boston pattern, but it does yield some valuable clues when used with due caution.

The most serious problem posed by the nature of the sources was the fact that in none of the samples except that from Laumann's Cambridge and Belmont study was there information about the occupational rank of all the fathers of sample members. The historical records available allowed a comparison of parental and filial status only in those instances in which both members of the pair resided in Boston. The 1880 and 1910 samples included many men who migrated to the city alone rather than in the company of their parents, and others whose fathers had lived in Boston but had died at some time prior to the date the sample was drawn. It was thus impossible to examine the impact of their social-class background on their career patterns. Similarly, although in the 1930 sample the occupations of all the fathers in the sample were specified in the birth records, the intergenerational mobility of the sons in the sample could not be estimated until these youths had reached the age at which they entered the labor market. Great numbers of them migrated out of Boston before they came of age, so once again the estimates of intergenerational mobility that could be made were based on the experiences of only a fraction of the total sample.

One consequence of this was that the number of cases from which generalizations about patterns of intergenerational mobility in Boston could be derived was substantially reduced. This did not pose a major difficulty, however, for statistically significant patterns did emerge from the analysis.

A more troubling problem is that my discussion of intergenerational mobility in Boston is based upon the experience of the more stable element of the population, and it is possible that migrants—men from the 1880 and 1910 samples who had come to Boston without their parents, and young men from the 1930 sample who later migrated out of Boston and followed their careers elsewhere—characteristically had quite different intergenerational mobility experiences than men from more settled local families.

This possibility cannot be ruled out decisively on the evidence at hand; the nature of the records available poses an insuperable obstacle.[4] There is, however, one indicator that suggests that the intergenerational mobility patterns of settled and migratory members of the Boston population may have been much the same. When rates of career mobility between first and last jobs are plotted separately for sample members with and without fathers living in Boston, no significant differences emerge. In the course of their own careers, at least, locals and outsiders experienced similar mobility. It could be, of course, that migrants were nonetheless more mobile than their fathers at the time when they first entered the labor market; no direct evidence on that point can be obtained. But one would expect that, if migrants were notably different from nonmigrants in characteristics that affected their intergenerational mobility prospects, some of that difference would show up in their later career patterns as well. If this reasoning is correct, my inability to examine levels of intergenerational mobility for father-and-son pairs in which one member did not live in Boston did not seriously distort the generality of my findings.

Scholars who derive social-mobility data from survey research rather than from historical archives can avoid this problem, of course, for they need only ask a respondent to specify his father's occupation, as Laumann did; where the father lives does not matter. The historian cannot administer a questionnaire, except insofar as he deals with the very recent past, and no attempt was made to do so in this study. But there was a certain virtue in the necessity of recovering direct information about the father's occupation from the sources, for it eliminated biases stemming from imperfect memory or from a deliberate desire to either upgrade or downgrade the family socially. The precise extent to which response errors in retrospective data of this kind have distorted previous studies dependent upon questionnaires is not clear, but there is reason to believe that the range of error has been quite substantial.[5] In any event, the present discussion rests on objective data specifying the father's occupation.

The question of *which* occupation held by a father to select as a base against which to measure his children's progress presents some difficulties. Previous investigators of social stratification and social mobility in American society have concentrated on intergenerational mobility to the neglect of career mobility, and this neglect has led some scholars to assume too readily that the typical American is securely and permanently lodged in an occupation by the time he becomes a father. This convenient but mistaken assumption underlies the common procedure followed in survey-research mobility studies, in which the respondent is asked to specify his father's "Regular occupation." That nicely glosses over the problem, by leaving it to the individual being interviewed to choose among what may in fact have been several different occupations held by his father at different points. The flaw in this procedure should be abundantly clear from a reading of the preceding chapter, for many of the restless men whose movement from stratum to stratum and from class to class was analyzed there, and indeed all of those in the depression generation (a sample drawn from Boston birth records for 1930), were already fathers. It would be leaving a good deal to the discretion of the sons of these men to let them determine what was their fathers' "regular occupation."

The ideal solution would be to take the shape of the father's entire career, or at least of his career during his son's lifetime, as the base against which to evaluate the son's career. Thus the father who had been the manager of a department store ever since his son was born would be distinguished from one who had worked as a badly paid clerk at the time he became a father and whose success came much later, perhaps after his son left school and began work himself. A method of this sort has been employed in at least one study, but the incompleteness of the available historical data and the restricted size of the samples made it impossible to do so here.[6] But at least we have a more uniform base than could be obtained from retrospective data pertaining to no clearly defined point in the father's career. The occupational achievements of young men in Boston are measured here against the status level attained by their fathers at the time the sons first entered the labor market (or at as close an approximation to that time as could be made on the basis of the available data).

OCCUPATIONAL INHERITANCE AND MOBILITY AT CAREER'S END

There were 1792 Boston residents about whom information was uncovered as to both their occupational status after they were well launched on their careers—past the age of 30, at a minimum, and in many cases into their 40's or 50's—and on the occupational rank of their fathers at the time the sons themselves entered the workaday world. They have been divided into age groups or cohorts, ranging from men born between 1840 and 1859 to a group born in 1930. Table 5.1 discloses how many of these men had, at the time they last were employed in Boston, held the same occupational rank as their fathers. No attempt was made to analyze the degree of occupational "inheritance" by specific occupation—to gauge the fraction of carpenters' sons who became carpenters, or of lawyers' sons who

TABLE 5.1. Intergenerational occupational inheritance, by stratum: percent of birth cohort with last job in same stratum as father's job

	Birth cohort				
	1840–1859	*1860–1879*	*1870–1889*	c. *1890–1930*[1]	*1930*
Entire sample	40	37	39	49[2]	47[3]
Father's job					
High white-collar	51	60	67	71	52
Low white-collar	53	58	55	57	57
Skilled	40	33	36	27	44
Semiskilled	21	28	33	48	39
Unskilled	25	10	5		0
Number in sample	208	784	193	405	202

[1] These figures are retabulated from Table 5.6 of Edward O. Laumann, *Prestige and Association in an Urban Community: An Analysis of an Urban Stratification System* (Indianapolis: Bobbs-Merrill, 1966). The sample was of adult male residents of Cambridge and Belmont, not of Boston proper. Some 48 percent of the employed males in these two communities held white-collar jobs according to the Census of 1960, as compared with 46 percent for the entire Boston S.M.S.A., and Laumann's sample was further skewed toward the middle class; 54 percent of its members were in white-collar occupations. This modest bias toward the middle class must be borne in mind in evaluating the findings. Note also that the age distribution of this sample was unfortunately quite broad, and more refined age controls could not be applied. The cohort is much less sharply defined temporally than any of the others. Unskilled laborers were not distinguished from semiskilled and service workers in the Laumann study, so a composite figure must be given for these two strata. If the unskilled and semiskilled categories were similarly combined for the other cohorts, the figures would read 43 percent for 1840–1859, 40 percent for 1860–1879, 37 percent for 1870–1889, and 44 percent for 1930.

[2] Significantly higher than the preceding cohorts, but only because the unskilled and semiskilled categories were not distinguished, and movement between the two was thus not registered.

[3] Significantly higher than 1860–1879.

became lawyers. Preliminary tabulations revealed that, Francis Walker's claims to the contrary notwithstanding, this fraction was negligible. It proved more fruitful to inquire whether sons typically obtained positions in the same occupational stratum as their fathers, whether carpenters' sons typically became skilled craftsmen of some kind, and whether lawyers' sons gravitated toward professional or other high-status business positions.

The answer is that the tendency toward occupational inheritance, even by stratum, was not very strong. In none of the five samples did a majority of men end their careers at their fathers' level. The figure was only 4 in 10 or less in the first three groups. That it was somewhat higher in the two groups born in the twentieth century probably reflects not a genuine trend toward increasing inheritance but rather some special features of these two samples. The highest figure, 49 percent for men born between *c.* 1890 and 1930, is partly due to the accident that Laumann did not distinguish unskilled from semiskilled and service workers and thus did not record movement between these two strata as mobility; when the unskilled and semiskilled categories are similarly combined for the other four cohorts the fractions of sons inheriting their father's occupation become 46, 44, 44, and 48 percent respectively, not different enough from 49 percent to be statistically significant. The cohort of men born in 1930 also appears to have been a little less mobile than the samples of men born in the nineteenth century, but these figures refer to the occupations they held at the relatively young age of 33; it is reasonable to surmise that the rate of occupational inheritance for this group would have been somewhat lower had it been possible to trace them at an age comparable to those of the other samples.[7] But for these peculiarities of the two twentieth-century samples, it seems likely that the rate of intergenerational occupational inheritance would have been exceedingly close to 40 percent in all five. The flow of Bostonians from one occupational level to another, not only within the span of a career but from generation to generation, went on at a relatively high and strikingly uniform rate over a period of almost a century. There was no indication that in this respect the class system was becoming less open and more rigid.

Although only about 4 in 10 young men in Boston ended their careers with the same occupational rank as their fathers, the fraction was much higher for families with high occupational status, and much lower for those with low status. As with the case of career mobility, those on the lower rungs of the class ladder, with most to gain from mobility, moved a good deal; those higher up, for whom mobility was likely to mean downward mobility, moved much less. At least half, and in two samples more than two-thirds, of the sons of professionals and prosperous businessmen reached that job level themselves, while 11 in 20 of the sons of clerks, salesmen, and small shopkeepers followed in their fathers' footsteps. (The uniformity of the tendency toward inheritance in lower white-collar families is especially remarkable; three of the figures are within a single percentage point of each other, and the spread between all five was an insignificant five points.)

Working-class sons, by contrast, were far less likely to gravitate toward jobs at their fathers' level. The fraction varied a good deal, from a high of 44 percent for children of skilled workers in the 1930 cohort (the 48 percent for the *c.* 1890–1930 group is inflated, of course, because it ignores movement between the unskilled and semiskilled levels) to a low of zero, but the mean was only 26 percent. Three out of four typically moved to an occupational status level other than that which they inherited. It could be argued, of course, that this movement was of slight significance because the status distinction between unskilled and semiskilled jobs was relatively minor, and that the relevant question is whether children born in families headed by unskilled or semiskilled blue-collar workers tended to cluster in the two low-skilled categories, though technically in a different stratum from their fathers'. But even if we collapse the unskilled and semiskilled levels together, the extent of occupational inheritance remains relatively low. In the five samples, 43, 40, 37, 48, and 44 percent of the sons of low-skilled workers themselves ended their careers in one of the two lower strata; between 52 and 63 percent, therefore, moved up to either a skilled or a white-collar job.

Many men who ended their careers working at a different occupational level from that which they had inherited had, of course, moved only a relatively short distance, shifting a notch up or down but remaining on the same side of the blue-collar–white-collar line as their fathers. Table 5.2 indicates how much interclass mobility there was between generations in the city—the fraction of men born in Boston middle-class homes who had skidded to a blue-collar post

TABLE 5.2. Intergenerational occupational inheritance and mobility across class boundaries (percent)

	Birth cohort				
Last job compared with father's	*1840–1859*	*1860–1879*	*1870–1889*	c. *1890–1930*	*1930*
In father's class	70	66	64	73	67
In different class	30	34	36	27	33
Working-class sons attaining white-collar jobs	41	41	43	36	34[1]
Middle-class sons skidding to blue-collar jobs	20	17	24	12[2]	29[3]
Ratio of upward to downward mobility	2.1	2.4	1.8	3.0	1.2
Number in sample	208	784	193	405	202

[1] Significantly lower than 1840–1859, 1860–1879, and 1870–1889.
[2] Significantly lower than 1870–1889 and 1930.
[3] Significantly higher than 1860–1879 and *c.* 1890–1930.

by the end of their careers, and of working-class youths who had found a secure niche in the white-collar world.

The rate of intergenerational inheritance of class status was, of course, considerably higher than the inheritance rate by stratum. Only 4 men in 10 ended up in their fathers' stratum; two-thirds to three-quarters of them remained in the class into which they were born, and from 27 to 36 percent moved to another class.

Over the entire period the escalators lifting men upward from blue-collar beginnings to white-collar careers carried many more passengers than those bringing *déclassé* men downward. The process of intergenerational mobility did not operate as a zero-sum game in which gains and losses were necessarily equivalent. In the three samples of men born in the nineteenth century the pattern was uniform, with fully 40 percent of all working-class children climbing to middle-class jobs and roughly half that fraction of middle-class sons falling into blue-collar positions. The two twentieth-century cohorts deviate somewhat from this, but it is doubtful that this represents a genuine change in the process of social circulation, given the special traits of those samples.

On the face of it, the evidence would seem to suggest that working-class men in Laumann's Sample had somewhat lower prospects for upward mobility than the earlier norm, and that men of middle-class origins were far more likely to retain their inherited positions. The occupational structure, it would seem, had tightened up considerably, and at the same time the ratio of upward to downward movement had become especially favorable, with climbers outnumbering skidders by nearly 3 to 1. But I suspect that Belmont and Cambridge were unrepresentative of Boston as a whole on this count, and that they contained unusual numbers of individuals with stable intergenerational career patterns. The very low 12-percent skidding estimate for this cohort seems especially questionable, and it may be suggested that Belmont in particular is not the kind of community in which downwardly mobile middle-class sons are likely to live.

Similarly, the deviant pattern displayed by the group of sons born in Boston in 1930—relatively low upward-mobility rates and usually high downward mobility—is not persuasive evidence of a real change in the occupational structure, because none of these men were older than 33. Since in every period in the modern history of Boston except the 1930's the volume of upward career mobility was larger than the volume of downward mobility, it seems likely that had this group been observed at a later age its occupational position would have been better, with fewer *déclassé* middle-class sons and more upwardly mobile working-class youths. If we used the mobility rates of the earlier samples as the basis for extrapolating the likely experience of the group of 1930 sons a decade into the future, the resulting estimate of intergenerational mobility would be very much in line with the figures for the earlier samples. Such an extrapolation does not, of course, prove anything, for it assumes that 1963–1973 for this group would be much like earlier decades for earlier groups, and that may not have been the case at all. But the exercise should suffice to show that the distinctive pattern of this sample could easily be due to its youthfulness relative to the other groups, and that it cannot be taken as solid evidence of a major alteration in the social structure. (It is regrettable that the limited size of the other samples made it impossible to isolate mobility rates for men at precisely the same age as the 1930 cohort attained in 1963, which would allow comparisons that would resolve the issue definitively.)

It is highly probable, therefore, though not certain, that there was little real change in the level of opportunities for intergenerational mobility in Boston in the twentieth century, and that more satisfactory data for the latter part of our period would disclose something quite like the older pattern, in which approximately 4 in 10 working-class youths moved into middle-class jobs by the end of their careers while about 2 in 10 children from middle-class homes skidded into a working-class calling.

Inspection of a more detailed mobility matrix, in which the occupational stratum of fathers is related to the stratum of their sons' last jobs, as in Table 5.3, provides further insight into the degree to which family origins determined the career patterns of Boston residents. It has already been made clear that young men born into middle-class homes in Boston had a very good prospect of attaining white-collar rank themselves; only 1 in 5 of them typically ended their careers in a manual job. The richer detail supplied in Table 5.3, however, indicates that it was far more advantageous to be of upper middle-class than of lower middle-class background. An average of only 9 percent of the sons of upper white-collar fathers in the various samples dropped into a blue-collar job in the course of their own careers. The only statistically significant variation from the 9-percent figure was in Laumann's sample, in which none of the children from the top white-collar stratum skidded to a manual post, but this is probably attributable to the special character of the sample.

There was, however, some significant variation in the extent to which upper white-collar sons fell one rung to the lower white-collar level, with the earliest group experiencing the maximum short-distance downward mobility of this kind—40 percent. Probably this high figure testifies to the stultifying effect of the prolonged depression of the 1870's. The final sample, of youths born in 1930, also had a poor record in this respect, but the number of cases was so small that this may be the result of sampling error, and there is the further fact that the youthfulness of this sample biases its occupational distribution downward. It does seem that it was a little harder for upper middle-class sons born before the Civil War and en-

TABLE 5.3. Intergenerational mobility by stratum (percent)

Stratum of father's occupation	*Birth cohort*	*Stratum of son's final job*				
		High white-collar	*Low white-collar*	*Skilled*	*Low manual*[1]	*Number*
High white-collar	1840–59	51	40	6	3	65
	1860–79	60	31	8	2	121
	1870–89	67	20	0	13	15
	c. 1890–1930	71	29	0	0	59
	1930	52	35	9	4	23
Low white-collar	1840–59	6	53	19	22	32
	1860–79	19	58	9	14	128
	1870–89	18	54	8	20	50
	c. 1890–1930	23	57	10	10	102
	1930	8	57	13	23	53
Skilled	1840–59	8	29	40	23	48
	1860–79	8	35	33	23	274
	1870–89	13	26	36	26	55
	c. 1890–1930	10	29	27	34	89
	1930	4	23	44	29	48
Low Manual	1840–59	8	35	14	43	63
	1860–79	5	34	20	40	261
	1870–89	5	41	16	37	73
	c. 1890–1930	5	30	17	48	155
	1930	5	33	18	44	78

[1] See Table 4.7, note 1.

tering the labor market in the 1870's to capitalize upon their inherited advantages than was the case later, though not harder to avoid skidding into the laboring class.

All in all, it was very helpful indeed to a man's career to come from a family headed by a professional or a prosperous businessman. From one-half to two-thirds—an average of 60 percent—of the sons born into the upper white-collar stratum found an occupation at that level themselves, as opposed to about 15 percent of the children of lower white-collar workers, 9 percent of the men of skilled manual origins, and 5 percent of those from unskilled or semiskilled backgrounds. Youths of upper white-collar origins, in other words, were overrepresented in upper white-collar jobs by about 400 percent as compared with lower white-collar sons, 650 percent as compared with skilled sons, and 1200 percent as compared with the sons of unskilled or semiskilled fathers. In the contest for jobs at the highest level, the disadvantage of "the poor man's son" was far greater than the *Pilot's* "double weight" metaphor would suggest.

It is noteworthy too that the majority of upper middle-class youths who did not reach the top occupational stratum customarily fell only a notch below it and no further. They were only a third as likely as working-class youths to end up as manual workmen. In the upper reaches of the Boston social structure, inherited advantages counted heavily.

The career prospects of the children of clerks, salesmen, small grocers, and similar lower white-collar workers were considerably less favorable. Some moved up to the upper white-collar stratum, but a substantial minority were downwardly mobile. The fraction of skidders varied, from a high of 41 percent for men born in the 1840's and 1850's to a low of 20 percent in the probably unrepresentative Laumann sample, but it averaged three times the skidding rate of the sons of professionals and prosperous businessmen.

There was virtually no fluctuation at all in the tendency of low white-collar sons to follow their fathers' occupations; 11 in 20 did so in each sample over this very long span of years. Nine in 20, therefore, moved to another stratum. But the balance between upward and downward intergenerational movement shifted considerably from sample to sample. Unfortunately, we cannot assess the impact upon intergenerational mobility rates of the greatest economic calamity of the period, the Great Depression of the 1930's. The preceding chapter revealed the disastrous impact of that experience upon the career patterns of low-skilled men and to some extent of lower white-collar employees too, but the sources provided no information about the social origins of members of the 1900–1909 cohort, who were at the most vulnerable age in the 1930's. Some of the men from Laumann's *c.* 1890–1930 sample were of the same age, but the age limits of this group were quite wide and no separate breakdown of the mobility rates of those actually born in the first decade of the century is available. It is evident that the rate of downward movement into blue-collar callings was high (on the order of 40 percent) and the rate of upward mobility to the high white-collar stratum unusually low (6–8 percent) in the first and last samples; in the 1860–1879, 1870–1889, and *c.* 1890–1930 groups the skidding rate ranged from 20 to 28 percent and the fraction of men rising to the top white-collar stratum was about 20 percent. The poor record of the 1930 group may be discounted, for reasons already mentioned, but the distinctiveness of the 1840–1859 cohort seems clear. Again we see evidence that the occupational structure was less favorable for men born into Boston middle-class homes before the Civil War. Only a third as many of the sons of lower white-collar workers climbed to the top nonmanual stratum as was common later, and unusually large numbers fell into laboring jobs.

This suggests the possibility that the Boston social structure became modestly but perceptibly less open at some point late in the nineteenth century, and that inherited advantages began to count more heavily as determinants of individual career patterns. Both upper and lower middle-class children entering the labor market after 1880 were somewhat less vulnerable to competition from below, somewhat more assured of being able to maintain white-collar status. The sons of professionals and important businessmen were increasingly able to attain their fathers' occupational rank, whereas the children of small businessmen, clerks, and salesmen found it easier to reach their fathers' level or to climb above it.

But so simple a generalization—that the occupational structure was tightening up—does gross injustice to the complexity of what was happening, for, if birth was coming to count for more for those of relatively high family origins, there was no corresponding change in the handicapping effect of a lowly social origin. A very large minority of the youths born into working-class homes from the first three samples—a little more than 4 in 10—found their way into white-collar jobs. The comparable figure for the two cohorts born in this century was a few points lower—36 and 34 percent respectively—but I have already cited grounds for believing that these estimates are on the low side, so that they do not constitute persuasive evidence that traditional channels of upward social mobility were becoming blocked. The details provided in Table 5.3 remind us of the important consideration that only about a quarter of these upwardly mobile working-class youths rose as high as the upper white-collar stratum, with the great bulk of them clustering in relatively routine and menial clerical, sales, or petty proprietary jobs, but the fact remains that access to jobs at the lower white-collar level at least was relatively easy throughout the period.

A further point of great significance is that there was significant upward intergenerational mobility *within* the blue-collar class as well as considerable movement into the nonmanual class. No fewer than 6 in 10 of the children born into the families of unskilled or semiskilled workers in the first three groups rose to either skilled or white-collar jobs; even in the latter two samples, which we have reason to believe yielded artificially low estimates of upward mobility, more than half of the sons from unskilled or semiskilled homes moved upward to become either skilled craftsmen or white-collar workers.

This is noteworthy in the light of the frequently advanced view that "poverty breeds poverty [and] passes from generation to generation in a cruel cycle of near inevitability." [8] The great majority of the low-skilled laborers of Boston were poor compared to their neighbors; their wages were low and irregular, and few of them could hope to accumulate significant property holdings (see Appendix B for supporting evidence). But a clear majority of the youths who grew up in households headed by such men managed to climb to an occupational level distinctly above that of their fathers in the course of their own careers. Further tabulations reveal that sons from the small minority of low-skilled families that owned property in the city fared somewhat better than those from propertyless families (see Table 5.6 below), but it is striking that even those youths whose fathers were doubly handicapped and lacked either occupational skill or property were more likely to enter skilled or white-collar jobs than they were to remain trapped in a low-skilled manual post.

The point should not be overstated. It is possible that employing a stricter definition of poverty, and examining not low-skilled laborers as a group but only men in the worst-paid and most menial occupations, would disclose a pattern that bore a somewhat greater resemblance to the "cruel cycle of near inevitability" that some commentators have hypothesized. The data here are not adequate to explore that question. Possibly, too, greater intergenerational transmission of poverty might be discerned if attention could be focused upon those persons who possessed the psychological traits emphasized by "culture of poverty" theorists, who locate the roots of poverty in early socialization experiences that are thought to produce inability to defer gratification and to plan for the future.[9] This notion, however, has not yet proved susceptible of empirical validation on a large scale, and it clearly is not amenable to testing with historical evidence. Whether the vast majority of fathers with these traits passed them on to their children, who were consequently unable to function productively, it is quite impossible to say.

What can be said is that, if there were indeed pockets of permanent poverty transmitted from generation to generation, they were just that—pockets. It was simply not the case that a major element of the society—the low-skilled laboring group included about a third of the city's population—was locked in a cycle that destined the great majority of children born into it to work at the same menial and ill-paid occupations that their fathers held. That upward mobility was more common than the transmission of low-skilled status from one generation to the next was a fact of profound significance. Doubtless poverty did breed poverty in some instances, but over the span of nearly a century the Boston social order has been sufficiently fluid to make that more the exception than the rule.

Close to 6 in 10 of the children of unskilled or semiskilled laborers became skilled craftsmen or white-collar workers in the course of their own careers. As we might expect, an even larger fraction of men from households headed by a skilled worker fared that well in the occupational competition; only about 1 in 4 of them skidded to a job at the unskilled or semiskilled level. It is somewhat surprising, though, that the chief advantage of youths with skilled fathers lay in their easier access to skilled positions. They were not more successful in penetrating the white-collar world; indeed, in three of the five cohorts they were slightly less successful than low manual sons in that respect. There is a hint in the data that skilled sons who did climb into nonmanual posts were a bit more likely to move all the way up to the high white-collar level, but the major difference in the career patterns of the two groups of sons was in their distribution within the blue-collar world, with the sons of skilled craftsmen obtaining skilled jobs in nearly double the proportion of low manual sons, and with correspondingly fewer of them confined to unskilled or semiskilled callings. The channels for entry into the skilled crafts—apprenticeship programs and union membership—were obviously more open to men whose fathers were already in a craft. But coming from a household on the upper rather than the lower level of the blue-collar hierarchy had no bearing upon access to opportunity of a quite different kind—the chance to wear a white collar and work in a nonmanual calling.[10]

Family social-class background, in sum, did exert a marked influence upon individual career patterns in Boston from the late nineteenth century to the present. About 9 of 10 sons of professionals and substantial businessmen, and from two-thirds to three-fourths of those of low white-collar workers, ended up in white-collar callings, but only 4 in 10 of the sons of blue-collar men did so. It is equally important, however, to note that children born into the working class were very far from being doomed to die in the working class. The odds of climbing into a white-collar job were only a shade less than even. And the chance that a youth whose father stood at the very bottom of the occupational ladder, in a menial unskilled or semiskilled job, would rise to a higher occupation himself—either skilled or white collar—was actually better than even. The background advantages of men from middle-class families were substantial; opportunities to rise in the world for men from working-class homes were also substantial.

FAMILY BACKGROUND AND MOBILITY FROM FIRST TO LAST JOB

There was some correlation between the occupational rank of an individual's father and where he himself stood on the social ladder at the time of his last job. We may now inquire *when* the advantages or disadvantages stemming from family background exerted their chief influence upon a man's career. One possibility is that social origins influenced eventual career lines largely via their impact in determining the level at which an individual entered the labor market in the first place. Middle-class parents, that is to say, and especially upper middle-class parents, produced children who found white-collar jobs when they first went to work, whereas the sons of laboring men were much more prone to take manual jobs initially. Since where one started influenced where one ended up in the occupational competition, as the preceding chapter demonstrated, this in itself might have accounted for the relation we have observed between last job and family origins. Another possibility, though, is that coming from a high- or a low-status family exerted a continuing pressure upon a man's subsequent career, in addition to its influence upon the level of his first job, so that by the end of his working life there was typically a closer relation between last job and family origins. Since we have information about the first job as well as the last job of at least some of the members of our samples, it is possible to explore this issue to some degree.

The data are less full, since the first occupations of many sample members could not be discovered. The group of youths born in 1930 had to be dropped because of the paucity of cases, as did Laumann's Belmont and Cambridge sample, for there was no question about first job in his survey. The sizes of the other three samples were sufficiently small to make it necessary to ignore movement from stratum to stratum and to deal solely with movement between the white-collar and blue-collar classes. Still, a finding of some interest emerged.

Table 5.4 indicates the fraction of middle-class and working-class Boston sons who began their careers at the white-collar level, the extent to which they moved upward or downward between their first and last jobs, and finally the fraction who ended their working lives in a middle-class calling of some kind. It reveals, first, that a high percentage of the children of white-collar workers did move directly into nonmanual posts when they first entered the labor market, from two to three times the fraction of working-class sons entering white-collar first jobs. Fewer than 1 in 10 of these middle-class youths were downwardly mobile in the course of their subsequent careers; working-class youths who had gotten a foothold in the white-collar world initially were from two to four times as likely to skid to a blue-collar job later. In this respect family origins exerted a definite influence after an individual's initial entry into the labor market, pulling unusually large numbers of aspiring working-class sons back to the level from which they sprang.

The same contrast appears in the records of young men who took a manual job initially. Half or more of the men from middle-class families who first entered blue-collar jobs—63, 51, and 50 percent respectively—were manual workers only temporarily; they later returned to their class of origin. By comparison, only a half to a third

TABLE 5.4. Influence of family origins upon career mobility from first to last job (percent)

Jobs	*Birth cohort* 1850–1859	1860–1879	1880–1889
White-collar first jobs			
Middle-class sons	79	81	67
Working-class sons	28[1]	42[1]	35[1]
White-collar to blue-collar			
Middle-class sons	7	9	11
Working-class sons	32[1]	24[1]	22[1]
Blue-collar first jobs			
Middle-class sons	21	19	33
Working-class sons	72[1]	58[1]	65[1]
Blue-collar to white-collar			
Middle-class sons	63	51	50
Working-class sons	30[1]	19[1]	28[1]
White-collar last jobs			
Middle-class sons	87	84	76
Working-class sons	40[1]	43[1]	46[1]
Number in sample	164	653	157

[1] Significantly different from middle-class sons.

as many youths of blue-collar origins and blue-collar first jobs later climbed to a nonmanual position. Family origins not only made a difference in initial job placement; they continued to make a difference in determining the shape of an individual's later career.

On the other hand, family background seems to have exerted a weaker influence upon working-class youths than upon their middle-class counterparts. Less than a tenth of the middle-class sons who began work wearing white collars like their fathers later moved across the class divide, but from 20 to 30 percent of the working-class sons who first worked at their fathers' level later moved out of their class of origin. Similarly, middle-class sons who might be called deviant in their choice of a first job—who initially entered a blue-collar occupation—later shifted to a white-collar post at least half the time, whereas less than a third of the deviant working-class youths—those who started work in the nonmanual class—later returned to their class of origin. Thus it was that the proportion of middle-class men who held jobs at their fathers' level increased from the time of initial entry into the labor market until retirement, whereas the proportion of working-class youths wearing blue collars like their fathers declined and the proportion holding white-collar jobs rose correspondingly. The influence of family origins was felt long beyond the first job. There was a continuing pull drawing men up or down toward the rank of their fathers. It is striking, though, that the upward magnetism of the middle-class family was stronger than the downward pull exerted by the working-class family.

THE SIGNIFICANCE OF FAMILY PROPERTY HOLDINGS

The single most important index of an individual's social-class origins is doubtless his father's occupation, but there is another dimension of the stratification system that should be examined. A family's command over economic resources—its income, wealth, and property holdings—obviously affects the character of the environment it offers children growing up within it. In popular discourse about the class system—the claim, for instance, that "the poor man's son carries double weight" in the contest for status—wealth tends to be referred to more often than occupation. Command over economic resources is, of course, closely related to occupation. Few laborers are rich; few bankers could be considered poor men. But there are some variations in wealth *within* broad occupational categories like those employed here, and it will be useful to see whether they had a significant bearing upon individual career patterns.

The evidence that can be brought to bear upon this issue is severely limited. No direct data were available on either individual earnings or liquid assets.[11] The sole source of information was the Boston tax records, which indicated the value of the real-estate holdings of sample members. This is a particularly grave limitation in the case of Boston, because it has long been a city with an unusually low proportion of single-family dwellings and thus a low rate of home ownership. Among major American metropolitan centers it has consistently ranked near the bottom, with New York, in home ownership. Real-estate records would be a considerably more sensitive index of a family's income and wealth in a city with a preponderance of single-family dwellings—Detroit or Los Angeles, say. In Boston, men who had the resources to purchase a home, and who would presumably have done so in another community, were more likely to keep their money in the bank or to invest it in other ways. This imparts a serious downward bias to estimates of property holdings derived from real-estate records, a bias not confined to middle-class apartment dwellers. A separate sample of 1000 Boston working-class families drawn from the manuscript schedules of the 1870 Census, which reported amounts of personal as well as real property held by citizens, disclosed that only 11 percent were homeowners but two and a half times as many (28 percent) had some assets. The median value of the personal-property holdings reported by workers who owned no real estate was $500, a not insubstantial amount in an era in which skilled workmen typically earned little more than that in a year. A sizeable minority of the fathers classified as propertyless in the analysis that follows probably were not in fact without significant financial assets; they simply were not homeowners.

A further limitation of the evidence is that attention must be confined to men born before 1880. The search through tax records had to be kept to those of the city of Boston; to extend it to the dozens of suburban communities in the metropolitan area would have been much too burdensome and costly. The fathers of a large fraction of the members of the post-1880 samples lived outside the Boston city limits and did not appear in the tax records; thus there were too few cases for analysis.[12] Some insights into the relation between home ownership and intergenerational occupational mobility in late-nineteenth century Boston, however, may be obtained from the available evidence.

Common sense would lead us to expect that the sons of property-owning fathers would generally fare better in the occupational competition than the offspring of propertyless men. Home ownership, some observers of the American scene have argued, symptomized dedication to values conducive to success: "A man is not really a true man until he owns his own home, and they that own their homes are made more honorable and honest and pure, and true and economical and careful, by owning the home." [13] If this seems excessive to modern ears, there is the practical consideration that men possessed of a property stake in the community were likely to be in a superior position to assist their offspring—to support their education beyond the legally required minimum, for instance, or to provide capital backing for business ventures.

A more complicated possibility, however, is that there was a positive relation between a father's property holdings and his son's occupational achievement in the middle class, but an inverse relation between the two for families on the lower rungs of the class ladder. Investing in a home and providing career backing for aspiring children, that is to say, may have been alternative rather than complementary choices. The earning capacity of manual laborers may have been so limited that accumulation of property was normally accomplished by sending the children to work at the earliest possible age and utilizing the additional income to purchase a small home. Investment in "human capital"—in formal education, lengthy low-paid apprenticeships, or other forms of assistance that would yield career benefits for the children in the future—would thus be sacrificed for the security and respectability of home ownership, for becoming "a true man," in the present. This seems to have been the trade-off made by the unskilled laborers who accumulated property in Newburyport, Massachusetts, in the middle decades of the nineteenth century.[14] Whether a similar pattern can be discerned in a major metropolis as well, and whether it held for semiskilled and skilled laboring families too, is the question.

For the sample as a whole, family wealth and intergenerational occupational achievement were positively correlated (Table 5.5). More than half of the fathers of sample members—56 percent—held no property at all; only 1 in 12 of the children of these men ended their careers as professionals or large businessmen, while almost a third of them became unskilled or semiskilled laborers. At the other end of the wealth pyramid was a group of fathers, 15 percent of the total, who were taxed on holdings of at least $10,000. More than 60 percent of their sons obtained jobs in the high white-collar category, and only 2 percent worked at low manual posts. Between the extremes there was the same general pattern; the larger the family holdings, the larger the fraction of sons employed in occupations in the upper echelons and the smaller the fraction confined to blue-collar posts. The possession of small or moderate amounts of property, however, was rather weakly related to a son's career prospects; the holding of at least $5000 was required to dramatically alter intergenerational mobility patterns.

A family's position on the property scale was associated with the career patterns its children were likely to follow, strongly associated

TABLE 5.5. Family wealth and the occupational achievement of sons, 1880 sample (percent)[1]

	Stratum of son's final job					
Father's property	*High white-collar*	*Low white-collar*	*Skilled*	*Low manual*	*Number*	*Percent of all families*
None	8	38	23	31	526	56
Under $2500	7	41	26	26	95	10
$2500–4999	16	41	27	16	113	12
$5000–9999	29	45	9	17	66	7
$10,000 or more	62	30	6	2	138	15

[1] Property figures were derived by tracing each sample member in the Assessor's Valuation Books of the city of Boston at 10-year intervals. Fathers are classified according to their maximum accumulation achieved before their sons reached adulthood. These men all had male offspring as of 1880, and were born (with a few exceptions) in the 1840's or 1850's. None of the differences between propertyless fathers and those with less than $2500 are significant. Fathers in the $2500–4999 class had significantly more sons in high white-collar jobs and significantly fewer in low manual callings than the propertyless. Those in the $5000–9999 class differed significantly from those in the $2500–4999 category in proportion of sons in high white-collar and skilled jobs. Those in the $10,000 and up category differed significantly from those in the $5000–9999 class in proportion of high white-collar, low-white collar, and low manual sons.

in the case of households at the upper ends of the scale. It is not clear, however, whether family property exerted any independent influence in the mobility process, or whether the correlation was simply attributable to the fact that relatively prosperous fathers were generally themselves in high-ranked occupations and propertyless fathers in low-ranked ones. Nor is it evident, from figures for the sample as a whole, whether there was any inverse relation between home ownership and a son's success for particular subgroups, such as low-skilled laborers.

It is thus necessary to examine the connection between family property holding and intergenerational occupational mobility within the various occupational strata (Table 5.6). There was, of course, a strong relation between a family's property position and the occupation of the household head. Almost three-quarters (74 percent) of fathers in high white-collar jobs held $5000 or more, but only 20 percent of clerks, salesmen, and petty proprietors, and a mere 6 percent of blue-collar workers.[15] Conversely, 72 percent of all unskilled or semiskilled fathers held no taxable property at all, and 69 percent of skilled fathers, compared with 56 percent of men in low white-collar jobs and only 10 percent of the professionals and large businessmen.[16] There were, however, some high white-collar workers and many low white-collar employees with little or no property, and there were laboring men who did own some, so that we may judge whether property ownership per se had any bearing on occupational achievement in the next generation.

TABLE 5.6. Family wealth and intergenerational occupational mobility, 1880 sample (percent)

		Stratum of son's final job				
Stratum of father's occupation	*Father's property*	*High white-collar*	*Low white-collar*	*Skilled*	*Low manual*	*Number*
High white-collar	None	28	50	17	5	18
	Under $5000	35	48	17	0	29
	$5000 or more	65	29	4	2	136
Low white-collar	None	11	60	8	21	87
	Under $5000	18	54	15	13	39
	$5000 or more	24	55	14	7	29
Skilled	None	9	34	31	26	200
	Under $5000	4	36	46	14	74
	$5000 or more	21	43	21	14	14
Low Manual	None	4	34	22	41	221
	Under $5000	8	34	15	43	65
	$5000 or more	14	41	9	36	22

Working-class fathers who accumulated property in Boston did not do so at the expense of their children, as had been the case in Newburyport. The great majority of laborers with property held amounts less than $5,000, and the sons of these men followed career lines closely resembling those of their peers from propertyless households. The children of low manual workers with small holdings actually fared a little better than their rivals, and the sons of skilled workers with property a little less well; neither difference, however, was statistically significant.[17] The ownership of a modest working-class dwelling simply made no difference either way.

The accumulation of substantial family property holdings, however, did make a difference in the careers of working-class youth, and that difference was positive. Only 5 percent of the skilled manual fathers in the sample and 7 percent of those in unskilled or semiskilled occupations obtained as much as $5000, an amount that was several times the average annual earnings of even skilled craftsmen in this period. The children of this select group of prosperous workingmen were distinctly more successful at penetrating occupations at both the high white-collar and low white-collar levels than those of fathers with small holdings or no property at all. By what means these families accumulated such impressive amounts is unknown, but clearly it was not by means that impaired the mobility prospects of the younger generation.

Even in this instance, however, the occupational level of the head of the household was a more powerful determinant of the son's occupational status than the family's property position. Forty-five percent of the sons of low manual workers in the highest property category and 35 percent of the sons of comparably prosperous skilled workmen remained in blue-collar jobs, whereas only 29 percent of the children of low white-collar employees with no property at all and 22 percent of comparable high white-collar sons became blue-collar workers. The gap between the sons of workers with large property holdings and the sons of propertyless white-collar workers was, to be sure, much narrower than that between white-collar and blue-collar sons in general, but there were elements of class culture linked to the father's occupation that did not vanish even when groups at the opposite end of the property scale are compared.

Within middle-class families, too, the possession of property holdings worth less than $5000 had only limited significance for the future career patterns of children, checking downward mobility little or not at all and increasing access to high white-collar posts only moderately. The sharpest distinction again was not between owning and nonowning families, but between the large holders and the rest. Possibly the possession of a home of his own made an individual "more honourable and honest and pure, and true and economical and careful"—about these qualities the historical record is silent—but it seems to have had no demonstrable effect upon the career prospects of his children.

This general point—the near irrelevance of home ownership per se to a son's success—may be reinforced by considering another measure of intergenerational achievement. Table 5.7 shows how the property position of Boston fathers affected the likelihood that their sons would themselves become property owners. Fully 83 percent of the children coming from propertyless households themselves obtained no property in the city; only 8 percent accumulated holdings as large as $5000. The sons of men owning homes of moderate value, however, were not in a dramatically different position. The large majority of them—two-thirds—did not become homeowners, and most of those who did obtained only small holdings. A mere 12 percent of them, little more than the 8 percent figure for the sons of propertyless men, succeeded in accumulating $5000 or more.

TABLE 5.7. Family wealth and property accumulations by sons, 1880 sample (percent)[1]

Maximum property of father	*Property accumulated by sons*			
	None	*Under $5000*	*$5000 or more*	*Number*
None	83	9	8	225
Under $5000	67	21	12	100
$5000 or more	37	18	45	105

[1] There are many fewer cases here than in Tables 5.5 and 5.6, in which the last known occupations of youths were related to family property holdings. The explanation is that many of the sons in the sample pursued their careers outside the city of Boston proper; their occupations could be traced through city directories, but it was impossible to trace the tax records of Cambridge, Waltham, Newton, and several dozen other communities outside of Boston proper to gather information as to their property holdings.

Men from households with large property holdings were far more successful. Little more than a third of them obtained no property; close to half (45 percent) reached the $5000-and-up bracket. More detailed tabulations, not given here, reveal that the connection between father's wealth and son's wealth became even tighter in the upper reaches of the property scale. Fifty-four percent of the youths who came into possession of as much as $10,000 ($N=49$) had fathers with that much property, whereas only 14 percent were from propertyless households. Fully 70 percent of those who obtained $25,000 or more ($N=27$) had fathers in that bracket, and a mere 7 percent came from families without any property at all.

At the top of the property scale, then, as at the top of the occupational scale, there was a good deal of rigidity in the Boston class structure. To be born into a wealthy family was a great advantage; it markedly increased one's chances both of becoming wealthy and of entering a highly desirable occupation. Below that level, however, the influence of family background was considerably weaker. In the competition for position and property, the sons of holders of moderate amounts of property fared only a little better than youths from propertyless homes. There was much shifting from generation to generation between the rungs of the social ladder that were most visible to ordinary people, but higher up—at the high white-collar level occupationally and the $5000 cut-off point in terms of family property—there was a relatively impermeable barrier.

THE CHANGING OCCUPATIONAL STRUCTURE AND THE QUESTION OF MOBILITY TRENDS: TWO ANALYTIC MODELS

Two broad conclusions are suggested by the evidence presented thus far. One is that, though inherited social advantages did count for a good deal in Boston, inherited disadvantages counted for less. The flow of men up the class ladder considerably exceeded the corresponding flow of men downward. Second, it appears that there was rather striking uniformity in the process of intergenerational occupational circulation in the community over this entire period.

This much seems clear from straightforward examination of intergenerational mobility matrices. One major issue has yet to be dealt with, however. The structure of the Boston economy changed over these several decades, altering the proportion of jobs in the various occupational strata. The change was by no means as dramatic as might have been thought, as was shown in the preceding chapter (Tables 4.1 and 4.2), but it did occur. The supply of high-status and low-status jobs, that is, did not remain constant over the period. Structural change in the supply of positions can, in a sense, *require* occupational mobility. If, for instance, the proportion of unskilled and semiskilled posts in the local labor force rises considerably in the course of three decades, the likelihood that sons of low manual workers beginning their careers then will inherit their fathers' occupation increases correspondingly, all other things being equal. If, on the other hand, low manual openings shrink and white-collar callings expand, increasing mobility on the part of low manual sons will result, in the absence of other offsetting changes. Sociologists have developed a number of analytic techniques that attempt to control for such changes in the occupational structure over time.

One such technique involves the application of a "maximum-stability" model in order to separate the bare minimum of mobility required by structural change from the total amount of mobility observed in a table. The extent to which mobility actually observed exceeds minimum structural mobility is a measure of what is termed "circulation" or "exchange" mobility. The method entails comparing the occupational distribution of a group of fathers and their sons, and calculating the proportion of sons who could conceivably have inherited their fathers' occupation, given the known distributions.[18] When this is done for the five Boston samples (Table 5.8), the level of minimum mobility is revealed to be close to 20 percent, except for the 1930 cohort, in which it was only 11 percent. Since in each sample observed mobility was much higher than this minimum, there was substantial circulation mobility. At least a third of the members of each group moved to a different occupational level for reasons unrelated to the supply of such positions in the local economy. There is a suggestion in the data of a trend toward diminished structural mobility and increased rates of circulation mobility, but this may be an artifact of the distinctive age com-

TABLE 5.8. Trends in intergenerational mobility (percent of sons mobile as of last job)

	Birth cohort				
Measure	*1840–1859*	*1860–1879*	*1870–1889*	c. *1890–1930*	*1930*
Observed [1]	54	56	56	51	52
Minimum from structural change	23	23	20	17	11
Circulation (observed minus minimum)	31	33	36	34	41
Expected, full-equality model	76	76	74	74	72
Ratio of observed to expected	0.71	0.74	0.76	0.69	0.72

[1] These figures differ from those in Table 5.1, indicating somewhat less mobility, because the semiskilled and unskilled categories were combined for this part of the analysis. The number of moves counted as mobility increases, of course, with the number of categories employed.

position of the 1930 cohort. What is clear is that there was no trend in the opposite direction, toward a more closed social system. Holding constant changes in the local occupational structure by means of the maximum-stability model leaves undisturbed the conclusion previously ventured on that point.

Another analytic model that has been used to control for changes in occupational structure and to measure circulation mobility defines a hypothetical condition of maximum mobility, in which the occupations held by a group of fathers and their sons are statistically independent of one another. Different investigators have employed a variety of terms to describe this technique—the "full-equality" model, the "random-mobility" model, the "perfect-mobility" model, the "index of association," and "social distance mobility ratios" are the most common—but the underlying logic is similar.[19] From a table classifying the occupations of a group of sons against the occupations of their fathers one calculates the occupational distribution of the sons that would be expected *if* the occupational rank of their fathers had no influence upon their own careers, if, that is, sons were randomly placed in the job market with respect to their social origins. The actual distribution of sons from the various social strata may then be compared with the distribution expected under the assumption of equal opportunity to see how far the two deviated from each other.

The extent to which the overall mobility patterns of the five samples fell short of the level that would have prevailed under circumstances of "perfect mobility" is indicated in Table 5.8. In fact, slightly more than half of the members of the five cohorts were occupationally mobile with respect to their fathers; had their career patterns been entirely uninfluenced by their social origins, about three-quarters of them would have been occupationally mobile. The amount of mobility that actually took place in the community was roughly 70 to 75 percent of what would have been expected if all sons had enjoyed equal occupational opportunity. Again there was no evident trend toward either increasing openness or increasing rigidity in the occupational structure; the ratio of observed to expected mobility was almost identical for men born as early as the two decades prior to the Civil War and as late as 1930.

The summary measures of observed mobility, minimum mobility, and expected mobility in Table 5.8 are useful in two ways. Controlling for changes in the local occupational structure in this manner, first of all, lends further support to a central theme of this chapter —that there was striking stability in the process of social circulation in Boston throughout the past century. Not only total intergenerational mobility, but the relation between total mobility, minimum structural mobility, and expected mobility varied remarkably little over this long span of years.

These summary measures computed by employing maximum-stability and full-equality models are helpful in another respect as well, in that they supply a pair of standards against which to judge the amount of mobility actually observed. A certain amount of intergenerational occupational shifting had to take place in Boston as a result of structural change in the economy, but it is revealing that this accounted for less than half of the mobility that was observed. There was much more mobility than there had to be to accomplish the net redistribution of the local labor force that occurred. Observed mobility, on the other hand, fell short of the maximal standard calculated from the full-equality model by a margin of 25 to 30 percent in the various samples. There was considerably less mobility than there would have been had the career patterns of sons been quite unrelated to family origins.

There are, however, severe limitations inherent in summary measures of mobility, in which all movements between occupational categories—upward and downward, short-distance and long-distance—are treated as equivalent. Two radically different communities, one with a high volume of downward mobility and little upward mobility and another with a great deal of upward mobility and little downward mobility, might be indistinguishable from each other by the measures employed in Table 5.8, for these two might display similar levels of total occupational shifting and similar ratios of observed to minimum and expected mobility. Despite the relatively constant level of observed, minimum, and expected mobility in Boston over the past century, therefore, the community mobility pattern may have changed significantly.

A more detailed examination of the extent to which the mobility patterns of Boston men of varying social origins deviated from the full-equality model is thus in order (Table 5.9). The index value in each cell registers the over- or underrepresentation of sons from high white-collar, low white-collar, skilled, and low manual families at each occupational level. A value of 5.0 for the concentration of sons of professionals and prosperous businessmen in high white-collar callings would mean that youths of privileged backgrounds reached the highest occupational stratum themselves five times as frequently as would have occurred in a community in which an individual's social origins had no bearing on his career prospects.

TABLE 5.9. Ratio of actual to expected occupational distribution of sons at last known job

Stratum of father's occupation and birth cohort	*Stratum of son's last job*			
	High white-collar	*Low white-collar*	*Skilled*	*Low manual*
High white-collar				
1840–1879[1]	3.2	0.9	0.3	0.1
1870–1889	4.3	.5	0	.5
c. 1890–1930	3.6	.9	0	0
1930	4.8	.9	.4	.1
Mean for all samples[2]	4.0	.8	.2	.2
Low white-collar				
1840–1879[1]	0.9	1.5	0.5	0.7
1870–1889	1.2	1.4	.4	.7
c. 1890–1930	1.1	3.1	.7	.3
1930	0.7	1.5	.6	.8
Mean for all samples[2]	1.0	1.9	.6	.6
Skilled				
1840–1879[1]	0.5	0.9	1.7	1.0
1870–1889	.8	.6	2.0	0.9
c. 1890–1930	.5	.8	1.8	1.2
1930	.4	.6	2.0	1.0
Mean for all samples[2]	.6	.7	1.9	1.0
Low manual				
1840–1879[1]	0.3	0.9	1.0	1.7
1870–1889	.4	1.1	0.9	1.4
c. 1890–1930	.2	1.1	1.2	3.0
1930	.5	0.9	0.8	1.4
Mean for all samples[2]	.3	1.0	1.0	1.9

[1] The 1840–1859 and 1860–1879 cohorts have been combined here. This simplifies the table, and it is justifiable because the two cohorts displayed nearly identical ratios.

[2] The mean is a simple unweighted mean which does not take into account differences in the size of the cohorts. It is intended merely to simplify interpretation.

Likewise, a value of 0.1 for the concentration of sons of unskilled and semiskilled laborers in the high white-collar category would mean that only a tenth as many of these youths as expected under conditions of full equality actually ascended to that level.

There was indeed some stickiness in the Boston occupational structure, some distinct deviation from the full-equality model. In each occupational category, in every sample, there was a greater than chance concentration of sons working at the occupational level of their fathers. The index values measuring the tendency toward occupational inheritance (those along the diagonal from upper left to lower right) were in no case lower than 1.4, and in 8 of 12 instances they were 2.0 or higher.

On the other hand, the importance of class origins was far greater for sons from upper middle-class families than for others. Youths of high white-collar origins reached that level themselves four times as often as chance would have dictated, while the mean index value for each of the other occupational groups was less than half that—1.9. Nor did those children of professionals and prosperous businessmen who failed to attain their fathers' status typically slip very far; four-fifths as many of them as expected entered other white-collar callings, but only one-fifth of the expected fraction became blue-collar workers.

Men from families headed by a clerk, salesman, or petty proprietor were quite successful at moving up into upper middle-class posts themselves, winning just about the share of these jobs that would have accrued to them under circumstances of equal opportunity and a much larger share than fell to youths of working-class origins. There was, on the other hand, substantial downward mobility on the part of this group, about 60 percent as much as would have been the case had middle-class origins been of no advantage in the job competition at all.

Jobs at the lower white-collar level were surprisingly accessible to sons of working class origins. The children of skilled craftsmen obtained 60 to 90 percent of their "fair share" of clerical, sales, and petty proprietary positions, and the sons of unskilled and semiskilled laborers were even more successful in this respect, winning a startling 90 to 110 percent of their quota. Sons from the lower stratum of the working class also found significant opportunities to enter skilled trades; in this category too they found as many openings as expected under circumstances of equal opportunity. It was only at the top of the occupational structure that men of low manual origins were dramatically disadvantaged. Less than a third of the expected number of low manual sons were able to obtain upper middle-class status. The children of skilled workers, who entered low white-collar posts considerably less often than low manual sons, fared quite a bit better in this respect. When they moved into the middle-class world at all they were twice as likely as the latter to rise to the top. Both groups of working-class sons, however, experienced significant upward mobility, less than would have been the case had their family origins been no handicap at all, but not dramatically less except in the case of movement from low manual origins to high white-collar jobs.

When changes in the local occupational structure are held constant by applying the full-equality model, in sum, the advantages of middle-class, and especially upper middle-class sons, remain striking. Really impressive, though, is the fact that youths born into working-class homes displayed substantial upward mobility.

The detailed mobility ratios in Table 5.9 also allow us to rule out the possibility that the relative constancy of the summary mobility measures in Table 5.8 masked important changes in the mobility opportunities of particular groups. No distinct trend toward either increased or diminished occupational inheritance is visible in the cells along the diagonal of Table 5.9, nor is there clear evidence of a long-term change in the direction and distance in which mobile sons moved. Some of the indexes fluctuate considerably, but this may be largely attributable to the small number of cases in many of the cells. In any event, there is no hint of *systematic* variation. Despite the dramatic social changes that have taken place in Boston, and in American society in general, over the past century, there was an element of remarkable, almost eerie, continuity. There was a calculus of probabilities that governed the likelihood that a young man from a particular kind of family would himself enter a given occupational stratum, a calculus that was nearly identical for youths born at any time between 1840 and 1930.

chapter six YANKEES AND IMMIGRANTS

One of the greatest themes of American history is the story of how millions of immigrants from distant shores entered the society and made their way in it, becoming new men and women, Americans, in the process. American folklore is full of metaphors to characterize the immigrant's experience in the New World: he was beckoned by the golden door, drawn into the melting pot, and eventually absorbed into the American mainstream. The historical and sociological literature devoted to some aspect of immigration and immigrant assimilation is rich, even superabundant. And yet there are some large gaps, some important questions for which more than impressionistic answers have yet to be given.

We know that more often than not newcomers to America came with little in the way of capital or of skills valuable in an urban industrial society, and that immigrants tended accordingly to begin at the bottom. We know that all groups experienced some social mobility in time, and produced men who attained wealth, power, and recognition in the larger society. But there has been surprisingly little systematic study of the rate, timing, and channels of mobility experienced by newcomers to America. If immigrants typically began their careers at a lower point on the occupational scale than native-born Americans, did they at least experience comparable upward mobility in the course of their careers, or did they fall further behind with the passing of time? Did the children of the foreign-born—second-generation immigrants—characteristically make far greater progress than their fathers, as legend would have it, or were they too sorely handicapped in the occupational competition? Did the presence of a massive immigrant population impair the prospects of old-stock Americans, as was argued by proponents of immigrant restriction, or did it rather stimulate upward mobility for this group? To what extent did differences in the cultural background of particular immigrant groups, or in the character of the economy and the labor market at the time they first arrived, speed or slow their progress? Did all groups, whatever their national background, have essentially similar forms and channels of mobility, or may we contrast "typically Irish" with "typically Italian" or "typically East European" patterns?

Boston affords an excellent laboratory in which to explore such questions; for more than a century the history of the community has been in large measure the history of immigrants and their children. Owing largely to the massive influx of peasants fleeing famine-ridden Ireland in the 1840's, immigrants made up a third of the city's population as early as 1850 (Table 6.1).[1] And, since the very young and the old were less likely to migrate than persons of working age, newcomers from abroad were an even larger fraction—45 percent—of the Boston labor force. The proportion of immigrants in the city remained roughly constant, at about a third of the population and nearly half of the male labor force, down to the ending of unrestricted immigration to the United States after World War I. The absolute number of foreign-born persons in the city increased enormously, however, from less than 50,000 in 1850 to almost 250,000 in 1920. The national origins of the newcomers shifted dramatically as well. In 1850 nearly three-quarters of Boston's immigrants were of Irish origin; by 1920 so-called "new immigrants" from eastern and southern Europe outnumbered the Irish by nearly two to one.

Immigration was even more important to the community than these figures suggest, for they fail to take into account the American-born children of the newcomers, the second-generation immi-

TABLE 6.1. Percent of white immigrants and their children in Boston, 1850–1960[1]

	Total population		
Year	*Foreign-born*	*Foreign or mixed parentage*	*Male labor force, foreign-born*
1850	35	46	45
1860	36	n.a.	n.a.
1870	35	n.a.	n.a.
1880	32	64	41
1890	35	68	44
1900	35	72	45
1910	36	74	48
1920	32	73	44
1930	30	n.a.	40
1940	23	n.a.	30
1950	16	n.a.	17
1960	12	41	16

[1] Taken from the respective *Population* volumes of the U. S. Census.

grants. First- and second-generation immigrants together—the foreign stock—comprised nearly half (46 percent) of the Boston population in 1850, nearly two-thirds (64 percent) by 1880, and almost three-fourths (74 percent) by 1910. In the classic era of heavy European immigration to the United States, the "minority" elements of the community together formed a large majority of the Boston population. In the simple demographic sense, it was the Yankees who were the minority. In this respect Boston closely resembled the other major American cities of the period(Table 6.2).

The flow of immigrants into the community was sharply reduced by World War I and the restrictive legislation that followed it, and there was a consequent decline first in the proportion of foreign-born residents and then in the second-generation group. The white immigrants of the earlier era were increasingly replaced by black newcomers, whose experience will be analyzed in Chapter 8. Persons of foreign stock, however, still made up 41 percent of the population in 1960. Nearly 40 years after the formal closing of the golden door, differences in national origin remained an important element of the Boston social fabric.

TABLE 6.2. Percent of white immigrants and their children in Boston and some other major cities, 1890–1920[1]

City	*1890*	*1900*	*1910*	*1920*
		Foreign-born		
Boston	35	35	36	32
New York	39	37	40	35
Chicago	41	35	36	30
Philadelphia	26	23	25	22
Detroit	39	34	34	29
Cleveland	37	33	35	30
St. Louis	25	19	18	13
Baltimore	16	13	14	11
		Foreign or mixed parentage		
Boston	68	72	74	73
New York	77	77	79	76
Chicago	78	77	77	72
Philadelphia	57	55	57	54
Detroit	78	77	74	64
Cleveland	75	75	75	69
St. Louis	68	61	54	44
Baltimore	42	38	38	34

[1] Niles A. Carpenter, *Immigrants and Their Children, 1920* (Washington, D.C.: U. S. Government Printing Office, 1927), p. 27.

THE OCCUPATIONAL CAREER PATTERNS OF IMMIGRANTS AND NATIVES

One simple measure of how successfully Boston's immigrants adapted to the local occupational structure is available from published census tabulations. Table 6.3 indicates the occupational distribution of first generation immigrant and native-born males employed in the city in 1890, 1910, 1930, and 1950. The categories "native" and "foreign" are, of course, gross. In due time consideration will be given to the critical second-generation group, which is included in the native population here; the best starting point for analysis, however, is the simple native–immigrant distinction. The tendency of newcomers to gravitate toward the lower rungs of the occupational ladder was pronounced throughout the entire period. Close to 45 percent of the city's immigrants held menial unskilled or semiskilled laboring jobs at each point; the vast majority of persons born abroad were blue-collar workers of some kind.

The gap between immigrants and natives, however, narrowed considerably over the period. In 1890 the fraction of foreign-born men in white-collar jobs was only 38 percent of the fraction of natives in such jobs; by 1910 the ratio was up to 50 percent. There was a slight reversal of this trend between 1910 and 1930, with the immigrant share of white-collar jobs dropping to 44 percent of the native proportion, but by 1950 it had resumed, and the immigrant middle class was almost two-thirds as large proportionately as the native middle class.

TABLE 6.3. Occupational distribution of natives and immigrants, 1890, 1910, 1930, and 1950 (percent)[1]

		Occupational level				
Year	*Nativity*	*Professions*	*Other white-collar*	*Skilled*	*Low manual*	*Ratio of immigrant to native middle class*
1890	U. S.	4	43	29	24	
	Foreign	1	17	37	45	0.38
1910	U. S.	6	42	19	33	
	Foreign	2	22	33	43	.50
1930	U. S.	9	46	20	25	
	Foreign	4	20	30	46	.44
1950	U. S.	13	33	21	33	
	Foreign	6	24	28	42	.65

[1] Calculated from the respective *Population* volumes of the U. S. Census. The cautionary note to Table 4.1, which was developed by the same method, applies here too. The occupational categories employed by the Census Bureau in 1890, and to some extent in 1910, were not sufficiently precise to distinguish skilled from unskilled or semiskilled workmen in all cases, and the 1890 data pertain to workers in 50 selected occupations rather than to the entire male labor force. It is doubtful, however, that these deficiencies give a misleading impression of the relative position of immigrants and natives. The figures given here and throughout the chapter refer to *white* natives and immigrants only; the situation of blacks in Boston will be treated in Chapter 8. Note also that the "other white-collar" category includes large as well as small businessmen. In data derived from the samples the former can be separated out and placed with professionals in the high white-collar stratum, but this cannot be done with published census data. The numbers on which percentages were based are not provided, nor is there any need to indicate levels of statistical significance, for these figures are from complete enumerations, not samples. All differences, however small, are real and not the possible result of sampling error. Since 1950, unfortunately, the census has not provided comparable tabulations.

These snapshot comparisons of the distribution of immigrants and natives at four moments in time are suggestive, but they leave many questions unanswered. Comparative distributional analysis of this sort has been a widely used tool in studies of the assimilation process, but insufficient attention has been directed to its grave limitations.[2] It is impossible to tell from evidence about changes in the distribution of "the foreign-born" from time 1 to time 2 how much of the change is attributable to advances made by the *individuals* who comprised "the foreign-born" at time 1 and how much to changes in the *composition of the group* between time 1 and time 2. It happens, for instance, that between 1930 and 1940 there was a rise in the proportion of German immigrants living in the United States who were businessmen or professionals, but the explanation is not that great numbers of German immigrants residing in America as of 1930 moved up into business and professional callings during the depression decade, but rather that the influx of Jewish immigrants fleeing Hitler altered the overall distribution of the "born in Germany" group by 1940. It has not been generally appreciated, but there can be considerable change in the composition of groups over even a relatively short period of time, owing to shifting patterns of fertility, mortality, and migration into and out of the unit under scrutiny; "the Irish" of Boston in 1890 were not simply "the Irish" of 1880 now 10 years older, and the caution applies even more forcibly when a broader group is treated or a longer time interval utilized. A large majority of "the foreign-born" employed in Boston in 1910 were not part of "the foreign-born" working there in 1890; many were too young to have been employed at all in 1890, and many others had not yet arrived in Boston. Some attention will be given below to changes over time in the distribution of groups whose composition was itself changing during the interval where there is no better alternative, but it is essential whenever possible to check conclusions derived by this method against data that reveal the position of *the same individuals* at different points in time.

The samples gathered for this study permit such refined analysis, though limitations of sample size and the spottiness of information about national background in certain of the samples have produced some unfortunate gaps. Table 6.4 indicates how four groups of immigrants and natives living in Boston during the past century fared

TABLE 6.4. Career mobility patterns of immigrants and natives

Birth cohort and nativity	Percent of group— Starting in white collar	Ending in white collar	Blue-collar climbers [1]	White-collar skidders [1]	Number
1850–1859					
U. S.	51	62	33	11	241
Foreign	18[2]	24[2]	13[2]	25[2]	68
1860–1879					
U. S.	55	56	22	16	614
Foreign	50	60	33	14	42
1880–1889					
U. S.	51	61	32	13	215
Foreign	23[2]	39[2]	28	23	206
1900–1909					
U. S.	40	47	23	17	146
Foreign	23[2]	31[2]	14	14	35

[1] Blue-collar climbers are men whose first occupation was manual but who were white-collar workers by the time of their last job; white-collar skidders made the corresponding shift from white collar to blue collar in the course of their careers. Note that the percentages given in these two columns refer not to the entire group, native or foreign, as the case may be, but only to that fraction of the group that *could* have been climbers or skidders. The 33-percent figure for U. S.-born climbers means not that 33 percent of the 241 native-born men in the sample moved from a blue-collar to a white-collar job in the course of their careers, but rather that 33 percent of those native youths who first worked as manual laborers were climbers. For this reason, one cannot subtract the skidding rate from the climbing rate and add the result to the figure in column 1 to arrive at the percentage ending in white collar (column 2). Unless skidding and climbing rates are computed on this basis—taking not the entire group but only those who began their careers in a position from which the move in question was possible—comparisons between groups are difficult to make. A higher percentage of the total foreign-born group, for instance, would be likely to move upward for the simple reason that a much larger fraction of the native-born started as white-collar workers and hence were by definition not able to move to a higher class. By computing the rate in the manner done here we control for the initial distribution of the group and see subsequent differences in mobility more clearly.

[2] Significantly different from the native-born.

occupationally at the time they first entered the labor market and in the course of their subsequent careers. (No such analysis is possible for men born after 1909; immigrant-native differences could not be explored in the sample of youths born in 1930, for all were

U. S.-born, and no information about ethnic background was available for either Laumann's Cambridge-Belmont sample or the sample from the 1958 Boston city directory.)

In all but one of the groups (the 1860–1879 cohort, whose exceptional character will be explained shortly), Boston's immigrants typically began their careers working with their hands—82 percent of the youths born before the Civil War, and 77 percent of those born in the 1880's and the first decade of the twentieth century. The sample data thus square nicely with the census evidence for the entire population of the city; they, too, indicate both that immigrant newcomers to Boston were heavily clustered in blue-collar callings and that there was a modest improvement in their access to middle-class jobs around the turn of the century.

The interest of the sample evidence, however, is that it allows us to explore a further question of critical importance, the question of what happened to typical immigrants and natives as their subsequent careers unfolded. It is quite possible, for instance, that a major barrier to immigrant entry into more attractive and better-paid jobs was the newcomers' sheer lack of familiarity with the culture and the language. If so, that obstacle might have been surmounted in time, and ambitious newcomers might later have pulled themselves up by their bootstraps, eliminating or narrowing the margin of disadvantage that obtained when they first entered the labor market. Thus the familiar folklore figure: the struggling immigrant lad who starts work as a newsboy, or perhaps as the operator of a sewing machine in a sweatshop, but whose superior ambition and drive win him business success once he has learned the ropes. This could have been a quite typical immigrant career without materially affecting distributional measures like those supplied in Table 6.3, because the group identified as "the foreign-born" at successive points in time was changing its composition rapidly, and was being constantly diluted by the influx of further newcomers who also started their careers in low-status blue-collar jobs.

It appears from Table 6.4, though, that such struggling immigrant lads were not very common in Boston. In only one of the four cohorts—and that an exception soon to be explained—did immigrants who first began work as manual laborers later find their way into middle-class jobs more frequently than the native-born, hence narrowing the gap between the two groups. In all other cases, the rate of upward career mobility for natives exceeded that for immigrants, leaving the latter even further behind at the end of the race than they were at the starting gun.[3]

What is more, the small select group of foreign-born youths who did gain an initial foothold in the white-collar world did not display any greater ability to retain their hard-won positions than the much larger fraction of native sons whose first job was nonmanual. In both the 1850–1859 and the 1880–1889 groups, indeed, immigrants were roughly twice as likely to skid downward into a blue-collar post as their careers unfolded. This aspect of the immigrant's handicap, however, appears to have been overcome after World War I. In the sample of men born in the first decade of the new century and entering the labor market around 1930, immigrant white-collar workers were slightly less likely to skid later than their native-born counterparts.

On every count, therefore, the foreign-born were at a disadvantage. Not only did they typically begin their careers on the lower rungs of the class ladder; they subsequently climbed to a higher rung less often than natives, and at least in the late nineteenth and early twentieth centuries were distinctly more prone to skid to a lower-ranked job. At the end of their careers they remained much more heavily concentrated in blue-collar callings than were native Americans.

The magnitude of the immigrant's handicap, however, diminished in the twentieth century. The proportion of immigrants entering white-collar callings at the start of their careers increased relatively; the very sharp differential in upward mobility that prevailed among men born before the Civil War shrank considerably; immigrants born in the twentieth century experienced less downward career mobility than natives. Immigrants remained somewhat behind natives in the contest for better jobs, but less far behind than they had been in the late nineteenth century.

The pattern displayed by the deviant 1860–1879 cohort fails to fit with any of these generalizations, and suggests the need for a further refinement in the analysis. Five out of 10 foreign-born men in this group started their careers as white-collar workers; 6 in 10 had reached the middle class by the end of their careers. The explanation lies in a distinctive characteristic of this sample—that it was composed of youths under 20 who were living in Boston in 1880.

Since the median age of this cohort was only 10 in 1880, the foreign-born youths in it had mostly left their homelands and arrived in Boston when they were still young children. Legally they were foreign-born, but in terms of experience they were less like true immigrants than like the native-born children of immigrants, second-generation immigrants. These *de facto* second-generation immigrants were exposed to immigrant ways at home, of course, but they were involved in American culture early in their formative years. They were young enough, for example, to attend American schools, which presumably made them better equipped to fill white-collar jobs than the typical immigrant. The most likely hypothesis is that the ability of these technically foreign-born but *de facto* second-generation youths of the 1860–1879 group to compete successfully with native-born Americans indicates that the children of immigrants to these shores did not face the same barriers to occupational success as their fathers.

THE SITUATION OF THE SECOND-GENERATION IMMIGRANT

Did second-generation immigrants indeed move rapidly into the mainstream of American life, or did they too find that certain doors were closed to them? A first clue may be gained from a simple comparison of census tabulations of the occupational distribution of foreign-born males, native-born sons of foreign parentage, and native sons of native parentage in 1890, 1910, and 1950 respectively (Table 6.5). Identifying first-generation immigrants by place of birth misclassifies a number of *de facto* second-generation youths as first-generation, and blurs the true difference between the two generations somewhat, but a reasonably clear picture emerges nonetheless. Second-generation immigrants were notably more successful than their fathers in moving into the upper reaches of the occupational structure. A third of the second-generation youths employed in 1890 held white-collar jobs, but less than 20 percent of the first-generation immigrants. Less than a quarter of Boston's immigrants in 1910 worked in middle-class callings, but 45 percent of their children did. The gap was narrower in 1950—43 percent vs. 30 percent—but still substantial. At each point of observation, furthermore, the American-born children of immigrants became professionals twice as frequently as their fathers.

Impressive though the gains of the second generation were, how-

TABLE 6.5. Occupational distribution (percent) of first- and second-generation immigrants and Yankees, 1890, 1910, 1950[1]

		Occupational level			
Year	*Ethnicity*	*Professions*	*Other white-collar*	*Skilled*	*Low manual*
1890	First-generation immigrant	1	17	37	45
	Second-generation immigrant	2	30	34	34
	Yankee	5	47	26	22
1910	First-generation immigrant	2	22	33	43
	Second-generation immigrant	4	41	21	34
	Yankee	8	43	16	33
1950	First-generation immigrant	6	24	28	42
	Second-generation immigrant	10	33	22	35
	Yankee	14	34	20	32

[1] Calculated from published census data, as in Table 6.3; 1930 data are unavailable, since the Census Bureau did not tabulate separately the occupations of native-born men of foreign parentage and of native parentage. All differences are significant because the data represent not a sample but a total universe.

ever, it was still something of a handicap to have a foreign-born father. Native-born sons of native parentage (who, for want of a better term, I label "Yankees" here) were more heavily concentrated in white-collar jobs, and especially in high-ranked professional callings, at each point.

Their margin of advantage, however, shrank dramatically during the period. In 1890 Yankee sons were about as far ahead of second-generation newcomers as the latter were ahead of their fathers. By 1910 the second-generation middle class was nearly as large as the Yankee middle class, and the same held true in 1950.

Admittedly, these figures give a somewhat too rosy impression of the situation of second-generation immigrants with respect to Yankees, for second-generation youths tended to cluster in the less attractive and less well-paid white-collar jobs, while Yankees obtained a disproportionate share of the better positions. Detailed evidence on this point is scanty, but some 1910 figures bear it out.[4] Yankees held jobs as manufacturers and officials in a proportion 2.6 times greater than second-generation immigrants; the Yankee margin of advantage as insurance agents was 2.2, as real-estate agents 2.3, as wholesale traders 2.0, as lawyers 2.2, as engineers 2.3, as physicians

3.3. The heaviest concentration of second-generation youths in white-collar callings was in less remunerative jobs. They outnumbered Yankees proportionately as store clerks and office clerks, and approached parity as salesmen. Precise information of this kind is not available for 1950, but it is plain from Table 6.5 that white-collar Yankees were still overrepresented in the professions in comparison with second-generation immigrants, and one suspects that there remained some tendency too for Yankees to hold more than their share of other white-collar jobs above the routine clerical and sales level. Still, it is evident that the very substantial occupational superiority Yankees enjoyed over second- as well as first-generation immigrants in late-nineteenth-century Boston was considerably eroded by 1910 and there was no reversal of the trend between 1910 and 1950.

The need for caution in interpreting changes in distributional indexes like these, however, has already been explained. Inferences about the experiences of individuals over time on the basis of group measures are risky when the composition of the group itself changes during the interval. The sample data are less rich in information about the career mobility of second-generation immigrants, regrettably, because the sources from which the samples of men born in 1880–1889 and 1900–1909 were drawn included no information about parental nativity. It is possible, however, to compare generational differences in career patterns for men born before 1880 and those born in 1930, to see if the seeming improvement of the position of second-generation immigrants in Boston that appears from distributional analysis can be confirmed.

In the sample of young men born between 1850 and 1879 and first entering the labor market in the late nineteenth century, generational differences in the level of individual's first jobs were very sharp (Table 6.6). Fewer than 2 in 10 immigrants began their careers as white-collar workers, but 4 out of 10 of the American-born children of immigrants and nearly three-quarters of the youths of old native stock did so. The subsequent experience of first-generation immigrants in the course of their careers, as was shown in Table 6.4, was discouraging; immigrants were less often upwardly mobile and more often downwardly mobile than natives. The sons of immigrants, however, displayed a radically different pattern. Not only did a much larger fraction of them enter white-collar jobs initially; those who began work as manual laborers were almost twice as likely as their father to move up into the middle class, later, nearly as likely, indeed, to climb to a white-collar job as Yankee youths who began their careers working with their hands.

If the second generation resembled old-stock native Americans in its propensity to rise from humble beginnings, however, it was notably less able to carve out a secure niche in the white-collar world after arriving there. Second-generation youths who began their careers in middle-class callings were more than twice as likely as Yankees to skid to a manual job later. Their downward-mobility rate

TABLE 6.6 Career mobility patterns of first- and second-generation immigrants and Yankees, late nineteenth century: men born 1850–1879[1]

	Percentage of group—				
Ethnicity	*Starting in white collar*	*Ending in white collar*	*Blue-collar climbers*	*White-collar skidders*	*Number*
Immigrant					
First-generation	18	24	13	25	68
Second-generation	41[2]	46[2]	24[2]	22	499
Yankee	73[3]	74[3]	29	9[3]	351

[1] The samples of men born 1850–1859 and 1860–1879 have been combined here, since there were no important differences in the pattern they reveal. First-generation immigrants born after 1860 have been excluded because an unknown but presumably large number of them were *de facto* second-generation.

[2] Significantly different from first-generation immigrants.

[3] Significantly different from second-generation immigrants.

(22 percent) was almost as high as that for the first generation, and only a shade below their rate of upward mobility.

In late-nineteenth-century Boston, second-generation immigrants thus were uniquely mobile, climbing after a lowly start as frequently as Yankees but moving in the opposite direction as often as new immigrants. For immigrants and Yankees there was a close relation between where one started and where one ended in the occupational competition—an association of 0.88 for Yankees and 0.70 for immigrants as measured by the statistic gamma.[5] The corresponding association for second-generation youths was a much weaker 0.40.

The measure of occupational mobility employed in much of this analysis—movement between manual and nonmanual callings—is, of course, a crude one. It might be thought that these findings are due to that crudeness—that, for example, the skidding syndrome manifested by men of foreign stock stemmed from the fact that such men were disproportionately concentrated in menial white-collar posts from which downward movement was common, whereas Yankees were disproportionately clustered in the upper echelons of the white-collar class. Utilizing more detailed occupational categories, however, allows us to rule out that line of argument. The group differences under consideration here did not evaporate when finer measures of status were employed; they remained clear-cut.

Indeed, more refined tabulations (not given here), which take into account upward and downward movement from stratum to stratum as well as shifts between the blue-collar and white-collar classes, give a heightened sense of the difficulties confronted by newcomers and their children. Not only did men of first- or second-generation immigrant stock who started their careers as white-collar employees of some kind lose those jobs and drop into the working class much more frequently than Yankee youths; a much smaller fraction of those of them who remained in nonmanual posts were able to move upward into highly paid professional, proprietary, or managerial positions. Two out of 10 Yankee white-collar starters climbed to the high nonmanual stratum in the course of their careers, whereas only 1 in 10 fell to a blue-collar job. For the first- and second-generation immigrants who started their careers wearing white collars, the proportions were reversed; the chance of skidding subsequently into a laboring job was twice the chance of climbing further.

In the late nineteenth century, native-born Americans had a distinct advantage in the competition for jobs on the higher rungs of the occupational ladder, and native-born Americans whose fathers were also native-born had a still greater advantage. Both immigrants and the native-born children of immigrants were far more likely both to begin and to end their careers working with their hands and wearing blue collars. Not only did the foreign-born start more often at the bottom; they were less often upwardly mobile after their first job, and those who started well were more prone to lose their middle-class positions and end up in a manual job.

The critical second generation, however, was somewhat more favorably placed, though not as favorably as the melting-pot folklore would have it. Having a foreign-born father, even though you yourself were born in this country, was a distinct handicap. It meant that you were more likely than the son of a native-born father to enter the labor market at the manual level, and it meant that if you did find a white-collar job at the outset, you were twice as likely to skid as to climb further. But unlike men actually born abroad, second-generation immigrants who began as manual laborers had relatively good prospects for subsequent upward mobility into clerical, sales, and petty proprietary positions; they were not left further and further behind the Yankee with each passing year.

Somewhere around the turn of the century, the distributional evidence in Table 6.5 suggests, the position of both immigrants and their children relative to old-stock native Americans began to improve. The immigrant middle class grew from a mere 18 percent in 1890 to 24 percent in 1910 and 30 percent in 1950, and the second generation made corresponding gains. The improvement registered by immigrants was partly the result of changes in the proportion of them entering white-collar jobs at the beginning of their careers, and partly caused by a rise in their upward-mobility rates and a decline in their downward-mobility rates compared with natives (Table 6.4).

There is a frustrating gap in the evidence available about the career patterns of second-generation immigrants as compared with immigrants and Yankees in the twentieth century, because of the absence of information about parental nativity in two of the samples. But there is one point at which sample data may be used to check the tentative conclusions drawn from the census distributional evidence. Nearly half of the members of the sample of young men born in Boston in 1930 were second-generation immigrants, and the remainder were Yankees. In 1963, when they were 33, 48 percent of the sons of immigrants in this sample held middle-class jobs, and only 46 percent of the youths of Yankee origin. Second-generation youths were not significantly ahead of Yankees, given the limited sample size (191), but they were not behind either. They remained disadvantaged in only one respect: only 7 percent were professionals or substantial businessmen, while 41 percent of them were in routine low white-collar jobs. Nearly double the fraction of Yankees (13 percent) were in upper white-collar callings, and correspondingly fewer (33 percent) were clerks, salesman, or small businessmen. Differences in ethnic background still affected access to jobs at the very top of the occupational structure, therefore. The second generation, however, no longer displayed any distinctive tendency to gravitate toward laboring jobs, a dramatic change from the pattern that prevailed in Boston in the nineteenth century.

THE INFLUENCE OF CLASS ORIGINS

It is possible that the foregoing has given a seriously misleading picture of the relation between ethnic background and occupational achievement. Neither the census distributional evidence nor the tabulations of sample data presented thus far take into account a major determinant of occupational career patterns—social-class origins. As the previous chapter demonstrated, the odds were heavy that the son of a laborer and the son of a lawyer living in Boston would follow quite different career lines. This simple fact could be the main explanation of the ethnic differences that have been disclosed by the analysis thus far. Suppose that the great majority of the fathers of first- and second-generation immigrants in late-nineteenth-century Boston were manual laborers, whereas the fathers of Yankees were heavily concentrated in business and professional callings. This, rather than any other characteristic of either the newcomers or the society in which they lived, might explain their inability to compete on equal terms with native Americans of native parentage. Likewise the improved relative position of both immigrant generations in the twentieth century might mean merely that a growing proportion of newcomers were of middle-class rather than working-class or peasant origins. The correlations observed thus far between ethnic background and occupational achievement, that is to say, may be spurious, the result of differences in class origins that happen to be correlated with ethnic background. It is necessary, therefore, to examine generational differences in occupational career patterns while controlling for inherited class position.

Such controls cannot be applied to census data concerning the occupational distribution of groups at one moment in time, another very serious limitation of distributional analysis that has not been generally appreciated. The sample evidence, however, may be exploited for these purposes to some degree. The results are limited because information about the class origins of sample members was available only for men whose fathers lived in Boston; in all but one of the samples the number of cases for analysis is too small to be anything but suggestive. But some useful conclusions emerge nonetheless.

Table 6.7 reveals the extent to which coming from working-class or middle-class homes affected the occupational attainments of second-generation immigrants and Yankees in the late nineteenth century. It shows plainly that the underrepresentation of second-gener-

TABLE 6.7. Social-class origins, ethnicity, and differential access to middle-class occupations, late nineteenth century: men born 1840–1879[1]

	Percent of group with—		
Ethnicity	*White-collar last job*	*High white-collar last job*	*Number*
	Sons of blue-collar fathers		
Second-generation immigrant	39	5	485
Yankee	51[2]	12[2]	143
	Sons of white-collar fathers		
Second-generation immigrant	75	26	126
Yankee	91[2]	44[2]	209

[1] The samples of men born 1850–1859 and 1860–1879 have been combined here. A group born in the 1840's has been added as well, men who could not be included in earlier tables pertaining to mobility between first and last job because they were over 30 at the time of the first occupational trace in 1880. There were insufficient cases to analyze the intergenerational mobility of first-generation immigrants.

[2] Significantly different from second-generation immigrants.

ation immigrants in white-collar callings (and especially in high white-collar jobs) was only partly attributable to their relatively low social origins. Thirty-nine percent of the youths from families headed by an immigrant laborer attained a white-collar job by the end of their careers, but 51 percent of the sons of Yankee laborers did so; Yankee working-class sons climbed higher on the occupational scale as well as more frequently, in that 12 percent of them, but only 5 percent of their second-generation rivals, became professionals or substantial businessmen.

Generational differences were even sharper among youths reared in the middle class. By the late nineteenth century there was an emerging immigrant middle class in Boston, but by one crucial criterion the position of that emerging middle class was terribly weak, for its members experienced a good deal of difficulty in transmitting middle-class rank to their children. Nine in 10 Yankee youths of middle-class origins ended their careers in white-collar jobs themselves; only 1 in 10 failed to maintain the status he had inherited. But fully a quarter of the second-generation youths from middle-class homes skidded to a blue-collar job. What is more, 44 percent of Yankee middle-class sons but only 26 percent of second-generation men from comparable families found their way into occupations in the upper white-collar stratum.

The distinctive career patterns of second-generation immigrants in late-nineteenth-century Boston thus cannot be explained away as the product merely of differences in social-class background. When these differences are controlled for by examining men from middle-class and working-class homes separately, second-generation newcomers still fared less well than Yankees in the occupational competition, and it is probable—though not certain, because there were too few cases for analysis—that first-generation immigrants were in an even weaker position.

Applying more refined controls for social-class origins does not alter this conclusion. It is true that middle-class Yankee sons often had fathers who worked in the upper white-collar stratum, whereas second-generation middle-class youths more frequently were from households headed by salesmen, clerks, or the owners of marginal businesses. This, however, only partly explains the superior occupational attainments of middle-class Yankees. Twenty-one percent of Yankee sons of clerks, salesmen, and small businessmen ($N=78$) ended their careers as professionals or large businessmen, but only 13 percent of second-generation immigrants from comparable backgrounds ($N=69$); 36 percent of lower middle-class sons of foreign stock skidded to a blue-collar calling but only 14 percent of their Yankee counterparts.[6]

After the turn of the century, it was shown earlier, the relative economic position of both immigrants and their children began to improve. This might indicate that newcomers of humble origins were encountering less prejudice than their nineteenth-century predecessors. Another possibility, however, is simply that a declining proportion of immigrants and their children were coming from humble backgrounds to begin with. That is, improved prospects for career mobility in the community might have stemmed largely from an increase in the proportion of first- and second-generation immigrants who came from middle-class homes.

The evidence available is woefully scanty and inadequate, but there are two suggestive clues in Table 6.8. The number of cases on which the percentages are based is small enough to be susceptible to considerable sampling error, and for men born between 1870 and 1890 only a crude comparison between the foreign-born and the native-born is possible because of the absence of information about parental nativity in this sample. It appears, however, that a good deal of the improvement in the position of Boston's immigrants visible in the early twentieth century was indeed attributable to a change in the social-class origins of newcomers.[7] When immigrant sons from households headed by laboring fathers are compared with native sons from similar households, the foreign-born show up as severely handicapped. Seven in 10 ended their careers wearing blue collars, but only half of the native-born Americans did so. It is

TABLE 6.8. Social-class origins, ethnicity, and differential access to middle-class occupations, twentieth century

Birth cohort and ethnicity	*Percent of group with—* *White-collar last job*	*High white-collar last job*	*Number*
	Sons of blue-collar fathers		
1870–1889[1]			
First-generation immigrant	30	0	40
Native	49[2]	13[2]	88
1930			
Second-generation immigrant	38	2	58
Yankee	31	8	65
	Sons of white-collar fathers		
1930			
Second-generation immigrant	74	22	23
Yankee	69	20	45

[1] A group of men born in the 1870's was added to this sample, men who could not be included in the earlier analysis because no job held prior to age 30 was known for them. The group of immigrant sons with white-collar fathers in this sample was too small to justify including the figures for them here.
[2] Significantly different from immigrants.

reasonable to surmise that had it been possible to break down the native-born group into second-generation immigrants and Yankees, the fraction of Yankee working-class sons reaching the middle class would have been well above the 49-percent figure for the two groups combined, and that the second generation would have been well below the 49-percent mark though distinctly ahead of their immigrant fathers. Native sons of working-class origins in this sample were also far more successful at penetrating into the upper reaches of the white-collar class; 13 percent of them did so, and not a single immigrant youth in the sample. The gains registered by first- and second-generation immigrants in early-twentieth-century Boston were real, to be sure, but they were the result of a shift in the social-class origins of the newcomers rather than of an increase in the ability of men of foreign stock to rise above the class status they inherited from their fathers.

By the time the sample of men born in Boston in 1930 had reached maturity, however, there seems to have been a genuine change in the opportunities open to men of varying national backgrounds when social-class origins are held constant. The sample is very small, and there is the further difficulty that its members were only 33 at the last point at which their occupations were plotted (1963), so that they were not far advanced in their careers. But it is impressive that second-generation sons from both laboring and middle-class backgrounds attained white-collar jobs more frequently than comparable Yankees. Yankee working-class sons appear to have had a shade of advantage in reaching the top white-collar stratum, but the difference is too small to be significant, and there was no similar advantage for Yankee middle-class youths on this count. By 1963, second-generation youths in Boston competed on equal terms with Yankees of similar class background, competed, indeed, a shade more successfully in most respects.

SOME HINTS OF DIFFERENCES BETWEEN PARTICULAR NATIONALITY GROUPS

It is not illegitimate to attempt to generalize about immigrants and their children, but it is possible that painting with such a broad brush obscures important variations in the way in which men of varying national background coped with the demands of the American environment. The sample data permit only a limited attack upon this problem, because in many instances the number of representatives of a particular nationality element was too small to sustain a valid generalization about the group. A combination of sample evidence and census distributional data, however, provides some useful insights.

In late-nineteenth-century Boston, immigrants were very heavily clustered at the bottom of the occupational ladder. Eighty-two percent of them worked with their hands, and a majority of these were relatively unskilled (Table 6.3). The differences between immigrants from particular countries were as marked, however, as those between foreign-born newcomers and native Americans. Table 6.9 compares the occupational distribution of native-born Bostonians with that of the largest immigrant groups residing in the city in 1890—the Irish, the British, English-speaking Canadians, the Germans, and the Scandinavians. More than a quarter of the German and British immigrants and 20 percent of the Canadians held middle-class jobs, much lower than the concentration of native-born Americans in such occupations but more than double the fractions of Irish and Scandinavian newcomers in white-collar callings. Men born in Sweden, Norway, and Denmark were as overwhelmingly

TABLE 6.9. Occupational distribution (percent) of natives and leading immigrant groups, 1890[1]

	Occupational level			
Nativity	*Professions*	*Other white-collar*	*Skilled*	*Low manual*
U. S.	4	43	29	24
Ireland	0[2]	10	25	65
Great Britain	2	24	43	31
Canada[3]	1	19	51	29
Germany	5[4]	22	48	25
Scandinavia	1	8	55	36

[1] Calculated from published census data.

[2] There were only 94 Irish-born immigrants in the four professions for which an enumeration was made. They composed 0.013 percent of the Irish males working in the city in 1890.

[3] Excludes French-speaking Canadians.

[4] The impressive German showing in the professions is somewhat misleading, since one of the four professions enumerated was "musicians and teachers of music," and 79 percent of the German professionals fell in this category.

clustered in manual jobs as the Irish, but were superior to them in one critical respect: more than half of them were in skilled trades, but only a quarter of the Irish were. Two-thirds of all Irish immigrants were ordinary unskilled or semiskilled workmen, nearly double the fraction of low manual workers among all other nationalities. The Irish of Boston were highly distinctive in their inability to find jobs that offered security, prestige, and financial rewards.

This is striking in the light of the fact that the Irish were very much the largest of the city's immigrant groups, and had already seized political control of the city of Boston. The first Irish mayors were elected in the 1880's, and soon thereafter the reins of government were almost exclusively in Irish hands. To translate group political power into group economic power, however, was to prove a slow and difficult task.

It could be, though, that the economic benefits of the Irish political conquest of Boston went not to the immigrant generation but to their children. The published census data provide no information about the position of the second-generation Irish, who comprised fully a fifth of the population of the community at the turn of the century. The sample evidence, however, allows us to isolate a group of them born in the 1860's and 1870's, youths whose careers unfolded subsequent to the Irish political conquest of Boston, and to evaluate their achievements against the record of other groups (Table 6.10).

The American-born children of Irish immigrants fared notably better than their fathers, it is plain. Nearly 40 percent had reached

TABLE 6.10. Occupational distribution (percent) of particular second-generation groups and Yankees at last job: men born 1860–1879

	Occupational level				
Ethnicity	*High white-collar*	*Low white-collar*	*Skilled*	*Low manual*	*Number*
Second-generation					
Irish	6	32	26	36	247
British[1]	13[2]	40[2]	24	23[2]	91
West European	15[2]	37	21	27[2]	106
Yankee	31[2]	42[2]	15[2]	12[2]	258

[1] Includes men of English-speaking Canadian descent.
[2] Significantly different from the Irish.

the middle class by the end of their careers, whereas only 10 percent of the first-generation Irish in the city in 1890 held white-collar occupations. Little more than a third (36 percent) of the second-generation Irish ended their careers in the unskilled or semiskilled laboring jobs in which two-thirds of the city's Irish immigrants were concentrated in 1890.

On the other hand, the growing political strength of the Irish community did not by any means put Irish-American youths on an equal footing with their Yankee rivals in the occupational competition. Only a quarter of the latter but nearly two-thirds of the second-generation Irish were manual workers at the time of their last job. Only 12 percent of Yankee youths ended their careers in menial unskilled or semiskilled callings, but three times as large a fraction among the American-born Irish. Conversely, fully a third of the old-stock Americans became professionals or substantial businessmen, but only 1 in 14 of the second-generation Irish did so.

Not only did the second-generation Irish fare badly by comparison with old-stock Yankee youths; they were less successful than other second-generation newcomers from groups that were politically much weaker. Eleven in 20 of the native-born sons of immigrants of British or West European (predominantly German and Scandinavian) descent ended their careers in middle-class occupations, but fewer than 8 in 20 of the Irish. Twice as many of the non-Irish second-generation Americans reached the upper white-collar stratum, and substantially fewer remained confined to unskilled or semiskilled laboring jobs. Both the British and the West European second generation were handicapped in comparison with Yankees, but they were climbing the occupational ladder with much greater speed than the Boston Irish.

This was very significant, but we must recall that 9 out of 10 of the first-generation Irish immigrants living in late-nineteenth-century Boston were manual workmen, a much larger fraction than in any other major group (Table 6.9). Since social-class origins strongly influenced career achievement, we could not expect the second-generation Irish as a group to fare as well as the second-generation members of groups with a more substantial middle-class element. It is necessary, therefore, to compare the attainments of second-generation Irish youths with those of other men of comparable class background.

When this is done (Table 6.11), the position of the second-generation Irish appears less dismal. Sons from households headed by an Irish immigrant laborer fared just as well as working-class youths of West European descent; an identical fraction of the two groups—35 percent—won white-collar jobs, and second-generation West Europeans were actually concentrated in unskilled or semiskilled posts slightly more than the Irish. British working-class youths were more successful than either, both at obtaining middle-class jobs and at avoiding menial laboring occupations, but the gap between the British and the Irish was narrowed considerably by taking class origins into account.

TABLE 6.11. Social-class origins and occupational achievement (percent) for particular second-generation groups: men born 1860–1879

	Level of last occupation				
Ethnicity	*High white-collar*	*Low white-collar*	*Skilled*	*Low manual*	*Number*
		Sons of blue-collar fathers			
Irish	4	31	28	37	223
British	8	37[1]	33	23[1]	71
West European	5	30	24	40	62
Yankee	11[1]	42[1]	23	24[1]	114
		Sons of white-collar fathers			
Irish	25	42	12	21	24
British	30	50	0	20	20
West European	30	45	16	9	44
Yankee	45	44	8	3[1]	144

[1] Significantly different from the Irish.

British sons from laboring families, however, did fare distinctly better than second-generation Irish youths of similar class origins. And among men born into middle-class homes, though the number of the cases is too small to yield statistically significant findings, it appears that both the British and the West Europeans outperformed the Irish. Much of the handicap of the second-generation Irish in Boston at the end of the nineteenth century, therefore, is explicable in terms of the near absence of an Irish immigrant middle class in the city, but by no means all of it. The second-generation Irish started several yards to the rear, as it were, in the occupational race, but this was only part of their trouble. Something else as well held them back, and it was something that the Irish political takeover of the city could not quickly overcome.

Neither the "immigrants" nor the "second-generation immigrants" of late-nineteenth-century Boston, then, were an undifferentiated mass. In many ways the differences between particular ethnic groups were as important as those between immigrants, the children of immigrants, and Yankees in general. The Irish, despite their political successes, ranked at the low end of the continuum of immigrant occupational achievement; men of British descent ranked at the high end. These differences remained visible even among the American-born children of the newcomers, and they were only partly attributable to differences in the social-class origins of typical members of the two groups.

The available information is less rich for the period since the turn of the century, but differences between particular national groups do not appear to have vanished. The volume of English and Irish immigration declined sharply, and there was a heavy influx of so-called "new immigrants" from Eastern and Southern Europe. By 1910 there were more than 31,000 Italians in Boston, and nearly 42,000 immigrants from Eastern Europe, most of them Jews. It was widely believed at the time that the new immigrants were an inferior breed, and were far les likely to become assimilated into the American mainstream than their predecessors.[8] There were indeed substantial differences in the economic adjustment of newcomers of various nationalities, but they did not correspond to the old-immigrant–new-immigrant dichotomy. What was thought to be the old-immigrant pattern applied to the British but not to the Irish; what was taken to be the new-immigrant pattern applied to the Italians but not to the East Europeans. A mere 10 percent of the Italian men employed in Boston in 1910 held white-collar jobs, just about the fraction (12 percent) of Irish in such posts in 1890; 65 percent of the Italians then and precisely that fraction of the Irish 20 years earlier were unskilled or semiskilled laborers (Tables 6.9 and 6.12). A quarter of the East European immigrants in the city in 1910 were white-collar workers, compared with 26 percent of the British in 1890; 40 percent of the former and 31 percent of the latter were in the low manual category.

These parallels between the Italians and the Irish and between

TABLE 6.12. Occupational distribution (percent) of Italian and East European immigrants, 1910 and at end of career

	Occupational level				
Ethnicity	*High white-collar*	*Low white-collar*	*Skilled*	*Low manual*	*Number*
		In 1910			
Italian	2	10	23	65	132
East European	3	22[1]	35[1]	40[1]	157
		At time of last known occupation			
Italian	10	25	27	38	48
East European	12	38[1]	28	23[1]	61

[1] Significantly different from Italian.

the British and the East Europeans apply not only to the initial occupational distribution of these groups but to the pace of their subsequent occupational advance as well. In the course of their careers, the late-nineteenth-century Irish enlarged their middle-class element from 10 percent to 38 percent, and reduced the fraction of low manual workers from 65 to 36 percent. Boston Italians in the next generation enlarged their middle class from 12 to 35 percent, and reduced the fraction of unskilled and semiskilled laborers from 65 to 38 percent (Tables 6.10 and 6.12). The British earlier saw their white-collar representation grow from 26 to 53 percent, and their low manual group shrink from 31 to 23 percent. Their East European counterparts increased their middle class from 25 to 50 percent, and their low manual group shrank from 40 to 23 percent. The sources from which the sample was drawn do not make it possible to distinguish second-generation newcomers from Yankees, but it is likely that there continued to be differences in the characteristic occupational trajectories of members of particular second-generation groups as well.

An investigation of Boston's immigrants conducted by the U. S. Immigration Commission in 1909 points to similar conclusions. (The figures supplied by the Commission are for East European Jewish immigrants, not for East European newcomers in general, but the overwhelming majority of East Europeans who migrated to Boston were Jewish, so the distinction is of little consequence.) The entrepreneurial bent of East European Jews was strikingly evident;

no less than 45 percent of these men were "engaged in business for profit," as opposed to only 5 percent of the first-generation Irish of the city (Table 6.13). Many of these Jewish "businessmen" were doubtless mere peddlers with very low incomes; despite the huge margin of advantage of the Jews over the Irish in business callings, the Commission found that the average annual earnings of Boston's Jewish immigrants were only $396, as opposed to $510 for the Irish. But that the Jews were heavily concentrated in callings that involved risk-taking and developed business skills was nonetheless very significant for the economic future of the group. The American-born children of Irish parents showed even less of a taste for business than their fathers; only 3 percent of them were in business for themselves. Italian immigrants were peddlers, small shopkeepers, and the like much more frequently than either Irish generation, though only about half as often as Jewish newcomers. Four out of 10 Italians, however, were unskilled laborers or servants, as

TABLE 6.13. Occupations of selected immigrant groups in Boston, 1909[1]

	"In business for profit"		*Unskilled labor or Domestic service*	
Ethnicity	*Percent*	*Number*	*Percent*	*Number*
First generation				
Jewish	45	226	3	374
Irish	5	139	24	188
Italian	22	309	39	698
Second generation				
Irish	3	58	11	156

[1] Tabulated from U. S. Immigration Commission, *Reports,* vol. 26 (Washington, D.C.: U. S. Government Printing Office, 1911), pp. 475–476. The figures for men in business are for male heads of households; those for unskilled and domestic workers include all sampled males 16 or older. The Commission's sample was not a random one of the Boston immigrant population, but rather of immigrants living in "the most crowded blocks inhabited as nearly as possible by members of one race" (p. 7). The failure to examine immigrants living outside the most ghettoized neighborhoods undoubtedly gave an unduly bleak impression of the economic situation of newcomers in general, and it may have yielded misleading estimates of the differences between particular groups, since only the most segregated portions of groups that differed widely in segregation were included in the sample. It is unlikely, though, that this bias was sufficient to create the sharply contrasting patterns visible here.

opposed to a quarter of the first-generation Irish, a tenth of the second-generation Irish, and 3 percent of the Jews.

Long after the flood of European immigration was checked by restrictive legislation, there remained large differences in the occupational distribution of particular ethnic groups. Some suggestive evidence may be gleaned from the 1950 Census. It was shown earlier (Table 6.5) that by 1950 the relative occupational positions of both immigrants and their children in Boston had improved somewhat, but neither group had attained full parity with the Yankees. Six percent of the foreign-born men employed in the city were professionals, compared with 10 percent of second-generation newcomers and 14 percent of old-stock Americans; 24 percent of Boston's immigrants held other kinds of white-collar jobs, as did 33 percent of their children and 34 percent of the Yankees. Seven out of 10 immigrants were manual workers, as opposed to 57 percent of second-generation men and 52 percent of the Yankees.

These, however, are composite figures that blur important distinctions between particular nationalities. Although the chances were 7 in 10 that the "typical" immigrant in Boston in 1950 held a blue-collar job, the fractions of manual workmen in the eight leading foreign-born groups actually ranged from 46 to 84 percent (Table 6.14). Of foreign-born men aged 45 or more, and thus in the late stages of their careers, less than half of those of British or Russian origin worked with their hands. At the other extreme were the Irish, the Italians, the Swedes, and the French Canadians, more than 8 in 10 of whom were laborers of some kind. German immigrants were midway between the British-Russian pattern and the overall immigrant average; men born in Poland were significantly more proletarian than the average, though a little less so than those from Ireland, Italy, Sweden, or French-speaking Canada.

In addition to these gross differences in access to white-collar or blue-collar jobs, there were more subtle but important group differences in the types of occupations characteristically held. These show up in a table giving indexes of over- and underrepresentation for each group at six occupational levels, from "professionals and technical workers" to "unskilled laborers." The measure relates the proportion of a given group in a particluar occupational category to the proportion of the entire city labor force in that category. A score of 100 indicates that the group has attained parity at this job

TABLE 6.14. Occupational distribution of first-generation immigrants by nationality: men 45 or over, 1950[1]

Occupation	Country of birth: England and Wales	Ireland	USSR	Italy	Sweden	Germany	Poland	French Canada
	Percent							
White-collar	52	18	54	18	16	40	24	19
Blue-collar	48	82	46	82	84	60	76	81
	Index of representation[2]							
Professionals and technical workers	108	11	70	22	45	133	33	38
Managers, proprietors, and officials	162	53	241	82	54	122	111	64
Clerks and salesmen	99	52	79	27	22	51	34	32
Craftsmen and foremen	119	97	97	114	283	152	103	197
Operatives and service workers	68	141	78	132	65	82	156	116
Unskilled laborers	43	298	38	273	55	47	123	78

[1] Calculated from U. S. Census of 1950.

[2] Computed by dividing the percentage of group members employed in the category by the percentage of the entire Boston male labor force in such jobs and shifting the decimal point two places to the right to give a value of 100 when the two distributions are identical.

level and is receiving its "share" of such jobs; a score of 200 means that it has twice as many persons employed at that level as would be expected if jobs were allocated without regard for group characteristics; a score of 20 means that the group has only a fifth as many such jobs as chance would dictate.[9]

As of 1950, the British and the Russian first generation had equally large middle-class elements, but their composition was quite different. The British were fairly evenly spread throughout the white-collar world, with just their share of clerical and sales positions, slightly more than their share of professional jobs, and about 60 percent overrepresentation as managers, proprietors, and officials. The Jewish immigrant middle class, by contrast, was far more specialized. Russians were distinctly underrepresented in both the professional and the clerical and sales category, and had nearly two and a half times as many jobs as expected as managers, proprietors, and officials. More detailed data are not available, but most of these Jewish immigrants were doubtless not managers or officials but proprietors. To what extent this distinctive concentration is attributable to prejudice against Jews on the part of Yankee employers and to what extent to a group preference for entrepreneurial callings is not clear, but the fact of distinctiveness is noteworthy.

Among the most heavily proletarian of the first-generation groups —the Irish, the Italians, the Swedes, the Poles, and the French Canadians—there likewise were important distinctions. Only the Irish and the Italians were drastically overrepresented in jobs at the very bottom of the occupational leader. They had nearly three times their share of unskilled laboring posts, whereas Swedes and French Canadians were actually underrepresented in those callings and Poles only moderately overrepresented; they had slightly less than their share of skilled manual jobs, only half the figure for French Canadians and a third that for Swedes. Irish and Italian immigrants had a much smaller professional class than the other three overwhelmingly blue-collar groups. The Italians at least had some entrepreneurial tradition, as had been evident as well from the 1909 data presented earlier, outperforming the Swedes and French Canadians there; the Irish lacked even that. Only in the category of clerical and sales employees did the Irish fare better than the Italians, Swedes, Poles, and French Canadians. The Irish immigrant middle class was not only very small; it was disproportionately composed of men who worked for others, and contained fewer independent professionals and businessmen than any other group. In 1950 as in 1880 the Irish were bottom dog. Closely resembling them, but a shade ahead, were the Italians. The other immigrant groups that were strongly clustered in blue-collar jobs—Swedes, Poles, and French Canadians—were in a distinctly stronger position, because they enjoyed greater access to the most attractive and rewarding posts within both the white-collar and the blue-collar worlds.

How did the children of these men, second-generation immigrants, fare in the occupational competition? Exact information is not available, but a fair approximation may be obtained by examining the situation of second-generation men aged 25 to 44 and living in Boston in 1950 (a group young enough, on the average, to have been sons of the city's first-generation immigrants, though many of them doubtless had fathers who either were living elsewhere or were deceased). As a group, it was shown earlier, second-generation immigrants moved up the occupational ladder at an impressive rate; 43 percent of them held white-collar jobs in 1950. The data on particular second-generation groups show a clear narrowing of the differentials that had prevailed in the first generation (Table 6.15). The fraction of second-generation Irish youths in middle-class occupations, for instance, was only a percentage point below the overall second-generation figure; the Swedish fraction was two points above, the German four points above, the English six points above. Most of the major second-generation groups partook of this progress. In only two of the eight did the second-generation middle class comprise less than a third of the group; in five the fraction exceeded 40 percent. The mean deviation of the fraction of white-col-

TABLE 6.15. Occupational distribution of second-generation immigrants by nationality: men 25–44, 1950[1]

	Father's country of birth							
Occupation	*England and Wales*	*Ireland*	*USSR*	*Italy*	*Sweden*	*Germany*	*Poland*	*French Canada*
	Percent							
White-collar	49	42	75	31	45	47	36	29
Blue-collar	51	58	25	69	55	53	64	71
	Index of representation[2]							
Professionals and technical workers	130	93	163	62	134	159	105	64
Managers, proprietors, and officials	112	63	217	78	94	104	74	64
Clerks and salesmen	105	125	153	75	95	83	79	67
Craftsmen and foremen	104	85	42	111	158	123	117	146
Operatives and service workers	85	111	52	125	66	86	128	121
Unskilled laborers	61	111	23	131	28	30	32	83

[1] Calculated from U. S. Census of 1950.
[2] See Table 6.14, note 2.

lar workers in the various second-generation groups was only 8 percent; for the first-generation groups it was nearly twice that (14 percent).

Despite this tendency for differences to narrow among the second-generation, however, some distinctive patterns remained visible. The achievements of the sons of Russian Jewish immigrants were most extraordinary. Three out of 4 of them entered middle-class callings, a far higher figure than that for any other second-generation group or even for native-born Americans of native-born parentage. Second-generation Jews, like their fathers, obtained far more than their share of proprietorships, but they also were highly successful at penetrating other white-collar callings as well; they outranked all other second-generation groups in both the professional and the clerical and sales categories.

The performance of second-generation Irish and Italian youths deviated from the norm in the opposite direction. Their concentration in unskilled laboring jobs was unusually high, as had been the case with their fathers, and they had fewer skilled craftsmen than any other group except the Jews (who, of course, were underrepresented in all manual callings). They were correspondingly slower to become professionals, proprietors, managers, or officials than most other groups.

The second-generation Irish, however, did find more openings in the white-collar world than their Italian counterparts. The distinctiveness of the second-generation Irish middle class was that it contained somewhat fewer professionals than normal for second-generation groups, a great many fewer managers, proprietors, or officials, and a high concentration of clerical and sales workers. Since clerical and sales employees typically rank below other white-collar workers in salary levels, economic independence, and social prestige, it is highly significant that much of the apparent success of the second-generation Irish involved only this short step up the social ladder.

CONCLUSION

Newcomers from abroad, then, did often edge their way a notch or two up the occupational ladder as they became more familiar with the American scene, and their children characteristically made further gains, but remained disadvantaged in comparison with their Yankee rivals. During the years of the massive transfer of population from the European countryside to the American city and for some time thereafter, there was a fairly clear-cut hierarchy of ethnic generations. Competition from European newcomers and their children did not seem to impair the career prospects of old-stock Americans; on the contrary, the first- and second-generation groups served as platforms that boosted the position of Yankees.[10]

Where you were born, however, and where your parents were born came to matter somewhat less over the span of years from the late nineteenth to the mid-twentieth century. Even in 1950 the occupational distribution of native-born children of native-born parentage was more top-heavy than that of second-generation newcomers, and far more so than that of immigrants, but the gap was much narrower than it had been earlier. The advantages that went with being a Yankee had diminished. Whether the rising tide of black migration to Boston supplied corresponding advantages to white residents of the city is a question to be explored below (Chapter 8).

The other principal conclusion to be drawn about immigration and social mobility in Boston is that particular groups moved ahead at different paces and through different channels. The Irish, for instance, lagged behind, and when they did make occupational gains typically became menial white-collar employees rather than professionals or entrepreneurs. Their political triumph in Boston was early and decisive; economic advancement, however, was slow to follow. Italians ventured into business for themselves more often than the Irish, but on the whole Italian occupational achievement too was on the low side. At the other end of the scale were the British and the Russian Jews, who were much less heavily concentrated in proletarian callings when they first arrived on these shores. The Jewish record was especially remarkable. Second-generation immigrants of British stock were distributed throughout the occupational structure in much the same proportions as their fathers, whereas the Jewish second generation thrust its way into a wide range of white-collar occupations that had been relatively closed to the first generation. Other groups, too, followed distinctive paths, as illustrated by the tendency of Swedes and French Canadians to cluster in the skilled trades.

The question of *why* particular groups moved upward at differing rates and via different channels obviously requires attention. An attempt at explanation, however, is best deferred until another issue can be clarified. Two of the groups that were conspicuously to the rear of the procession—the Irish and the Italians—were, of course, predominantly Roman Catholic, whereas those in the lead were largely Protestant or Jewish. Religious affiliation thus might have been a more significant influence upon occupational adjustment than nationality.

chapter seven PROTESTANTS, CATHOLICS, AND JEWS

Religion, like nationality, has long been a crucial ingredient of the Boston social fabric. The two, indeed, have always overlapped, at times to the point of inseparability. The city into which tens of thousands of Irish immigrants poured in the 1840's was a Protestant as well as a Yankee city; the newcomers, in turn, were Catholic as well as Irish. Religious affiliation as well as national background defined the lines of conflict and accommodation that emerged in the years that followed. Subsequent waves of immigration further changed the religious complexion of the community, adding some Protestants, a great many more Catholics, and substantial numbers of Jews. My aim here is to compare the social-mobility patterns of Boston's major religious groups in the late nineteenth and twentieth centuries, and then to offer some explanations of the religious and ethnic differences in mobility that were visible in the city.

The question of the relation between religious orientations and worldly success was raised in a challenging form by Max Weber in his classic, *The Protestant Ethic and the Spirit of Capitalism,*[1] and has been hotly debated ever since. Although Weber's chief aim was to establish the connection between religious ideology and the emerging "spirit of capitalism" in precapitalist society,[2] a corollary of his analysis was the proposition that exposure to "the Protestant ethic" would continue to predispose Protestants to success in the marketplace in later historical periods, and that Catholicism would continue to inhibit the worldly aspirations of its adherents.

The Weberian corollary about Protestant-Catholic differences in achievement has come under heavy but not entirely persuasive attack of late. Thus Lipset and Bendix found no differences in the occupational mobility of Catholics and Protestants in a 1952 national sample of the U.S. population, but, as Gerhard Lenski points out, they ignored the fact that a much larger fraction of the Catholics in the sample had been reared in big cities and should for that reason have fared better occupationally than Protestants, more of whom were of rural or small-town origins.[3] In an analysis of career patterns in Detroit in the mid-1950's Lenski found substantial differences of the kind predicted by Weber, and subsequent research in Detroit points in the same direction.[4] It has been argued, however, that Lenski confounded religion and ethnicity, that Detroit Catholics happen to have come from such relatively unsuccessful ethnic groups as the Poles more often than American Catholics in general.[5] Two major studies by Andrew M. Greeley and Peter Rossi, based upon national samples rather than upon data gathered in a single community, portray Catholic occupational achievement in a far more favorable light.[6] About the worldly success of the Jews there is little disagreement: they outperform both Protestants and Catholics according to every recent study.[7]

The assumption that recent surveys uncover timeless social patterns that must have existed in the past is, however, a questionable one. Catholic doctrine and ritual may have changed relatively little in the past century but it does not follow that the social and cultural traits of the Church's communicants have changed equally little. It is quite possible that there were substantial Protestant-Catholic differences in social-mobility patterns, political preferences, and other matters a generation or two ago, and that these have only recently been eroded away as the Church has become more fully "Americanized." It is even conceivable that Jews were notably less successful at the turn of the century than they have been in recent years. These, of course, are hypotheses that cannot be tested by contemporary survey research, however sophisticated. They are propositions about the past, about a time when the social characteristics of particular religious groups may have been quite different than they are now, and they must be tested against evidence drawn from the historical record.

One important limitation of this inquiry must be kept firmly in mind. In American society for at least the past century religion has been so closely tied to ethnicity that it is difficult to disentangle the two analytically. Both American Catholicism and American Judaism have until recently been religions of immigrants and their children; the Protestant churches have had much less than their share of first- and second-generation newcomers. What is more, Catholics and Jews of immigrant background have not been drawn in equal proportions from the various European countries that dispatched newcomers to the United States. Each religious group has rather had a distinctive nationality mix, and this poses a serious problem in interpreting any religious differences in occupational achievement that night be observed. Are they indeed genuine religious differences, or are they spurious ones, the result of differences in ethnic origins that happen to be correlated with religion?

It might seem that a multivariate analysis in which nationality is held constant could resolve the problem, but this did not prove to be a practical alternative. Even an enormous (and prohibitively costly) sample of the population of Boston would not include enough Irish Protestants or Italian Jews to allow analysis of religious differences uncontaminated by the effects of nationality. The great majority of the Boston Catholics dealt with below were first- or second-generation Irish or Italian immigrants, and there was no way to circumvent that fact. If religion and nationality were so intertwined historically that they cannot be pulled apart for analysis, there is little to be done except to note that the patterns disclosed below are not to be understood as universal "Catholic" patterns, but rather as Irish and Italian Catholic patterns that manifested themselves in a particular city in a particular historical epoch. They may well not have appeared in either communities in which, for instance, the bulk of the Catholic population was of German origin.[8] This chapter is thus not so much a test of the Weber thesis as it is a further exploration of the subject of the preceding chapter—the process of immigrant assimilation—aimed at assessing the significance of the religious dimension of ethnicity.

DATA PROBLEMS

Evidence about the religious affiliations of Americans in the past is dismayingly difficult to uncover. The United States Census and most other records suitable for a study of this kind contain no information about individual religious preferences; unlike nativity, race, and other social characteristics, religion is assumed to be a private matter. Precise information about religious affiliations was available in the case of only two of the six samples utilized in this chapter.

The 1910 marriage-license applications of the city of Boston indicated the type of wedding ceremony that was performed. It was thus possible to distinguish men married by Protestant ministers, Roman Catholic priests, and Jewish rabbis. There was, in addition, a fourth group, those joined in marriage by a justice of the peace. But these were only a modest fraction of the total—17 percent of the marriages, and only 11 percent of the marriages by those men about whom there was enough information for mobility analysis. The overwhelming majority of Boston's young men at this time were sufficiently religious to marry under church auspicies, so that group differences in mobility patterns may be analyzed without worrying that large numbers of individuals were part of a religious subcommunity in some sense but could not be identified because they were married by civil ceremony. The religion of sample members was known with some accuracy in that case and it was known for the data drawn from Edward Laumann's survey of Belmont and Cambridge residents in 1963, which included a question concerning religious affiliation. Laumann did not gather any information about career mobility, one of the principal concerns of this study, but he did examine intergenerational mobility, so that his data provide a secure foundation for part of the analysis here.

With two secure points of reference—accurate information about the religious affiliations of members of two of the samples—it seemed appropriate to take an otherwise indefensible liberty with the other samples. I decided to guess the religious affiliation of individuals on the basis of such data as nationality and name, and to see if the patterns revealed in the samples in which religion was definitely known resembled those in which religion was merely assumed. If not, if the differences were glaring, then obviously the guessing procedure was of doubtful accuracy. But happily the guessing game seems to have been reasonably accurate, for the same patterns do recur in both types of samples.

This is not surprising, for the guessing was not as difficult and arbitrary as might be thought. Men of Irish or Italian birth or parentage were assumed to be Roman Catholics. Likewise for those with Irish names, though actually born in England or Canada. Men from Catholic South German states like Bavaria were also classified as Catholic, as were French and Portuguese immigrants. Those of Russian or Polish origins, and those from Germany with common Jewish names, were taken to be Jewish. (In this instance attention was paid to the first names of all members of the family; many German surnames could be either Jewish or non-Jewish, but the presence of a wife or a child named for a New Testament figure resolved the difficulty in many instances.) There was often a further clue in the sample of fathers and sons from the 1930 birth records, for it was known what hospitals the sons had been born in, and patronage of a Catholic or a Jewish hospital was regarded as one indication of possible Catholic or Jewish affiliation.

Some check upon the accuracy of this guessing game was made by examining the 1910 data cards, on which religion was known, and assigning individuals to religious categories on the basis of these other clues without looking at the column indicating type of religious ceremony. This check indicated that proper judgments were made in roughly 9 out of 10 cases. Given this range of probably error in classification, the differences observed below are clearly significant.

PATTERNS OF CAREER MOBILITY

Catholics, Protestants, and Jews in late-nineteenth- and twentieth-century Boston characteristically began their careers at different occupational levels and had different prospects of moving up or down the occupational ladder between their first jobs and their last jobs (Table 7.1). At the time they first entered the labor market, Jewish youths were disproportionately concentrated in white-collar callings (though the number of cases on which the percentages were computed was too small to make the results more than suggestive). Boston Catholics, by contrast, typically gravitated toward jobs in the lower reaches of the occupational structure. In three of the four cohorts they were far more heavily concentrated in blue-collar callings that Protestants at the start of their careers, and in the fourth somewhat more so. Young Jews, it seems, quickly found jobs working with their heads; Catholics tended to start out working with their hands; Protestants were more evenly distributed between blue-collar and white-collar occupations.

TABLE 7.1. Religious differences in career mobility from first to last job

	Percent of group—				
Birth cohort and religion	*Starting in white collar*	*Ending in white collar*	*Blue-collar climbers*	*White-collar skidders*	*Number*
1840–1859					
Catholic[1]	14[2]	33[2]	28	33[2]	105
Protestant	59	65	26	9	196
1860–1879					
Catholic[1]	41[2]	43[2]	20	24[2]	297
Protestant	65	64	25	14	340
Jewish	73	85[2]	57	5	26
1880–1889					
Catholic	32[2]	44	29	23[2]	203
Protestant	41	50	23	10	151
Jewish	43	60	43[2]	19	37
Unknown[3]	33	53	33	6	49
1900–1909					
Catholic[1]	6[2]	22[2]	18	20	76
Protestant	38	39	13	20	133
Jewish	71[2]	82[2]	55[2]	7	38

[1] As explained in the text, the religious-group labels here are not based on hard evidence about individual affiliations, except in the case of the sample from the 1910 marriage licenses—the 1880–1889 birth cohort in this table.

[2] Significantly different from the Protestant figure.

[3] These 49 men were married by a justice of the peace.

A cautionary note is in order, however, for these generalizations do not apply so clearly to the 1880–1889 cohort, which is the one in which religious information is most reliable. Men married by a priest wore a white collar at the outset somewhat less often than men married by a Protestant minister or by a rabbi, but the disparity was not striking, and the Jewish-Protestant difference visible in the other cohorts does not show at all in this one, which suggests the possibility that the patterns displayed by the other cohorts are perhaps due to errors in religious classification. In the case of the Jews this seems unlikely, for another explanation is readily available: the Jews in the early cohorts were largely of German origins, whereas those born in the 1880's and married in 1910 were much poorer, recently arrived newcomers from Poland and Russia. By 1930, when the 1900–1909 cohort first worked, the East European Jews were sufficiently established to give their sons as large a head start as the German Jews had in the late nineteenth century—compare the 73 percent and 71 percent rates of initial white-collar jobholding for the second and fourth cohorts—but in the 1880–1889 cohort young Jews, like young Protestants and young Catholics, started their careers working with their hands in a majority of cases. And it is likely that Catholic-Protestant differences in first jobs were smaller in the 1880–1889 group than earlier because this sample, unlike the earlier ones, was composed entirely of married men aged 21 to 30 in 1910; quite possibly disproportionate numbers of Protestant white-collar workers in this age bracket were still unmarried and were thus unrepresented in the sample. A similar argument, however, would apply to the group of men born in 1900–1909, all of whom were married too. Since the religious differences observed in the first two cohorts reappeared there also, there remains some puzzle about the 1880–1889 group. In any event, even in that somewhat distinctive cohort Catholics differed from Protestants and Jews in the same way as in the other cohorts, that is, they gravitated toward proletarian callings. The point is only that this tendency was not as marked.

With respect to religious differences in rates of movement up and down the occupational ladder between first and last jobs, there was a clear and uniform pattern, so uniform as to allay any doubts that may be occasioned by the smallness of the samples and the uncertain accuracy of the information about religious affiliations. Three points stand out clearly.

It is evident, first, that Catholic youths who began their careers as blue-collar workers were just as likely as their Protestant counterparts to move upward later into a white-collar position. At the end of their careers, Boston Catholics were more often working with their hands than Boston Protestants, but the difference was due chiefly to the fact that they were more prone to enter the labor market initially at the manual level. There is no indication, in other words, that Catholic manual workers were less eager for upward mobility into the white-collar world than Protestants, or less successful at realizing their ambitions. Approximately 1 in 4 made this move in the course of their careers; in three of the four cohorts the Catholic rate of upward career mobility was actually a shade higher than the Protestant. It was not insufficient upward mobility after their first job that held Boston Catholics back, but the circumstance that destined them so often to take laboring jobs when they first left school and began to work.

A second conclusion suggested by this evidence is that popular folklore concerning the mobility achievements of the Jews is indeed well founded. Not only did an unusually high proportion of Jewish youths in Boston start their careers in the upper reaches of the occupational structure; those who were forced to work in blue-collar callings at the outset were extraordinarily successful at moving into the white-collar world later. Only about half of the Jews who began their careers as laborers—43,57, and 45 percent—were still employed in manual work at the time of their last job. The Jewish rate of upward mobility was double that of other groups!

Perhaps the most important pattern visible in Table 7.1, however, is a third—the dramatic tendency of Catholic youths who had begun their careers in nonmanual jobs to lose those jobs and to end their lives wearing a blue rather than a white collar, with all that this shift implied for wage levels, employment security, and social prestige. In the 1880–1889 cohort, where religious affiliation is reliably known, Catholics who began their careers in the white-collar world were more than twice as likely as Protestants to fall into a laboring job later on. The differential was a little smaller but still clear for one of the two earlier cohorts, and even larger for the other. Only in the last cohort, men born in the first decade of the twentieth century and at a critical point in their careers during the Great Depression of the 1930's, did the Catholic propensity for high downward mobility fail to manifest itself. Whether this indicates a basic long-term improvement in the position of Boston Catholics, or merely a temporary blurring of religious differences in the face of dismally hard times, cannot be answered definitely with the data available, but something more will be said about this issue at a later point.

That there was a distinctive Catholic mobility pattern, a skidding syndrome in which youths who started with a foothold in the white-collar occupational world were unable to maintain it for long, is further evident from an inspection of detailed data on the occupational shifts made by sample members from decade to decade (Table 7.2). (Sample attrition made it necessary to leave Jews out of consideration here.) There was little difference between the two groups with respect to upward mobility from manual to nonmanual jobs over the span of a decade. The Protestant rate of upward

TABLE 7.2. Religious differences in career mobility during a decade: percent (number)

Birth cohort and decade[1]	*Blue-collar climbers*		*White-collar skidders*	
	Catholic	*Protestant*	*Catholic*	*Protestant*
1840–1859[2]				
1880–1890	12 (169)	12 (155)	19[3] (37)	10 (161)
1890–1900	9 (102)	11 (95)	11[3] (35)	2 (121)
1900–1910	7 (62)	9 (47)	3 (29)	0 (85)
1860–1879[2]				
1880–1890	13 (40)	17 (36)	50 (24)	35 (34)
1890–1900	17 (83)	21 (57)	22[3] (37)	12 (113)
1900–1910	12 (137)	14 (93)	14[3] (94)	6 (161)
1870–1889				
1910–1920	24 (119)	20 (81)	12 (66)	10 (72)
1920–1930	9 (65)	11 (45)	10 (62)	9 (54)
1930–1940	6 (53)	5 (40)	12 (42)	5 (38)
1890–1909[1]				
1930–1940	10 (126)	10 (146)	22 (23)	20 (94)
1940–1954	9 (69)	12 (85)	7 (15)	2 (52)
1954–1963	4 (28)	10 (31)	15 (13)	6 (34)

[1] The age limits of some of these cohorts have been broadened beyond those given in the preceding tables, so as to include men whose "first" jobs—those held prior to age 30—were unknown because they were already 30 or over at the time the sample was taken. It seemed worth sacrificing the more precise age controls employed earlier to obtain a larger number of cases for analysis.

[2] See Table 7.1, note 1.

[3] See Table 7.1, note 2.

movement was a shade higher than the Catholic in 8 of the 12 decades observed, but not one of these differences was large enough to be significant at the 0.90 level, so that the Catholic handicap on this count was slight. With respect to downward mobility, however, the Catholic figure was higher in all 12 instances, and in two-thirds of the cases it was more than 50 percent higher. Four of these differences were statistically significant.

It could, however, be argued that this apparent skidding syndrome is attributable to the crudeness of the occupational categories employed in the analysis. Suppose that Catholic white-collar workers were heavily concentrated in jobs in the lower reaches of the white-collar class, as minor clerks, salesmen, and petty proprietors, and that white-collar Protestants were typically professionals, prosperous merchants, or managers of large enterprises. That downward mobility from jobs of the former kind would be more common is obvious. If this were the case, the mobility handicap of Boston Catholics would not be that a Catholic white-collar worker was more likely to skid to a manual job than a Protestant who started work in the same occupation; the problem would be the excessive concentration of Catholics in jobs from which downward mobility was common, and their underrepresentation in more secure nonmanual posts.

Inspection of more detailed mobility matrices (not included here) which reveal the career patterns of workers in the high and the low white-collar strata separately does not, however, alter the conclusion previously advanced. It is indeed true that the Catholic white-collar class included fewer bankers, physicians, and factory managers than its Protestant counterpart, and more menial white-collar employees. But this fact is not sufficient to explain the prevalence of the skidding syndrome among Catholics, for it appears even when we confine our attention to the experience of men in low white-collar callings. Protestant clerks, salesmen, and small proprietors were sometimes downwardly mobile; similarly situated Catholics were so far more often.

One could, however, push this line of attack still further, and maintain that such categories as "low white-collar" and "high white-collar" are still too crude and heterogenous. Suppose, for instance, that Catholics in the low white-collar stratum were typically clerks in small groceries, whereas Protestants white-collar youths were typically bank clerks. Though the job designation is the same —"clerk"—the jobs themselves differ radically in many respects, one obvious one being that the bank clerk is situated on a ladder with higher rungs which are clearly visible and quite possibly within his grasp, whereas the grocery clerk may be in a "way-station" calling which he might abandon (or be forced to abandon) a few years hence, older but otherwise no better equipped for other white-collar positions than he was when he started. That a group of grocery clerks should experience more downward mobility in the course of their careers than a group of bank clerks would hardly be surprising.

I cannot explore this issue much further, alas, both because the sources of occupational information did not unfailingly make the necessary distinctions, often supplying no more than the datum that so and so was a "clerk," and because the sizes of the samples limited the possible breakdowns by precise occupational title even when it was provided. But there was enough evidence on this point to persuade me that the Catholic skidding syndrome cannot be explained away in this manner. The sample taken from the manuscript schedules of the U. S. Census of 1880 permitted some analysis of this issue. It revealed that Catholic youths were somewhat more frequently store clerks and less often office clerks than Protestants; of all low white-collar employees, 53 percent of the Catholics and 41 percent of the Protestants clerked in stores rather than in offices. Clerking in a store was indeed a less secure white-collar job than clerking in an office; downward mobility from such positions was a little more common. But it was not so much more common, nor was the disproportionate concentration of Catholic youths in these posts so great, as to fully account for the Catholic propensity to skid.

There were, in sum, important religious differences in career mobility patterns, with Jews enjoying a clear advantage over Protestants, and with Catholics bringing up the rear. The Catholic handicap, however, lay not in insufficient upward mobility in the course of a typical career, but in two other weaknesses: an initial heavy concentration on the lower rungs of the occupational ladder, and a pronounced tendency for those Catholics who did start out reasonably well situated to lose their white-collar posts and to drop down into a blue-collar calling as they grew older.

FATHERS AND SONS

It is possible, however, that these apparent differences are spurious, the result of differences in the social-class background of the various religious groups. Some attempt to measure religious differences in intergenerational occupational mobility is thus necessary. The number of cases available for such analysis is modest, since the social origins of many sample members were unknown. No estimates of the intergenerational mobility of Boston Jews can be offered for this reason. There are, however, fragments of evidence from two samples that could not be exploited earlier. Laumann's 1962 survey of Belmont and Cambridge inquired into intergenerational but not career mobility. There is, in addition, useful information from a sample of youths born in Boston in 1930. No tabulation of religious differences in the career mobility of these youths was given earlier because many were not working in Boston in 1954, our first trace year for the cohort, presumably because they were in the armed services. But substantial numbers had reappeared by 1963, making it possible to relate their job level at age 33 with that of their fathers' regular occupations. It will be possible, thereafter, with these two sources of evidence from the early 1960's to say something more about the issue mentioned at the outset of this chapter—the question of religious differences in mobility patterns in contemporary America.

The career attainments of Catholic and Protestant youths of similar social-class origins are indicated in Tables 7.3 and 7.4. The overall rate of upward mobility for working-class sons in general was quite impressive; neither the Catholic nor the Protestant sector of the laboring class was a closed caste (Table 7.3). But clear religious differences in opportunities for advancement were evident in all but the last of the five samples. In the first four, Protestant youths climbed to the top of the occupational ladder more frequently than Catholics; in each, Catholics were more prone to end their careers in unskilled or semiskilled laboring jobs. It was only in the earliest two cohorts, however, that Catholic working-class sons had less access to jobs at the low white-collar level—clerical, sales, and petty proprietorships—and then their margin of disadvantage was slight. In the later samples Catholics actually gravitated toward these positions more frequently than Protestants. Even then, though, their suc-

TABLE 7.3. Religious differences (percent) in occupation of working-class sons at end of career

Birth cohort and religion	Last Job: High white-collar	Low white-collar	Skilled	Low manual	Number
1840–1859					
Catholic[1]	5	31	21	44	62
Protestant	13	35	29	22	48
1860–1879					
Catholic[1]	4[2]	33	25[2]	37[2]	298
Protestant	9	36	30	24	226
1870–1889					
Catholic	6	41	17	37	66
Protestant	10	33	30	28	40
c. 1890–1930[3]					
Catholic	16[2]	16	21	47	170
Protestant	26	15	21	38	62
1930					
Catholic[1]	5	32	20[2]	42	49
Protestant	6	22	35	37	69

[1] See Table 7.1, note 1.
[2] See Table 7.1, note 2.
[3] These figures are derived from a retabulation of the data from Edward Laumann's previously-described sample of Cambridge and Belmont. No breakdown of intergenerational mobility by religion is supplied in the published version, *Prestige and Association in an Urban Community,* but the author very kindly performed the tabulation upon request and furnished the results to me. The relatively high rate of upward mobility into the high white-collar class for both groups is doubtless attributable to the fact that residents of Cambridge and Belmont hold such jobs with somewhat greater frequency than the labor force of Boston proper, a feature that is evident from Table 7.4 as well.

cess was limited, for they clustered more than their Protestant rivals in the less rewarding and demanding middle-class positions. And those Catholic youths who were unable to climb out of the working class were less likely to obtain a skilled job and correspondingly more likely to work in the least desirable low manual callings.

In the very last sample, of youths born in Boston in 1930, Catholics seem to have fared a little better than Protestants. It is difficult to know how seriously to take this evidence, because the men in question were still in mid-career, but it is possible that the development Greeley and Rossi discern in their national sample—the apparent thrust of Catholic working-class sons into middle-class callings at about the same pace as Protestants—is apparent in these Boston figures. If so, however, it was a quite recent development, a distinct departure from the historic pattern manifested by previous generations of Catholic residents of the city.

A similar shift of pattern did not take place among Catholics and Protestants of middle-class origins (Table 7.4). The number of cases for analysis is dismayingly small in most of the samples, but the consistency of pattern is striking. In every cohort, Protestant middle-class youths ended their careers in the high white-collar category far more frequently than Catholics of similar class background; in each, Catholic men skidded into blue-collar jobs, and especially

TABLE 7.4. Religious differences (percent) in occupation of middle-class sons at end of career

	Last Job				
Birth cohort and religion	*High white-collar*	*Low white-collar*	*Skilled*	*Low manual*	*Number*
1840–59					
Catholic[1]	29	18[2]	35[2]	18	17
Protestant	38	49	5	8	78
1860–79					
Catholic[1]	24[2]	50	13	13[2]	46
Protestant	42	42	9	6	179
1870–89					
Catholic	16[2]	48	8	28[2]	25
Protestant	40	48	4	8	25
c. 1890–1930[3]					
Catholic	53[2]	20[2]	14	13[2]	74
Protestant	84	6	9	1	67
1930					
Catholic[1]	0[2]	57	14	28	14
Protestant	21	47	16	17	43

[1] See Table 7.1, note 1.
[2] See Table 7.1, note 2.
[3] See Table 7.3, note 2.

low-skilled manual jobs, much more often than Protestants. For instance, in the case of the sample of men born in the 1870's and 1880's, in which religious identification is precise, Catholic middle-class sons obtained only 40 percent as many high white-collar posts as Protestants, and three and a half times as many ended their careers at the very bottom of the occupational heap.

It might be thought that the relative inability of Catholic middle-class youths to penetrate the upper reaches of the occupational structure and their unusual propensity to skid into manual jobs indicates only that the control for social-class background employed in the analysis is too crude. If the typical "middle-class" Protestant father was a lawyer and his Catholic counterpart the proprietor of a small grocery, we could expect the career trajectories of Protestant and Catholic sons to differ greatly, for we would be comparing a marginal lower-middle-class group with a solidly upper-middle-class group. When the data are tabulated so as to distinguish high white-collar from low white-collar families, Catholic fathers prove to have indeed been more often in the latter category. But this did not explain away the distinctive career patterns of their children. The same tendencies manifest in Table 7.4 reappear in these more refined tabulations (not given here).

Taking into account the social-class background of sample members, in sum, does not modify the conclusions ventured earlier concerning the occupational handicaps of Boston Catholics. In one way, indeed, the relative position of Catholics seems worse than had appeared earlier. Though in the course of their careers Catholic youths climbed from blue-collar to white-collar callings about as frequently as their Protestant rivals, Catholics from working-class families experienced less upward intergenerational mobility than Protestants in all the samples except that of men first entering the labor market in the post-World War II period. Catholic working-class sons moved into the lower reaches of the middle class in large numbers, but less often attained top-ranked professional and managerial posts and were more likely to end their careers as mere unskilled or semiskilled laborers.

What is more, Catholic youths who grew up in relatively privileged circumstances—those whose fathers held a middle-class job of some kind—were much less successful than Protestants of comparable class origins. They won their share or more than their share of routine clerical and sales jobs but were heavily underrepresented in upper white-collar and heavily overrepresented in menial low manual jobs in all five.

TOWARD AN EXPLANATION OF GROUP DIFFERENCES IN ACHIEVEMENT

Differences in ethnic origins and religious affiliations were clearly associated with differences in occupational achievement. Some groups fared notably better than others in levels of initial occupational placement and in subsequent mobility up and down the social scale. To explain why this was the case is extraordinarily difficult with the sketchy evidence at hand. Adequate data about a number of variables of possible relevance—information, for instance, on the educational background of sample members—was simply not available. A rough estimate, however, may be made of the relative importance of a few of the factors most likely to be significant.

1. *Discrimination: Active and Structural.* One invitingly straightforward explanation of the difficulties experienced by Boston's Catholic immigrants and their children is that they were treated unfairly in the marketplace—that prejudiced Protestant employers were unwilling to give Catholics jobs for which they were duly qualified, and that Protestant bankers unfairly refused needed credit to aspiring Catholic businessmen.

It certainly is true that in late-nineteenth-century Boston the overwhelming majority of those who were in a position to hire, promote, fire, or lend money to others were Protestant Yankees, and even today this element of the population is overrepresented in management and banking. That many such persons were very unfavorably disposed toward Catholics is well known. Back in the 1880's Boston upper-class circles warmly applauded the anti-Catholic tirades of Edward A. Freeman, whose ingenious solution to America's social problems was to hope that every Irishman would kill a Negro and then be hanged for it! [9] As late as the 1920's the word "Protestant" frequently appeared as a necessary qualification in want ads published in the Boston *Transcript*.[10] Joseph P. Kennedy left Boston for New York in those years because of his conviction that certain doors in the local business world would always remain closed to him because of his religion. It is undoubtedly true that until fairly recently religious and ethnic prejudice restricted the opportunities open to Boston Catholics to some degree, especially at the top of the economic structure in such areas as finance.

Sheer prejudice, however, cannot be more than part of the explanation of the difficulties experienced by Catholic newcomers, because other groups that fared much better seem to have encountered similar hostility, most notably the Jews. Prejudice against immigrants in general, and especially against the so-called "new immigrants" from Southern and Eastern Europe, was rising sharply in the late nineteenth and early twentieth centuries. Freeman directed his attack not only against the Irish but against all "non-Anglo-Saxon" immigrants, and the animus of groups like the Immigration Restriction League was felt chiefly by more recent newcomers, many of them non-Catholic.[11] By the turn of the century Boston School Committee members of Irish descent had arrived at a certain *modus vivendi* with their Yankee colleagues, both groups deploring the "new immigrants" and calling for more strenuous efforts to "Americanize" them via the public school system.[12] Whatever the importance of blatant discrimination in holding back newcomers in general, therefore, it is doubtful whether it suffices to explain the sharply different experiences of Catholic and non-Catholic immigrants and their children.

More significant, in all likelihood, than sheer prejudice—active discrimination—is what has been termed "passive" or "structural" discrimination. This refers to features of the labor market that, without deliberate prejudicial intent on the part of employers, serve nonetheless to restrict the opportunities open to members of certain groups.[13] For instance, the common practice of recruiting new employees through networks of primary-group affiliation yields a tendency for labor forces to reproduce themselves. Relatives, friends, and neighbors of groups already well established in an industry enjoy superior access to openings as a result, and this limits the prospects of individuals from other groups who do not have such personal ties. This is at least part of the explanation for the pattern of "ethnic sponsorship" that has been observed in some firms.[14] When a particular group has won a substantial share of low-level supervisory posts, other members of the group employed at lower levels have the inside track in gaining promotions and avoiding lay-offs. Similarly, requirements that job applicants have "suitable" training or experience can operate to exclude outsiders or to keep them in subordinate positions. Even the use of seemingly universal criteria for job allocation—such as level of education—can entail structural discrimination if the criterion specified is not in fact closely related to on-the-job performance and if access to education is not open equally to all groups. In these and other ways there is a certain inertia in the job market that silently and unconsciously preserves the status quo.

Important as structural discrimination may be, though, in explaining the difficulties out-groups in general face in attempting to improve their position, it is again hard to see how it could account for the differentials between particular out-groups that have been pointed up in this and the previous chapter. Once the Irish had established a solid base in local government, and the Jews in retail trade, for example, structural factors would tend to keep them there and to limit the entry of other groups into that sphere of the economy, but we are left with the question of how and why they were able to create that base in the first place.

2. *Background Handicaps.* A second circumstance that influenced the economic adjustment of different groups was that some arrived with background handicaps that impaired their ability to compete: illiteracy, inability to speak English, lack of vocational skills, unfamiliarity with the rhythms of urban life.

Such factors inevitably influenced the adjustment of newcomers to American life. Ireland and Italy (at least southern Italy, from which most immigrants came) had experienced little industrialization and urbanization when the flow of migrants across the ocean was at its height. Thus it was that approximately half of the English, Scotch, and Welsh immigrants to the United States between 1875 and 1910 had worked in skilled jobs before migrating, but barely a tenth of the Irish and not many more of the Italians.[15] Of the Irish immigrants living in Boston in 1909 who had been employed before their departure to America, 64 percent had done agricultural work, and 42 percent of the Italians, as opposed to a mere 2 percent of the Jews.[16] The latter had been city dwellers in the Old World. Although not as many Jews as legend would have it were merchants and professionals, about two-thirds had been in skilled trades, and this clearly gave them an important initial advantage over some of their rivals.[17]

It is impossible however, to account for the differential occupational adjustment of the various immigrant groups in these terms alone. If ability to speak English was a significant asset—a plausible assumption—the Irish obviously had it. If literacy was of consequence, the kinds of Irish newcomers arriving in the late nineteenth century, unlike their predecessors, were again better equipped for the competitive struggle than many other groups. Only a tenth of the first-generation Irish male heads of household in Boston in 1909 were unable to read and write, but twice as many Jews (22 percent) and four times as many Italians (41 percent).[18] Nor was it the case, as has sometimes been thought, that Jews typically brought substantial amounts of capital with them to the New World and enjoyed a head start for that reason. This was true to some extent of the German Jews, but the predominantly East European Jewish groups arriving in the late nineteenth and early twentieth centuries entered the country with no more money in their pockets than the Italians and less than the Irish, who had about the same mean wealth as Scandinavian immigrants.[19] There are, in short, a good many discrepancies between the ranking of immigrant groups in terms of various background handicaps and their ranking in terms of occupational performance after their arrival.

Even if the background-handicap argument could be developed so as to explain virtually all of the variation in the performance of the different first-generation groups, it would leave the problem of the differential achievements of members of the succeeding generation. There were group differences that remained visible after the immigrating generation had passed from the scene and that do not disappear when the occupational achievements of the first generation are held constant analytically. Thus the skidding syndrome exhibited by the children of Irish and Italian Catholic newcomers who had already gained a foothold in the white-collar world. Old World background handicaps per se can hardly explain this. Something about the organization and culture of ethnic groups in the New World must have been involved.

3. *The Ghetto as a Mobility Barrier.* One feature of ethnic-group life in American cities that has often been identified as an obstacle to assimilation and mobility is residential segregation. The tendency of groups to form clusters, it has been argued, "maintains visibility and awareness of the status of the ethnic group both for its

own members and for other segments of a city's population," and blocks access to opportunity in a variety of ways.[20] Children growing up in the ghetto, it is thought, are confined to an environment that limits their aspirations and impedes their development as productive citizens.

Certain of Boston's immigrants have been heavily concentrated in particular neighborhoods. The index of dissimilarity between Italian immigrants and native-born Americans living in the city in 1880 was 74, which means that 74 percent of the Italians would have had to move to other areas of the city for the group to be distributed in the same residential pattern as natives, and the figure for Russian-born newcomers was 55. In 1910, similarly, 66 percent of the Italian and 48 percent of the Russian immigrants where ghettoized by this measure.[21]

There are, however, two crucial weaknesses of the ghetto hypothesis as an explanation of the differential occupational achievement of Boston's immigrants and their children. First, as was shown in Chapter 3, the population of the city was amazingly fluid during the entire period, and the turnover rate was especially high on the lower rungs of the class ladder, where immigrants were characteristically located. Though there were distinct clusters of particular groups at different points in time, not very many of the *same individuals* composed the group over time. If the presumably pathological effects of ghetto living depended upon being trapped there for long periods of life, rapid population turnover was an important solvent.

It could, of course, be that some ethnic groups were much less mobile spatially than others, and that the Irish and Italians of Boston were slow to move up the occupational scale because they were strongly rooted in their respective ethnic subcommunities and unaware of or uninterested in the opportunities that might have been available to them in other cities. In fact, however, the persistence rates of Catholics in the samples were not dramatically higher, on the average, than those of Protestants in comparable occupations, and it was the highly successful Jews who were the least migratory of all groups (Table 7.5).[22]

A second objection to the ghetto hypothesis as an explanation of differential occupational achievement is that there was no consistent relation between the extent to which the city's ethnic groups were

TABLE 7.5. Religion, occupation, and persistence (percent) of sample members in the city in three decades

Religion and occupation	*1880–1890*[1]	*1910–1920*	*1930–1940*[1]
Catholic	61	43	59
Protestant	66	42	56
Jewish	74	44	75
High white-collar[2]			
Catholic	83	75	[3]
Protestant	74	50	55
Low white-collar			
Catholic	69	56	84
Protestant	68	51	58
Skilled			
Catholic	63	39	67
Protestant	60	36	62
Low manual			
Catholic	58	37	50
Protestant	50	38	51

[1] See Table 7.1, note 1.
[2] There were too few Jews in the sample to permit cross-tabulation of persistence rates by occupational level.
[3] There were too few cases for calculation of percentage.

concentrated in ghettos and their occupational ranking. The least segregated of Boston's immigrants (as measured by an index of dissimilarity for 1880 and 1950) were the highly successful English and the relatively unsuccessful Irish; the most segregated groups were the highly successful Russian Jews and the unsuccessful Italians. When the city's immigrants are arrayed in two lists, according to their degree of residential segregation and to the fraction of their members in laboring jobs, the ordering of the two lists is almost completely unrelated. The rank correlation (Spearman's r) between the two is a mere 0.10 for 1880 and an even lower 0.08 for 1950.[23] Important though it may have been in affecting other realms of behavior, residential segregation was apparently not an important source of differential group mobility.

4. *Differential Fertility*. A simple demographic explanation of the relatively poor occupational performance of Boston's Irish and Ital-

ian Catholics is that they tended to have larger families than members of other groups and consequently found it more difficult to provide career assistance to their sons. The more children there are in need of aid, presumably, the less a father can do to encourage and finance their education and to provide capital backing for business ventures. The historical data available to test this explanation are very sketchy, but they do not seem to sustain it. In the late nineteenth century, the birth rate of Irish immigrants living in Boston was only a shade higher than that of Scotch and English newcomers, and was lower than the German and Swedish rates.[24] What is more, the Irish death rate, much of it due to infant mortality, was the highest of any group, and this further limited the number of second-generation youths who lived long enough to avail themselves of career backing from their families. The Italian birth rate, it is true, was extraordinarily high then, but so too was the birth rate of Russian Jews. In 1919, when the U. S. Immigration Commission conducted its survey in Boston, Jewish immigrant families in the city were distinctly larger on the average than Irish immigrant households and nearly as large as Italian families; the respective figures for mean family size were: Jewish, 5.28; Irish, 4.80; Italian, 5.52.[25] The second-generation Irish household, moreover, contained 4.30 persons, not many more than the typical Yankee household (3.49) of the day (no figures are available for other second-generation groups). There were more Jewish than Irish sons and nearly as many Jewish as Italian sons to draw upon family resources.

A subsequent study that traces some 700 couples marrying in Boston around 1910 through local birth records down to 1930 also provides only limited support for the differential fertility hypothesis as an explanation of differential intergenerational mobility.[26] In these years both working-class and middle-class Catholic families were considerably more fertile than their more successful Protestant counterparts. But Italian Catholic families were much larger on the average than Irish Catholic families, and yet these two groups were equally slow to move ahead occupationally. What is more, Jewish families were larger than Protestant and only a little smaller than Irish Catholic families, again a pattern that fails to square with the observed differences in mobility rates between these groups.

No post-1930 evidence pertaining to Boston specifically is available, and the information from other American communities is generally crude, revealing only broad religious differentials and neglecting ethnic distinctions within religious groups. But the general American pattern in recent decades was that Catholics tended to have larger families than Protestants of similar class status, and Jews smaller families. The religious differential, furthermore, was relatively small at the lower socioeconomic levels and greatest at the higher levels.[27] If Boston conformed to this pattern, it may indeed have had some bearing upon the skidding syndrome of middle-class Catholic youths in the city. But since that mobility syndrome was operating well before the differential in family size first appeared, the latter obviously cannot be a sufficient explanation for the former. Nor is it likely that family size was an important cause of the limited upward intergenerational mobility of Catholics of working-class origins, for religious differences in family size seem to have been slight within the working class.

5. *Institutional Completeness.* It may seem paradoxical, but it is possible that the very strength and cohesiveness of the Boston Irish and Italian Catholic communities negatively affected the mobility prospects of many of the children growing up within them. Raymond Breton has suggested that there may be an inverse relation between the "institutional completeness" of an ethnic community—the degree to which ethnic organizations can perform all of the services its members require, whether religious, educational, political, recreational, or economic—and the likelihood that members of the group will be upwardly mobile in the larger society.[28] To the degree to which a group is inward-looking and insulated from contact with "outsiders," its members may develop values that are deviant by the standards of the larger society, or, even if they hold the same values, they may not learn socially accepted methods of pursuing them. It is, of course, true that a cohesive, disciplined group can act in concert to attain certain objectives; a classic example often mentioned in contemporary discussions of the racial crisis is the Irish take-over of the big-city political machines in the late nineteenth century. But what is too often overlooked is that such a victory—winning control of 3000 jobs in the Public Works Department, let us say—may involve seizing one kind of opportunity *at the expense of other opportunities.* The success of the Irish in the political sphere was not matched by comparable gains in the private economy.

The solidarity of the Boston Irish, and the completeness with which the community was organized, were certainly notable. In his study of nineteenth-century Boston, Oscar Handlin noted that the Irish were the only group with a full, independent institutional life, the only group that "felt obliged to erect a society within a society." [29] Among more recent comers to the community, the Italians would also rank very high in this regard. But then so too would the Jews, or, to take another highly successful group not present in significant numbers in Boston, the Japanese Americans. Institutional completeness, it would seem, can be associated with worldly success or with a lack of worldly success, depending upon the values of the ethnic group in question.

6. *Cultural Values.* It is with some reluctance that I turn to group values as a possible explanation of differences in occupational achievement—reluctance because explanations of this type tend to be tautological and difficult to verify independently. "Why did the Irish move up the occupational scale less rapidly than other groups? Because the Irish placed less value on worldly success, or defined success in a different way. How do we know that Irish values were truly different from those of other groups? Because the Irish moved less rapidly up the occupational scale." Even when such interpretations are buttressed by evidence that makes them more than merely tautological, there is always a question whether the subculture of the group is truly a cause or only a *consequence* of the group's status. Nevertheless, it does appear that there was something distinctive about the cultural patterns of the Boston Irish and Italians that exerted an influence upon the career patterns of their children that may be distinguished from the general influence of parental social status.

Unlike Boston's other major immigrant groups, the Irish and the Italians were largely of peasant origin, and this, it is likely, gave them a distinctive value system that was passed on from generation to generation via the family. Particular attitudes toward education, work, thrift, and consumption patterns were inculcated in the Irish and the Italian family, and these influenced the occupational placement of children reared in such families.

This hypothesis, of course, cannot be systematically tested against evidence drawn from the historical record. But a plausible case can be made for it. With respect to the Irish, Oscar Handlin's magisterial account of their painful adjustment to Boston in the middle decades of the nineteenth century provides a wealth of material consistent with this view, and a host of descriptions by contemporary observers of the late-nineteenth- and twentieth-century Irish community indicate that the basic cultural pattern endured long after.[30]

There is no equally rich body of historical writing and contemporary observation about the Boson Italians, but a number of excellent sociological studies conducted in the past 30 years have delineated a distinctive Italian subculture which directed energies away from the world of work, or at least from those callings that are most highly valued and rewarded in the larger society.[31] One of these accounts describes the Italians as "urban villagers," and finds that even among the second-generation "the idea that work can be a central purpose of life, and that it should be organized into a series of related jobs that make up a career is virtually nonexistent."[32] These studies, it is true, have focused on two particular and quite special Italian neighborhoods, the North End and the West End. These are the most heavily Italian districts of Boston and the great majority of their inhabitants are manual laborers. Middle-class Italians and those aspiring to become middle class are least likely to be found there, and one suspects that similar studies of Italians in the more mixed and higher-status neighborhoods of such surrounding communities as Medford, Malden, or Arlington would yield a different impression of the values of the group as a whole, but it is certainly significant that large numbers of Boston Italians have been exposed at some point in their lives to the subculture of the North and West Ends.[33]

Though a sizable Irish-Catholic lower middle class emerged fairly early, and later a comparable Italian group, they did not provide a solid launching pad for greater gains in the next generation, perhaps because their members neither hungered for further advancement for their sons nor feared loss of face if they became policemen or plumbers, so long as the work was safe and steady. It is this, we may surmise, that accounts for one of the intriguing findings in Laumann's study of social stratification in Cambridge and Belmont. Laumann asked his respondents a series of questions designed to reveal the extent to which they made sharp distinctions between the status levels of various occupations. "High-status discriminators" were those who conceived the occupational structure as a ladder with many rungs; "low-status discriminators" made fewer distinctions, and were less inclined to believe that a clerk was socially superior to a carpenter and an accountant to a bus driver. It turned out, interestingly, that Catholics scored lower on the index of status discrimination than Protestants, and men of Irish descent notably lower than those of any other ethnic background.[34]

Another possibly distinctive aspect of the culture of the American Irish and Italians concerned attitudes toward property ownership and investment in education. In an earlier study of the Irish laborers of Newburyport, Massachusetts, in the nineteenth century, I suggested that the relative lack of upward occupational mobility by the sons of these men was part of a cultural pattern that placed a very high value upon home ownership, which in that setting was attainable only by putting children to work at an early age and consequently depriving them of an education that might have furthered their own careers.[35] As noted in Chapter 5, however, the sketchy evidence available on property ownership in Boston did not reveal a similar inverse relation between family property accumulation and intergenerational occupational mobility for members of the 1880 sample, the only one for which suitable property data were available. Nor, it should be added, was there any indication from an analysis of ethnic differences in property holding that the Boston Irish displayed the same hunger for real estate as the Newburyport Irish. (There were not enough Italians in the 1880 sample to discuss their behavior on this count.) Possibly this was because of a special characteristic of the Boston housing market: it contained a very low proportion of single-family dwellings that could be purchased inexpensively. Possibly, too, the failure of the study to gather data on property ownership for the large numbers of sample members fleeing to the suburbs obscured a pattern that was in fact present. Perhaps the Irish and Italians who moved from Boston proper to Cambridge, Somerville, Watertown, and similar communities in such large numbers were more like their Newburyport brethren and made the same trade-off that they did.[36] At present, however, it cannot be established that the distinctive occupational mobility patterns of the Boston Irish and Italians were linked to distinctive attitudes toward the relative importance of property ownership and the education of their young.

Although there is no support at present for the claim that the desire to accumulate property led Irish and Italian parents to underinvest in their children's education, there is direct evidence that their children did obtain less schooling than those from other groups, and that Jewish youths were unusually well educated. The U. S. Census of 1950 reported the educational and occupational attainments of first- and second-generation immigrants in the Boston area in some detail (Table 7.6). From 27 to 31 percent of the members of the three predominantly Protestant second-generation groups in the 25–44-year age bracket had attended college for a year or more, and a striking 44 percent of the largely Jewish second-generation Russians had done so. The figures for Irish and Italian Catholics were much lower—21 percent and 11 percent respectively. This was doubtless a major reason why second-generation Catholics held a much smaller share of jobs at the high white-collar level—only two thirds as many as the Protestants and less than half as many as the Jews—and were similarly underrepresented in the top sixth of the income-distribution pyramid.

One cannot, of course, draw the immediate inference that these Catholic immigrants tended to value education less highly than their Protestant or Jewish counterparts, for the explanation may lie in the differing social characteristics of the immigrating generation. Some groups had much less education in the Old World than others; some, as a result of the background handicaps they brought with them and other circumstances, were more heavily clustered on the lowest rungs of the occupational ladder. It is well known that the children of relatively uneducated and unskilled fathers tend to obtain less education than those from better-educated and more prosperous families. A study of students who graduated from Boston high schools between 1916 and 1934 disclosed that almost two-thirds of those from well-to-do homes but less than one-third from families in the lower occupational brackets continued their education further.[37] It is possible, then, that the educational and consequent occupational handicaps of second-generation Catholics revealed in Table 7.6 were due entirely to the fact that their fathers were more frequently uneducated workingmen.

The Census did not report this information in a manner that permits a direct test of that hypothesis, but some gauge of its validity may be gained by assuming that the educational and occupational rank of the fathers of these second-generation men was roughly

TABLE 7.6. Education, occupation, and income of second-generation immigrants (ages 25–44) by father's education and occupation, 1950[1]

	Percent of second-generation men with—			Family background (estimated)[5]	
Ethnic background and dominant religious affiliation[2]	*One year or more of college*	*High white-collar occupation*[3]	*High income*[4]	*Median school years of father*	*Percent of fathers with white-collar job*
Catholic					
Irish	21	19	13	8.3	18
Italian	11	17	9	5.2	18
Protestant					
English	27	29	19	10.3	52
Swedish	28	27	23	8.7	16
German	31	31	23	10.3	40
Jewish					
Russian	44	46	27	8.1	54

[1] Calculated from published U. S. Census data.

[2] The religious classification is, of course, quite imperfect. Many of the Germans were Jews in fact, and many others were Catholics. There were English Catholics, and even a few Irish Protestants. The Census does not, alas, supply similar tabulations for religious groups, so this is the best approximation that can be made.

[3] This is the proportion employed in the two census categories "professional, technical and kindred workers" and "managers, proprietors and officials, except farm," and thus is not precisely comparable with the high white-collar category used for the sample data elsewhere in the present study. Petty proprietors cannot be separated out from the census tabulations. If that had been possible, some of the group differences visible here would doubtless be accentuated. In particular, it is highly likely that many of the Italians in "high white-collar occupations" by this classification were in fact proprietors of small fruitstands, newsstands, and the like.

[4] Percent earning more than $4000 the previous year, which placed them in the top sixth of the income distribution for all second-generation persons earning income in the city. The income figures unfortunately include females, which tends to lower them in general.

[5] In the absence of direct evidence about the education and occupation of the fathers of second-generation men, figures for first-generation males aged 45 or more were taken as a rough base line.

equivalent to that of the city's first-generation immigrants aged 45 or more in 1950. (The correspondence is obviously imperfect, for some of the foreign-born males aged 45 or older had no sons who lived in Boston, and many of the second-generation men aged 25 to 44 did not have a father residing in Boston as of 1950, but it is hard to see why these flaws would appreciably impair the validity of the measure for the purposes to which it is put here.)

Applying this rough control for parental attainments reveals that part of the educational and consequent occupational handicap of second-generation Catholics did stem from their father's lack of education. Italian fathers ranked far below all others in median number of school years completed, and the Irish fell well behind two of the three Protestant groups. But there are two important anomalies: Russian immigrants had even less education than the Irish, and yet their children attended college much more frequently than those from any other group; Swedish fathers had less than half a year more schooling on the average than Irish fathers, and yet substantially more of their children were educated beyond the high-school level.

That the children of Jewish immigrants were more than twice as likely to attend college as their Irish counterparts with equally uneducated fathers appears less surprising when the occupational achievements of Jewish fathers are taken into account. More than half of them held middle-class jobs, but less than a fifth of Irish fathers did so. Despite their lack of education, Jewish immigrants moved very rapidly into white-collar callings, particularly as proprietors of small shops and manufacturing concerns, and this, of course, put them in a far better position to educate their sons than any of their Catholic rivals. The special Jewish commitment to education, however, stands out as remarkable when they are compared not with the Irish but with a Protestant group with an equally large and better-educated first-generation middle class, namely, the English. Almost the same fraction of both immigrating groups attained middle-class jobs, and the English immigrants had attended school an average of 2 years more than the Russians. But 44 percent of the second-generation Russian Jews and only 27 percent of their counterparts of English stock attended college, and a correspondingly larger fraction of the former found employment in the upper reaches of the middle class and were in the top income bracket.[38] This seems to be a clear example of the way in which the cultural values of a group can shape the career patterns of its children in a distinctive manner.

The second anomaly in the rankings—the relatively high educational, occupational, and income position of second-generation men of Swedish stock whose fathers had little more schooling than Irish immigrants—is suggestive of a cultural difference too. The comparison between the Irish and the other two Protestant groups—English and German—is perhaps unfair, because the first-generation English and Germans had more schooling and better jobs than their Catholic rivals. But immigrants from Sweden closely resembled those from Ireland both in their low educational level and in their overwhelming concentration in blue-collar jobs, and yet the second-generation Swedes outperformed the Irish by all three measures of achievement.

The educational and occupational achievement of second-generation Jews and the relative lack of achievement of Catholics thus cannot be explained away by holding the educational and occupational attainments of their parents roughly constant. There were very large group differences in the characteristics of the immigrating generation, to be sure, and these left a clear imprint upon the record of their children in school and at work. But a residue of unexplained variation remains when this is taken into account, a residue which suggests that Jews placed an especially high value on education and the careers it was the key to, whereas Catholics were somewhat less dedicated to educational and occupational achievement for their sons than Protestants from the same class and educational backgrounds.

If we knew more about the quality, as opposed to the sheer quantity, of the education received by these groups, it is likely that differences would stand out even more sharply. Large numbers of Boston's Irish and Italian Catholics attended parochial schools, and one wonders how effective these institutions were in providing the kind of training that was conducive to occupational success. Careful historical investigations of the effects of the parochial educational system are badly needed, but it is obvious that one basis for choosing a parochial over a public school was that the former was more closely attuned to the value system of Catholic immigrant parents. What this may have meant is that the parochial system, although it offered the security of the familiar, muted rather than heightened aspirations and fostered a sense of alienation from the larger society.

The evidence in Table 7.6 pertains to second-generation men born between 1906 and 1925 and observed in 1950, and it is, of course, possible that things have changed since then. Although

Catholic adults still were sharply underrepresented in the ranks of college graduates in 1961, younger Catholics were completing college in about the same proportion as Protestants.[39] Had the Boston sample data been more extensive in their coverage of the past two decades, permitting a closer analysis of recent trends, they might have disclosed the same improvements in the Catholic achievement level that have shown up in the two national studies by Greeley and by Greeley and Rossi.

If there was such a change in Boston, however, it was indeed a change, a sharp departure from a well-established historical pattern. Whatever the relation between religion and social mobility in present-day America, there were distinct ethnic and religious subcultures in the American city of the past. Although a wide range of circumstances influenced the ability of different groups to make their way in the workaday world, differences in group culture played a significant role. Whether these cultures are best described with religious labels, as Weber presumably would argue, or with labels based upon country of origin cannot be determined from a study of a community with Boston's particular ethnic and religious mix. But it can be said that immigrants from both Catholic peasant societies and the Jewish communities of Eastern Europe brought with them distinctive habits and attitudes that were slow to disappear and that influenced the occupational trajectories of the two groups long into the future.

chapter eight BLACKS AND WHITES

Among the newcomers who flocked to Boston in the late nineteenth and twentieth centuries were some who carried with them a special burden, the burden of being black men living in a white society. Despite the swelling volume of publications in the field of black history, there have been few systematic historical investigations of the fate of Negro migrants to the city. The literature of American Negro history emphasizes politics, organized group activity, leadership, the perceptions of the articulate. In other areas of scholarship this traditional emphasis is being challenged by those who are attempting to write the history of the inarticulate, history "from the bottom up," but we have yet to see much in the way of history from the bottom up dealing with the group that has the longest and bitterest acquaintance with life on the lowest rungs of the American class ladder.

THE "LAST-OF-THE-IMMIGRANTS" THEORY

My aim is not merely to provide some fresh descriptive material about the economic position of the Negro residents of a major Northern city since the late nineteenth century, but to use this evidence to test the validity of a theory which has often been advanced to *explain* the economic handicaps that Negro city dwellers have faced and continue to face even today. That theory holds that the core problem of the black urban population is that it is composed largely of uneducated, unskilled migrants from backward rural areas, much like the masses of European peasants who made their way into the American city in the late nineteenth and early twentieth centuries. Both groups, the argument goes, were ill prepared for urban industrial life and were forced to work at the least desirable menial jobs for that reason.

In time, however, the European immigrant struggled a notch or two upward on the economic scale, as he became better adapted to the environment in which he lived, and his children—the second generation—moved ahead more rapidly. The chief problem of black city dwellers, in this view, is that Negroes came to the city much later, and that the tide of mass in-migration from rural areas has not yet run its course. Second- and third-generation urban blacks are making progress like their European predecessors, but their gains are not visible in statistics that measure the status of the group as a whole, because this element is far outnumbered by recent rural migrants.

The necessity of considering the influence of rural migration upon the black city population was recognized long ago by W. E. B. DuBois in his classic study, *The Philadelphia Negro* (1899), in which he cautioned:

> No conclusions as to the effects of Northern city conditions on Negroes, as to the effect of long, close contact with modern culture, as to the general question of social and economic survival on the part of this race, can be intelligently answered until we know how long these people have been under the influence of given conditions, and how they were trained before they came.[1]

At least half of the black population of Philadelphia at that time, he went on to note, "cannot in any sense be said to be a product of the city, but rather represents raw material, whose transformation forms a pressing series of social problems."[2]

Although he stressed the negative effects of rural migration upon the black community, DuBois did not go so far as to suggest that Negro newcomers to the city faced no greater handicaps than white immigrants from Europe. But a number of later observers have emphasized the similarities. "The Negro today is like the immigrant yesterday," it has been argued; blacks are simply "the last of the immigrants," and will be drawn into the mainstream of American life at about the same pace as earlier newcomers.[3] More cautious formulations of the same general view recognize that particular immigrant groups in the past followed significantly different trajectories after their entry into American society, but emphasize that the experience of Negro newcomers to the city has not been very different from that of those European groups which were least well prepared for American life, such as the Irish.[4]

The literature on this subject, though stimulating, has been impressionistic. Systematic comparison of the experience of representative first- and second-generation European immigrants, black rural migrants, and blacks born and reared in an urban setting is badly needed.[5] The evidence gathered for this study provides an opportunity for one such comparison.

MIGRATION AND THE GROWTH OF THE BOSTON BLACK POPULATION

Though not a great center of black population like New York, Chicago, or Detroit, Boston is a satisfactory site in which to explore these issues. Its small Negro community—numbering 2348 persons in 1865—was highly attractive to the first generation of freedmen who made their way North. The city had an old, well-established Negro community; it had been a center of abolitionist activity, and a leader in the attack upon institutional segregation. At that time, it has been argued, Negroes were better off in Boston than in any other place in the United States.[6] The migratory wave that began after Appomattox swelled the black population by nearly 50 percent in the next 5 years, and by another 68 percent in the subsequent decade (Table 8.1). Between 1865 and 1900 the number of Negroes in the city increased nearly fivefold.

Even in 1900 blacks were only slightly more than 2 percent of the population of Boston, but this indicates not that Boston was an unimportant destination for Negro migrants in this period, but rather that the volume of black migration to virtually all Northern cities prior to World War I was modest compared with what took place later. Throughout the entire period from the Civil War to World War I, Boston had as large a proportion of Negro residents as New York, Chicago, Detroit, or Cleveland; only Philadelphia, among leading Eastern and Midwestern cities, had a substantially higher fraction of black inhabitants (Table 8.2).

TABLE 8.1. Growth of the black population of Boston, 1865–1970[1]

Year	*Number*	*Percent increase*	*Percent of city population*
1865	2,348	—	1.2
1870	3,496	49[2]	1.4
1880	5,873	68	1.6
1890	8,125	38	1.8
1900	11,591	43	2.1
1910	13,564	17	2.0
1920	16,350	20	2.2
1930	20,574	26	2.6
1940	23,679	15	3.1
1950	40,157	70	5.0
1960	63,165	57	9.1
1970	104,596	66	16.3

[1] From Massachusetts State Census, 1865, and U. S. Census, 1870–1970. All figures pertain to Boston city.
[2] Forty-nine-percent growth for the 5 years 1865–1870. For the entire decade 1860–1870 the figure was 53 percent. Thus 95 percent of the decadal gain took place after 1865.

It is true that Boston was somewhat distinctive in attracting less than its share of Negro newcomers during the Great Migration of World War I and its aftermath. The black population continued to edge upward, both in absolute numbers and as a proportion of the

TABLE 8.2. Proportion (percent) of black population in selected major Northern cities, 1870–1970[1]

Year	*Boston*	*New York*	*Chicago*	*Philadelphia*	*Detroit*	*Cleveland*
1870	1.4	1.3	1.2	3.3	2.8	1.4
1880	1.7	1.6	1.3	3.7	2.4	1.3
1890	1.8	1.6	1.3	3.8	1.7	1.2
1900	2.1	1.8	1.8	4.8	1.4	1.6
1910	2.0	1.9	2.0	5.5	1.2	1.5
1920	2.2	2.7	4.1	7.4	4.1	4.3
1930	2.6	4.7	4.1	11.3	7.7	8.0
1940	3.1	6.1	8.2	13.0	9.2	9.6
1950	5.0	9.5	13.6	18.2	16.2	15.2
1960	9.1	14.0	22.9	26.4	28.9	28.6
1970	16.3	21.2	32.7	33.5	43.7	38.3

[1] Central cities only. The 1970 figures are from Census advance reports.

total, but at a somewhat slower rate than in the prewar period. The Boston Negro population grew by only half between 1910 and 1930, while Detroit was registering gains of 1900 percent, Cleveland 800 percent, Chicago 430 percent, New York 250 percent, and Philadelphia 160 percent.

The next great wave of Negro migration, however, affected Boston in much the same way as other major cities. The proportion of Negro residents in the city nearly tripled between 1940 and 1960, a rate of increase exceeded only by Detroit and Cleveland, and continued to grow very rapidly in the 1960's. There were proportionately more blacks in Boston in 1970 than in New York in 1960 or in Chicago and Cleveland in 1950 (though fewer in absolute numbers, of course).

By this simple demographic measure, therefore, Boston is a fairly representative case in which to examine the adjustment of black migrants to urban life. The one distinctive feature about it is the relatively low rate of black in-migration between the two world wars, a factor that should have worked to the advantage of the community's Negroes in those years if rural migration was indeed a prime source of their economic difficulties.

It is obvious from the population totals in Table 8.1 that Boston must have been attracting substantial numbers of black migrants, for the rate of natural increase for Negro city dwellers was not high enough to account for the growth that took place. Until after the turn of the century, indeed, life was so hazardous for black Bostonians that the death rate exceeded the birth rate and net in-migration had to be heavy enough to offset a natural decrease. Noting that the black death rate was nearly double that for whites, the City Registrar observed in 1884 that "were accessions from without to cease, the colored population would, in time, disappear from our community." Rising fertility rates and declining mortality rates soon obliterated this pattern, but even in the post-World War II period the nonwhite rate of natural increase was insufficient to produce the dramatic gains that were observed.[7]

Information on the place of birth of Boston blacks for scattered dates indicates clearly that migration was the chief source of population growth and sheds some light on the geographic origins of the newcomers (Table 8.3). It has sometimes been assumed that the black community of Boston was distinctive in containing an unusually high proportion of descendants of free Negroes of the antebellum period. It is true that an elite of old families who trace their lineage back this far can be identified, and there is evidence that such persons have played an important role in the social life of the community.[8] But the simple fact is that the black population of Boston since at least 1870 has been made up largely of migrants who were born elsewhere, a majority of them in the South.

TABLE 8.3. Nativity (percent) of Boston black population, 1870–1970[1]

	Place of birth			
Year	*Massachusetts*	*South*	*Other U. S.*	*Foreign*
1870	37	38	14	11
1880	31	48	13	8
1890	28	46	11	14
1900	25	53	12	10
1910	29	n.a.	n.a.	13
1920	30	n.a.	n.a.	18
1930	38	37	9	16
1960	43	n.a.	n.a.	8
1970	49	29	16	6

[1] Place-of-birth data for blacks are not published routinely by the Bureau of the Census; only this incomplete series is available. Figures for 1870, 1890, and 1900 are taken from John Daniels, *In Freedom's Birthplace: A Study of Boston Negroes* (Boston, 1914), pp. 468–469. The 1880 data were compiled from the manuscript schedules of the U. S. Census by Elizabeth H. Pleck of Brandeis University, as part of a doctoral dissertation in progress on "The Black Community of Boston, 1870–1900." The 1910, 1920, and 1930 figures are to be found in the U. S. Bureau of the Census, *Negroes in the United States, 1920–1932* (Washington, D.C.: U. S. Government Printing Office, 1935), pp. 32, 74, 75, 216–218. The 1960 and 1970 figures are from the Massachusetts *Population* volumes of the 1960 and 1970 Censuses.

Little more than a third (37 percent) of the Negroes enumerated by the Boston census taker in 1870 were born in the state of Massachusetts; a slightly larger group was made up of migrants from the South, chiefly from Virginia, Maryland, and North Carolina; the remaining quarter were newcomers who had been born elsewhere in the United States or abroad, with the foreign immigrants evenly divided between West Indians and the Canadian-born descendants of fugitive slaves. Even these figures minimize the significance of migration, for a substantial fraction of the Massachusetts-born black population was made up of young children whose parents were migrants. Among Negroes old enough to be in the labor force in 1870, fully 54 percent were Southern-born newcomers. A decade later, no less than 61 percent of the employed black males in Boston were Southern migrants.[9]

The black population of the city tripled between 1870 and 1900, and in that period the fraction of black residents who were born in Massachusetts fell from 37 to 25 percent, while the fraction of Southern-born persons increased from 38 to 53 percent. (Note that this is almost precisely the fraction of Southern blacks in the Philadelphia population—54 percent—at the time DuBois made his survey.) No figures are available on composition of the black labor force in 1900, but the best estimate is that approximately 3 out of 4 employed Negroes were newcomers from the South, and no more than 1 in 10 were born in Massachusetts.[10] Nearly half (47 percent) of a large sample of Negroes working in Massachusetts then had migrated into the state within the past 10 years; 7 out of 10 had lived in Massachusetts less than 20 years.[11]

Between 1900 and 1930 the growth rate of the Boston black population slowed considerably. Instead of tripling, as in the preceding 30 years, the total rose by only 77 percent. By 1930 the proportion of Masschusetts-born Negroes had risen back to its 1870 level, and the proportion of Southern migrants had likewise fallen to its 1870 level. Even so, 62 percent of the entire black population, and probably 80 to 85 percent of the black labor force, consisted of migrants from outside the state.

After 1930, and particularly after 1940, the rapid growth rates that had prevailed in the late nineteenth century were resumed. The Negro population more than tripled between 1930 and 1960, and increased another two-thirds in the 1960's. This time, however, natural increase contributed more to the growth than in the past, for there was no new decline in the proportion of Massachusetts-born blacks, but rather a small further increase, and a distinct decline in the percentage of foreign-born Negroes. Still, in 1970 a majority (51 percent) of Boston's blacks had been born outside the state and had migrated into it, and most of the newcomers (29 percent of the entire black population) were of Southern origin. The fraction of

Southern migrants in the labor force was doubtless higher still. More than half (52 percent) of the respondents in a 1958 sample of black household heads were Southern migrants, whereas only 26 percent were Boston-born.[12]

The initial premise of the "last-of-the-immigrants" theory, then, is correct. The Boston black community has indeed undergone a heavy continuing influx of newcomers, the bulk of them migrants from the rural South. But was it true that those blacks who were, in DuBois' phrase, "a product of the city" fared notably better than their migrant brethren from rural backgrounds? Were black newcomers to the city in a situation basically analogous to that of any of the major European immigrant groups? Did the children of Negro migrants to the city, second-generation blacks as it were, move upward at about the same rate as second-generation whites? Or was there a difference in kind between the experience of Negroes and that of white immigrants?

It must be recognized at the outset that the answers given to these questions below will be far from definitive, because the bulk of the evidence available for analysis is of a different character from that employed earlier in my discussion of ethnic and religious differences in occupational achievement. The samples on which I relied in examining patterns of movement through careers and between generations did not include sufficient numbers of blacks to yield reliable results. I have been forced, therefore, to base this account largely on patterns displayed in gross census tabulations for different points in time. The limitations of such distributional evidence have already been made plain. A finding that a particular group had essentially the same occupational distribution at two dates does not by any means prove that the individuals who composed the group at the initial date experienced no change in occupational status over the interval. Nor does a dramatic change in distribution over the interval necessarily indicate that the individuals remaining in the community during the period were affected by the change. Whether or not this was the case depends upon both the volume and the characteristics of in- and out-migrants in the years in question. Such evidence, furthermore, tells us little about whether or not intergenerational mobility was taking place on a significant scale.

Indeed, even if there were available a body of historical evidence about the mobility of individual blacks in a particular community, it would be insufficient to measure what might have been a critical type of black social ascent—out-migration to a new destination coupled with "passing" in the white world and movement into a higher-ranked occupation. The analysis offered here is thus more tentative and more open to revision than that in the preceding chapters. I believe, though, that it is correct in its main outlines, and that future work will reinforce rather than overturn the conclusions I have drawn.

THE ECONOMIC POSITION OF BLACKS IN LATE-NINETEENTH-CENTURY BOSTON

Southern black migrants who made their way to Boston in the late nineteenth century did indeed, as Table 8.4 shows, cluster on the lowest rungs of the occupational ladder. In both 1880 and 1900, 12 out of 13 worked in blue-collar jobs, the overwhelming majority of them unskilled laborers, janitors, domestic servants, or porters. What is striking, however, is that their presumably more "prepared" Northern-born brethren had only a small margin of advantage over them in the occupational competition.[13]

Though most of the Northern-born blacks employed in Boston in 1880 could presumably trace their roots back to the antebellum free black community, more than 90 percent of them were manual laborers; the tiny middle-class element in this group was only a shade larger than among black migrants from the South, most of them ex-slaves, or from outside the United States. The only significant occupational advantage that came with "long, close contact with modern culture" was that 2 in 10 of these second-generation Northern Negroes and only half as many first-generation black newcomers had found their way into a skilled trade. That was something, but the overriding fact was that almost 3 out of 4 of those Boston Negroes who had been born and reared in the urban North held jobs that entailed little in the way of skill, prestige, responsibility, or monetary reward. In another important respect, indeed—vulnerability to unemployment—Southern blacks were actually better off than their Northern counterparts. Only 7 percent of the former, but nearly twice as large a fraction (12 percent) of the latter were unemployed during the year preceding the 1880 Census.

The situation was little different in 1900. Massachusetts-born Negroes may be distinguished from migrants from other Northern

TABLE 8.4. Occupational distribution (percent) of Boston black males, by place of birth, 1880 and 1900[1]

Year	Place of birth	Occupational level			Number
		White-collar	*Skilled*	*Low manual*	
1880	North	9	19	73	901
	South	7	9	84	1895
	Foreign	7	12	81	298
1900	Massachusetts	12	14	74	530
	Other North	6	11	83	2476
	South	8	12	80	824
	Foreign	6	16	78	479

[1] The 1880 data, and subsequent data on blacks in 1880, were gathered from the manuscript schedules of the U. S. Census of 1880 by Elizabeth H. Pleck of Brandeis University, for Thernstrom and Pleck, "The Last of the Immigrants? A Comparative Analysis of Immigrant and Black Social Mobility in Late-Nineteenth Century Boston," unpublished paper for the 1970 meetings of the Organization of American Historians. The 1900 evidence is from Massachusetts Bureau of the Statistics of Labor, *34th Annual Report* (Boston, 1904), pp. 249–251. The occupational categories employed in the Bureau's survey were somewhat unsatisfactory, so the figures for skilled and low-manual workers are estimates. On the basis of careful study of census data for 1890, 1900, and 1910 I concluded that approximately half of the blacks the survey classified as workers in transportation or manufacturing were skilled, and the remainder were not. The estimates above were developed on that assumption. One curious feature of the data raises a question about either the accuracy of the survey or the tabulation of the place-of-birth information. The proportion of Southern blacks in the survey seems much too low (cf. Table 8.3) and the proportion of migrants from Northern states much too high. Precisely what states were classified "Southern" is not clear from the report, but it seems impossible that this could account for the large discrepancy. The consistency between these figures on occupation by nativity and those for 1880, however, makes it seem likely that the survey accurately gauged the occupational distribution of Southern blacks, even though they were underrepresented as a group in the returns.

states in this instance, and it is significant that the former were considerably more successful than other blacks at penetrating into the white-collar world. The Massachusetts-born middle class, however, was still pathetically small; 3 out of 4 of these men were only unskilled or semiskilled laborers. It is significant, too, that Southern migrants to Boston were not a whit worse off than newcomers born in the North outside of Massachusetts; Northern migrants, in fact, were actually a little more heavily concentrated at the bottom than Southern migrants.

The continued influx into the community of ill-prepared first generation migrants from the rural South, therefore, can hardly be the fundamental explanation of the dismal economic status of blacks in late-nineteenth-century Boston. It was the fate of most black residents of the city to be hewers of wood and drawers of water; where they were born and reared, North or South, in a city or in the countryside, appears to have made very little difference.

This is damning evidence against the "old-resident" theory of the sources of Negro poverty. And, coupled with the evidence in Chapter 6, it exposes the inadequacy of crude versions of the "last-of-the-immigrants" argument. The second-generation offspring of European newcomers to Boston typically made impressive advances over their fathers. Second-generation black city dwellers, by contrast, were only a shade better placed occupationally than migrants from the rural South.

If the question, however, is not simply whether Negroes fared about as well occupationally as European immigrants in general, but whether the experience of blacks fits *anywhere* on the spectrum of immigrant occupational achievement, further analysis is required. The obvious point of comparison is the Boston Irish, the least successful of the "old-immigrant" groups to arrive in the community in the nineteenth century. There were indeed some pronounced similarities between the Irish and the Negroes. As of 1860, according to the leading student of Boston's immigrants, the Irish actually ranked *below* the blacks in the city occupationally.[14] The editor of the Irish Catholic paper, *The Pilot,* was so depressed at the difficulties experienced by his countrymen that he declared: "The Irish came out of slavery, with many of the marks still visible upon them . . . They also labor under other disadvantages—an inferior culture and a consciousness of lower-classness."[15] Some of the marks of this heritage remained visible within the Boston Irish community long after; as late as 1890, 90 percent of the Irish immigrants in the city were manual laborers, as compared with 92 percent of local Negroes.

The crucial question, however, is whether the process of assimilation into the social structure was operating in a broadly similar fashion for both groups. To resolve that issue requires a comparison not between first-generation Irish immigrants and all Negroes, but rather between Irish and black newcomers to the city, and between the second-generation offspring of these men. Such a comparison reveals a radical contrast between the experience of the two groups (Table 8.5).

Only 12 percent of the first-generation Irish employed in Boston in 1880 were white-collar workers, and 7 percent of the black migrants from the South—not an impressive margin of advantage for the Irish. Twenty percent of Irish immigrants but only 10 percent of blacks, however, were in skilled trades; 84 percent of Southern Negroes and only 67 percent of the first-generation Irish were unskilled or semiskilled laborers. Though heavily concentrated in blue-collar callings, Irish immigrants were distinctly less confined to the least attractive and rewarding manual occupations.

TABLE 8.5. Occupational distribution (percent) of Irish and black males by generation, 1880

Ethnicity	*Occupational level*			*Number*
	White-collar	*Skilled*	*Low manual*	
First-generation[1]				
Irish	12[2]	21	67	417
Black	7	9	84	1895
Second-generation				
Irish	24	24	52	277
Black	9	19	73	901

[1] "First-generation" blacks are those of Southern birth; "second-generation" those of Northern birth.

[2] All differences in the table are statistically significant.

A sharper and more important contrast, however, was to be found among second-generation city dwellers from the two groups. Almost a quarter of the American-born youths of Irish parentage found their way into a middle-class job; white-collar callings were twice as accessible to the second generation as to their fathers. The second generation of Northern blacks, however, made hardly any progress in this area; in a generation the middle-class element grew by a mere 2 percent.

This snapshot at one point in time—1880—may be supplemented with some evidence about the unfolding career patterns of members of these groups between 1880 and 1890 (Table 8.6). Of the first-generation black migrants to Boston who were employed there

TABLE 8.6. Percentages of blacks and immigrants in white-collar occupations in 1880 and 1890, by generation, for men aged 20–39 and employed at both dates

Generation and group	*1880*	*1890*	*Number*
First-generation			
Blacks	9	11	315
Irish	11	14	99
Other European	27[1]	33[1]	112
Second-generation			
Blacks	12	17[2]	141
Irish	25[1]	32[1]	72
Other European	39[1]	41[1]	41
Third-generation			
Blacks[3]	17[2]	17[2]	87

[1] Significantly different from blacks.
[2] Significantly different from first-generation blacks.
[3] Third-generation blacks are Northern-born men whose fathers had also been born in the North.

in 1880 and still to be found in 1890, there was virtually no occupational progress; a mere 9 percent held white-collar jobs at the outset, and only 2 percent more a decade later. Immigrants from Ireland, however, fared only slightly better; their margin of advantage over first-generation blacks was not large enough to be statistically significant at either the beginning or the close of the decade. Fully a third of the non-Irish immigrants in the city had found their way into the white-collar world by 1890, but only 14 percent of the Irish. There was no resemblance between the pattern of black migrants and that of European immigrants in general, but a rather close one between those for black migrants and Irish immigrants.

Within both the Irish and the non-Irish European immigrant groups, however, the second generation moved ahead impressively. The Irish continued to lag behind other European whites, a third of them attaining white-collar status by 1890, as contrasted with 41 percent of other second-generation males. But the glaring gap in occupational achievement was not between the Irish and other second-generation groups but between Northern-born second-generation Negroes and second-generation whites. Five-sixths of those blacks who had been in "long, close contact with modern culture" all their lives (to the extent to which mere physical presence in the city provides much contact, as the "last-of-the-immigrants" theory holds) worked in the same manual jobs as the generation fresh from the rural South. By 1890 second-generation blacks held only 6 percent more white-collar jobs than Southern black migrants, and with respect to entry into skilled trades their margin was even less impressive; 17 percent, as opposed to 15 percent of the first-generation newcomers, had reached that level (table not included here).

Even more striking evidence that the economic difficulties of black men in late-nineteenth-century Boston did not stem largely from the continued influx of ill-prepared rural migrants may be obtained by isolating a group of Negroes with even more prolonged contact with Northern urban ways: those whose *fathers* had been born in the North and who thus had deep family roots in the free black community of the antebellum years. These third-generation Northerners comprised less than a fifth of the black male labor force in 1880, and they should have been an economic elite if familiarity with the culture indeed made a great difference. In no way were they "raw material" with respect to length of exposure to city life. In fact, however, they fared not one whit better than Northern-born second-generation blacks and very little better than first-generation rural migrants. Eighty-three percent of them were still manual workmen in 1890, most of these in precisely the characteristic jobs of black migrants—laborer, servant, waiter, janitor, or porter. The second-generation Irish middle class, though smaller than that of other European second-generation groups, was nearly twice as large proportionally as that of third-generation Northern Negroes.

It was only among the small group of third-generation Negroes who reported their race as "mulatto" in the Census that there was much upward occupational mobility. These men ($N = 37$) moved ahead during the 1880's at about the same rate as the second-generation Irish, while third-generation blacks who identified themselves as Negro ($N = 50$) remained on the bottom rungs of the occupational ladder to precisely the same degree as black migrants fresh from the rural South. It is difficult to know what this signifies, given the ambiguities of the term "mulatto." [16] Perhaps these mulattoes were men whose race was less indelibly stamped on their countenance, and who encountered less discrimination for that reason. Alternatively, this self-identification may have born little relation to skin color, and have been symptomatic of greater determination to act in ways acceptable to white employers. Either way, the striking lack of occupational achievement by third-generation black males who were not identified as mulattoes is damning to theories that trace the problems of blacks to the rural South.

A further piece of suggestive evidence indicates that even the apparent resemblance between the most impoverished and ill-prepared of the European immigrant groups of the late nineteenth century—the Irish—and the blacks was somewhat superficial. Data from the

TABLE 8.7. Index of relative concentration of Irish immigrant and black males in selected occupations, 1890[1]

Occupation	*Irish*	*Blacks*
Unskilled and menial service		
Laborer	329	328
Servant	114	1128
Porter	135	848
Janitor	63	720
Semiskilled		
Factory operative		
Iron and steel	125	8
Tobacco	9	12
Wood	50	20
Shoes	117	64
Transportation		
Steam railroads	146	56
Street railways	70	20
Teamsters	111	40
Watchman and policeman	102	24
Skilled		
Barber	84	28
Blacksmith	169	20
Cabinetmaker	33	12
Carpenter	55	16
Machinist	47	8

Occupation	Irish	Blacks
Mason	164	36
Painter	58	20
Plumber	59	4
Printer	35	20
Tailor	92	52
Low white-collar		
Agent	36	4
Clerk	24	20
Commercial traveler	21	8
Salesman	28	12
High white-collar		
Merchant, dealer, and peddler[2]	64	40
Manufacturer	46	8
Professional[3]	15	25

[1] Calculated from the 1890 U. S. Census. An index value of 100 means that the proportion of the members of the group in the occupation was identical to the proportion of all employed males holding such jobs in the city. Indexes below 100 indicate underrepresentation for the group, those over 100 overrepresentation.

[2] Peddlers and small shopkeepers cannot be distinguished from substantial merchants here, which doubtless helps to explain the relatively favorable showing of both blacks and Irish.

[3] Engineers, lawyers, and physicians only.

U. S. Census of 1890 permit us to go beneath very broad categories like "white collar" and to measure the extent to which blacks and Irish immigrants had penetrated particular occupations (Table 8.7). The figures for blacks pertain to all Negro males, rather than merely to Southern migrants, whereas the Irish figures are only for immigrants and do not include the second generation. The comparison is thus biased in favor of blacks, in that a substantial minority of them had lived their entire lives in the North.

Despite this, Negroes in the city were in a far weaker economic position than Irish immigrants. Both groups contained disproportionate numbers of ordinary unskilled day laborers—almost 3.3 times as many as would be expected had men been distributed throughout the occupational structure without regard to ethnic characteristics (or traits, such as literacy, correlated with ethnic characteristics).[17] But in each of the other menial unskilled occupations of the city blacks were far more heavily overrepresented. There were 7 times as many black janitors, 8 times as many black porters, 11 times as many black servants as would be expected if jobs had been allocated randomly. The Irish, by contrast, were only slightly overrepresented as servants and porters, and underrepresented as janitors.

More striking evidence of the extraordinary thinness and imbalance of the black occupational structure, even compared with the lowly Irish, lies in the fact that it was *only* in those four menial jobs, out of 31 major occupations isolated for analysis, that there were as many Negroes as chance would dictate. Indeed, in only three more—shoe-factory operative, railroad worker, and tailor—did blacks have as much as *half* of their expected share of the available jobs.[18] The Irish, on the other hand, were overrepresented in 7 of the 27 occupations above the unskilled and menial service level, and had at least half of their share of jobs in 15 of the 27.

There were few professionals in either group, not surprisingly in the light of the educational qualifications generally required for such posts even in 1890, and the Irish were even more markedly underrepresented at this level than blacks.[19] Outside of the few learned professions, however, in the broad range of entrepreneurial and commercial occupations that provide critical leverage for aspiring groups, Negroes found many fewer opportunities than even first-generation Irish immigrants. There were 40 percent as many black merchants, dealers, and peddlers as chance would have had it, but 64 percent as many Irish in such callings (both figures are doubtless inflated by the inclusion of lowly peddlers). There were less than a twelfth of the "expected" number of Negro manufacturers, whereas the Irish had 46 percent of their share of such jobs. The Irish were likewise much more successful at finding posts as insurance and real-estate agents, commercial travelers, and salesmen. It was only in the white-collar occupation that probably offered least in terms of income and future prospects—routine clerical work—that blacks were at all close to parity with the Irish.

Probably the most significant feature of the economic plight of blacks in Boston, however, was their lack of access to blue-collar jobs above the most menial level. By 1890 the Irish immigrants had found their way into skilled trades in large numbers. They had won much more than their share of openings in two of the crafts—blacksmithing and masonry—and in only 3 of the 10 skilled trades were they underrepresented by as much as 50 percent. Blacks, by contrast, were underrepresented by 50 percent or more in 9 of the 10. The black index of representation in skilled jobs averaged only 22, as opposed to 80 for the Irish.

Similarly, the Irish found the factory doors open to them (except for the German-dominated tobacco industry) and moved into operative positions—not very glamorous or well paid but a distinct cut above unskilled and menial service jobs. Negroes, by contrast, were largely bypassed by the Industrial Revolution; only the small local shoe industry, which employed 23 Negroes in 1890, appears to have been at all receptive to black labor. Other semiskilled jobs in transportation and public service were likewise open to large numbers of Irish newcomers, but relatively inaccessible to blacks.

All of the evidence from the late nineteenth century thus points in the same direction. Black residents of the city were not simply located on the low end of the immigrant spectrum, in a situation broadly comparable to that of the Irish. Both groups were largely composed of relative newcomers to the city, newcomers whose formative years had been spent in an environment that left them ill prepared for life in the modern metropolis, but the differences in their subsequent experience in the city were far more important than the similarities.

Part of the difference was visible immediately. First-generation newcomers of both groups had little opportunity to escape the manual laboring class, but blacks were largely confined to four menial jobs at the very bottom of the blue-collar hierarchy, whereas the Irish solidly established themselves in semiskilled jobs in factories or transportation and were well represented in the skilled trades. And, though both groups had a white-collar elite of roughly comparable size, the Irish were stronger in job-generating entrepreneurial posts, whereas middle-class blacks were mostly either lone-wolf professionals or subordinate employees of others. These contrasts would have been even sharper had it been possible to separate Southern-born from Northern-born Negroes in this portion of the analysis and to compare Irish immigrants with the former.

Even larger differences appeared within the second generation. Although American-born youths of Irish background moved ahead more sluggishly than most of their second-generation rivals, they fared much better than their fathers had. The Northern-born son of a black migrant from the South, by contrast, had but a slight chance of ending up in a better job than his father. Indeed, *his* children—unless they were mulattoes—were no closer to arriving in the white-collar world than their grandparents.

STASIS—1900–1940

There was virtually no improvement in the occupational position of black men in Boston between the late nineteenth century and the beginning of World War II. In 1890, 56 percent of the black males employed in the city were unskilled day laborers, servants, waiters, janitors, or porters; three decades later the fraction was 54 percent, and in 1940 it was 53 percent. As of 1890, a mere 8 percent of Boston's blacks held white-collar jobs; half a century later the figure was only 11 percent.

There were some modest gains in black representation in particular callings during the period, but in 1940 Negroes remained heavily underrepresented in every single major occupation except the menial-labor and service tasks to which they had traditionally been confined (Table 8.8). At the opening of the century the Negro index of representation in such jobs stood at 347; on the eve of World War II it was actually a shade higher (365). By then there had been a considerable opening up of semiskilled operative posts but blacks still had less than two-thirds of their share of those jobs. In only one of the nine occupations in the "craftsmen, foremen, and kindred workers" category were there even half as many blacks as random distribution would have produced, although the index of representation had at least edged upward in seven out of the nine since 1900. Among the major lower white-collar callings, blacks remained radically underrepresented as bookkeepers and salesmen, but found somewhat greater opportunities to become clerks or agents. (The latter gain, however, was due entirely to the increase in the number of Negro real-estate agents, probably employed in black firms; only 6 of the city's 1541 insurance agents in 1940 were black, a tenth of the expected number.) Blacks were slightly better represented as wholesale merchants by 1940, but less well repre-

TABLE 8.8. Index of relative concentration of black males in selected occupations, 1900 and 1940[1]

Occupation	*1900*	*1940*
Unskilled and menial service	347	365
Semiskilled operative	24	63
Skilled		
Cabinetmaker	0	18
Carpenter	24	45
Foreman	20	17
Machinist	5	24
Mason	57	38
Painter	23	72
Plumber	13	24
Printer	23	26
Tailor	26	38
Low white-collar		
Agent	25	53
Bookkeeper	5	5
Clerk	30	47
Salesman	9	12
High white-collar		
Merchant, retail	21	18
Merchant, wholesale	21	28
Manager or official	8	25
Professional[2]	34	38

[1] Calculated from published volumes of 1900 and 1940 U.S. Census. Index as explained in Table 8.7, note 1.

[2] Architects, dentists, engineers, lawyers, and physicians only.

sented as retail traders. There were distinctly more black managers and officials than before, but still only a quarter as many as chance would dictate. In the learned professions there was only the tiniest of changes—the black index rose from 34 to 38.

The evidence for this period, regrettably, does not permit any analysis of differences between first-generation black migrants and long-term Northern residents, but it is extremely doubtful that the lack of economic progress of the city's Negroes in these years was any more attributable to the influx of Southern newcomers than it had been in the late nineteenth century. Had the migration of ill-prepared Southerners been the core of the problem, there should have been a marked improvement in the situation of Boston blacks in these decades, for the pace of Southern migration slowed considerably after the turn of the century. The proportion of Southern-born Negroes in the city fell from 53 percent in 1900 to 37 percent in 1930 (Table 8.3), and likely fell still more by 1940, given the very slow growth of the black population in the depression years and the rising rate of natural increase that occurred then. This substantial decline in the proportion of Southern migrants would have been accompanied by a distinct upward shift in the occupational distribution of the city's Negroes *if* the predominance of rural migrants had in fact been the prime source of the economic difficulties of the black community. But no such pronounced upward shift took place.

Nor did the occupational patterns of blacks and of European immigrants display any signs of converging during these years (Table 8.9). If the "last-of-the-immigrants" hypothesis had been accurate, Boston's Negroes should have ranked somewhat ahead of first-generation immigrants and somewhat behind second-generation newcomers, since the black group contained a mix of first-generation mi-

TABLE 8.9. Occupational distribution (percent) of blacks and first- and second-generation immigrants, 1890, 1910, and 1930[1]

		Occupational level		
Year	*Ethnicity*	*White-collar*	*Skilled*	*Low manual*
1890	First-generation immigrant	18	37	45
	Second-generation immigrant	32	34	34
	Blacks	8	11	81
1910	First-generation immigrant	24	33	43
	Second-generation immigrant	45	21	34
	Blacks	10	8	82
1930	First-generation immigrant	24	30	46
	Blacks	11	12	77

[1] Calculated from published census data; no information on the occupations of second-generation immigrants was given for 1930.

grants and settled men long familiar with city ways. Black men, furthermore, should have enjoyed a growing margin of advantage over European immigrants in this period, since the proportion of Southern migrants in the former group was declining substantially.

In fact, however, Negroes ranked far behind even the city's first-generation immigrants in 1890, 1910, and 1930 (no data on the occupational distribution of immigrants in 1940 are available). Less than half as many blacks as immigrants held middle-class jobs, and nearly twice as many were unskilled or semiskilled laborers. Second-generation immigrants were even further ahead of blacks in the occupational competition, with a middle-class element four times the size of the Negro middle class.

The inferences that can be drawn from these distributional data as to the barriers to black social mobility find further confirmation from some fragmentary information about the career patterns of Negroes and immigrants married in Boston in 1910 and still employed there in 1920. Twenty-one percent of the immigrants working in 1910 ($N = 538$) held white-collar jobs, but only 12 percent of the blacks ($N = 88$). After the passage of a decade, a third of the European newcomers still to be found in the city ($N = 171$) were in middle-class occupations. The black middle class, by contrast, grew not at all; it remained at a mere 12 percent of the group ($N = 22$). During these 10 years almost a fifth (19 percent) of the immigrant laborers who remained in the city moved up into the white-collar class; *not a single one* of the black manual workers in the sample made a comparable advance. Native-born Americans made their way into the white-collar world during the decade at a somewhat more rapid pace than immigrants—24 percent of them made this shift ($N = 235$)—but the glaring contrast, obviously, was not between immigrant and native but between black and white.

PROGRESS AT LAST

Three-quarters of a century after Emancipation, Boston's blacks were still at the bottom of the class ladder. As late as 1940 6 out of 7 of them worked in manual occupations; more than half were still confined to traditional "Negro jobs" as unskilled laborers, janitors, porters, servants, or waiters.

Between 1940 and 1970, however, a breakthrough occurred. The proportion of black men in these menial jobs fell from 53 percent in 1940 to 23 percent in 1960. Equally detailed tabulations of the occupational distribution of Negro males were not provided in the 1970 Census, but the figure was doubtless lower still. The overall concentration of blacks in unskilled laboring and service jobs, Table 8.10 discloses, dropped strikingly over the period, from almost two-thirds (65 percent) in 1940 to little more than one-quarter (27 percent) three decades later.

TABLE 8.10. Occupational distribution (percent) of black males, 1940–1970[1]

Occupation	*1940*	*1950*	*1960*	*1970*
Professional	5	4	7	11
Manager, proprietor or official	2	3	3	5
Clerical worker	5	6	9	11
Sales worker	2	2	2	3
Craftsman	9	13	15	17
Operative	12	23	31	25
Service worker	52	32	22	19
Laborer	13	17	11	8

[1] Calculated from published U. S. Census data. The 1940 figures are for Boston proper; subsequent ones are for the Boston metropolitan area.

One source of the dramatic decline in black employment in the most menial laboring and service tasks was the widening of opportunities to work as semiskilled operatives. On the eve of World War II, only 1 in 8 Negro males held such jobs. In the booming labor market of the 1940's that proportion nearly doubled, and it rose further in the 1950's, to almost 1 in 3, before dropping moderately to 1 in 4 by the close of the 1960's.

Most of the massive net shift upward of the black labor force after 1940, however, resulted from gains at higher occupational levels, in the skilled trades and the white-collar world. Less than a tenth of the Negro males employed in Boson at the close of the depression were skilled workers. The figure grew steadily over the next three decades, and by 1970 it stood at 1 in 6. Access to occupations at the white-collar level improved at an even more impressive pace over the period, but here progress was less even. Virtually no gains were made during the 1940's, but between 1950 and 1970 the proportion of blacks holding white-collar jobs doubled.

These were striking changes, certainly, but it is essential to ask how much they reflected overall changes in the Boston occupational structure during the period and thus left unaltered the relative position of blacks and whites. The precipitous decline in the proportion of Negroes employed in unskilled or service jobs, and the corresponding gains made by blacks at higher occupational levels, would obviously appear in a rather different light if whites working in the city experienced the same net upward shift in these years.

This, however, was not the case. In only one stratum above the unskilled and service level, the professions, were the gains revealed in Table 8.10 attributable only to overall shifts in the local occupational structure (Table 8.11). Although there was a dramatic increase in the proportion of blacks employed as professionals between 1940 and 1970—a rise from 5 percent to 11 percent—the proportion of professional workers in the entire Boston labor force nearly tripled during the same interval. Despite their advances in this area, blacks were thus actually slipping back relative to whites; their index of relative occupational concentration in the professions fell from 68 to 56.

This seeming decline, however, is somewhat misleading. In both 1940 and 1950 the two largest groups of black proeessionals were clergymen and musicians, callings that did not necessarily require extensive training and were generally ill paid. Some 39 percent of Negro professionals in 1940 and 32 percent in 1950 were in these marginal professions. During the 1950's the proportion dropped suddenly to a mere 11 percent, and there was at the same time a sharp rise in the number of black professionals with technical skills. The number of Negro engineers, designers, and draftsmen, for example, increased five times faster than the rate of increase in such jobs in the entire Boston labor force (273 percent vs. 56 percent.) Similarly detailed tabulations are not available in the 1970 census, regrettably, but it is likely that the further swelling of the black professional class that occurred in the 1960's entailed further advances on the technical front. If Negroes had a somewhat smaller share of professional jobs in 1970 than they did in 1940, they had at least as great and perhaps a greater share of posts in the most demanding and well-rewarded professions.

TABLE 8.11. Index of relative occupational concentration of blacks, 1940–1970[1]

Occupation	*1940*	*1950*	*1960*	*1970*
Professional[2]	68	38	47	56
Manager, proprietor or official	22	22	25	40
Clerical worker	44	67	90	107
Sales worker	18	19	21	40
Craftsman	46	60	70	93
Operative	63	117	169	177
Service worker	352	366	259	181
Laborer	166	237	187	159

[1] Indexes computed as in Tables 8.7 and 8.8. The figures for 1940–1960 differ in minor ways from the indexes for the same years given in Leon H. Mayhew, *Law and Equal Opportunity: A Study of the Massachusetts Commission Against Discrimination* (Cambridge, Mass.: Harvard University Press, 1968), because Mayhew has computed the ratio of black to white workers in each category rather than the ratio of black workers to all workers.

[2] The 1940 index for black professionals is higher than that given in Table 8.8, because this one includes all professionals, whereas that in Table 8.8 was calculated for persons in the traditional learned professions only so as to maximize comparability with the 1900 data. As noted in the text, the strong black showing in the professions in 1940 and the apparent decline thereafter is somewhat misleading in that it is attributable partly to the shrinking of the marginal professions of clergyman and musician. If these are excluded from the indexes, the 1940 and 1960 figures are a nearly identical 47 and 43.

At all levels of white-collar employment other than the professional, blacks were forging ahead and narrowing the gap between the races. Most impressive were the gains in clerical occupations. At the close of the depression Negroes had less than half of their share of clerical jobs; by 1970 they were actually overrepresented in such occupations by 7 percent. In the two other major white-collar strata —managers, proprietors, and officials, and sales workers—blacks remained greatly underrepresented even at the close of the 1960's, with only 40 percent as many jobs of this kind as would be expected if they were randomly distributed through the labor force. But if the racial gap in these two categories was still enormous, it had been cut in half during the period.

The pace of black advance relative to whites in higher-status blue-collar occupations was striking too. The shift of Negro males out of service occupations did not stem merely from the overall shrinking of those jobs in the labor force. That was indeed the cause of the great decline in black service employment during the World War II decade; in 1950 Negroes were even more overrepresented in service work relative to whites than they had been a decade earlier. But in the 1950's and 1960's they moved out of such jobs in greatly disproportionate numbers, and reduced their relative concentration by almost half. They nearly doubled their representation in the ranks of semiskilled operatives in the 1940's and won further gains in the 1950's. Most significant, they made steady inroads into the skilled crafts, and by 1970 had almost attained parity at that occupational level; during these years the index of Negro employment in skilled trades rose from 46 to 93.

Despite these undeniable gains, however, the occupational distribution of Negro males in Boston remained quite distinctive in 1970. Seven of ten black men, but slightly less than half of the white males of the city, were manual workmen of some kind. As compared with the entire Boston labor force, there was a black excess of 59 percent among unskilled laborers, 81 percent among service workers, and 77 percent among semiskilled operatives. And there was a corresponding black deficit of 44 percent among professionals and 60 percent among managerial and sales personnel.

What is more, the distinct narrowing of the racial gap in the various occupational strata that took place between 1940 and 1970 does not seem to have yielded a similar narrowing of the income gap between the races. Tabulations of black and white earnings are not available for 1940, but in 1950 the median income of employed Negro males was only 0.719 of the white median. Despite the thrust of blacks into the higher occupational categories during the next decade, their median earnings relative to whites actually fell significantly, to 0.662. It is true that this disconcerting pattern of occupational advance but income retreat did not continue into the 1960's —both the occupational distribution and the median earnings of Negroes as compared with whites improved between 1960 and 1970—but the income gains achieved then were only large enough to make up for the losses of the 1950's. In 1970 as in 1950 Negro males in Boston earned less than three-quarters of what their white counterparts earned.[20]

The explanation of this seeming paradox—abrupt occupational upgrading for Negroes but virtually unchanged relative income position—lies in the fact that the upward occupational movement of blacks in these years was movement into precisely those occupational categories in which the racial gap in income was widest. The median earnings of Negro unskilled laborers in 1970 were 95 percent of the median for all persons working in such jobs. But with each step up the occupational ladder the relative income of blacks was less and less favorable. Negro operatives earned only 85 percent of the city median for such work, skilled craftsmen 75 percent, professionals and managers a mere 66 percent.[21] So sharp were the disparities in the relative earnings of blacks and whites at the higher occupational levels that attaining complete racial equality in distribution between these broad occupational categories without narrowing the racial gap in income within each category would do very little to shrink the overall income gap between the races. A trial calculation assuming 1970 earnings differentials within the major occupational strata and equal distribution of blacks and whites throughout the occupational structure indicates that under these hypothetical conditions the median earnings of Negro males would be 0.770 of the median for the entire Boston labor force, certainly not a dramatic improvement over the 0.720 figure that actually held in 1970.[22]

This is not, of course, to say that the large-scale movement of blacks up the occupational scale between 1940 and 1970 did not represent a significant advance. Negro professionals, managers, and proprietors, after all, earned almost two-thirds (63 percent) more than black unskilled laborers in 1970, Negro craftsmen an average of one-third (34 percent) more, black operatives 27 percent more. Each step up the occupational ladder meant very real gains in income, as well as in job security, working conditions, and the like. But it is noteworthy that the impressive occupational upgrading of blacks relative to whites in these three decades was apparently accomplished largely via entry into the least well-paid jobs in the higher categories. Whatever the gains for the individuals involved, these shifts did not perceptibly alter the overall income position of Boston blacks in comparison with whites.[23] It thus will take something more than a simple continuation of the patterns of black occupational mobility that have been operating in recent decades to bring about greater racial equality in the distribution of income.

THE SOURCES OF INEQUALITY

What accounts for the overwhelming concentration of Negro males in the most menial and ill-paid occupations from the late nineteenth century down through the Great Depression, and the persistence of substantial economic inequality between the races even after the major advances made between 1940 and 1970? The evidence at hand, though far from adequate to yield definitive answers, does permit an evaluation of some of the chief explanations that might be offered.

1. *Rural-Background Handicaps.* The claim that the fundamental source of the black man's economic difficulties has been the continued influx into the city of masses of ill-prepared Negroes of Southern rural origins has found little support here. It is indeed true that Southern migrants, most of them from rural backgrounds, have comprised a substantial fraction of the Boston population throughout the past century, and it is undeniable that many of these newcomers arrived without the training and skills needed for most jobs at the skilled or white-collar level.

But the preceding analysis has offered two grounds for insisting that this was by no means a sufficient explanation of the dismal economic position of blacks in Boston. One is that a series of comparisons between Negroes and various European immigrant groups of predominantly rural origin have revealed clear contrasts in occupational status, with blacks far to the rear of any of the immigrants. Even the least successful of the immigrant groups, like the Irish, moved into a much wider range of occupations than did blacks.

A second means of critically examining the hypothesis that the rural origins of so many blacks constituted the prime obstacle to the occupational advance of the group was to compare the situations of Northern-born and Southern-born Negroes in Boston. The requisite data were available only for 1880 and 1900, but for that period at least the results were clear-cut. Those blacks who had lived all their lives in the North, and who presumably experienced "long and close contact with modern culture," were in almost precisely the same miserable economic position as the rawest black migrants from the South.

For these reasons, it would seem that this line of explanation can be flatly ruled out. It is not implausible, certainly, but the empirical data simply do not support it.

2. *Education.* Another possible explanation focuses on the alleged educational deficiencies of the black urban population. This point is sometimes raised as part of the rural-background hypothesis, since children growing up in rural areas tend to have less access to educational facilities than their urban counterparts. But a related and complementary argument would be that urban blacks drop out of school earlier than whites and consequently enter the labor market with inferior qualifications. The evidence indicates, however, that although the relatively low educational level of the black population of Boston has impeded their occupational advance, the educational gap between Negroes and other groups in the city has not been great enough to account for more than a fraction of the disabilities of blacks in the economic competition.

The pertinent data are supplied in Table 8.12. The first section of the table indicates the proportions of immigrants, second-generation Americans, Yankees, and blacks aged 10–14 and 15–20 who were attending school in Boston in 1900. At the turn of the century Negroes were only half as likely as Yankee whites to continue their education past the age of 14, and it is tempting to identify this as a prime cause of the extremely constricted occupational opportunities these young blacks were to find in the course of their careers. The availability of comparable evidence about first- and second-generation immigrants in the city, however, provides two control groups for evaluating the assumption that a genuine causal relation was involved. That assumption appears dubious. Negroes in Boston in 1900 were receiving substantially more education than European immigrants, and they were to fare far less well in the later occupational competition. In 1910, for example, there were two and a half times as many immigrants as blacks holding white-collar jobs (24 percent vs. 10 percent) and four times as many in skilled posts (33 percent vs. 8 percent), and the differential was still almost as sharp another two decades later (Table 8.9). A comparison between blacks and second-generation immigrants further indicates the weakness of education as an explanation of the economic condition of blacks. In 1900 Negroes in Boston were attending school in about the same proportion as native-born children of immigrant parentage, but fully two-thirds of the second-generation group were able to enter skilled or white-collar jobs later and less than a fifth of the blacks (Table 8.9).

TABLE 8.12. Educational attainments of blacks and other groups, 1900–1970[1]

I. Percent attending school, 1900

Age	*Immigrant*	*Second generation*	*Yankee*	*Black*
10–14	80	92	94	89
15–20	7	23	39	20

II. School years completed (percent), 1940

School years	*Immigrant*	*Native white*	*Black*
6 or less	41	6	26
7–8	36	31	39
9–11	9	21	15
12 or more	13	42	20
Median years	7.5	10.8	8.5

III. School years completed and occupational level (percent) 1950

	Irish	*Italian*	*French Canadian*	*Black*
Median school years	8.4	6.1	8.5	9.5
Occupational level				
White-collar	19	19	20	15
Skilled	21	25	39	13
Low manual	60	56	41	72

IV. Median school years of blacks relative to total population, 1940–1970

Year	*Total population*	*Blacks*	*Black median as percent of city median*
1940	8.9	8.3	93
1950	11.8	9.5	81
1960	12.1	10.5	87
1970	12.4	11.6	94

[1] The 1900 figures are census data, as given in Massachusetts Bureau of the Statistics of Labor, *34th Annual Report,* p. 273. All other data are from the respective *Population* volumes of the U. S. Census.

The evidence for 1900 is seriously limited in one respect. It pertains only to education received in Boston, and reveals nothing about the schooling that migrants may have had before they arrived in the city. It is conceivable, though not very likely, that the typical European immigrant had an advantage over the typical black rural migrant in that respect and that this accounted for his superior occupational success. It is fortunate that similar data for 1940 do not share this limitation. They indicate group differences in years of school completed, whether in Boston, Mississippi, Ireland, or some combination thereof. (It is, of course, possible that these and other figures on school years completed given in Table 8.12 conceal important *qualitative* differences in education received. Eight years of schooling in Boston may have meant something quite different from 8 years of schooling in Mississippi. This caution must be borne in mind in interpreting educational data for blacks and native whites, but it probably does not substantially affect the validity of comparisons between Negroes and immigrants, in that the schools of Ireland or Italy were likely not the equivalent of Boston schools either.)

The group differences in educational attainments visible in 1940 again suggest that something more than their lack of education was driving the majority of Boston's blacks into menial unskilled or service jobs. That the Negro population of the city then had 2.3 fewer median years of schooling than native whites would seem, on the face of it, an important source of the occupational disparities between the two groups. But a comparison between blacks and immigrants once more calls into question the explanatory power of education. Even though Negroes had a full year more of schooling, on the average, than foreign-born whites, they were much more heavily concentrated at the bottom of the occupational structure.[24]

The data for 1950 offer a comparison not between blacks and immigrants in general, but between Negroes and three of the lowest-ranking of Boston's first-generation groups—the Irish, the Italians, and the French Canadians. Blacks were substantially better educated than all three, with a year more of education than the Irish and French Canadians, and no less than 2.4 years more than the Italians. But this advantage did not yield a comparable occupational advantage for blacks. On the contrary, Negroes had lower occupational status than each. The Negro white-collar class was smaller than that of immigrant groups with less schooling. More important, the proportion of skilled craftsmen among blacks was only a third as high as among French Canadians, half as high as among Italians, and about 60 percent of the Irish figure.

A final item pointing in the same direction, against the hypothesis that their lack of education was the prime source of the economic inequality of blacks, is the set of figures comparing the median education of Negroes and of the total population of Boston from 1940 to 1970. At the close of the Great Depression, when blacks were far more strongly clustered in traditional "Negro jobs" than they were to be later, they were nearly as well educated as the average resident of the city; median school years completed for blacks stood at 8.3, some 93 percent of the median for the total population, and yet blacks were radically underrepresented at all occupational levels except unskilled labor and service work. Opportunities began to open up significantly in the 1940's, particularly in the clerical, skilled, and operative categories, but this did not come about as a result of advances made on the educational front. During the decade the median schooling of the Boston population as a whole increased by nearly 2 years, while the black figure rose by only 1.2 years, which reduced the black median from 93 to only 81 percent of the city-wide median.

It is true that the impressive occupational progress made by Boston Negroes since 1950 has gone hand in hand with a narrowing of the educational gap between the races, and may have stemmed in part from those educational advances. Rising educational levels for blacks were no doubt necessary conditions for some of the gains won in those years. The growth of the black professional class, which nearly tripled between 1950 and 1970, could hardly have taken place without a sharp increase in the stock of college-educated Negroes; the dramatic rise in the proportion of black clerical workers might not have taken place without a substantial rise in the percentage of blacks graduating from high school.

If a necessary cause, though, these educational advances were far from a sufficient cause of the occupational breakthroughs made by Negroes in recent years, for the educational gap between the races did not narrow over the 1940–1970 period as a whole. In 1970 the black median for years of school completed relative to the city median stood almost precisely where it stood 30 years before—at 93 percent in 1940 and 94 percent in 1970—and yet the distribution of Negroes throughout the occupational structure had become far more favorable.

It would be foolish to deny that further occupational progress for blacks will require, among other things, further gains in educational attainments. Although blacks ranked only a little behind the city-wide median in school years completed in 1970, these median figures conceal very substantial inequality at the higher educational levels. Only 17 percent of black males aged 25 or more had some college training, but almost twice as high a proportion (31 percent) of the total population; 20 percent of the residents of Boston but only a third as many blacks (7 percent) were college graduates. This was obviously an important barrier limiting the entry of Negroes into the professions and into many posts in bureaucratic hierarchies in both the private and the public sectors of the economy.

True as this is, the main point suggested by the historical record is that education, that cherished American panacea for so many social problems, has been a tool of distinctly limited use for aspiring blacks. The economic status of Negroes in Boston from the late nineteenth century down to 1940 was much too low to be explained as the result of their educational deficiencies; the progress made by blacks in the three decades since then was not the result of the educational gains they made in those years.

3. *The Ghetto.* The residential clustering of Negroes in certain areas of the city and their exclusion from others, it can be argued, has seriously limited the economic opportunities open to them. Residential segregation, it has been suggested, promotes occupational segregation as well.[25]

It was shown in Chapter 7 that this hypothesis is of little utility in explaining the differential occupational achievements of Boston's immigrants during the past century. There was virtually no relation at all between the extent of residential segregation and the occupational status of such groups as the Irish, Italians, English, and Jews.

A comparison of blacks with immigrants on this count only reinforces that conclusion. True, in 1950 Negroes were both far more heavily concentrated in ghettos than other ethnic groups in Boston, and also much more strongly clustered at the bottom of the occupational ladder (Table 8.13.) But there could hardly have been a causal connection between these two facts, because the next most ghettoized element of the population was the largely Jewish Russian-born immigrant group, who were actually better represented in white-collar callings then than even old-stock Yankees (Tables 6.5 and 6.14). The Irish, by contrast, who ranked barely ahead of blacks occupationally, were among the least segregated of all groups residentially. It should also be noted that the Russian Jews in 1880 and the Italians in both 1880 and 1910 were less evenly distributed through the neighborhoods of the city than Negroes but were distinctly better off economically. A further challenge to the ghetto hypothesis posed by this evidence is that the degree to which blacks were residentially segregated in Boston rose substantially over this period—the segregation index increased from 51 in 1880 to 84 in 1960—without producing any corresponding decline in their occupational status. The major advances made by blacks in the occupational sphere during the 1940's and 1950's, furthermore, were not accompanied by declining segregation; the index stood at 86 in 1940 and only an insignificant two points lower in 1960.

TABLE 8.13. Residential segregation indexes for blacks and selected first-generation immigrant groups, 1880–1960[1]

Group	*1880*	*1910*	*1930*	*1940*	*1950*	*1960*
Black	51	64	78	86	80	84
English	13	11	15	n.a.	19	n.a.
Irish	15	19	26	n.a.	24	n.a.
Swedish	27	23	32	n.a.	31	n.a.
German	31	31	35	n.a.	31	n.a.
Russian	55	48	65	n.a.	65	n.a.
Italian	74	66	54	n.a.	48	n.a.

[1] The figures for 1880, 1910, 1930, and 1950 were computed by Stanley Lieberson, for his *Ethnic Patterns in American Cities* (Glencoe, Ill.: Free Press, 1963), p. 206. The 1940 and 1960 indexes for blacks are from Karl and Alma Taeuber, *Negroes in Cities* (Chicago, Aldine, 1965), p. 39. These indexes indicate the percentage of the group in question that would have to have shifted into another area of the city to have been distributed identically to the native-born white population. The 1880 and 1910 figures were computed on a ward basis, the 1930 and 1950 ones from census tracts, and the 1940 and 1960 ones from block data. The finer the unit employed in such analyses, generally, the greater the segregation that will be found; one cannot, therefore, infer much about long-term trends from these indexes. But they do accurately measure the relative segregation of different groups at each point in time.

None of this, it need hardly be said, is intended to minimize the evil of the circumstances that have confined so many of Boston's blacks to ghetto areas in the past century. That certain European immigrant groups at various times in the past have been highly segregated too does not necessarily mean that the same causal mechanisms were responsible. Not enough is yet known about the influences that led many immigrants to huddle together in segregated neighborhoods, but it is clear that not only external hostility but internal factors—a preference for living with others of one's own kind, the prevalence of chain migration patterns, and the like—were involved. In the case of blacks it seems that external hostility played a far more important role, as is suggested by the well-known phenomenon of the "color tax," the fact that Negroes pay substantially higher rents than whites for housing of comparable quality.[26] Immigrants seem to have participated in the same housing market as other whites; most blacks have had to make housing choices in a quite separate market. With respect to residential as well as occupational opportunities the "last-of-the-immigrants" theory appears deficient. The point at issue here, however, is only whether the residential segregation of Negroes was a significant cause of their economic disabilities, and the answer to that question seems to be no.

4. *Family Patterns.* The hypothesis that blacks may have been economically impeded by the excessive size of the typical Negro family, and the limitations that imposed upon the capacity to provide education and capital backing for children, has little to be said for it. The relevant evidence is extremely scanty, but it is highly unlikely that black families in Boston have been unusually large relative to other groups. The murderously high death rates for blacks, particularly for black infants, that prevailed until the early twentieth century constituted a powerful restrictive influence on family size. As late as 1900, nearly a third (32 percent) of the Negro children born in the city died before they reached the age of 1, but only 19 percent of white infants.[27] This became a less significant check later, because both the general level of infant mortality and the racial differential in mortality declined, but racial differences in fertility were not large enough to make the typical black family in Boston much larger than its white counterpart. As of 1960, the

number of children ever born to Negro women aged 35 to 44 was only 2.35, a lower figure than for all women in that age bracket in the city (2.58.) By 1970 black women were somewhat more fertile than the average woman in the city, with 3.41 children ever born as opposed to 3.16 for the total population, but the difference was far too small to explain the enormous racial gap in economic status.[28]

It could be, though, that Negroes who migrated to Boston from the rural South typically came from very large families, and that this was a major source of the difficulties they encountered in the city. No direct evidence bearing on this question is available, but there are three reasons for doubting that this possibility has much explanatory utility. First, Northern-born blacks, whose families were not notably larger than the city norm, seem to have fared little better economically than Southern-born migrants. Second, it is unlikely—though precise data are lacking—that the families in which European immigrants were typically reared were notably smaller than the black rural family, and yet the contrast between Negroes and immigrants in occupational achievement was sharp. Finally, one of the chief ways in which being reared in a large family is thought to impede economic success is in limiting access to education. But blacks, it has already been shown, had substantially more schooling than the immigrants who outranked them occupationally.

A quite different argument about the crippling effect of a supposedly distinctive feature of the black family has attracted much attention recently—the claim that the Negro family is "disorganized." The prevalance of black households with only one parent present, and particularly of female-headed households, it has been suggested, has negatively affected the development of black children and impaired their ability to perform successfully in later life.[29]

Evidence that, at least at first glance, seems to support this view was provided in the 1970 Census. Barely half (50.3 percent) of the Negro children under 18 in Boston were living with both of their parents, but fully 7 out of 8 (87.9 percent) white children, a radical contrast indeed. Since it has been established that "a background of living in a broken family . . . has some adverse effect upon educational attainment," and that this "educational handicap is, in turn, translated into poorer than average occupational achievement," it may seem that the disorganization of the black family has indeed been a key source of the economic inequality of Negroes in Boston during the past century.[30]

Such a conclusion, however, would be too hasty. It is essential to demonstrate not only that the average black family was more often broken than the average white family, but that Negro families were substantially less stable than white families *of similar economic status*. No analysis of racial differences in family patterns controlled for income or occupation has yet been made with 1970 data, but 1960 evidence reveals that broken families were common among poor people in general, and that the apparently greater stability of the average white family was largely the result of its superior economic status; racial differences were negligible among whites and blacks at the same income level.[31] Since whites had "a background of living in a broken family" about as frequently as Negroes from families of comparable economic status and yet were generally more successful in their subsequent careers, the disorganization of the black family cannot have had the profound causal significance that has been attributed to it.

This is evidence from the very recent past, and too much should not be made of it. It could be argued that even if economic level rather than race was the prime determinant of family stability in post-World War II America, there may have been a genuine racial difference independent of economic status in the late nineteenth and early twentieth centuries. It has long been assumed that slavery prevented most blacks from establishing stable families before 1865, and it has been suggested that the appalling conditions of life in black urban slums thereafter had a similarly destructive impact upon the family.[32]

Recent historical investigations indicate, rather surprisingly, that this view is quite erroneous. A pioneering study by Herbert G. Gutman discloses that even under slavery there was remarkable strength and vitality in the family life of blacks, and that in a wide sampling of Northern and Southern cities from Reconstruction down to the early years of this century the Negro family displayed impressive stability.[33] Some evidence pertaining specifically to Boston points in the same direction. Elizabeth Pleck has discovered that in 1880 some 82 percent of the black households in Boston had both husband and wife present, and only 16 percent were female-headed.[34]

This finding may be set against the results of Tamara Hareven's wider inquiry into Boston family patterns at the same time.[35] Some 18 percent of the households in South Boston in 1880, 22 percent of those in the Back Bay, and 19 percent of those in Dorchester were female-headed. Among the Irish living in the South End, the figure was an even higher 27 percent. Although Negroes ranked below every other group in the city on any measure of economic status, their families were strikingly stable in comparison with other elements of the population. The highly constricted economic opportunities that black children growing up then found when they entered the labor market later therefore could not have been the result of the scarcity of stable two-parent families in the black community.

These crude statistical indicators do not, of course, necessarily establish that the black family *functioned* as effectively as white families at the same class level. Some ingenious future investigator may devise some way of exploring that issue. What can be subjected to empirical testing at this time is the simple claim that the distinctive concentration of Negroes on the lowest rungs of the class ladder during the past century has followed inexorably from the distinctive instability of the Negro family and the "tangle of pathology" associated with it. That hypothesis appears to be false.

5. *Discrimination and the Nature of Black Culture.* We remain far from having a sufficient explanation of the observed facts, it seems, and only two further possibilities come to mind. Blacks in Boston must have been held back either by something in their own culture that limited their desire or capacity to compete in the marketplace, or by discrimination directed against them by others.

I suggested in the previous chapter that at least part of the reason for the differential economic success of Boston's ethnic and religious groups was indeed differences in group culture. Elusive as this factor is, the other variables that could have been responsible for the patterns that were found did not appear sufficient to explain them. It seemed necessary to introduce group culture as a kind of residual factor to account for the variations that could not otherwise be explained.

Studies of the economic problems of blacks often employ a residual argument of a quite different sort. Residual differences between the races that remain after such variables as education, urban-rural background, and the like are controlled for are attributed not to the cultural characteristics of the Negro population but to the discriminatory treatment to which they presumably were subjected.[36] This is not an assumption that can be put forward as a self-evident truth. Did the confinement of Boston's black workers to the lower rungs of the occupational ladder stem entirely from prejudice directed against them *in Boston?* Could it be that the long and bleak historical experience of Negroes in the United States, an experience of more ruthless subordination than that, say, of the Irish peasantry, produced an enduring black lower-class culture that rendered the average Negro objectively less qualified for economic pursuits than the average white? If it is admitted that the nature of Irish culture and Jewish culture had something to do with the different occupational trajectories followed by these two groups, how can we dismiss differences between black culture and white culture as an explanation of the economic differences between the races? It could be said, of course, that such a black culture—if it did indeed exist—was ultimately the product of white racism, an inevitable adaptation to centuries of oppression. But there remains at least a question how and where white racism took its toll. Was the heart of the problem quite simply the persistence of discriminatory practices in a supposedly enlightened Northern city, or was there a lag between possibility and performance that was caused by a cultural heritage that limited the ability of blacks to seize opportunities that actually lay open to them?

The evidence at my command will not permit a thorough and dispassionate assessment of the validity of these alternative explanations; I could not attempt the immense task of surveying the records that might contain clues about the extent of discrimination and the nature of black culture in the past. But it seems plain to me that down to World War II discrimination, both active and structural, was far more important than any distinctive feature of black culture, and that even after that some important sectors of the economy remained relatively closed to well-qualified Negroes. It would not be surprising if the bitter experience of generation after generation of blacks in this country has left a cultural memory, a defeatist complex, that could endure after the oppressive conditions that originally generated it have vanished. But those conditions remained so unfavorable until quite recently that we need not posit a defeatist complex among blacks to explain their economic failures. Even if it had existed, it could not have mattered very much in the circumstances.

Perhaps the most unambiguous expression of prejudice against blacks in the economic sphere was their exclusion from most semi-skilled jobs in manufacturing and transportation down to about 1940. These occupations were no more demanding, though distinctly better paid, than the "Negro jobs" blacks were holding down successfully, and it is hard to believe that it was anything but their race that prevented Negroes from entering them in large numbers. The tight labor market of the World War II years and the waning of historic prejudices in the society at large that began about the same time effected a dramatic change at this level, so that by 1950 blacks were overrepresented by 17 percent in operative positions. Both the extreme degree of exclusion that prevailed before the war and the rapidity of the change that occurred thereafter point toward discrimination as the key factor involved. The culture of urban blacks before 1940 cannot have been so radically deviant as to render so few Negroes capable of performing adequately as operatives, and if we do assume that it was indeed that different we will be hard pressed to explain how such a deviant culture could have been modified so suddenly, in the span of but a decade.

The skilled trades remained relatively closed to blacks until even later; even in 1970 blacks had not quite attained parity at that level. Direct discrimination against Negro artisans by employers and unions was doubtless partly responsible. Structural discrimination that kept blacks out of the social networks that governed access to apprenticeship programs, union membership, and job openings was certainly important as well. Perhaps, too, the absence of an artisan tradition in black culture kept young Negroes from an awareness of the possibilities there. That absence, however, was not a permanent feature of black culture; there had been a flourishing artisan tradition among both slaves and free blacks before the Civil War, but Negroes were deliberately and systematically excluded from the skilled trades shortly after the war.[37] It may be, though, that expectations about the barriers to black entry into the crafts that were quite realistic in the late nineteenth century were transmitted to subsequent generations of Negro youths and blinded them to opportunities that were in fact open. The cultural argument may have some measure of validity in this instance. But it is hard to believe that it provides anything like a sufficient explanation of the pattern of exclusion that prevailed for so long.

There was substantial discrimination against Negroes in the white-collar world as well. The most glaring manifestation was in sales positions, where even in 1970 blacks had only 40 percent of their share of available jobs. The contrast with clerical occupations, in which Negroes were actually overrepresented by 1970, is revealing. Since educational and skill requirements for jobs in these two spheres were much the same, and since it cannot reasonably be argued that black culture was somehow more successful at producing satisfactory clerks than adequate salesman, the explanation must surely lie in the aversion of employers to placing blacks in jobs that involved extensive contact with the general public. Whether that aversion stemmed from invidious racial stereotypes in the minds of employers, or from accurate perceptions on their part of the prejudices of the public, the result was the same.

It was only in the 1950's and 1960's that clerical jobs became available to large numbers of Negroes. Again it seems likely that the source of this dramatic change was not a seismic shift in the nature of black culture that improved the personal qualities of black job aspirants but rather a shift in employers' attitudes about the appropriateness of allowing Negroes in positions at that level.

In the professions, by contrast, discrimination does not appear to have been the key factor at work. Though severely underrepresented in professional callings, blacks fared about as well as could be expected given their educational attainments, as well, for instance, as European immigrant groups with an equally small class of highly educated persons. In 1970 Negroes actually held more professional posts than their education would seem to justify. Their index of representation in the professions was 56; a similar index indicating how many blacks had completed at least 4 years of college was only 36, a fact that doubtless helped to account for the concentration of Negroes in the least well-paid professions and the consequent earning gap between black and white professionals. The paucity of Negro college graduates I would attribute not to something intrinsic to black culture but to the greater incidence of poverty among Negroes and a variety of other inequities in American social arrangements. But if discrimination was the ultimate cause that restricted black access to the professions, it operated not directly in the labor market but indirectly, by inhibiting educational attainments.

In the other major white-collar occupational category—"managers, proprietors, and officials"—blacks have been about as conspicuous for their absence as they have been in sales work. As late as 1960 they held barely a quarter of their share of such posts, and even in 1970 the index stood at only 40. Among salaried managers and officials, the largest subgroup within the category, Negroes have been still more drastically underrepresented. In 1950 and 1960, the only recent years for which detailed tabulations are available, the black index for such jobs was a mere 15. Given the educational requirements for managerial positions in bureaucratic hierarchies, one could hardly expect Negroes to have attained parity at this level, but it is certainly hard to believe that the distinctiveness of a hypothesized deviant black culture could be so great as to account for disparities of so striking a magnitude. More likely is the simple explanation, offered in 1968 by a careful observer of race relations in Boston, that Negroes "still face considerable discrimination," particularly in the competition for posts that would give them authority over white employees.[38]

A more complicated explanation, however, is probably required to understand the scarcity of self-employed black businessmen. Certainly it is hard to explain the very sharp differences between various European immigrant groups on this count—between the Jews and the Irish, for example—except in terms of differential cultural inclinations about entrepreneurial activity. And it is striking that Negroes have been even less prone to mount business ventures of their own than even the least entrepreneurially oriented of the immigrants. Clearly blacks encountered more discriminatory treatment than European newcomers, but was a cultural pattern—an emphasis on consumption rather than saving, and an aversion to risk-taking investment—also involved?

I suspect that it was. A variety of observers with divergent ideological stances, from Booker T. Washington and W. E. B. DuBois down to Malcolm X and the Black Muslims, have described American black culture in these terms, and the other explanations that have been suggested for the weakness of black business do not seem sufficient. The simple claim that Negroes "lacked the capital" to launch business enterprises does not take us very far, for few of the immigrants who came to Boston in the late nineteenth and early twentieth centuries brought significant amounts of capital with them. The point is that many of them *accumulated* the capital to become business proprietors, and blacks did not. Detailed studies of possible discrimination in the granting of commercial credit have yet to be made, but I doubt that this was important; Irish grocers probably received no more help from Brahmin bankers than did black grocers.

It may be, though, that the market open to Negro entrepreneurs was severely circumscribed by prejudice. It could be that white consumers who would patronize an Irish, Italian, or Jewish business without a qualm balked at dealing with a black businessman. If black enterprises were more heavily dependent upon black consumers than Irish businesses were upon Irish consumers, that and the greater poverty of Negroes in the city would have seriously limited the development of black business. But it has yet to be demonstrated that this was indeed the case, and until it has been the cultural argument would seem to have some force here.

In any event, in virtually every other area of the economy it appears that the main barriers to black achievement have been not internal but external, the result not of peculiarities in black culture but of peculiarities in white culture. For three-quarters of a century following Emancipation there was a pervasive belief in Negro inferiority that fostered overt racial discrimination in many industries, and left most blacks with little choice but to accept traditional "Negro jobs." Within the past generation there has been a marked softening of these historic prejudices, and this has allowed Negroes to make unprecedented economic gains. Some pockets of active discrimination still remain, and there are alarming signs of growing white ethnic backlash in some areas, but it is likely that the main factor that will impede black economic progress in the future will be the forces of inertia that have been called passive or structural discrimination, and that whatever may be distinctive about black culture will play some role too. By now, that is American Negroes may face opportunities and constraints that are fairly analogous to those experienced by the millions of European migrants who struggled to survive in the American city of the late nineteenth and early twentieth centuries. But until very recently, it seems clear, the problems of black men in a white society were different in kind from those of earlier newcomers. We can only hope that the cruel experience of the past will not leave scars visible long into the future.

chapter nine THE BOSTON CASE AND THE AMERICAN PATTERN

This book deals with a particular community, but it seeks to reveal something not only about that community but about the larger social order of which it was a part. Each city has some distinctive features, to be sure—a shape, a texture, a tradition all its own. Having myself recently lived in both one of America's oldest cities—Boston—and in one of its newest and most dynamic—Los Angeles—I am acutely conscious of this. These differences have preoccupied many previous scholars, who believe that "however much the historian talks of common urban problems, he will find that his most interesting task is to show in what respects cities differed from each other." [1]

I have found my most interesting task, however, to be quite the opposite—to show that the patterns of mobility that existed in Boston were not peculiar to that city, but rather were products of forces that operated in much the same way throughout American society in the nineteenth and twentieth centuries. Boston had many special attributes, but with respect to those features of its social life that have been examined in this study the city was "a fraction of the civilized world," just as its harbor was "part of the ocean." In both, as Oliver Wendell Holmes saw, there operated "general laws . . . modified more or less in their aspects by local influences." [2] These "general laws" or societal patterns may be discerned from a comparison of the chief findings of this study with the results of similar investigations conducted in other American communities.

PATTERNS OF PERSISTENCE

The population of Boston in the late nineteenth and early twentieth centuries was remarkably fluid. Although conventional methods of calculating net migration yielded results that suggested the city's population was changing very sluggishly, new techniques for estimating gross flows into and out of the community indicated that the contrary was the case. Thus the actual volume of movement into Boston during the 1880's was approximately *twelve* times larger than estimated net in-migration, because huge numbers of people were leaving the city at the same time that huge numbers of others were entering it. Another investigation employing similar methods has shown that much the same generalization can be made about the population of antebellum Boston. Actual in-migration into the city exceeded net in-migration by six times in the 1840's and by eleven times in the 1850's.[3]

Historians have not yet subjected other American communities to similarly close demographic scrutiny, but there are strong indications that Boston was not a deviant case. Although other detailed studies of in- and out-migration flows on an annual basis have not been made, one crude indicator of levels of population turnover—decadal rates of persistence for adult males—is available for some twelve American cities at various points in time between 1800 and the present (Table 9.1).

The persistence rate for Boston for 1880–1890, a decade of dizzying population turnover, was 64 percent. Something over a third of the males living there in 1880 had disappeared before a decade had elapsed; the volume of in-migration during these 10 years, therefore, had to exceed this very large outflow for there to be any *net* inflow at all. If this persistence rate—64 percent—had been unusually low, it would follow that the Boston findings could not be generalized to other communities.

In fact, however, the Boston persistence rate for 1880–1890 was not unusually low. It was actually the *highest* rate of the 31 given in Table 9.1. In all 30 of the remaining cases the urban population

TABLE 9.1. Persistence rates in selected urban communities, 1800–1968 (percent of residents still in community at end of decade)[1]

Decade	*Community*	*Percent*
1800–1810	Salem, Mass.	52
1830–1840	Boston	44
	Philadelphia	30
	Waltham, Mass.	54
1840–1850	Boston	39
	Philadelphia	38
	Waltham	56
1850–1860	Boston	39
	Philadelphia	32
	Waltham	44
	Northampton, Mass.	53
1860–1870	Waltham	45
	Poughkeepsie	49
1870–1880	Waltham	50
	Poughkeepsie	50
	Atlanta	44
	San Antonio, Texas	32
	San Francisco	48
1880–1890	Boston	64
	Waltham	58
	Omaha	44
	Los Angeles	54
	San Francisco	50
1900–1910	Omaha	44
1910–1920	Boston	41
	Los Angeles	49
	Norristown, Pa.	59
1930–1940	Boston	59
	Norristown	50
1940–1950	Norristown	53
1958–1968	Boston	46

[1] Salem and Northampton data are from Robert Doherty, "Industrialization and Social Change: A Comparative Study of Five Massachusetts Communities," unpublished manuscript in progress; Waltham, from Howard Gitleman, "Men in Motion: Mobility in the Urban and Industrial Development of Waltham, Massachusetts," unpublished manuscript in progress; Boston 1830–1860 from Peter R. Knights, "Population Turnover, Persistence and Residential Mobility in Boston, 1830–1860," in Stephan Thernstrom and Richard Sennett, eds., *Nineteenth-Century Cities: Essays in the New Urban History* (New Haven, Conn.: Yale University Press, 1969), pp. 257–274; Philadelphia, from Stuart M. Blumin, "Mobility in a Nineteenth-Century American City: Philadelphia, 1820–1860," unpublished dissertation, University of Pennsylvania, 1968; Poughkeepsie, advance tabulations from Poughkeepsie Mobility Study kindly made available by Clyde Griffen; Atlanta, computed from Richard Hopkins, "Occupational and Geographic Mobility in Atlanta, 1879–90," *Journal of Southern History*, 34 (1968), 200–213; San Antonio, computed from Alwyn Barr, "Occupational and Geographic Mobility in San Antonio, 1870–1900," *Social Science Quarterly*, 51 (1970), 396–403; San Francisco, from an unpublished study in progress by Allen Emrich; Omaha (for 1880–1891 and 1900–1911), from Howard Chudacoff, *Mobile Americans: Residential and Social Mobility in Omaha, 1880–1920* (New York: Oxford University Press, 1972); Los Angeles, 1880–1890, from Charles Slosser, "Mobility in Late-Nineteenth Century Los Angeles," unpublished seminar paper, U.C.L.A., 1970; Los Angeles, 1910–1920, from Michael Hanson, "Occupational Mobility and Persistence in Los Angeles, 1910–1930," unpublished seminar paper, U.C.L.A., 1970; Norristown, from Sidney Goldstein, *Patterns of Mobility, 1910–1950: The Norristown Study* (Philadelphia: University of Pennsylvania Press, 1958). Figures for Boston 1830–1860, 1910–1920, and 1930–1940, Salem, Waltham, Northampton, and Omaha 1900–1910 are for heads of households; all others are for adult males. In most of these studies there was no attempt to correct persistence estimates for deaths that occurred during the interval. Removing men who died in the city during the decade from the base population yields somewhat higher persistence rates, but not drastically higher. In the case of Norristown, both raw persistence figures and figures corrected for death are available; the latter were 7 percent higher for 1910–1920, 8 percent higher for 1930–1940, and 4 percent higher for 1940–1950.

was apparently even more volatile than it was in Boston during the 1880's.

Despite differences in the sampling techniques and tracing methods employed in these various studies that might have produced spurious variations in the findings, there was a striking consistency of pattern. In more than three quarters (24 of 31) of all the cases, the 10-year persistence rate was in the 40- to 60-percent range. Rather surprisingly, there does not seem to have been any systematic variation between time periods or community types.

Over the span of a century and two-thirds, there was no clear long-term trend toward either increased or decreased population mobility in the United States. The figures for Salem, Massachusetts, in the first decade of the nineteenth century differ by only one percentage point from those for Norristown, Pennsylvania, in the fourth decade of the twentieth century.[4] The Boston persistence rate for 1830–1840 was only two points below that for Boston 1958–1968. High rates of population movement in the United States were not a product of the automobile age, nor even of the industrial age. Nor does the opposite assumption—that the fluid and chaotic nineteenth century may be contrasted with the more ordered and settled twentieth century—find any support here. The migratory impulse seems to have been surprisingly strong and uniform over a period of almost 170 years.

Neither was there any consistent relation between population stability and either city size or population growth rates. I once suggested, on the basis of much less complete evidence, that persistence rates tend to be higher in very large cities, on the grounds that individuals may be able to move further (both physically and socially) and still remain within the community boundaries.[5] But when the cities in Table 9.1 are arrayed according to size, it is difficult to see a consistent pattern of this kind. The largest city examined in the 1880's—Boston (363,000)—had a higher rate than Omaha (30,000) and Los Angeles (11,000), but between 1830 and 1860 persistence was lower in Boston and Philadelphia than in much smaller Waltham and Northampton. The Boston population was more fluid than that of Norristown in the World War I decade but less so during the Great Depression.

It also seems plausible to assume that cities which are growing very rapidly and attracting unusually large numbers of newcomers would be more likely to retain their existing population than those which are growing sluggishly or not at all, but this does not seem to have been the case either. The low growth rate in Boston in the 1880's (24 percent) went with high persistence; the exceptionally high growth rates of Los Angeles (351 percent) and Omaha (233 percent) in that decade were accompanied by much lower persistence rates. Atlanta, Georgia, grew by a healthy 71 percent during the 1870's, San Francisco by a substantial 57 percent, Waltham by a moderate 29 percent, and Poughkeepsie grew not at all, but the persistence rates in the four communities were much the same. There were some differences between cities and within cities over time, but no consistent patterning with respect to growth rates.

Rates of *in*-migration, of course, and hence of net migration, varied widely from community to community. Given the limited range over which rates of natural increase could fluctuate, they *must* have done so to produce the drastic differences in overall population growth rates that existed. Los Angeles, for instance, must have been attracting a much larger flow of in-migrants than Boston around 1910; Atlanta must have been attracting many more newcomers than Poughkeepsie in the 1870's.[6] In this sense the populations of Los Angeles and Atlanta were more fluid than those of Boston and Poughkeepsie. The interesting and surprising point, however, is that rates of outflow from these four cities so closely resembled each other. In this respect, the populations of all four—and of all other American cities that have yet been studied—were equally volatile. Communities differed enormously in their power to attract outsiders into them; they varied hardly at all in their ability to hold on to their existing population.[7]

The probability that only between 40 and 60 percent of the adult males to be found in an American community at one point in time could still be located there a decade later held not only for most cities throughout the nineteenth and twentieth centuries; it applied in farming communities untouched by urbanization as well. Persistence rates in the 40- to 60-percent range have been found in agricultural towns like Ware, Northampton, and Pelham, Massachusetts, in the first decade of the nineteenth century and in dozens of Kansas townships in the early twentieth century (Table 9.2).

The only marked deviation from this pattern appeared in the earliest years of settlement on the frontier, in which population

TABLE 9.2. Persistence rates in selected rural communities, 1800–1935 (percent of residents still in community at end of decade)[1]

Decade	*Community*	*Percent*
1800–1810	Ware, Mass.	56
	Northampton, Mass.	52
	Pelham, Mass.	43
1850–1860	Wapello County, Iowa	30
1860–1870	Trempealeau County, Wis.	25
	Eastern Kansas	26
	East Central Kansas	31
	Central Kansas	42
1870–1880	Trempealeau County	29
	Roseburg, Ore.	34
	Eastern Kansas	44
	East Central Kansas	59
1885–1895	Grant County, Wis.	21
	Eastern Kansas	51
	East Central Kansas	51
	Central Kansas	46
1895–1905	Eastern Kansas	48
	East Central Kansas	51
	Central Kansas	40
	West Central Kansas	47
	West Kansas	33
1925–1935	Eastern Kansas	55
	East Central Kansas	56
	Central Kansas	58
	West Central Kansas	58
	West Kansas	51

[1] 1800–1810 data refer to male heads of households, from Robert Doherty, "Industrialization and Social Change"; Iowa data are for employed males, from Mildred Throne, "A Population Study of an Iowa County in 1850," *Iowa Journal of History,* 57 (1959), 305–330; Trempealeau County data are for employed males, from Merle Curti, *The Making of an American Community* (Stanford, California: Stanford University Press, 1959); Grant County, Wis., figures are for households, from Peter J. Coleman, "Restless Grant County: Americans on the Move," *Wisconsin Magazine of History,* 66 (Autumn

turnover was exceptionally rapid. No more than a third of the adult male residents of newly opened farm areas remained there as long as a decade—whether it was Wapello County, Iowa, in the 1850's, Trempealeau County, Wisconsin, and various townships in eastern and east central Kansas in the 1860's, Roseburg, Oregon, in the 1870's, Grant County, Wisconsin, between 1885 and 1895, or West Kansas from 1895 to 1905. After an initial period of extraordinarily rapid reshuffling of the population, however, a distinct settling-in took place, and rural persistence rates tended to rise to the general level of those in cities.

However glaring the differences between tiny farming communities, small industrial cities, and major metropolitan centers in other respects, they had in common a crucial demographic characteristic —their populations were leaving them for other destinations at a rapid and surprisingly uniform rate. Approximately half of their residents at any date were destined to disappear before 10 years had elapsed, to be replaced by other restless newcomers who had lived elsewhere a decade before. This was not a frontier phenomenon, or a big-city phenomenon, but a national phenomenon.

This similarity between communities of such radically different types, over such a long span of time, is so surprising that one wonders if it is not somehow an artifact of the measurement technique. When an instrument registers the same result under many different circumstances, the suspicion arises that there is something wrong with the instrument, something that mistakenly gives the same reading on the gauge every time. All I can say is that a careful methodological examination of all of the separate studies from which I derived this conclusion has left me unable to see how this could be

---

1962), 16–20. Kansas data are for farm operators in sample townships from various parts of the state; James C. Malin, "The Turnover of Farm Population in Kansas," *Kansas Historical Quarterly*, 4 (1935), 339–372. The failure to include farm laborers and persons in urban occupations probably accounts for the tendency of even the earliest Kansas figures to be higher than those for Iowa, Wisconsin, and Oregon, but this could not explain the clear trend toward increased persistence with the passing of frontier conditions. Roseburg, Oregon, data are for adults; from William G. Robbins, "Opportunity and Persistence in the Pacific Northwest: A Quantitative Study of Early Roseburg, Oregon," *Pacific Historical Review*, 39 (1970), 279–296.

the case. I am persuaded that there has indeed been a fairly constant migration factor operating throughout American society since the opening of the nineteenth century.

One implication of this is that the society appears to have been nationally integrated considerably earlier than has usually been thought, at least in the simple demographic sense that transiency was part of the American way of life—remaining in one community over a lifetime was extremely uncommon. One leading historical study argues that as late as the 1870's America was "a nation of loosely connected islands," a society of small, tight-knit local communities in which face-to-face relations predominated, and that it was only later that local loyalties became attenuated.[8] This is perhaps an accurate observation about the changing orientation of that element of "the community" visible to historians through newspapers and similar sources, but this group, one study suggests, comprised little more than 5 percent of the actual population.[9] The masses of invisible men whose presence was recorded not by the newspaper but by the census taker, city-directory canvasser, or tax collector have been men on the move throughout most of the past two centuries of American history. If the communities in which they lived were somehow "islands" until late in the nineteenth century, in one crucial respect they long before were part of the main: their inhabitants moved back and forth between them with astonishing frequency.

This may help to explain the rapidity of America's economic development in the past century and a half. Migration is the prime mechanism by which the labor force is redistributed in response to shifts in the location of industry brought about by technological innovation, the discovery of new resources and other circumstances. A geographically rooted work force unwilling to migrate to seize new employment opportunities can significantly retard productive growth. As early as the opening of the nineteenth century, it seems, American society was prepared for the great transformation of industrialization and urbanization. The country had an enormous reservoir of restless and footloose men, who could be lured to new destinations when opportunity beckoned.

The restlessness of the American people was more or less constant over the course of nearly two centuries. There was, however, a major shift in the *kinds* of men who were most transient. In nineteenth- and early-twentieth-century America, persons on the lower rungs of the class ladder were far more likely to move than those of higher rank (Table 9.3). Out of the ten available tabulations of occupational differentials in persistence rates for city dwellers in the period down to 1920, men in high white-collar callings persisted in larger numbers than those in more lowly ones in all but one case; this was Boston 1850–1860, a decade in which middle-class men seem to have been fleeing the city, perhaps because of the massive influx of famine Irish. In all but two of the ten pre-1920 cases, workers in low white-collar jobs remained in the community more frequently than skilled laborers. And in all but one case, low-skilled manual employees in turn persisted less often than skilled craftsmen. An average of almost two-thirds of the men at the top of the occupational structure were still to be found a decade later, but only 4 in 10 of those at the bottom. The same pattern holds when individuals are ranked by property rather than by occupation; both in cities and in rural areas property owners persisted more frequently than propertyless men, and those with large holdings tended to be more settled than those with smaller amounts.[10]

Soon after World War I, however, there was a fundamental alteration of this historic pattern, though the evidence necessary to date the shift with precision is lacking. By the 1930's, at least, in two cities—Boston and Norristown—men in high white-collar jobs were no more persistent than low-skilled laborers, and skilled workmen were the most stable occupational group of all. In the country as a whole between 1935 and 1940, professionals and technical workers remained living in the same county much less often than members of all other occupational strata. Much the same pattern appears in data for the United States as a whole between 1940 and 1947, for Norristown 1940–1950, and for Boston 1958–1968. In the two cities there was a greater resemblance in the persistence rates of the high and low white-collar strata, and a more conspicuous tendency for skilled workers to persist, which may reflect some special characteristics of Boston and Norristown, but all of the evidence points to a reversal of the long-established pattern in which the tendency of men to remain rooted in the community varied directly rather than inversely with socioeconomic rank.

Just what this shift means is not altogether clear. It may suggest that in the earlier period intercommunity variations in economic

TABLE 9.3. Occupational differentials in persistence rates in selected urban communities, 1830–1968 (percent of occupational group still in community at end of period)[1]

		Occupational level			
Decade	*Community*	*High white-collar*	*Low white-collar*	*Skilled*	*Low manual*
1830–1840	Boston	66	60	37	39
1840–1850	Boston	69	40	44	36
1850–1860	Boston	38	40	50	32
1870–1880	Atlanta	58	51	42	40
1880–1890	Boston	80	71	63	56
	Omaha	59	48	39	34
1900–1910	Omaha	55	43	47	39
1910–1920	Boston	58	50	36	35
	Los Angeles	72	58	45	29
	Norristown	70	62	59	58
1930–1940	Boston	56	68	66	51
	Norristown	50	54	59	50
1935–1940	United States	75	85	87	86
1940–1950	Norristown	54	54	60	55
1940–1947	United States	68	79	81	80
1958–1968	Boston	40	39	59	51

[1] Lack of sufficiently detailed occupational data made it difficult to regroup some of the material into the occupational categories used in the present study, but these are reasonably accurate approximations. Sources as cited in the note to Table 9.1, except for Boston, 1830–1860, from Peter R. Knights, *The Plain People of Boston, 1830–1860: A Study in City Growth* (New York: Oxford University Press, 1971), pp. 98–99, and data for the U. S., 1935–1940 and 1940–1947. The latter are estimates derived from more detailed census figures, as given in Donald J. Bogue, *The Population of the United States* (Glencoe, Ill.: Free Press, 1950). They refer to the proportion of persons still living in the same county at the terminal date; note that the interval was only 5 and 7 years in these instances, and all of the rates were thus higher than the decadal figures from the other studies.

opportunity were widest in the blue-collar world, and that the incentive to move on was strongest for men with the fewest resources and skills. (The absence of sharp intercommunity differentials in career mobility rates that will be demonstrated below does not necessarily challenge this interpretation; it may have meant that there was enough migration of this type to cancel out the differentials that would have existed without a large volume of migration.) Movement out of the community by workers thus would have been an economically rational effort to improve their situation.

This, however, is only an assumption, and perhaps an unduly complacent one. Whether low-skilled migrants leaving the cities of nineteenth- and early-twentieth-century America did in fact typically succeed in improving their lot as a result of migration is simply unknown; the question cries out for further study. Economic historians have shown that the net flow of the labor force was toward areas of greater economic opportunity as measured by wage levels, unemployment rates, and the like.[11] But inferences about the experiences of individuals on the basis of these analyses of net migration are questionable, because gross migration flows in and out vastly exceeded net movements. Positive correlations between net in-migration and levels of economic activity may obscure what happened to many, perhaps even most, of the men who were moving about in the period. Some working-class migrants must have benefited from moving, given these correlations, but there could still have been a large group of Americans who drifted helplessly from place to place for a lifetime, forming a permanent but invisible floating proletariat. The relative size of this element of the population must have diminished some time between World War I and the Great Depression, but how large it was in either period cannot be determined without further research.

Whatever the proportions of successful and unsuccessful blue-collar migrants in the nation as a whole, it surely is significant that at the local level prior to the 1930's it was the successful who stayed and the unsuccessful who vanished. The people who were stable enough to constitute the visible community were, by and large, making it; those who were not making it locally were not around long enough to make their presence felt. The extreme transiency of the urban masses must have severely limited the possibilities of mobilizing them politically and socially, and have facilitated control by more stable and prosperous elements of the population.[12] Effective organization demands some continuity of membership, and this was glaringly absent among the poorest city dwellers of nineteenth- and early-twentieth-century America. There are, of course, a good many complicated reasons for the inability of generations of dedicated labor organizers to establish strong unions among the semiskilled employees of major American industries until the 1930's, long after their counterparts in European countries at a comparable stage of economic development had done so, but it is perhaps not coincidental that success came at last at just the point at which low-skilled laborers had become not the most transient but among the least transient elements of the population.

What was true of poor people in general in the nineteenth and early twentieth centuries was true as well of poor immigrants and their children. To present detailed tabulations of ethnic differences in persistence in Boston and other communities would burden the text unduly, but the major foreign-born and second-generation groups in various cities that have been studied were about as transient as Yankees of comparable socioeconomic status. The familiar ghetto model of the immigrant experience is thus seriously misleading. The extent to which foreign-born newcomers typically huddled together in neighborhoods composed largely of their fellow countrymen has often been exaggerated, and even where there were highly segregated ethnic neighborhoods there was little continuity of the *individuals* who composed them over time. Just as there was a radical distinction between the visible portion of the community immortalized in the local newspapers and the masses of ordinary citizens, so too there was a distinction between what was most visible in the ethnic subcommunity—the groceries, restaurants, bars, churches, meeting halls, and the rest—and the nature of the ethnic community defined in a more comprehensive demographic sense. There were indeed Irish, Italian, Jewish, and other ethnic neighborhoods that could easily be discerned, but the vast majority of anonymous immigrants who lived in them at one census were destined to vanish from them before 10 years had elapsed. Some institutional continuity there was, but little individual continuity.

LEVELS OF CAREER MOBILITY

There was impressive consistency in the career patterns of Boston residents between 1880 and 1968. About a quarter of all the men who first entered the labor market as manual workers ended their careers in a middle-class calling; approximately 1 in 6 of those who first worked in a white-collar job later skidded to a blue-collar post. There were particular decades that were less favorable than others —upward mobility rates were unusually low in the 1880's, for instance—but in only one instance did such short-term fluctuations have an enduring effect upon lifetime career patterns. The Great Depression of the 1930's had serious and permanent consequences for a portion of one cohort—men born in the first decade of the century who held unskilled or semiskilled jobs as of 1930. These men never recovered from the depression and were much less successful over their lives than was normal for Boston workers. With that one exception, the structure of opportunity was extremely stable.

Few comparable studies of career mobility from first job to last have been made in other communities, but at least a partial answer to the question of how typical Boston was in this respect may be ventured. Two rough indexes of mobility—the proportions of blue-collar workers climbing to white-collar jobs and of white-collar workers skidding to blue-collar jobs in the span of a decade—have been calculated in a number of recent historical investigations. One study treats antebellum Boston, thus providing the basis for an examination of mobility trends in the city from 1830 all the way down to 1968. Another analyzes mobility patterns in Poughkeepsie from 1850 to 1880, and there are comparable data for Atlanta in the 1870's and '80's, Omaha 1800–1890 and 1900–1910, Los Angeles 1910–1920, and Norristown 1910–1950 (Table 9.4).[13]

Before the middle of the nineteenth century there was relatively little occupational career mobility in Boston. Only about a tenth of the city's manual laborers moved upward into middle-class callings in the 1830's and '40's; hardly any of its white-collar workers were displaced by competitors. In 1830 Boston was a fairly large city, with some 61,000 residents, and it grew by a substantial 38 percent in the 1830's and a very substantial 63 percent in the 1840's, but its occupational structure was rather tight. In the 1850's, however, there was a distinct loosening up, and a sharp increase in the flow of men up and down the occupational ladder; rates of both upward and downward mobility were double what they had been in the 1830's.

Whether the constricted pre-1850 Boston pattern was typical of

TABLE 9.4. Career mobility in selected urban communities, 1830–1968 (percent climbing or skidding)[1]

		Blue-collar climbers		*White-collar skidders*	
Decade	*Community*	*Percent*	*Number*	*Percent*	*Number*
1830–1840	Boston	9	58	3	80
1840–1850	Boston	10	60	0	96
1850–1860	Boston	18	83	7	42
	Poughkeepsie	17	758	7	410
1860–1870	Poughkeepsie	18	1172	8	601
1870–1880	Poughkeepsie	13	1661	9	866
	Atlanta	19	188	12	250
1880–1890	Boston	12	334	12	209
	Omaha	21	n.a.	2	n.a.
	Atlanta	22	299	7	435
1900–1910	Omaha	23	n.a.	6	n.a.
1910–1920	Boston	22	248	10	165
	Los Angeles	16	95	13	154
	Norristown	8	549	4	232
1920–1930	Norristown	9	543	8	217
1930–1940	Boston	11	301	16	166
	Norristown	10	629	19	278
1940–1950	Norristown	10	671	15	301
1958–1968	Boston	17	206	9	193

[1] Sources for Poughkeepsie, Omaha, Los Angeles, and Norristown data as given in note to Table 9.1. Boston 1830–1860 calculated from Knights, *The Plain People of Boston,* pp. 98–99. The Atlanta evidence is not from the Hopkins article cited in the note to Table 9.1, but from advance tabulations of two larger samples gathered by Hopkins from the manuscript census schedules for 1870 and 1880. These figures are for whites only, since none of the samples from other cities included a large proportion of blacks and since the experience of blacks was so different from that of other groups. In Atlanta the rate of black upward mobility from blue-collar to white-collar jobs was only a quarter of the white rate for 1870–1880 and a third of that for 1880–1890. For further discussion of black mobility, see pp. 254–256. The number of cases is not available for the two Omaha samples, but the full 1880 sample included 696 manual and 278 nonmanual workers, and the corresponding numbers were 449 and 288 for the 1900 group. Applying the 10-year persistence rates given in the study would

American society in that era is uncertain in the absence of other comparable studies. What is very clear, however, and extremely striking, is that the post-1850 Boston pattern was manifest in a wide range of other cities. Poughkeepsie, for instance, was less than a tenth the size of Boston in 1850, but rates of climbing and skidding for 1850–1860 were nearly identical in the two places. Of a dozen samples for the period from 1850 to World War I, drawn from six different communities, there were only two in which the upward-mobility rate differed by more than 5 percent from that for Boston in the 1850's and only one in which the downward mobility rate did so.

City size seems to have mattered not at all. Boston in 1910 was some 60 times larger than Poughkeepsie in 1850 and yet there was virtually no difference between their mobility patterns. Nor did rates of urban growth have any effect. In the World War I decade the Boston population increased by only 12 percent while the Los Angeles population more than tripled, but there was actually a little less upward mobility in booming Los Angeles than in relatively stagnant Boston.

No clear signs of a long-term trend toward either heightened or diminished mobility since 1850 is evident either. Laborers in Poughkeepsie at the time of the presidency of Millard Fillmore, in Los Angeles during the Taft administration, and in Boston in the Eisenhower era had almost precisely the same prospects of moving up into white-collar jobs (17, 16, and 17 percent respectively would do so within a decade). The chances that a white-collar worker in those three eras would be displaced and forced into manual work varied little more.

The only exceptions to this strikingly uniform post-1850 pattern were in Poughkeepsie in the 1870's, Boston in the 1880's and 1930's, and Norristown for each of the four decades from 1910 to 1950. What explains the relative constriction of the Poughkeepsie occupational structure in the 1870's and that of Boston in the 1880's is not clear, but it is significant that at least in Boston the constriction was temporary. By the end of their careers, Boston men who first en-

leave approximately 255 blue-collar and 140 white-collar workers in the 1880–1890 group, and about 180 manuals and 130 nonmanuals in the 1900–1910 group. An 11-year rather than a 10-year trace interval was employed in the Omaha study, which imparts a slight upward bias to the figures.

tered the labor market around 1880 had moved ahead at just about the same pace as in other eras (see Table 4.7). Whether this was also the case in Poughkeepsie cannot be determined. The low rates of upward mobility and high rates of downward mobility that were found in both Boston and Norristown during the 1930's are not surprising; the depression had devastating impact in both communities.

Norristown, however, seems to have had a relatively tight occupational structure throughout. Not only in the depression decade, but in the two that preceded it and in the one that followed it, rates of upward mobility for manual laborers in Norristown were well below the national norm, and indeed were at the low level of those in Boston prior to 1850. Since Norristown is the site of a very thorough and valuable analysis of career mobility patterns in a twentieth-century American city, it is important to note that it seems to deviate considerably from the general American pattern. Although it is at least possible that Norristown is representative of other twentieth-century cities of approximately its size (28,000 in 1920, 38,000 in 1950) on this count, it is doubtful, since mobility rates did not vary consistently with city size in all the other cases in Table 9.4. The Norristown pattern may possibly have manifested itself in many other American communities, but it appears likely that Boston was a good deal more typical.

The measures of mobility employed in this comparative effort are admittedly crude. More refined comparisons between these communities cannot be attempted, because some studies failed to report the data in sufficient detail and in others there were significant variations in the detailed occupational classification schemes used. Two closer comparisons, however, each involving a city of a radically different type from Boston, can be made here.

It is possible, first, to compare lifetime career patterns from first job to last, rather than over merely a decade, for men living in Poughkeepsie around the middle of the nineteenth century and in Boston shortly thereafter (Table 9.5). The comparison strongly reinforces the conclusion suggested earlier on the basis of cruder evidence, that the structure of career opportunities was remarkably similar in what was then the country's fourth largest metropolis and a city with only 20,000 inhabitants.

There was no more than a single percentage point of difference

TABLE 9.5. Career mobility from first to last occupation in two nineteenth-century cities (percent)[1]

Level of first occupation, and city	*Level of last occupation* *High white-collar*	*Low white-collar*	*Skilled*	*Low manual*	*Number*
High white-collar					
Boston	92	8	0	0	26
Poughkeepsie	93	5	1	1	96
Low white-collar					
Boston	25	61	9	6	109
Poughkeepsie	25	61	6	8	389
Skilled					
Boston	4	22	60	15	82
Poughkeepsie	8	23	60	10	830
Low manual					
Boston	4	24	13	59	93
Poughkeepsie	2	13	17	68	685

[1] Poughkeepsie data are from advance tabulations supplied by Clyde Griffen. Both studies traced men from first known occupation held prior to age 30 to last known occupation held later than age 30. Poughkeepsie sample members were born between 1820 and 1850, Boston men between 1850 and 1859, so that the time periods are only roughly, not precisely, comparable.

between Boston and Poughkeepsie in the proportion of professionals and large businessmen who retained their initial high white-collar status throughout their careers; of clerks, salesmen, and small proprietors who moved up into the upper middle class, were stable, or skidded into a blue-collar job; and of skilled workers who remained stable or entered a low white-collar post. There were but two small hints of any difference at all in the opportunity structures of the two communities, and they pointed in opposite directions. Men who began their careers in a skilled trade moved up into high white-collar posts a little more and fell into low manual jobs a little less in Poughkeepsie than their counterparts in Boston. Unskilled and semiskilled laborers in Boston, on the other hand, had somewhat greater opportunities to move up into jobs in the lower echelons of the white-collar class. Neither difference was dramatic. What is dramatic is that the flow of men between occupational strata in the course of their careers took place in almost precisely the same manner in two such very different kinds of cities.

A similar comparison of occupational mobility during the decade 1910–1920 in Boston and Los Angeles reveals similarities that are slightly less close but even more striking (Table 9.6). In this case

TABLE 9.6. Occupational mobility patterns in two cities, 1910–1920 (percent)[1]

Occupational level in 1910, and city	*Occupational level in 1920*				
	High white-collar	*Low white-collar*	*Skilled*	*Low manual*	*Number*
High white-collar					
Boston	90	7	0	3	31
Los Angeles	88	8	4	0	25
Low white-collar					
Boston	10	79	2	10	134
Los Angeles	7	78	11	4	129
Skilled					
Boston	2	21	66	11	103
Los Angeles	0	13	79	9	61
Low manual					
Boston	2	19	6	73	145
Los Angeles	0	21	12	67	34

[1] Los Angeles data from Hanson, "Occupational Mobility and Persistence in Los Angeles." The sample was drawn from the 1910 Los Angeles city directory, and the age range is thus wide, whereas the Boston sample was taken from marriage-license records and was composed mostly of men in their 20's and 30's. Since mobility rates decline somewhat with advancing age, this difference in age distribution of the two samples probably accounts for the somewhat higher rates of mobility in Boston.

mobility was observed over a much shorter period, and short-term fluctuations attributable to the business cycle or to other causes are more likely to distort the findings. There also were differences in the age distribution of the two samples that render the comparison less precise. These could produce some variations between the findings even if the opportunity structure had been identical in Boston and Los Angeles.

Few observers, however, would expect to find much similarity between these two communities. Boston seems the archetype of the

Eastern metropolis, long-established, slow-growing, conservative. Los Angeles, by contrast, seems the quintessentially dynamic, open, vital Western city, the ideal spot for the young man on the make.

The evidence at hand does not sustain this expectation at all. The kind of job a man held at one point in time influenced the probability that he would hold a different kind of job 10 years later to almost exactly the same extent in these two cities 3000 miles apart. Ninety percent of Boston's professionals and major businessmen in 1910 were still employed in the high white-collar stratum 10 years later, and 88 percent of those in Los Angeles. Only 3 percent of the members of this stratum in Boston and 4 percent in Los Angeles had skidded into a manual job. In Boston, 79 percent of the clerks, salesmen, and small proprietors held jobs at the same level a decade later, in Los Angeles 78 percent. A slightly higher percentage skidded in Los Angeles than in Boston, and correspondingly a slightly higher proportion moved up into the high white-collar stratum in the Eastern city, but the differences were trivial.

It could, however, be argued that the real difference between a dynamic, burgeoning place like Los Angeles and a more settled, slow-growing place like Boston would not be visible in the upper reaches of the occupational structure. It is not so surprising, perhaps, that upper-middle-class men in the two communities were equally successful at preserving their status, and that those in the lower middle class had very similar prospects too. It would be more reasonable to expect that it was men lower down on the occupational scale in booming Los Angeles who would reap disproportionate advantages over their Eastern counterparts, and that they would find greater opportunities to move up into the business world. In fact, however, precisely the same proportion of unskilled and semiskilled laborers in the two cities—21 percent—climbed into the white-collar class during the decade, and among skilled workers the rate of upward mobility was distinctly higher in Boston than in Los Angeles. It is doubtful that the Boston occupational structure was truly more open than that of Los Angeles—there was a difference in the age distribution of the samples, explained in the note to Table 9.6, that probably accounted for the somewhat higher mobility of the Boston sample—but it is quite clear that the opposite was not the case.

Boston and Los Angeles certainly differed in many important respects. But differences in life styles, residential patterns, ethnic composition, city size, timing of growth, rates of growth, and the like apparently have little effect upon the process of occupational mobility at the local level. A shattering historical event like the Great Depression can disturb the normal process temporarily (and with permanent consequences for some individuals), and there are, apparently, some communities like Norristown that are outside the main current. But the process itself seems to be a national one, which has operated in much the same way in many different communities for more than a century.

Part of the explanation lies in the fact that the occupational structure of American communities of various sizes and types varies much less than is commonly believed. Gigantic metropolitan centers do indeed typically have a higher proportion of professionals and managers than small cities, and fewer blue-collar workers, but the difference is usually too slight to have more than the most subtle effect upon mobility opportunities. In 1950, 11.0 percent of the labor force in American cities with more than 3 million residents were professionals, and 11.1 percent were managers, proprietors, and officials; in small cities (10,000–25,000) 9.6 percent of workers were professionals and 10.2 percent were managers, proprietors, or officials.[14] Blue-collar workers comprised 57.1 percent of the labor force in small cities, 53.2 in giant urban centers. There were, to be sure, variations between particular cities within a given size class, and they may have been larger in the nineteenth and early twentieth centuries than they are today.[15] Lowell, Massachusetts, for instance, was roughly the size of Omaha and Atlanta in 1880, but its massive concentration of semiskilled textile workers gave it a very different occupational structure, and it is extremely unlikely that there were similar opportunities for occupational mobility in the three communities. Further study of such local variations and their consequences is certainly needed. It must be recognized too that the similarities in rates of movement between fairly broad occupational *levels* that have been revealed here may conceal important intercommunity differences in the composition of the levels and in the particular avenues of mobility open to residents. Finer-grained studies of this question could be very valuable. But the first generalization to make is that the occupational structures of American communities have deviated from the national norm less than had been previously suspected.

Another factor that surely served to minimize local variations in occupational mobility patterns is the rapid population turnover that has prevailed throughout American society since at least 1800. The striking volatility of the American people must have served as an equilibrating mechanism that tended to iron out differences between local opportunity structures. If, for instance, the chances of rising in the world had been far less in Boston than in New York, this should have induced migration from the former to the latter, to the point of increasing the competition for scarce places in New York and easing it in Boston.[16] Of course the economist's assumption of perfect mobility of labor did not apply fully in the real world—there were barriers to movement that produced immobilities and made for disparities between regions and communities in such matters as wage levels—but the evidence at hand on patterns of persistence and turnover in nineteenth- and twentieth-century America suggests that there was an extremely large pool of transient workers who moved in this fashion. Whether these migratory men typically improved their lot as a result of migration cannot be said at present—this is one of the great unexplored topics in American history—but it is likely that the fluidity of the labor supply helped to account for the surprising similarity between career mobility rates in different communities.

MOBILITY BETWEEN GENERATIONS

Youths born into working-class homes in Boston had rather good prospects of moving upward into middle-class jobs in the course of their own careers. No more than 1 in 10 succeeded in becoming professionals or substantial businessmen—movement all the way to the top of the occupational ladder was far less likely for them than for sons from upper-middle-class families—but about a third of them ended up as clerks, salesmen, or small proprietors. Downward mobility on the part of middle-class youths was much less common. In all but one of the five Boston samples, probably a misleading case because its members were still in the early stages of their careers, white-collar skidding occurred only a half to a third as frequently as blue-collar climbing. There was a continuing cycle of migration and social mobility, in which the bottom rungs of the class ladder were occupied by successive waves of relatively uneducated and unskilled newcomers to the community.

The task of assessing to what extent these findings may be generalized to American society as a whole over the past century or so is complicated by a methodological difficulty. The bulk of the studies available for comparative analysis did not examine a particular age cohort and measure intergenerational mobility attained toward the *end* of an individual's career; most investigations selected samples of men ranging in age from 21 to 65, and plotted the occupational attainments of respondents at the time of the survey, whether they were in the early, middle, or late phases of their career. The first three Boston samples, by contrast, were of a particular age cohort of individuals whose careers were traced until they retired or left the city; intergenerational mobility was measured at the end of a man's career or as close to it as possible. (This procedure could not be followed in the later Boston samples, one of which was gathered for another study and had a wide age range, and the other of which was composed of men who were only 33 at the last time for which information was available.) This seems to me the most revealing way of gauging the effect of family origins upon career patterns, but comparisons with other studies that measure mobility at an undefined point in an individual's career must take into account this methodological difference. Since upward mobility in the course of a career is more common in American society than downward mobility, investigations that include large numbers of relatively young men underestimate the extent of upward intergenerational mobility that takes place in a typical American's lifetime.[17]

This is at least part of the explanation of the apparently greater opportunities for upward mobility enjoyed by working-class sons in Boston (Table 9.7). From 41 to 43 percent of the men in the three early Boston samples made this advance, a rate higher than in any other study except the 1949 Oakland inquiry (which was based on a biased sample; see the note to Table 9.7). At the time they first entered the labor market, however, they were much less successful; only 22, 38, and 33 percent of them, respectively, held white-collar jobs. This is one indicator of the extent to which other studies that included men in the early stages of their careers underestimated actual lifetime intergenerational mobility. Further evidence of this may be seen in the record of the two later Boston samples, which unavoidably did include men whose careers were far from complete. The upward mobility rate for working-class sons was several points lower in these samples—36 percent and 34 percent. It is likely that the true mobility rate for these men at the time of their retirement from the labor force would have been close to the 40 percent figure observed in the three earlier ones.

If one bears this in mind—that the mobility rate found in samples including men in the early stages of their career will be several points lower than the true rate at career's end—it follows that the Boston pattern did not deviate much from that observed in San Jose, California, in 1933, in Indianapolis in 1940, in Norristown in 1952, and in the nation as a whole in 1945, 1956, and 1962. In all of these instances about 30 percent or more of the men born into blue-collar households themselves obtained middle-class jobs, and the proportion would presumably have been higher still had it been possible to trace them through to the end of their careers.

It is not certain, however, that this is the full explanation of the modest contrast between Boston and these communities, and there are some contrasts that are so sharp that this cannot have been the cause. The Poughkeepsie study measured intergenerational mobility by the same method employed here, and there was distinctly less ascent into white-collar jobs by working-class sons there. The rate of upward mobility in Indianapolis on the eve of World War I was likewise exceedingly low—roughly half the Boston rate. The lack of precise comparability in the data renders any definite conclusion impossible, but there is a suggestion that the structure of opportunities for intergenerational mobility may have varied more widely from community to community than the structure of career mobility opportunities. The high rate of upward mobility found in the Bay Area study—47 percent—may indicate this. The exclusion of poverty areas from the sample imparted an upward bias to this estimate, but the failure to trace sample members to a late point in their careers may have offset that bias. Perhaps it is significant that Boston and Oakland were the largest urban centers of those studied, and probably offered greatest educational opportunities to working-class children, but it would take much more evidence than is presently available to be at all sure.[18]

Perhaps the most striking finding about intergenerational mobil-

TABLE 9.7. Intergenerational occupational mobility in selected communities: blue-collar sons attaining white-collar status[1]

City	*Date*	*Percent*	*Number*
Poughkeepsie	1880	26	223
Boston	*c.* 1890	41	111
Boston	*c.* 1910	41	535
Indianapolis	1910	22	940
Boston	*c.* 1920	43	128
San Jose	1933	32	606
Indianapolis	1940	31	1026
U. S.	1945	29	323
Oakland	1949	47	252
Norristown	1952	29	383
U. S.	1956	31	291
U. S.	1962	38	n.a.
Boston	1962	36	244
Boston	1963	34	126

[1] Precise comparison of the findings of these studies is impossible. Some of the differences that appear are attributable to sampling error; some to differences in the population studied (adults, adult whites, men marrying in a particular year, heads of households); some to differences in occupational coding; some to labor-market conditions at the time the data were gathered. Small proprietors could not be distinguished from large ones in most studies, so mobility into high and low white-collar jobs could not be analyzed separately. The most important variation, however, concerns the point in the individual's career at which his status is compared with that of his father's. In the first three Boston samples intergenerational mobility was measured at career's end, but this procedure was not followed in the other samples and there were wide variations in the age and career stage of sample members. The Poughkeepsie data are for men between 30 and 40; both Indianapolis samples are for men 30 or over, but a possible special portion of that age group (namely, men marrying at that relatively advanced age); San Jose, men 30 or over; U. S. 1945, adult whites; Oakland, heads of households; Norristown, whites 25 or over; U. S. 1956, adults; U. S. 1962, men 25 to 64; Boston 1962, adult whites; Boston 1963, men 33. Studies that fail to measure intergenerational mobility attained by the late-career stage probably underestimate rates of upward mobility, for reasons suggested in the text.

The Oakland results must be used with particular caution, for they are based on a sample excluding 17

ity patterns in Boston had to do with a particular stratum of the working class, the mass of unskilled and semiskilled laborers who held the jobs that demanded the least in terms of training, education, or capital and offered the least in income, security, or prestige. Analysis of the career patterns of sons of these low manual workers revealed that most of these families were not trapped permanently in a "culture of poverty." Poverty there was aplenty, but intergenerational *transmission* of low manual status was less common than upward mobility. In the five Boston samples an average of 4 in 10 of the youths from families on the lowest rung of the occupational ladder found their way into middle-class jobs of some kind, and a significant proportion of the remainder—roughly 1 in 6—entered a skilled trade. In none of the samples did as many as half of these youths fare no better than their fathers in the occupational competition.

This general pattern of intergenerational ascent from the low

of the city's census tracts that were characterized by extremes of wealth or poverty. Most of the excluded tracts were in the poverty category, and there was thus substantial underrepresentation of unskilled laborers in the sample, which doubtless inflated the estimates of upward mobility for working-class sons.

Poughkeepsie figures are advance tabulations from the Poughkeepsie Mobility Study; Indianapolis, from Natalie S. Rogoff, *Recent Trends in Occupational Mobility* (Glencoe, Ill.: Free Press, 1953), pp. 122, 125; San Jose, Calif., from Percy E. Davidson and H. Dewey Anderson, *Occupational Mobility in an American Community* (Stanford, California: Stanford University Press, 1937), p. 29; U. S. 1945, from Richard Centers, "Occupational Mobility of Urban Occupational Strata," *American Sociological Review*, 13 (1948), 197–203; Oakland, from S. M. Lipset and Reinhard Bendix, *Social Mobility in Industrial Society* (Berkeley: University of California Press, 1959); Norristown, from Sidney Goldstein, ed., *The Norristown Study; An Experiment in Interdisciplinary Research* Training (Philadelphia: University of Pennsylvania Press, 1961), p. 109; U. S. 1956, from a preelection national sample gathered by the Survey Research Center of the University of Michigan, as reported in S. M. Miller, "Comparative Social Mobility: A Trend Report and Bibliography," *Current Sociology*, 9 (1960), 78; U. S. 1962, from U. S. Bureau of the Census, "Lifetime Occupational Mobility of Adult Males, March 1962," *Current Population Reports: Technical Studies*, Series P-23, No. 11. The number of cases was not given, but there were approximately 20,700 men in the total sample.

manual stratum was not at all peculiar to Boston. It has manifested itself in many American communities during the past century (Table 9.8). The proportion of sons from unskilled or semiskilled laboring families who became low manual workers themselves was 43 percent for youths born in Poughkeepsie in the 1840's, 49 percent for men who took out marriage-license applications in India-

TABLE 9.8. Intergenerational occupational mobility in selected communities (percent of sons of unskilled or semiskilled laborers climbing or not moving)[1]

		Occupational level of son			
City	*Date*	*White-collar*	*Skilled*	*Low manual*	*Number*
Newburyport	*c.* 1880	10	19	71	245
Poughkeepsie	*c.* 1880	22	35	43	121
Boston	*c.* 1890	43	14	43	63
Boston	*c.* 1910	39	20	40	261
Indianapolis	1910	22	29	49	278
Boston	*c.* 1920	46	16	37	73
San Jose	1933	29	16	55	311
Indianapolis	1940	28	25	47	440
U. S. (nonfarm)	1946	24	22	57	160
Norristown	1952	27	27	46	223
U. S. (nonfarm)	1956	27	25	48	147
U. S. (nonfarm)	1962	29	25	45	n.a.
Boston	1962	35	17	48	155
Boston	1963	38	18	44	78

[1] The obstacles to precise comparison described in the note to Table 9.7 and in note 17 of this chapter apply equally here, of course. Sources as cited there, plus Stephan Thernstrom, *Poverty and Progress: Social Mobility in a Nineteenth-Century City* (Cambridge, Mass.: Harvard University Press, 1964), p. 218. The Newburyport data are for sons of unskilled laborers only, but this does not account for the low rate of mobility observed. Comparable figures for unskilled sons in Poughkeepsie and Boston are as follows:

City	*Date*	*White-collar*	*Skilled*	*Low manual*	*Number*
Poughkeepsie	*c.* 1880	20	32	48	76
Boston	*c.* 1890	39	14	48	44
Boston	*c.* 1910	35	23	41	137

The prospects of reaching the white-collar world were twice as high in Poughkeepsie as in Newburyport, and three and a half times as high in Boston.

napolis in 1910, 46 percent for adult males living in Norristown in 1952, 45 percent for the entire U. S. nonfarm population in 1962. In only 1 of the 14 samples did as many as 60 percent of the sons of unskilled or semiskilled laborers remain in the low manual stratum themselves; in only 3 of the 14 cases was the figure as high as 50 percent. It is likely that, had the other studies available for comparison plotted mobility at career's end, the generality of the Boston findings would be even more striking.

The one glaring exception was Newburyport, Massachusetts, in the late nineteenth century, where fully 7 out of 10 low manual sons failed to climb above the low manual level themselves, and only 1 in 10 attained white-collar status. In an earlier attempt to compare mobility rates in Newburyport and in various twentieth-century cities, based upon much scantier evidence, I apparently erred in taking the Newburyport findings as a base line for gauging levels of mobility in nineteenth-century America.[19] How much it was Newburyport's relative economic stagnation in the period, and how much the preponderance of second-generation Irish in the sample that produced notably lower upward-mobility rates there than in other communities is not clear, but the deviant character of Newburyport is quite evident.

Although the chance that the offspring of unskilled or semiskilled laborers would escape the low manual occupational universe themselves varied little from place to place—with the exception of Newburyport—how far up the ladder they climbed was susceptible of greater fluctuation. Again there is the problem of methodological differences between the studies that limit comparability, but there clearly was less chance in the white-collar world for a low manual son in nineteenth-century Poughkeepsie and pre-World War I Indianapolis, and there was in general a substantial gap between rates of upward mobility into white-collar jobs in Boston and in other communities.

The relative position of low manual sons in Boston, that is to say, was unusually good. The children of unskilled or semiskilled laborers there had just as much chance of entering nonmanual occupations as the sons of skilled workmen; in three of the five samples, indeed, they had a slight advantage over skilled sons in this respect. In seven of the eight cases in which a similar comparison can be made in other communities, however, skilled sons climbed into white-collar posts more frequently than their rivals of low manual origins (table not given here). There was, then, something like "a labor aristocracy" in other American cities, at least in this mild sense of the term. Whether its absence in Boston, and the greater ease of access to middle-class jobs enjoyed by men of the most lowly origins, was at all peculiar to Boston or was a more general big-city phenomenon is not clear, since there are no comparable data for other big cities (the Bay Area findings were not presented with a breakdown for skill level). But the possibility that major metropolitan centers offered the most favorable habitat to aspiring men born on the lowest rungs of the class ladder is an interesting one.

Only a brief and crude attempt at a comparative analysis of the achievements of middle-class sons in different American communities of the past can be made here. In addition to the methodological problems already discussed, there is the further difficulty that virtually none of the previous studies that have been made drew the critical distinction between large and small businessmen, and instead lumped them together as "managers, proprietors, and officials." This makes it impossible to recode the data into the high white-collar and low white-collar strata, and we have already seen how radically the career patterns of men born into these two strata differed in Boston. Only the crudest of comparisons—of the proportion of white-collar sons who skidded to blue-collar jobs in the cities that have been studied—can thus be made (Table 9.9).

The overwhelming majority of American youths from middle-class homes retained the white-collar status they had inherited. In Boston the proportion ranged from 74 to 83 percent. (Both the lower figure of 71 percent for the sample of youths born in 1930 and traced to 1963 and the higher one for the 1962 Cambridge and Belmont sample may be discounted, the former because these men were still in the early stages of their careers, the latter because it is attributable to the unusually high proportion of sons of professionals and large businessmen in the sample, which distorted the average for the white-collar group as a whole.) There was slightly more retention of middle-class status and less intergenerational downward mobility in Boston than in the United States in general as of 1945, 1956, and 1962, but this slight difference probably stems from the failure of these studies to trace individuals to the end of their careers. Skidding rates were only a shade higher in nineteenth-century

TABLE 9.9. Intergenerational occupational mobility in selected communities (percent of white-collar-sons not moving or skidding)[1]

City	Date	Occupational level of son: White-collar	Blue-collar	Number
Poughkeepsie	*c.* 1880	70	30	149
Boston	*c.* 1890	80	20	97
Boston	*c.* 1910	83	17	249
Indianapolis	1910	65	35	577
Boston	*c.* 1920	76	24	65
San Jose	1933	61	39	941
Indianapolis	1940	70	30	903
U. S.	1945	81	19	267
Oakland	1949	68	32	225
Norristown	1952	64	36	161
U. S.	1956	74	26	154
U. S.	1962	72	28	n.a.
Boston	1962	88	12	161
Boston	1963	71	29	76

[1] Sources as cited in the note to Table 9.7. The highest skidding rate nere—that for San Jose—is probably inflated, both because the study was conducted during the depression and because fathers who were farmers were classified as proprietors and considered white-collar workers. The sons of farmers, many subsequent studies have shown, fare less well occupationally than sons of urban white-collar workers.

Poughkeepsie, in Indianapolis in 1940, and in Oakland, again not a very impressive difference. The pattern in Indianapolis in 1910, in San Jose during the Great Depression, and in Norristown in 1952 differed more substantially (though the San Jose case too is somewhat special, for reasons indicated in the note to Table 9.9), but even in those cases more than 6 in 10 middle-class sons obtained white-collar jobs themselves, which was 2 to 3 higher than the proportion of working-class sons entering nonmanual occupations in those communities.

Throughout the United States for at least the past century, the evidence suggests, there has been a fairly high and relatively constant rate of upward intergenerational mobility, with a very large minority of working-class sons moving up into at least the lower echelons of the white-collar class, and with a clear majority of youths born into what has sometimes been taken as a "culture of poverty" finding their way into either a skilled trade or a white-collar post. Not many men from laboring households succeeded in obtaining jobs that offered the greatest autonomy, power over others, and financial rewards, it appears from the few studies that make it possible to distinguish movement into the high as opposed to the low white-collar stratum. In this respect there was a high degree of inequality in the American social system. But the volume of more short-distance upward mobility into skilled and minor white-collar posts was substantial, and presumably was enough to sustain the national faith that opportunities for advancement were widespread.

At the same time, there was much less downward mobility on the part of middle-class sons. In American society generally, as in Boston, the escalators lifting men upward from blue-collar beginnings to white-collar careers carried many more passengers than those carrying *déclassé* middle-class sons downward into working-class occupations.

ETHNIC DIFFERENCES IN OCCUPATIONAL ACHIEVEMENT

There were sharp ethnic differences in economic opportunity in Boston. In the late nineteenth and early twentieth centuries, immigrants fared much less well than natives in the occupational competition. The American-born children of European newcomers were typically more successful than their fathers, but distinctly less so than men of old native stock. The Yankees of the city, it seemed, stood on the shoulders of the second generation, which in turn stood on the shoulders of the first generation. The restriction of mass immigration in the 1920's eventually began to blur these differentials, but half a century later they remained visible to some degree still.

A second chief finding about the ethnic factor in Boston economic life was that there were important variations between particular national groups, variations as striking as the overall differences between immigrants, second-generation men, and Yankees. Among the major groups to be found in Boston, the Irish and the Italians moved ahead economically only sluggishly and erratically; the English and the Jews, on the other hand, found their way into the higher occupational strata with exceptional speed. A fully convincing explanation of these differentials cannot be provided, but there is some basis for believing that something more than readily measurable Old World background handicaps—illiteracy, inability to speak English, poverty at the time of immigration, and the like —was involved, and that certain features of the cultures the immigrants brought with them had some effect.

The other major finding was that Negroes in Boston were in a drastically different position from other newcomers. The dismal economic situation of black men in the city was not attributable to the continuing influx of ill-prepared rural migrants; even the second- and third-generation Negro city dweller had only the barest chance of entering a secure, well-paid, respectable job. Blacks were not, in this respect, "the last of the immigrants," but were instead on another spectrum altogether. Only in the years since 1940, which saw substantial changes in the attitudes and behavior of white Americans, did Negroes begin to progress at anything like the pace of European immigrants earlier.

A thorough comparative analysis of ethnic mobility patterns in other communities that would reveal whether or not much the same situation prevailed throughout American society cannot be attempted here, because the available data are severely limited. Quantitative studies are rare; studies distinguishing second-generation newcomers and providing detail upon particular nationalities are even rarer. What I can offer here is thus more a critical comment about the difficulties involved in such comparative analyses and a suggestion of research that should be done than a substantive argument about ethnic mobility patterns in American society.

It is clear that European immigrants were not equally handicapped economically in all American cities of the past. In Omaha in the 1880's, it is true, the foreign-born were clustered on the lower rungs of the occupational ladder to about the same degree they were in Boston, and, as in Boston, they experienced much less upward mobility and more downward mobility than natives during the decade. In South Bend, Indiana, too, immigrants were a more heavily proletarian group in the 1850–1880 period, but there they were strikingly successful at climbing upward after their initial low start.[20] In Atlanta, Georgia, and San Antonio, Texas, in the late nineteenth century, men born abroad were spread quite evenly through the occupational structure, and their rates of occupational mobility were about the same as those of natives.[21] In Omaha during the first decade of the twentieth century, contrary to the earlier pattern, immigrants climbed the occupational ladder more rapidly than natives, though they also skidded somewhat more frequently. Men with foreign-born parents displayed patterns of upward and downward intergenerational mobility similar to those of old-stock Americans in Indianapolis around 1910; three decades later immigrants and their children were distinctly more successful than Yankees in Indianapolis.[22]

What explains these divergent patterns, however, is difficult to determine. One possibility is that sharp differentials between immigrants and natives are most likely to be found in cities with a large immigrant population; in places with only a small or modest concentration of the foreign-born, it has been suggested, immigrants are less visible and less the target of dislike by the native majority. The number of cases available for comparison is much too small to draw firm conclusions, but I am doubtful about this hypothesis. It cannot explain the shift in pattern in Omaha between the 1880's and 1900–1910, for the proportion of immigrants there was relatively low and constant over the period. The San Antonio case is also inconsistent with this interpretation, for European immigrants were a surprising 38 percent of the labor force there in 1870, very close to the Boston figure, and yet they were just as successful occupationally as natives.

A related notion has been advanced to explain the favorable position of the foreign born in San Antonio and Atlanta—the argument that the masses of black laborers in Southern cities served as "surrogate immigrants," whose presence deflected hostility away from true immigrants from abroad. There may be something to this, but the supply of black "surrogate immigrants" was small in Omaha at the turn of the century and in Indianapolis in 1910 and 1940 and yet European immigrants fared very well.

Another line of explanation is that the immigration streams bringing newcomers to different communities may have varied in selectivity. Immigrants who traveled long distances away from the seaport cities they first entered, it may be surmised, were more ambitious and venturesome than those who remained in places like Boston, New York, and Philadelphia. This hypothesis certainly deserves systematic exploration, but the few cases for which data are now available do not conform very closely to that pattern.

I suspect that the chief source of the differences between these communities in the relative economic position of natives and immigrants had to do not with the size of the foreign-born population, the presence or absence of a black proletariat, or differential migration selectivity, but with the precise nationality mix of the immigrant population and the character of the native-born group with which they competed in each.

As I have emphasized, an index of the average status of "first-generation immigrants" in Boston is a composite figure that blurs important distinctions between particular groups. That the Boston average for an entire ethnic generation deviated from that found in another community thus may indicate not a genuine difference in the two opportunity structures but only a difference in the ethnic mixture that composed the generation. Cities in which first-generation immigrants were in an unusually favored economic position may simply have been cities in which an unusually large proportion of the immigrant population was from nationalities that typically flourished in the occupational competition. In Atlanta, for instance, the highly successful foreign-born group included relatively few Irish—the proportion of Irish among Atlanta's immigrants was less than half that in Boston—and the proportion of Germans, many of them probably Jewish, was five times as high as in Boston, which undoubtedly had a good deal to do with the contrast between the communities.

Most of these studies unfortunately do not provide sufficiently detailed evidence to judge whether the economic prospects of an Irish, English, Italian, or Jewish immigrant were different in those communities than in Boston. The South Bend inquiry, however, allows some comparisons between particular ethnic groups. Comparative analysis reveals that immigrants in general fared better in South Bend than in Boston largely because the South Bend population included more newcomers from Germany and England and fewer from Ireland. When the occupational distributions of each group in the two cities are compared, there are no significant differences.[23] There are, in addition, a number of other investigations that suggest that one of Boston's major immigrant groups—the Irish—were in much the same economic situation throughout the United States in the latter half of the nineteenth century. There were marginal differences from place to place—with Boston and South Bend most advantageous on the whole, and Newburyport least—but in these three cities and in Worcester, Massachusetts, Providence, Rhode Island, and Poughkeepsie, New York, Irish immigrants were strongly clustered in low-skilled laboring jobs and unusually slow to climb out of them over time.[24]

More needs to be known about the economic adjustment of other immigrant groups in other American cities. But the literature currently available does not indicate that Boston was a special case.[25] Future inquiries that focus more upon the anonymous immigrant than the conspicuous immigrant may, of course, disclose such differences. It would seem particularly important to examine cities outside of the Northeast, which has attracted disproportionate attention thus far. For now, however, there is reason to suspect that, in this respect as in so many others, the Boston findings point up broader societal patterns.

It must also be recalled that the relative positions of immigrants and natives in a community depend not only upon who the immigrants were—Irish or German, Italian or Jewish—but also upon who the natives were. Did immigrants perhaps compete on relatively equal terms with natives in Atlanta and San Antonio but not in Boston because the "natives" in these Southern cities were mostly ill-educated poor whites from the backwaters of the rural South, and much less formidable competition than the Yankees of Boston? The proportion of native migrants from rural areas was doubtless higher in Atlanta and San Antonio than in Boston, and the *kind* of rural migrants in these cities differed as well. Youths from the farms of New England seem to have fared quite well in late-nineteenth-century Boston (see Table 3.2); sociological studies of Southern rural migrants in twentieth-century Southern cities suggest that they did not.[26] Probably this reflects differences in the social structure of the rural areas of the two regions. The presence of large numbers of Southern rural migrants in Indianapolis may likewise help to explain the relatively favorable position of European immigrants there. Nothing definitive can be said at this point, but the need for more finely calibrated comparative analyses is certainly clear.

The lack of adequate studies of the black urban population in the American past is particularly glaring. That the Negro has long been situated at the bottom of the class ladder is a surprise to no one, but there has been very little historical analysis that has illuminated the sources of black poverty in the city. Two recent studies of Atlanta and San Antonio challenge the "last-of-the-immigrants" theory and question the handicapping effect of rural background for black migrants by showing a radical contrast between the mobility patterns of Negroes and European immigrants over time. Foreign-born men made rapid economic progress in these two Southern cities; blacks made virtually none at all.[27]

The Boston evidence reinforces and significantly extends this line of argument. It suggests that the situation was by no means peculiar to the South. From 1880 down to at least 1940, the barriers to black occupational achievement were much the same in a "liberal" Northern metropolis as in two much smaller, provincial, reactionary Southern cities in the period of not-so-benign neglect that followed the failure of Reconstruction. The Northern city may have been more attractive to blacks on many other grounds, to be sure, but unless Boston was for some reason atypical of the North, in this fundamental respect American society was quite uniform. Whether the community was south or north of the Mason-Dixon line, whether it contained a massive black population and a small immigrant population or vice versa made very little difference.

The North was much like the South, and within the Northern city the fate of blacks born in an urban setting was much the same as that of ill-prepared Negro newcomers from the rural South. Direct evidence to challenge the hypothesis that it was the rural origins of the urban black population that accounted for its economic plight is available for only the 1880–1900 period and is confined to Boston, but I strongly suspect that this was a national pattern until quite recently. European immigrants to the American city—even those of peasant origins like the Irish and Italians—made fairly steady economic progress from generation to generation. The children of the foreign born moved to higher occupational positions, on the average, than those held by their fathers; their children in turn made further gains. At least until World War II blacks simply did not experience the same process of assimilation to urban life and consequent mobility. There are promising indications in the gross data available that this may no longer be the case, that Negroes in recent decades have begun to edge their way up the occupational ladder in something like the fashion of earlier white newcomers from Europe. But there is negative evidence as well—for instance, the fact that the racial gap in income was as wide in 1970 as it was 20 years before—and more extensive and refined inquiries will be required to gauge the full impact of recent developments. Whatever the judgment that may be rendered on the pace of progress of late, it is clear from the historical record that for previous generations of black city dwellers the promise of American life was not fulfilled.

THE SIGNIFICANCE OF THE AMERICAN MOBILITY PATTERN

This has been a long and often quite technical attempt to delineate as precisely as possible how the process of mobility operated in nineteenth- and twentieth-century America. It should not be necessary, in these final pages, to reiterate the chief conclusions that I have advanced. It may be useful, though, to add a few comments about the broader significance of the findings.

The promise of mobility has been a key theme in American life because it mediates between the competing values of equality and inequality. Americans have long been committed to the ideal of equality, and yet they have constructed a social order characterized by sharp inequalities in the distribution of resources. The explanation of this seeming paradox, the prime justification for the acute economic and social inequalities that have in fact existed in a supposedly egalitarian society, is to be found in the ideology of mobility. It is not equality of *condition* but equality of *opportunity* that Americans have celebrated. If careers are genuinely open to the talented, if all have an equal chance to compete for wealth, power, and prestige, the distribution that results is deemed just, however unequal. Is this an accurate assessment of the possibilities for individual advancement in American society during the past century, or is it sheer fantasy? The materials at hand help us to gauge to what extent the ideal of equal opportunity was in fact realized.

Only a limited and tentative verdict can be returned. The data analyzed here pertain chiefly to freedom of movement between broad occupational classes. With the minor exception of some fragmentary evidence about the ownership of real estate in late-nineteenth-century Boston, I have no direct information about the extent of opportunities to acquire wealth or power; the study bears on them only to the extent that they are correlated with occupational level. Historical studies focused on these dimensions of social stratification are badly needed, and they may well yield a quite different impression of the fluidity of the American social system.

This much, however, seems clear. There were definite rigidities in the occupational structure, a series of barriers that impeded mobility and perpetuated inequality. The level at which a young man entered the labor market strongly influenced the course of his subsequent career. His point of entry into the occupational competition was in turn significantly related to the social-class position of the family in which he was reared. Thus it was that sons of professionals and substantial businessmen were four times as likely as children from low white-collar homes to attain upper white-collar status themselves, 6½ times as likely as the sons of skilled workers, and no less than 12 times as likely as youths from households headed by an unskilled or semiskilled laborer. There were marked disabilities connected with ethnic status as well. To have been foreign-born, or even the native-born child of an immigrant parent, was a serious handicap; to have been Irish or Italian was a still greater handicap. The most glaring contradiction to the ideal of equal opportunity was the case of blacks, who at least down to World War II faced nearly insuperable obstacles in advancement.

The height and impermeability of the barriers that divided the social strata, however, should not be overestimated. At any one point in time, whether 1880 or 1970, a cross-sectional view of the social system yields an impression of rigid stratification along class and ethnic lines. But scrutiny of the experience of representative individuals traced over time, a dynamic rather than a static view, indicates that the impression of rigidity was partly an optical illusion. The social system was more fluid than could be seen at any one moment. The middle class, and particularly its high white-collar stratum, was relatively successful in transferring status from father to son, but upward mobility both from blue-collar to white-collar callings and from low-ranked to high-ranked manual jobs was quite common. If Horatio Alger's novels were designed to illustrate the possibility not of rags-to-riches but of rags-to-respectability, as I take them to have been, they do not offer wildly misleading estimates of the prospects for mobility open to Americans. Runaway carriages containing the helpless daughters of prosperous merchants can hardly have been as common in reality as they were in Alger's fictional world, but social types like Ragged Dick and Mark the Match Boy were not mere figments of his imagination.

It is true that the climb up the class ladder was harder for men of foreign stock than for Yankees, and harder for some immigrant groups than for others. But part of the explanation, at least, was not simple prejudice or even passive structural discrimination but objective differences in qualifications to perform demanding occupational tasks. And all of the major immigrant groups, however dismal their plight when they first arrived, experienced substantial upward mobility in subsequent years. The only group that could be considered a truly permanent proletariat was the blacks, and even they have found new opportunities for advancement in recent decades.

The American class system, in short, allowed substantial privilege for the privileged and extensive opportunity for the underprivileged to coexist simultaneously. It is tempting to argue that this has been a key distinguishing feature of American society, and that it explains some of the other distinctive features of our national life—such as the dominant individualism of our national ethos and the relative absence of acute class conflict in our political history. Thus it has been suggested that the fluidity of the American social system has defused class resentments and generated a politics of consensus. American workers, the argument runs, failed to flock into labor and socialist parties to the same extent as their European counterparts in the late nineteenth and twentieth centuries because of the greater permeability of the class structure that governed their lives. Large numbers of them were able to improve their lot as individuals within the existing order, and hence were not strongly motivated to mount collective protests against the existing distribution of rewards. And those who were not individually successful witnessed enough mobility on the part of their peers to believe that their own failure was the result of individual inadequacy rather than of unjust social arrangements. Politically explosive anger was thus transformed into self-deprecating guilt.[28]

The hypothesis is tantalizing, but nothing like an adequate basis for testing it is available at the present time. I think that I have demonstrated that American workers did indeed enjoy rather impressive opportunities for self-advancement, but the proposition at hand asserts that they had markedly greater opportunities than the workmen of such countries as Germany, France, and England. This is a problem of comparative historical analysis, and as yet there have not been enough quantitative studies of mobility in the European past to make systematic comparison possible.[29]

Some speculative remarks about what such a comparative analysis will disclose, however, may be in order. First, it is likely that the sharp dichotomy that has so often been drawn between the "open" social system of the New World and the "closed" system of the Old World will not be sustained. There probably was neither so much mobility in America nor so little in Europe as this facile contrast suggests. Second, mobility will not prove to be the only significant variable. Obviously there were other distinctive features of American life—the uniquely high levels of real wages generated by economic growth and the absence of feudal institutions, to name only two—that shaped our political institutions and fostered the integration of the working class into the two-party system. Cultural expectations about mobility may prove as important as objective rates and patterns. The meaning of mobility—whether a given level of it is perceived as high or low, whether it satisfies the people who experience it or only whets greater appetite—is influenced by societal values. Even if 40 percent of American working-class children found their way into middle-class callings and only 10 percent, say, of French working-class youths, Americans may have *expected* to experience four times as much mobility; indeed, they may have expected something like 100-percent upward mobility and have been more frustrated and embittered than their objectively less-mobile French counterparts. This extreme example is perhaps implausible, but the general point—the need to examine subjective perceptions and expectations as well as objective measurements—must be kept firmly in mind.

Despite these cautions, my hunch is that future research will on the whole support the contention that the American social order has been distinctly more fluid than that of most European countries, and that the availability of superior opportunities for individual self-advancement in the United States did significantly impede the formation of class-based protest movements that sought fundamental alterations in the economic system. A comparison of the American evidence reviewed earlier in this chapter with a careful study of mobility in mid-nineteenth-century Marseilles reveals glaring contrasts of the kind hypothesized here, and an ongoing project treating Frankfurt, Rotterdam, and San Francisco in the late nineteenth century points in the same direction.[30] The national differences disclosed by these inquiries obviously do not constitute a full explanation of the varying political histories of these nations. It is hard, however, to believe that they are entirely irrelevant to such an explanation.

How long the buoyant character of the American social system will continue in the future is uncertain. The dynamic quality of the mobility process stemmed from certain historical influences—most notably the cycle of migration that drew into the cities newcomers from across the oceans or from the farms of America to fill the blue-collar jobs that demanded least in the way of education and skills, long-term changes in the occupational structure that opened up new room at the top from generation to generation, and the demographic vacuum created by the failure of upper-status men to produce enough sons to fill the vacancies created by their retirement. When the United States becomes a fully urbanized country in the not-too-distant future, and the supply of low-skilled rural migrants is hence exhausted, escape from the lower rungs of the class ladder can come from only three sources: (1) further changes in the occupational structure that create room at the top; (2) class differences in fertility that produce an insufficient stock of sons among high-status groups; and (3) downward mobility from high- to low-ranked occupations. There clearly are limits to how much further the first of these can proceed, and since World War II class differences in fertility have narrowed so as nearly to eliminate the demographic vacuum. It thus seems problematical whether the mobility pattern that has prevailed in the United States for a century or more will continue into the indefinite future. It seems likely that the mobility process will tend to become more of a zero-sum game, in which the number of climbers and skidders will have to be in approximate balance, which will entail either a sharp diminution in rates of upward mobility or a dramatic increase in the volume of downward mobility.

Such a departure from the historic American mobility pattern would doubtless embitter large numbers of people and heighten social conflict. It could, however, promote a reexamination of the opportunity ethic itself, a questioning of the fundamental principle that extreme disparities in command over resources are justifiable so long as they result from "fair" and "open" competition. Out of this process of questioning might emerge a richer and more humane conception of the just society.[31]

APPENDIXES NOTES INDEX

Nothing is easier than to choose from a given population so many hundreds or so many thousands of individuals . . . whose circumstances, duly set down in arithmetical terms, shall constitute a picture of economic life thoroughly biased and misleading . . . When, therefore, an inquiry, instead of covering all possible instances in a given population, is necessarily and confessedly based upon selected units, it is imperative . . . that the selection be made by a strictly objective test, and that the nature of the test shall be explicitly made known to all who read and venture to use the results.

F. H. GIDDINGS [1]

appendix A. THE SOURCES AND THE SAMPLES

True enough, and particularly so in the present instance. This book makes assertions about basic social processes and patterns that affected the lives of some millions of individuals who lived in the city of Boston at some point in the past nine decades on the basis of actual study of only a few thousand persons. The question of how the "selected units" under scrutiny were chosen is important in any inquiry that employs a sample and generalizes to a large population. It is doubly important here because historians have not yet developed any generally accepted guidelines for sampling records of the kind utilized in this study, and I thus encountered a number of problems that have not been discussed and resolved in the literature.

THE SOURCES AND THE TRACING PROBLEM

The skeleton of this book was constructed from raw material pertaining to five samples of the male population of Boston.

The first sample, for the year 1880, was drawn from the richest source of historical population data available to American researchers, the manuscript schedules of the United States Census. The manuscript schedules of later censuses, alas, have not yet been opened to scholars, and thus could not be utilized.[2] Their unavailability makes the systematic study of recent American social history considerably more difficult than would otherwise be the case. The alternative sources that can be used for a study of this kind are neither as comprehensive in coverage nor as rich in detail. Despite these limitations, however, it was possible to glean enough evidence from other local records to make this inquiry possible.

A second sample, designed to illuminate mobility patterns in early-twentieth-century Boston, was drawn from city marriage records for the year 1910. The marriage-license applications indicated the age, occupation, nativity, and religious affiliation of the groom, as well as the name of his father. The occupations of at least those fathers of the grooms who were then living in Boston could be discovered from a search of the city directory, which allowed analysis of patterns of intergenerational as well as career mobility. A sample of men getting married is not, of course, representative of the entire adult male population; its age distribution, for one thing, is skewed toward the young-adult years, and it leaves out men who never marry (who might possibly have career patterns that differ from those of married men.) [3] But these did not seem crippling flaws; indeed, the relative youth of the sample members was something of an advantage, in that it assured abundant information about the criticial early and middle stages of these men's careers. So long as comparisons with the other samples employed proper age controls, as was done, the skewed age distribution of the sample posed no great problem.

The chief difficulty with the 1910 sample, preliminary analysis revealed, was that not very many of the fathers of the sampled grooms could in fact be located in Boston, so that the number of cases in which intergenerational mobility could be measured was disappointingly low. This led me to abandon my original plan of drawing a similar sample of men marrying in Boston two decades later, and to select a third sample from a source that supplied definite information about the fathers' occupations, namely, local birth records for 1930. To obtain the evidence about the social rank of fathers contained in the birth records seemed worth the loss of the precise comparability that sampling another set of marriage records would have provided. However, my hope of accumulating fuller data on intergenerational mobility from the birth records was disappointed.

All of the fathers in the sample could be ranked occupationally from information in the birth certificates, but the intergenerational mobility of their sons could not, of course, be estimated until these infants had reached maturity and entered the labor market. And it happened, regrettably, that a great many of these youths disappeared from Boston before that. This 1930 sample did, however, provide extensive evidence about the career patterns of the fathers included, and at least some suggestive clues about mobility between generations.

I initially thought that an analysis of the experience of the sons from the 1930 sample would be a sufficient basis for generalizations about the process of social circulation in Boston in the 1950's and 1960's, but the departure of so many of these men from the city convinced me of the need for supplementary information. Two sources of such information were found.

One was a fourth sample of the Boston population drawn from the 1958 city directory. The directory included no data on age, father's occupation, or ethnic background, which limited the analytical possibilities of this sample considerably, but it did provide a firmer base for discussing patterns of persistence and career mobility in the most recent period.

The major gap in the 1958 city directory sample—the absence of any evidence on intergenerational mobility—was filled with a fifth sample, one gathered by another investigator for other purposes. This was Edward Laumann's stratified, area-probability interview survey of residents of Cambridge and Belmont, Massachusetts, in 1963. These two suburban communities were not, of course, fully representative of Boston proper, but the data on intergenerational occupational mobility that this sample yielded were revealing when used with due caution.[4]

The information provided in the sources from which these samples were drawn was deficient in one crucial respect. It revealed the situation of individuals at one moment in time, as in a snapshot. But the critical unexplored questions about urban social life in the past are dynamic in character. We wish, for example, to know if young men who began their careers as ditchdiggers at the age of 14 were doomed to remain unskilled laborers for a lifetime, or whether there were channels of social ascent open to them. We wish to know if men born into upper-middle-class homes were far more likely to obtain well-paid, respectable white-collar jobs themselves than youths of proletarian origins. We wonder how occupational mobility in the past was related to other forms of social mobility—the acquisition of property, for instance—and whether men of different national, religious, and racial origins had equal opportunities for advancement. The sources from which the samples were taken, alas, did not in themselves provide sufficient evidence to deal with these issues. They provided information about the social rank of sample members at one moment, but not at any subsequent time.

The ideal country in which to study the dynamics of migration and social stratification would be one whose historical records provided, for every inhabitant, a full occupational history for himself and for his father, a list of all of the communities in which he lived during his lifetime, an indication of how much property he had accumulated at various points of his career, and information about a number of other social characteristics, such as his religion, his ethnic background, and the amount and type of education he had received. The population registers of nations like Holland and the Scandinavian countries are the closest approximation to such a record, though even they fall short of this ideal. In any event, nothing remotely like this exists for the United States. There are many records which provide fragments of relevant social data, but the time dimension is always missing. A sense of process, a dynamic view of the American class structure, therefore, cannot be obtained without tracing representative individuals over time, through a series of *separate* records.

The most satisfactory method of carrying out this task would be via a computerized linkage system. The information from two or more sets of records can be put in machine-readable form and placed in the memory cells of a computer. Given a set of rules which specify the criteria for deciding that a set of records pertains to the same individual, the computer can readily perform the linkage.[5] It was not possible, however, to employ this technique in the present study, because of the monumental labor and expense that would have been involved. To trace the members of the 1880 sample in this fashion, for instance, would have required that data about the *entire* male population of Boston in 1890, 1900, 1910, 1920, and 1930 be coded and transferred to cards or tape. To carry out by machine all of the linkages that were made in this inquiry would have required the processing of more than 2 million cases. The modest resources I had at my disposal rendered this impossible.

A much simpler and more economical alternative was fortunately available. There were historical sources suitable for tracing men over time that had the immense advantage of being alphabetized, namely, the local city directories and the city tax records. Straightforward manual linkage of separate records was thus possible. Information about the occupation, place of residence, and wealth in 1890 of a member of the 1880 sample could be obtained by consulting the appropriate pages of the 1890 city directory and the tax records.

THE SAMPLING PROCEDURE

There was, however, a serious difficulty in the tracing process, a difficulty that affected the sampling procedure I employed. The information provided in the directories and tax records was very scanty —first and last name and sometimes middle initial, occupation, address, and property holdings. How could it be established that the John Murphy who was identified as a common laborer residing in East Boston in the 1880 Census schedules was the same John Murphy who lived in East Boston and was employed as a carpenter according to the Boston city directory of 1890? It happens that there were no fewer than 235 John Murphys listed in the local directory for 1890, 120 of them without even a middle initial to assist identification! There were, in addition, 122 John Smiths, 88 Patrick Sullivans, and 90 Michael Murphys. If the tracing sources had provided much fuller information—age, first names of wife and children, place of birth, and the like—many of these cases of doubtful identity could have been cleared up, but the directories and tax records, the only suitable alphabetized tracing sources available, did not. Some arbitrary rules for resolving the difficulty might have been devised.[6] It could, for instance, have been assumed that men are more likely to remain working at the same job than to remain living in the same neighborhood, and to take similarity of occupation as a stronger indication of identity than similarity of neighborhood. But this seemed to me to assume answers to the very questions the study sought to explore, and possibly would have biased the findings in serious and unknown ways.

A different and unorthodox, but not quite unprecedented, solution to the problem was therefore adopted. I decided to draw a random sample from the sources—to take every *x*th name—but to discard individuals selected by this procedure who had common names, and to take the next name on the list as a substitute.[7] Before accepting a randomly selected name as sufficiently distinctive to be traceable at the next stage of data gathering, my research assistant checked it in the Boston city directory for the year in question. If two or more persons with identical first and last names were recorded there, the individual was passed over in favor of the next name in the source. The John Murphy problem was thus solved by leaving the John Murphys of the city out of the study altogether. As a result, the samples utilized here are not true random samples, but random samples of Bostonians with relatively uncommon names.[8]

I am now of the opinion that this was not the wisest strategy to adopt, and that future investigators confronting similar problems would do well to follow a different procedure. Instead of rejecting a randomly selected case when the name in question was likely to be untraceable, it would be preferable to include it. Lest this produce too small a sample of traceable cases, a quick pilot study should be made to reveal the extent of the problem and the sample size could then be adjusted accordingly.

It is important to realize that pursuing this strategy would not have yielded samples whose *traceable* members had significantly different characteristics from those of the members of the samples in the present study. People with common names would still have had to be ignored in the subsequent mobility analysis. But the original samples would at least have been true random samples, and it would have been possible to go on to show precisely how its traceable and untraceable components differed from each other. I cannot do this, regrettably, and this is a mistake others should avoid.

Despite this methodological error, there are grounds for confidence that the departure from orthodox sampling procedure made here did not in fact result in samples that were grossly unrepresentative of the population of the entire city. A good deal of information about the social and economic characteristics of the people of Boston is available in the published volumes of the United States Census. A comparison of the study samples with these census check data will disclose whether the sampling method I followed was seriously biased, and if so in what ways.

Appendix A

SAMPLE REPRESENTATIVENESS AS MEASURED BY CENSUS CHECK DATA

One could not, of course, expect to find a perfect correspondence between the distribution of population characteristics in a sample and in a full census enumeration. All but one of the samples employed in the study were drawn from information collected by organizations other than the Bureau of the Census, which in the best of circumstances would produce some variations. The census itself was far from perfect; even today there are quite substantial census errors in the enumeration of certain groups, such as young Negro males, and similar errors were doubtless made in past censuses as well.[9] Nor is it likely that the Boston birth and marriage records and city directories were perfectly accurate. In addition, in any sample of a larger population there is a margin of sampling error; even the relatively large samples employed here produce estimates that might be expected to vary from the true population figure by a few percentage points.

Given these cautions, the check data seem reassuring on most, though not all, counts. One important point of comparison between the samples and the census figures for the population of Boston as a whole is occupational distribution. Did the decision to exclude men with extremely common names greatly distort the occupational distribution of the samples, giving them either a much more heavily proletarian or a much more heavily middle-class composition than the city as a whole? It does not seem so from Table A.1.

Given the existence of normal sampling error, the impossibility of precisely coding the tabulated census data into the categories employed in the study, and the special age and marital characteristics of the 1910 and 1930 samples, the samples display a resemblance to the entire Boston labor force that is impressive. The only discrepancies of any magnitude—and those not enormous by the standards set by similar previous investigations—appeared in the samples from the 1958 city directory and from Cambridge and Belmont in 1962 which had respectively 10 and 8 percent more white-collar workers than the 1960 Census reported.[10] The first of these discrepancies is doubtless attributable to the selectivity of the city directory from which the sample was drawn, a matter explored at length below, and the second reflects the special characteristics of Cam-

Appendix A

TABLE A.1. Sample representativeness by occupational level: distribution (percent) of entire Boston male labor force and of samples)[1]

	1880		*1910*		*1930*		*1960*		
Occupational level	*Census*	*Sample*	*Census*	*Sample*	*Census*	*Sample*	*Census*	*Directory sample*	*Laumann sample*
White-collar	32	35	35	30	36	32	46	56	54
Blue-collar	68	65	65	70	64	68	54	44	46
Skilled	36	27	22	27	21	29	21	19	17
Semiskilled	17	20	32	27	30	31	27	21	23
Unskilled	15	18	11	16	13	8	6	5	7

[1] A more detailed distribution of white-collar workers into high and low white-collar jobs cannot be given because the Bureau of the Census did not distinguish large from small proprietors. Absolutely precise coding of the census data into the blue-collar skill levels used for the samples was not possible either, and this is responsible for some of the discrepancies here. The 1910 and 1930 samples were younger than the labor force as a whole, since they were composed of newlyweds and new fathers respectively, and this, as well as class differences in marriage and fertility rates, probably accounts for the slight overrepresentation of blue-collar workers in them.

bridge and Belmont. Generalizations derived from the patterns displayed in either of these samples must therefore be made with some caution, but the extent to which they were skewed occupationally was by no means so great as to render them useless for my purposes.

A number of other checks between sample characteristics and census data attest to the general reliability of the sampling procedure, despite its one unorthodox feature. For instance, men in the samples were distributed throughout the neighborhoods of the city in proportions closely similar to the population as a whole. Thus 40 percent both of the men in the 1880 sample and of the entire population of Boston resided in the inner core of the city, 8 percent of the sample and 9 percent of the total population lived in East Boston, 10 percent of both lived in Charlestown, 15 percent of both lived in South Boston, and so forth. The percentage of illiterate males in the 1880 sample was 4.4, as opposed to 4.5 for the entire city. The mean size of sampled families corresponded closely to the mean for the city as a whole.

The balance between immigrants and natives in the samples also squares well with the census check data in the three instances in which the data permitted a comparison (Table A.2). There was a

TABLE A.2. Sample representativeness by national origin (percent)

	1880		1910		1930	
National origin	*Census*[1]	*Sample*[1]	*Census*[2]	*Sample*[3]	*Census*[1]	*Sample*[4]
Native-born	58	57	48	46	59	52
Foreign-born	42	43	52	54	41	48
Distribution of foreign-born[5]						
Britain	29	28	22	19	26	19
Ireland	48	46	23	8	16	6
Italy	2	1	16	24	18	32
Other	21	25	39	49	40	43

[1] Employed males.
[2] Males of voting age.
[3] Bridegrooms.
[4] Fathers.
[5] The U. S. Census of 1880 did not tabulate the national origins of Boston's immigrants for males separately, and even the more detailed tabulations in Carroll D. Wright, *The Social Commercial and Manufacturing Statistics of the City of Boston* (Boston, 1882) do not provide sufficient evidence about particular immigrant groups. These figures were therefore taken from the Massachusetts State Census of 1885. Similar checks of the 1958 and 1963 samples cannot be made, because the city directory included no information concerning ethnic background, and Laumann's tabulations are not comparable with available census figures.

difference of but 1 percent in the native:immigrant ratio in the 1880 figures, and of only 2 percent in 1910. The foreign-born were overrepresented by 7 percent in the 1930 sample, but this is probably attributable not to the decision to exclude individuals with common names from the sample, but rather to the fact that the census check data pertain to employed males, whereas the sample was of men whose wives bore sons during the year. The higher fertility of the immigrant population doubtless led to some overrepresentation of foreign-born men in the birth records. The moderate excess of immigrants in the 1930 sample suggests the need for some caution in generalizing from the population listed in the birth certificates to the total adult male population of the city, but it does not call into question the procedure by which the sample was selected from the birth records.

More important discrepancies between the samples and the census check data appear when we examine the particular nationality groups that composed Boston's immigrant population. The 1880 sample seems to have had just about its proper share of men of British, Irish, Italian, and other nationalities. But both the 1910 and the 1930 samples had much too low a proportion of Irish immigrants, and a corresponding excess of Italians and East Europeans. Part of the explanation lies in the fact that particular immigrant groups varied considerably in their propensity to marry and in their fertility, and hence in the likelihood of their appearing in samples from marriage licenses and birth certificates. The available evidence is very spotty, but it is plain that Irish immigrants failed to marry at all in much larger numbers than other groups, and tended to have rather small families compared with other groups of comparable occupational rank. Italians and East Europeans, by contrast, who seem substantially overrepresented in the 1910 and 1930 samples, had very high marriage and fertility rates.[11]

There is little doubt, however, that part of this imbalance in the samples stems from the decision to exclude men with common names. Of the seven names most frequently listed in the Boston city directories—John Murphy, John Smith, John Kelly, John McDonald, Michael Murphy, Patrick Sullivan, and John Shea—five were patently Irish. Italian and East European names, conversely, exhibited much wider variation, and this helped to produce the excess of men with these backgrounds in the samples.

This is unfortunate, but I doubt that it distorted my findings as much as might be imagined. The conclusion, for instance, that both the Irish and the Italians ranked low in occupational achievement should be unaffected by the underrepresentation of the former and the overrepresentation of the latter in two of the samples. In an analysis in which nationality is the independent variable, the question is not whether there are too many or too few Irish immigrants in the sample, but whether the particular Irish included were representative of the entire group of Irish in the city. One might legitimately compare samples of 500 Irish and 500 Italian newcomers even if there were four times as many Irish as Italian immigrants in the city as a whole. Only if the John Murphys and Patrick Sullivans of Boston had had different characteristics than their compatriots with less common names—which is difficult to believe—would the sampling procedure followed have produced misleading conclusions about the Irish as a group.

The imperfect representation of particular ethnic groups in the

1910 and 1930 samples might, however, have yielded a somewhat erroneous picture of the relative mobility of immigrants and natives and of overall mobility rates in the city. If, for instance, there were too few Irish and too many Italians in the sample and Irish and Italian mobility patterns differed sharply, estimates of the overall mobility of immigrants in general would be thrown off. In fact, however, it happens that both the most underrepresented and the most overrepresented groups in these samples had similar mobility patterns. Both, that is, experienced less upward mobility than the city norm, so that these biases in the samples tended to cancel each other out. There was, though, also a 10-percent excess of East Europeans in the 1910 sample, which probably inflated the overall mobility estimates for this sample because East European newcomers were an especially successful group. This probably explains the slightly higher rates of upward career and intergenerational mobility that were in fact observed for this sample.

A further check on the representativeness of the samples is provided in Table A.3, which compares the occupational distribution

TABLE A.3. Sample representativeness by nativity and occupation: foreign-born males in white-collar occupations (percent)

Year	*Census*	*Sample*
1880	18[1]	21
1910	24	20
1930	24	22

[1] In the absence of a breakdown of occupation by nativity in the published 1880 Census material, 1890 Census data were used here.

of foreign-born sample members with that of all immigrant males as reported by the census. In none of the three samples did the proportion of immigrant white-collar workers deviate as much as 5 percent from the census figure.

It does not, in sum, appear that the somewhat unorthodox sampling procedure that was followed to solve the John Murphy problem produced samples that were seriously unrepresentative of the Boston population in most significant respects. Two of the samples, of course, represented not the entire adult male population of the city but only the sector getting married in a particular year in one instance and having male children in a particular year in the other. This limitation was unavoidable, given the records available for sampling, and it poses no grave problems for the analysis if proper age controls are applied. The only troubling feature of the samples that was apparently the result of the sampling procedure itself was the imperfect representation of some of the major ethnic groups of the community. This imbalance, I have suggested, does not necessarily call into question my conclusions about ethnic differences in mobility patterns, but it is a real weakness of the study. Future investigators, I hope, will deal with this difficult problem more successfully than I have.

SAMPLE SIZE AND SAMPLE ATTRITION

The purpose of sampling "selected units" is to discover something about the characteristics of an entire population without going to the excruciating labor of examining it item by item. We may generalize about a class of objects on the basis of a number of individual specimens, with a known probability of being accurate. If an adequate sampling procedure is followed—the reasons for believing that the procedure adopted here was broadly satisfactory have now been reviewed—the main determinant of the reliability of the generalization is the size of the sample. However carefully selected, a sample of 10 will not supply very reliable information about the population of a very large entity, such as the city of Boston. A random sample of 100,000 individuals, on the other hand, would guarantee a tremendously accurate estimate, but at so great a cost that there might be little point in sampling at all; the job of sampling would approach in magnitude the task of surveying the entire population man for man. As this suggests, there is no single "correct" sample size. A sample of proper size is one large enough to permit generalizations within a range of error the investigator finds tolerable, and yet small enough to be feasible, given his energies and his budget.

These considerations governed the size of the samples drawn for the study. The largest sample was that for 1880, both because the source utilized—the manuscript census schedules—was unusually rich and because so little was known about social mobility in late-nineteenth-century America. The 1880 sample included 3730 individuals, half of them adults and half children. The 1910 marriage-license records yielded 1078 new bridegrooms; the 1930 sample consisted of 861 newborn male infants and the 861 men who sired them; the 1958 city directory provided another 1030 men. With Laumann's 1962 sample of Cambridge and Belmont ($N = 405$) this gave a total of 7965 males.

These samples seemed suitably large for my purposes. At first blush, indeed, they seemed extremely large by comparison with those of similar studies conducted by social scientists in other communities. Two important prior investigations of social mobility in the United States employed samples of only 637 and 784 individuals. Lipset and Bendix's well-known Oakland study was based upon a sample population of 935; Sidney Goldstein's Norristown study utilized samples ranging from 544 to 973; Gerhard Lenski's generalizations about religious differences in mobility patterns in Detroit draw on annual surveys of from 520 to 766 individuals.[12] By these standards the Boston samples seemed highly satisfactory.

These comparisons, however, are somewhat misleading, because the aforementioned studies were based on questionnaires, which directly provided the evidence necessary to analyze social mobility. In none of them was there the slippage or attrition that plagues the historian who must piece together the information needed for mobility analysis from a variety of different sources. Of the 1809 sample members employed in Boston in 1880, only 1158 were still to be found in the city in 1890. Evidence about career mobility between 1880 and 1890 was thus available for less than two-thirds of the original group; 36 percent had vanished from the scene. The attrition problem was even more severe in the other samples. Some 59 percent of the 1910 sample of newlyweds, 43 percent of the fathers in the 1930 sample, and 54 percent of the members of the 1958 city-directory sample disappeared from Boston before a decade elapsed. This still left a number of cases suitable for analysis that was reasonably large relative to other comparable investigations, but by no means as comfortably large as it had seemed at first.

The problem of missing information for a large fraction of the sample, and hence of small numbers, was more bothersome when it came to exploring the impact of social-class origins upon the careers of Boston residents. The occupation of an individual's father is the most convenient and generally satisfactory index of his social-class background. But the sources sampled did not supply this information, except in the case of youths who were still living in their fathers' households at the time of the 1880 Census. Though there were nearly 1100 father-son pairs in the sample taken from 1910 marriage-license files, the record did not specify the occupations of these fathers, only their names. To place them occupationally required a search in the city directory, and it happened that only about a fifth of the newlyweds had fathers who were employed in Boston at that time. A comparable problem existed with the 1930 sample, of 861 fathers and their newborn sons. The social-class origins of all of these infants could be judged well enough, but only about a quarter of them were living and working in Boston as grown men three decades later, when a trace of their occupations was attempted. In both cases, then, samples of the magnitude of about 1000 yielded something on the order of only 200 cases usable for the analysis of intergenerational mobility.

Generalizations about the population of a major metropolis on the basis of 200 cases are not as reliable as one would wish, but there are a number of more reassuring considerations. First, some of the samples supplied more cases suitable for intergenerational analysis; there was the 1880 Census sample, and in addition Laumann's 1962 survey of Cambridge and Belmont, which offered 405 father-son comparisons.

A second comforting point is that the adequacy of the sample size depends upon the magnitude of the difference being observed. We could for instance, conclude with a good deal of confidence that the Boston Irish were less successful than the Yankees on the basis of representative samples of 20 of each, if 100 percent of the Yankees and none of the Irish were upwardly mobile. The probability that chance fluctuation could produce so dramatic a difference as this is tiny. There are standard tests of statistical significance which indicate the likelihood that a given finding may be attributed to mere chance, and these have been employed throughout.

Finally, and most important, the central conclusions of this study depend, for the most part, not upon a pattern observed in any one sample, but rather upon patterns displayed in all of them. Consistency of pattern between separate samples is powerful testimony that something more than chance produced the finding. Consider a finding which, because of the small size of the sample, can pass only a very weak test of statistical significance; it is significant, let us say, only at the 0.10 level. Then in 1 case out of 10 we could expect this finding to appear out of sheer chance, which is too great a likelihood for most social scientists, who prefer a 0.05 or even 0.01 level of significance. But the chance of this same finding's occurring in *two* separate samples is 0.10×0.10, or 0.01; the chance of its occurring in three samples is $0.10 \times 0.10 \times 0.10$, or 0.001. Small samples which achieve only a weak level of statistical significance can nonetheless yield findings that are almost certainly not the result of chance variation, when the same pattern appears in each of them.[13]

To say that the problem of sample attrition was not so severe as to undermine the main conclusions of this study is not, however, to deny that it limited the analytical possibilities at many points, requiring the use of broad rather than precise categories so as to avoid tables in which the percentages in some cells were based on a mere handful of cases. Thus it has been possible to say more about differences between immigrants and Yankees than about differences between say, Irish immigrants and Italian immigrants. Similarly, much of the analysis concerns rates of movement between manual and nonmanual occupations, whereas ideally it would have been preferable to employ a more finely calibrated occupational scale, which distinguished between the upward mobility of two carpenters who moved into the white-collar world, one of them by becoming a prosperous contractor and the other by becoming a small grocer. Such distinctions have been recognized at many points, but in some instances the limits of the sample size prevented it. Certain of the findings of this study, therefore, are merely suggestive, and might well be revised or overturned by fuller investigations in the future.

PERSISTENCE, OUT-MIGRATION, AND THE ACCURACY OF THE TRACING OPERATION

The accuracy with which I have measured the movement of sample members into and out of the city and up and down the social ladder within it depends upon the accuracy of the tracing process employed in the study. If many of the men who seem to have left the city and were recorded as out-migrants were in fact still present there and missed in the tracing operation, the study's estimates of out-migration rates are exaggerated, and even the estimates of occupational mobility are called into question, since the career patterns of persisting men mistakenly missed in the traces may have differed considerably from those of men who were successfully traced. A fuller discussion of the tracing process and the tracing sources is thus in order.

The chief instrument used in tracing sample members over time was the Boston city directory, a privately printed publication derived from a careful annual door-to-door canvass of each house in the community.[14] Sample members were traced in successive city directories at 10-year intervals; even when an individual was recorded as absent on one trace he was checked in later directories as well, to guard against erroneous nonlistings and to pick up cases of out-migrants who later returned to Boston. (City tax records were used as well for supplementary tracing, but they proved less useful in identifying persisters and migrants because they supplied no information about address or occupation and there were thus many instances in which definite identification could not be made.) The sources of potential error in the tracing process are the following.

First, some men classified as out-migrants may have been still listed in the directories but missed in the tracing process. Two ways in which this might have happened come to mind. One is simple error on the part of a research assistant whose mind was wandering and who made a mistake as a result. The students who assisted me were extremely diligent and conscientious workers, as the periodic quality checks I conducted revealed.[15] But a few mistakes were doubtless made, and these mistakes probably tended to bias the findings in one direction. It was easier to overlook and to record as absent a man who was actually still present in the city than it was to code a sample member present when in fact he was not. Failing to spot the appropriate name in a directory could have happened through a lapse of attention, but probably not a mistaken identification of a missing sample member as present. The persistence estimates given in the study probably err on the low side for this reason, but I doubt that the error is of much magnitude.

A related source of error is that some men may have been untraceable not because they had actually disappeared from the city but because they were listed in the directory under a different name. This could stem from spelling errors on the part of directory canvassers, or from deliberate name changes, most commonly the

Anglicization of European names. My assistants were alerted to the problem, and many name alterations that involved only slight modifications, such as omission of a syllable, were caught through diligent searching. But some name changes, especially radical ones, were doubtless missed, and those persons were erroneously identified as out-migrants. That this significantly distorted any of the chief findings is doubtful. The most careful attempt that has yet been made to conquer the problem of name changes in linking historical records—in Sidney Goldstein's Norristown study—reported only "a few instances" of drastic change.[16] It is reassuring, too, that the persistence estimates made in that inquiry, arduously corrected for name changes, so closely resemble the less carefully corrected Boston rates given here (see Table 9.1).

Few sample members who were actually listed in the city directories, it is safe to conclude, were missed in the tracing process. But what of the possibility that many of those classified as nonpersisters were in fact still living in the city but were for some reason not included in the directories? The directories may, that is, have provided an incomplete and biased listing of the population of the city. This is an important issue, not only because it raises doubts about the conclusions of this book but also because increasing numbers of other investigators are now turning to the city directories as a source of historical population data.[17] Unless it can be demonstrated that the city directory is a reasonably comprehensive and accurate source, much of the new work in urban history will stand upon shaky foundations.

One serious question concerns the extent to which the Boston city directories enumerated persons living within the metropolitan area but outside the limits of Boston proper. Even in 1880 less than half of the population of the area later designated by the Census Bureau as the Boston Standard Metropolitan Statistical Area resided in the city of Boston itself, and by 1970 suburbanites outnumbered central-city residents 3 to 1. If individuals moving from Boston proper to the suburbs were thereby lost to the study, the persistence and out-migration estimates given here are much less striking than would otherwise be the case. And the findings concerning occupational mobility might be seriously in error as well, if it happened that men moving to the suburbs had different career patterns from those remaining in the central city.

Fortunately, however, there were means of tracing a substantial fraction of Boston's inner-city residents after they joined the suburban exodus. First of all, the Boston directories were not in fact confined to persons living within the city boundaries. The policy followed by the firm responsible for producing the directories is not altogether clear, but it is evident from close inspection of the listings that coverage extended to all persons employed in the city proper, wherever they lived, and to substantial numbers of persons who both worked and lived in the suburbs. Thus 45 percent of the men listed in the 1958 Boston directory lived outside the city proper. This is less than comprehensive coverage of the suburban communities within the Boston SMSA, for they then contained 73 percent of the SMSA population, but it establishes that directory listings were very far from being confined to inner-city residents.

There remained, though, a substantial gap in the coverage of the suburbs provided by the Boston directories, and this demanded an additional research effort. Separate directories were available for the following independent cities and towns within the metropolitan area: Cambridge, Chelsea, Everett, Lynn, Malden, Medford, Quincy, Revere, and Somerville. Sample members were searched for in the directories for these nine suburban communities, which contained 37 percent of Boston's suburban population in 1880 and 33 percent in 1960. At least a third of the men who moved outward from Boston proper into a suburb thus entered communities whose directories were combed, and a further very large, if indeterminate, fraction of movers remained within tracing range because they were included in the Boston directories.

A more precise assessment of the magnitude of this problem cannot be made, regrettably, from the evidence at hand. Despite my efforts, there was substantial slippage stemming from the migration of sample members to places within the metropolitan area but outside the orbit of any city directory.

This limitation of the study suggests two caveats about my conclusions. First, it must be noted that much of the heavy flow of out-migration from Boston entailed movement outside the metropolitan area, but by no means all of it; an unknown but sizable minority of out-migrants made short-distance intrametropolitan moves only. Second, it is possible that my inability to track down all of the out-migrants whose destinations were the suburbs led to some underestimation of the level of upward occupational mobility in the community, since the suburbs may have attracted disproportionate numbers of aspiring men who were rising in the world. This possible bias, however, only serves to strengthen the main point I have emphasized—that the Boston social structure over the past century has been strikingly fluid. A fuller canvass of sample members who fled to the suburbs would presumably have only underlined that conclusion.

Another important issue is whether the Boston city directories were incomplete and socially skewed in their enumeration of even the population of Boston proper—whether there were class and ethnic biases that led to the exclusion of some elements of the population. The only extensive discussion of this important issue presently available is in a chapter on "The Validity of City Directories as Sources of Migration Data" in Sidney Goldstein's valuable study of Norristown, Pennsylvania, 1910–1950. Goldstein is optimistic about the coverage of the Norristown directories, but it is by no means clear that his case for the validity of the directories in a small twentieth-century city applies to a much larger metropolis over a longer historical span. There is, furthermore, an important flaw in Goldstein's defense of the Norristown directories, for he did not directly compare individual listings in the directories with those from another independent source, but instead relied upon the general resemblance between the population totals and occupational distributions derived from the directories and the census.

It seemed important, therefore, to discover whether the Boston city directories included all of the individuals who appeared in the samples drawn from other sources. Each sample member was checked in the city directory for the sample year 1800, 1910, or 1930 (since the 1958 sample was itself taken from the directory, no such check for that year was possible). The results were, at first glance, surprising and disconcerting. Only 73 percent of the adult members of the sample from the U. S. Census of 1880 were listed in the 1880 city directory, and 77 percent of the sample from the 1930 birth records were to be found in the 1930 directory. And, most troubling, a mere 43 percent of the young men marrying in Boston in 1910 were listed in that year's directory.

Not only were the Boston directories less than fully inclusive in coverage; even worse, there were systematic biases in whom they included and whom they excluded. Some 27 percent of the members of the 1880 sample were not to be found in the city directory of that year, but the rate of exclusion for the various occupational strata ranged from a low of 7 percent for men in high white-collar callings to a rate five times that for unskilled and semiskilled laborers. Similar occupational differentials in coverage held in the other samples as well. Likewise, Negroes were less often listed than whites, immigrants than natives, the propertyless than the propertied.

This suggested an ominous possibility. If the city directories consistently discriminated against lower-status groups, the findings of the study might be badly distorted. Any conclusions drawn about occupational differentials in persistence and out-migration would obviously be rendered suspect. Less obviously, the occupational mobility rates estimated could be distorted as well. A finding that 30 percent, let us say, of the low-skilled laborers residing in Boston in a given decade climbed to a skilled or white-collar job during these years would be erroneous if the source used for tracing was more likely to list upwardly mobile laborers than unsuccessful ones. Suppose, for instance, that there were 200 laborers in the 1880 sample, but only 100 of them listed in the city directory of 1890, 70 of these still laborers and 30 of them now in higher-ranked jobs. This would give a 30-percent rate of upward mobility during the decade. But if the 100 men seemingly absent in 1890 were all in fact still in the city and still laborers, and were merely left out of the directory because of its class bias, the proper base to employ in computing the mobility rate would be 200 and the correct rate would be only 15 percent. Clearly it is essential to inquire more closely into the sins of omission of the compilers of the Boston city directories to see if this example is farfetched.

The remarkably poor rate of coverage of the 1910 city directory, let it be said, probably does not indicate that this directory was of a poorer quality than the others, but only that a large number of the men who married in the city of Boston were not truly residents of the community, and instead had come into the city just to be married. But even in the other two samples roughly a quarter of the men who should have appeared in the directories did not, and in all three those of low status were least likely to be included. How can we account for the poor overall coverage of the directories, and for these apparent socioeconomic biases in coverage?

One source of the discrepancy between the directories and the sources from which the samples were drawn is that the directories were compared with other sources compiled the same year but not the same month or day; some sample members, therefore, were missed by the city directory canvassers for the good reason that they were not residents of the city at the precise time of the canvass. The Boston city directories were based on a door-to-door canvass conducted annually in May. Two of the samples were drawn from files of records for an entire year; they included, therefore, men who were married in Boston or who became fathers in Boston several months before or several months after the directory staff had made its rounds, and who may have left the city before the directory canvass or have migrated into it after the directory was compiled. In the case of the 1880 sample there could not have been so many instances of this sort, for the census was completed only 2 months after the directory. Even in 2 months, however, substantial numbers of men moved into Boston, as my earlier analysis of annual in- and out-migration flows suggested. More direct evidence of the possible volume of migration over a very short interval may be found in a recent analysis of the population of a mid-nineteenth-century Canadian city that revealed that fully 23 percent of the persons listed in the city's assessment rolls for 1852 were missing from the census conducted only 3 months earlier, and that a comparable percentage of household heads enumerated in the census were absent from the assessment rolls.[18] At least some fraction of the city-directory omissions in 1880 can be attributed to in-migration in the 2 months between the canvasses, and a more sizeable portion of the discrepancy between the directory and the two later sources may be similarly explained.

It still seems likely, however, that substantial numbers of men who were physically present in Boston at the time of the directory canvasses of 1880, 1910, and 1930 were not counted in them, and that these men were disproportionately of low socioeconomic status. The main explanation for these two disconcerting facts is that in practice the city directory defined "the population of Boston" in a way fundamentally different from that of the sources from which the original samples were drawn. Two of these sources were simply lists of all individuals who had performed a particular legal act in Boston during the year of the sample—signed a marriage-license or a birth-certificate application—and who had no necessary connection with the community other than that. The U. S. Census aimed at a complete enumeration of everyone who was physically present in Boston at the time of the canvass, the temporary inhabitants of a rooming house as well as the owner of a house on Beacon Street, the traveling salesman as well as the banker. The census takers were not perfectly successful, doubtless. But in principle the census was catholic in coverage, and in practice it did include a great many people who were only passing through Boston at the moment of the canvass. The central aim of the census takers was to find out how many people there were in the community at one point in time.

The central aim of the city directory appears to have been quite different. The compilers of the directory did not make their policy explicit, but the main function of the directories was not to count heads but rather to indicate the whereabouts of those inhabitants of the community who belonged there and whom one might reasonably expect to find still in the city by the time the directory had come off the printing press. It was a list of the *residents* of Boston, not of every inhabitant at one moment in time or of all persons registering a marriage or birth. Just as there was a legally specified residence requirement that had to be met before an individual could vote in a local election—6 months residence in the city, and 1 year in the state—there was an implicit residence requirement, it seems, for inclusion in the city directories. A careful analysis of mid-nineteenth-century census schedules and Boston city directories by Peter Knights reveals that the directory practice then was to include newcomers to the city only after they had lived there for 2 years. It is possible that this requirement was relaxed somewhat in the 1850's —the preface to the directory of 1858 remarks that "within a few years very many names have been inserted which previously it was not deemed necessary to give"—but it is clear that long after that the directory canvass was based on a conception of who was a true resident of the community, a conception that excluded substantial numbers of men whose presence was registered in the U. S. Census, marriage-license files, birth certificates, and similar records.

Demographers distinguish between an "actual" census and an "ideal" census. The former lists all persons actually present at the time of the canvass; the latter includes all those who should have been present but were not (vacationers, for example) and excludes those who were present but would not ordinarily have been so.[19] The city directories of Boston must be classed as ideal rather than actual censuses, and this accounts for the startling imperfection of their coverage of persons who appeared in sources that were of the actual-census type. Perhaps the city directories of twentieth-century Norristown about which Goldstein was so enthusiastic were closer to the actual-census type, but it is very doubtful; it is more likely that the distinction eluded him because there were fewer transients in that small city and it was thus less important. In any event, in Boston the difference was considerable.

That a good many men appearing in the sources from which the samples were drawn were not true residents of the community as the city directory defined residents, an "ideal" rather than an "actual" definition, is the main reason for the failure of the directories to include a quarter or more of the men who appeared in other lists of the Boston population in 1880, 1910, and 1930, and the main reason, as well, for the higher rate of omission of persons of low socioeconomic and ethnic status. There were upper-middle-class as well as lower-class transients, to be sure, but many more of the latter in the late nineteenth and early twentieth centuries. It was because, as compared with the population of the city as a whole, they were more often recent arrivals and temporary residents that men on the lower rungs of the social ladder were less likely to be listed in the three directories in which the cross-check was made.

This is extremely important, because it means that the directories did not deliberately and consistently fail to include men on the lower rungs of the social ladder per se. The directory policy of neglecting to include transients had the incidental effect of leaving out disproportionate numbers of low-status individuals, of course, and for some purposes it would amount to the same thing. But with respect to the question of the validity of the directories as a tracing instrument, the difference is crucial, for it means that the city directories did provide reasonably accurate information about long-term residents of the community whatever their social rank. It means that those laborers who did settle down in Boston and remain living there over a decade were not excluded from the directory compiled at the end of the period even if they were still mere laborers, which in turn means that my estimates of rates of migration and social mobility were not seriously distorted because of inadequacies in directory coverage.

Further support for this line of reasoning appears in the fact that a good many of the men who were not included in the directories of 1880, 1910, or 1930 were listed in a subsequent directory. Initial exclusion did not mean permanent exclusion, which again suggests that it was their transient status initially rather than the class bias of the directory compilers that accounted for their omission originally. Some 35 percent of the low-skilled workers who appeared in the 1880 census sample but not in that year's city directory did turn up in the directory of 1890, the great majority of them low-skilled laborers still, and similar rates of subsequent directory inclusion held in the later samples as well—29 percent and 32 percent. It was not low status per se, but transient status, which happened to be correlated with low status, that led to exclusion. Once settled in Boston for any length of time, it seems, sample members did typically find themselves listed in the prime source used for tracing, and they were thus properly counted in the foregoing calculations.

The city directories, in sum, do offer something rather different from an "actual" census of a city's population, but the respect in which they differed was not such as to impair the estimates of migration and social mobility offered in the present study. All of the figures provided here are susceptible to error, of course, but there is no apparent source of large and sysematic error that would call the principal findings into question.

appendix B. ON THE SOCIO-ECONOMIC RANKING OF OCCUPATIONS

This study draws conclusions about rates and patterns of movement up and down the Boston social ladder on the basis of evidence pertaining to certain kinds of occupational changes made by sample members, namely, job shifts across the boundaries of one of five occupational strata or two broad occupational classes. It is time to explain how these occupational groupings were devised, to indicate just what occupations fell into each category, and to justify the assumption that the five strata were arranged in a hierarchy, so that movement from one to another represented significant vertical social mobility.

The detailed occupational classification scheme employed to group the jobs held by sample members is reproduced in Table B.1. This, it will be seen, is simply a variant of the "social-economic grouping" of occupations originally devised by the census statistician Alba M. Edwards in the 1930's and employed, with minor modifications, in most American mobility studies that have been carried out since then.[1] That fact was in itself an important consideration, in that I hoped to be able to compare my findings with those of other investigators so as to arrive at larger conclusions about mobility trends in the United States during the past century.

Appendix B

TABLE B.1. Occupational rankings

WHITE-COLLAR OCCUPATIONS

I. HIGH WHITE-COLLAR

Professionals

Architect
Chemist
Clergyman
Editor
Engineer (except locomotive or stationary)
Lawyer
Pharmacist
Physician
Scientist
Social worker
Teacher
Veterinarian

Major Proprietors, Managers, and Officials

Banker
Broker
Builder, Contractor (with sufficient property[1])
Corporation official
Government official (upper ranks only[2])
Hotel keeper or manager
Labor-union officer
Manufacturer
Merchant (with sufficient property)

II. LOW WHITE-COLLAR

Clerks and Salesmen

Accountant
Advertising man
Agent
Auctioneer
Auditor
Baggageman
Bank teller
Bill collector
Bookkeeper
Canvasser
Cashier
Clerk
Collector
Credit man
Dispatcher
Insurance adjuster or salesman
Mail carrier
Messenger
Office boy
Salesman
Secretary
Typist

Semiprofessionals

Actor
Airplane pilot
Artist
Athlete
Chiropractor
Dietician
Draftsman
Embalmer
Entertainer
Journalist
Librarian
Musician
Newspaperman
Optician, Optometrist
Osteopath
Photographer
Surveyor
Technician—medical, dental, electrical, etc.
Writer

Appendix B

White-Collar Occupations

II. Low white-collar

Petty Proprietors, Managers, and Officials

- Foreman
- Huckster, Peddler
- Minor government official
- Proprietor or manager of a small business
- Railroad conductor
- Self-employed artisan[3]

Blue-Collar Occupations

III. Skilled (Apprentices in IV, Self-employed in II)

- Baker
- Blacksmith
- Boilermaker
- Bookbinder
- Bricklayer, Mason
- Carpenter, Cabinetmaker
- Caulker
- Compositor, Printer
- Confectioner
- Coppersmith
- Craneman, Derrickman
- Electrician
- Engineer (locomotive or stationary)
- Engraver
- Fireman (locomotive)
- Furrier
- Glazier
- Goldsmith
- Jeweler
- Lithographer
- Machinist
- Master mariner
- Mechanic
- Millwright
- Molder
- Painter
- Paperhanger
- Patternmaker
- Plasterer
- Plumber
- Roofer
- Shoemaker (except in factory—IV)
- Silversmith
- Slater
- Steamfitter
- Stonecutter
- Tailor
- Tinner
- Tool-and-die maker
- Upholsterer

IV. Semiskilled and service workers

- Apprentice
- Barber
- Bartender
- Brakeman
- Bus, cab, or truck driver, Chauffeur
- Cook
- Cooper
- Deliveryman
- Elevator operator
- Factory operative
- Fireman (stationary or city)
- Janitor
- Lineman
- Longshoreman
- Meatcutter
- Milkman
- Motorman
- Policeman
- Sailor
- Servant
- Soldier (except officers)
- Stevedore
- Switchman

TABLE B.1. Occupational rankings (*Continued*)

BLUE-COLLAR OCCUPATIONS	
IV. SEMISKILLED AND SERVICE WORKERS	
Fisherman	Teamster
Gas-station attendant	Waiter
Guard, Watchman	Welder
Hospital attendant	
V. UNSKILLED LABORERS AND MENIAL SERVICE WORKERS	
Coachman	Laborer
Gardener	Lumberman
Hostler, Liveryman	Porter

[1] The crucial distinction between large and petty proprietors was made from the search through the city's assessment rolls. Men in entrepreneurial callings assessed for at least $1000 in personal property or $5000 in real estate were classified as large proprietors. The arbitrary cutoff point may seem low, particularly for the later samples, but I was more interested in keeping a reasonable homogeneity of status in the petty-proprietor than in the large-proprietor category. In any event, the available information about property holdings, as explained previously, was scanty for the later samples and absent altogether for that drawn from the 1958 city directory, so that raising the cutoff to adjust for changes in income and price levels seemed unnecessary. A more fine-grained analysis of this whole problem, based upon fuller information, would be desirable.

[2] Important posts were defined as chief elective offices and appointive positions at the level of police captain or above.

[3] Self-employed artisans were identified by means of the business-directory section of the city directories. This group, however, had largely disappeared from Boston by 1880, so that the category was less useful than it might have been in a study of a less fully industrialized community.

The possibilities for comparative analysis opened up by use of a similar classification scheme, however, would be of limited value if the scheme were not an adequate representation of the occupational hierarchy, and I must establish that in fact it was. There are two problems here. First, it must be shown that most of the specific occupations assigned to a given stratum on the basis of a classification scheme developed in recent decades fell into the same stratum at a point more remote in time. Second, it must be demonstrated that the relative positions of the five strata—the hierarchy ranging from high white-collar workers on top to unskilled laborers on the bottom—remained largely unchanged over the period dealt with here.

The first of these issues—the accuracy with which particular occupations were assigned to a stratum—is rather easily disposed of.

Obviously there have been substantial changes in the world of work since the late nineteenth century. Certain callings—harnessmaker, blacksmith, coachman—have become obsolete, and a host of new ones—airplane pilot, auto mechanic—have been created. This could be a grave problem for studies that extend back into preindustrial settings, but it did not bulk large here.[2] By 1880 Boston was already a highly industrialized community with an occupational structure and division of labor that was essentially modern. A careful scrutiny of the detailed occupations listed in Table B.1 suggests that the overwhelming majority of the labor force was employed at jobs that fell in the same broad stratum in 1880 and 1970.

The difficult problem, however, is whether the five strata were indeed hierarchically arranged in the manner I have suggested, and whether that hierarchy remained essentially the same over the entire period. The overall shape of the Boston occupational structure certainly changed during the period. Less than a third of the city's workers held white-collar jobs in 1880; 80 years later the proportion had risen to nearly half (Table 4.1). There was a striking expansion of the professional category, and a dramatic shrinking of unskilled laboring jobs. If the relative positions of the various occupational groups changed as well—if, for instance, the status of skilled craftsmen was drastically altered compared with that of low white-collar employees—occupational shifts that have been counted as significant mobility in the preceding analysis did not have the same meaning at each point in time. What was genuine upward mobility at one time might have been merely horizontal mobility or even downward mobility at another. Many of the findings of this study—for instance, the apparent constancy of mobility patterns in Boston over the span of nearly a century—would be called into question if the nature of the occupational hierarchy itself was basically transformed during the period.

How can it be established that a particular occupation is socially superior to another? A wide range of criteria have been suggested in the literature: [3]

1. Levels of earnings (including fringe benefits, expense accounts, and other perquisites);
2. Regularity of earnings, and vulnerability to unemployment;
3. Levels of education and skill required;
4. Prospects for future career advancement;

5. Attractiveness of working conditions—clean work or dirty, physically exhausting or not, and so forth;

6. Opportunities to exercise authority over others, and freedom from control by others;

7. The social prestige attached by the public to the position.

Information about some of these matters, particularly historical information, is very difficult to obtain. Enough evidence is at hand, however, to justify the ranking scheme employed here. First, we will examine its validity against data from the contemporary period, and then consider the late-nineteenth- and early-twentieth-century situation.

The average educational and income levels of men in an occupation or group of occupations are important determinants of its ranking, for "education is a very large factor in the social status of workers, and wage or salary income is a very large factor in their economic status." [4] Table B.2 supplies some pertinent data on these matters: the median earnings of the various major occupational groups in Boston in 1959, comparable figures on the educational attainments of men in these groups in the northern and western United States in 1950 (in the absence of such tabulations for males in Boston a decade later), and a composite "socioeconomic index" that measures the relative income and educational status of the groups in the country as a whole in 1950.

It is, of course, true that such summary measures of the position of broad occupational groups conceal considerable variations within each. Surgeons, for instance, earned higher incomes on the average, and had completed more years of school, than elementary-school teachers, although both of these callings fell in the professional category. For that matter, there was some variation even within precisely defined occupations; some surgeons and some teachers earned a good deal more than others. There was even some overlapping between broad occupational groups. Approximately 15,000 of the city's professionals had incomes below the median for unskilled laborers ($3543); there were in turn some 1500 unskilled laborers who earned more than the median for professionals ($6741). There was, in short, heterogeneity within these groups that averages, whether medians or means, necessarily obscure. But these poorly paid professionals were in the bottom 15 percent of the income distribution for professionals; the prosperous laborers represented the top 4 percent

TABLE B.2. Median earnings, median education, and socioeconomic index, by major occupational group, 1950–1960[1]

Occupational group	Median earnings (dollars)	Median education (years)	Socio-economic index
I. High white-collar			
Professional, technical, and kindred workers	6741	16+	75
Managers, officials, and proprietors	7420	12.2	57
II. Low white-collar			
Sales workers	5345	12.4	49
Clerical workers	4598	12.2	45
III. Skilled			
Craftsmen and foremen	5378	9.5	31
IV. Semiskilled			
Operatives	4501	8.9	18
Service workers	3864	8.8	17
V. Unskilled			
Laborers	3543	8.4	7

[1] Median earnings are for 1959, and apply to males 14 or over in the Boston Standard Metropolitan Statistical Area; from the 1960 Census. In the absence of Boston data on education, or even any national tabulation for 1960, the education figures are for males in Northern and Western regions of the U. S. as of 1950; from the 1950 Census. The socioeconomic index, devised by Otis Dudley Duncan, ranks the groups by income and education (controlled for age) from national data for 1950; A. J. Reiss, Jr., *Occupations and Social Status* (Glencoe, Ill.: Free Press 1961), p. 155.

of wage earners in their category. Although predictions of the income (or education) of a given individual on the basis of knowledge of his occupation cannot be made with a high degree of reliability, the figures given in Table B.2 do indicate the central tendencies and supply reasonable grounds for generalizing about the relative positions of the groups themselves.[5]

The data reveal the distinctly superior ranking of high white-collar workers and the distinctly inferior position of semiskilled and unskilled laborers in contemporary America. Professionals and large businessmen earned about twice as much, on the average, as unskilled laborers and over 50 percent more than semiskilled workers, and these differentials would have been even larger if the census classification procedures corresponded exactly to those used in the study. The margin of advantage in educational attainment was about as large.

There seems to be more of a question, however, about the ranking of low white-collar and skilled workers. The former were much superior to the latter in education, but sales workers earned slightly less than craftsmen and foremen, and clerks earned substantially less. Figures such as these have led some observers to conclude that what was once a wide income gap between these two occupational groups has been eliminated in recent years.[6] The evidence for convergence in the earnings of skilled craftsmen and lower white-collar workers, however, is not entirely persuasive.

For one thing, the skilled median is inflated by the inclusion of highly paid foremen, who might more properly be classified in the low white-collar group, as has been done in the present study. Furthermore, the data are not standardized for age, which is important because of a fundamental difference in the age distributions and characteristic career patterns that prevail in the skilled and low white-collar strata. The moderately comfortable earnings of the craftsman represent his peak career attainment in most instances, whereas clerical and sales jobs are classic entry occupations for young men. Although clerks employed in Boston in 1960 took home substantially less pay than skilled workers, fully a third of the former and only 18 percent of the latter were less than 30 years of age. If the later careers of these young clerks unfolded in anything like the same manner as those of their predecessors in earlier years (see Table 4.10), a sizable minority of them would find their way into jobs in the upper income brackets in time. A crucial difference in the dynamics of the earning situation of skilled and white-collar workers is thus obscured by income data that fail to measure the differences in age and career prospects characteristic of the two groups.[7]

The rather crude evidence available on median earnings, therefore, does not deal a devastating blow to the assumption that low white-collar workers generally outranked skilled workers toward the end of the period dealt with here. That evidence is ambiguous, in the light of the considerations advanced above, and a number of other bases of white-collar superiority were clearly evident. Clerks and salesman were much better educated, on the average, than all of the laboring groups, including skilled craftsmen. Their earnings, even when low, tended to be far more regular; unemployment rates for clerical and sales personnel are far lower than those for skilled workers. "The assured and stable income of lower white-collar persons," concludes a recent study, is a "principal differentiating dimension between them and blue-collar workers." [8] Their prospects for future advancement, furthermore, were better. The chances that their children would rise to a high-status occupation were also far better (see Table 5.3). Their working conditions were probably better on the average, at least with respect to such matters as dirt, noise, and the like. Finally, there is evidence from contemporary studies of how the public rates occupations in terms of prestige that suggests the existence of a "halo effect"that elevates the prestige imputed to even those with white-collar jobs that "require less skill and command less income than many blue-collar occupations." [9]

Such is the case for believing that there were significant differences in the average status of men employed in high white-collar, low white-collar, skilled, semiskilled, and unskilled occupations in post-World War II Boston, and that shifts from one to another of these categories, either during a career or between generations, usually entailed a change in social status. We may now ask whether essentially the same occupational hierarchy existed in the city several decades earlier.

The evidence is spotty, pertaining chiefly to the most narrowly economic dimensions of occupational status: levels of earnings, regularity of earnings, and prospects for career advancement. There is, in addition, the technical difficulty that most of the figures available are means rather than medians (which in this instance might reveal sharper group differences because they are more affected by the extremes of the distribution). A reasonably definite positive verdict, however, may be returned.

According to a study of the incomes of men employed in Boston (Suffolk County) in 1875, white-collar workers had on the average almost twice the earnings of blue-collar workers (Table B.3), and skilled craftsmen took home roughly 50 percent more than unskilled laborers. Manual workmen, the inquiry revealed, were equally disadvantaged in another respect; they averaged 61 days unemployed during the previous year, as opposed to only 16 days for nonmanual employees.

No details were provided to distinguish professionals and large

TABLE B.3. Mean annual earnings in Suffolk County, 1875[1]

Occupational group	*Earnings (dollars)*
White-collar	1054
Blue-collar	576
Skilled	603
Unskilled	415

[1] From a survey of 1616 white-collar and 5921 blue-collar employees in Suffolk County; Massachusetts Bureau of the Statistics of Labor, *Seventh Annual Report* (Boston, 1876). Men who would be ranked as semiskilled factory operatives in the present study could not be distinguished in the report. Most of them seem to have been ranked as unskilled, which inflates that figure. The mean earnings of ordinary day laborers were probably substantially below $415 per year.

businessmen from low white-collar workers, unfortunately, nor was there any report on the earnings of semiskilled and service employees, but these gaps may be closed with some supplementary evidence. That semiskilled workers ranked ahead of unskilled laborers and behind skilled craftsmen economically is indicated in 1880 Census data which indicated that median wages of skilled workers in Massachusetts were $2.50 per day, and of semiskilled employees $1.50 per day.[10] The same differential appears in an examination of the property holdings of a sample of 1000 Boston wage earners from the manuscript schedules of the Census of 1870. Thirty-seven percent of the skilled, 27 percent of the semiskilled, and 17 percent of the unskilled workers reported some property, typically personal savings of a few hundred dollars (Table B.4). The same hierarchy within the blue-collar class appears, though less sharply, in the more limited property information available for 1880. These data pertain only to holdings taxed by the city of Boston—real estate, primarily—and in a city with few single-family dwellings most

TABLE B.4. Property ownership by occupational stratum, 1870 and 1880[1]

Occupational stratum	Percent of group owning—	
	Real or personal property, 1870	*Taxable property, 1880*
I. High white-collar	n.a.	65
II. Low white-collar	n.a.	18
III. Skilled	37	11
IV. Semiskilled	27	9
V. Unskilled	17	7

[1] 1870 data are from a sample of 1000 Boston wage earners taken by the investigator from the manuscript schedules of the Census of 1870, which included questions about the ownership of personal as well as real property. The 1880 property information, from the Boston Assessor's Valuation Lists for 1880, unfortunately pertains to real property only; the Census of 1880 included no property questions.

working-class property was in the form of savings, but the differences between the manual strata are in the same direction as those in 1870.

Direct evidence about the earnings of high white-collar, as opposed to low white-collar, workers in this period is unfortunately not available, but there is little doubt of the greatly superior economic position of the former. The 1880 tax data disclose that 65 percent of the city's professionals and large businessmen owned taxable property, but only 18 percent of the clerks, salesmen, and small proprietors did so. It is reasonable to surmise that the $1054 mean annual earnings for all white-collar workers in Boston in 1875 concealed a large income gap between the two groups, with many low white-collar workers likely averaging not much more than the best-paid skilled craftsmen.

It has often been assumed that even the lower stratum of the white-collar workers earned far more than skilled artisans in the nineteenth century, and that the current relative income position of the two groups, with skilled workers ranking a little ahead of clerks and salesmen in figures that do not control for differences in age distribution and career patterns, represents a dramatic change, a remarkable leveling of a historic difference.[11] It is by no means clear, however, that this is anything very new.

TABLE B.5. Weekly earnings and unemployment rates for selected occupations, *c.* 1900[1]

Occupation	*Weekly earnings (dollars)*	*Percent unemployed— 1 month or more*	*3 months or more*
Low white-collar			
Bookkeeper	20	7	4
Clerk			
Office	12	7	4
Shipping	13	7	4
Unspecified	10	7	4
Commercial traveler	28	5	3
Salesman	15	7	4
Skilled			
Carpenter	15	39	20
Electrician	16	13	4
Gasfitter	16	n.a.	n.a.
Latheman	18	n.a.	n.a.
Machinist	15	14	7
Mason	22	54	31
Moulder	17	n.a.	n.a.
Painter	15	40	21
Plasterer	20	45	27
Plumber	19	28	16
Roofer	15	34	20
Tinsmith	15	24	13
Semiskilled and service			
Driver	11	n.a.	n.a.
Motorman	15	n.a.	n.a.
Packer	11	9	5
Teamster	12	n.a.	n.a.
Watchman	14	n.a.	n.a.
Unskilled			
Laborer	10	41	24
Porter	10	9	6

[1] White-collar mean wages are from a 1902 survey of salaries in 455 Boston mercantile establishments; Massachusetts Bureau of Statistics of Labor, *33rd Annual Report* (Boston, 1903). Blue-collar data are from a 1904 survey of Massachusetts wage earners; *35th Annual Report* (Boston, 1905). Unemployment figures are from the Census of 1900. High white-collar workers were not included in these studies. Figures from the 1910 Census, however, disclose that salaried officials, superintendents, and managers in Boston industry had mean earnings 2.89 times as large as those for clerks and 4.47 times as large as for blue-collar workers.

The earliest direct evidence available for Boston is for 1902 (Table B.5). At that date Boston's clerks averaged $10 to $13 per week, ordinary salesmen $15, and bookkeepers $20. Weekly wages in the dozen leading skilled trades of the city were substantially above the clerical and sales average. These, however, are weekly figures, and blue-collar workers were far more likely to experience unemployment in the course of a typical year. From a quarter to half of them in most trades were out of work for at least a month, but only 7 percent of the city's low white-collar workers, and a substantial fraction were unemployed for more than 3 months. It is impossible to calculate whether these differentials in unemployment were sufficient to reduce the annual earnings of skilled workers to the level of low white-collar employees or not, but it is certainly doubtful whether they were of a magnitude to pull the annual earnings of craftsmen far beneath the low white-collar average.

At the opening of the twentieth century and probably earlier, as well as in the post-World War II period, the basis for ranking men in the lower echelons of the white-collar class above skilled craftsmen was not amount of income per se, though there doubtless were differences in the typical *lifetime* earnings of men in the two groups, given the entry status of many low white-collar jobs and the superior career prospects of workers beginning their careers in that stratum. There certainly were crucial differences in the predictability and security of earnings, and in the likelihood of future occupational success by the children of low white-collar and skilled workers. The former were also better educated than the latter, on the average, and probably enjoyed superior social prestige as well, though direct evidence on these two matters is lacking.

Despite the substantial changes in the overall shape of the Boston occupational structure that took place over the long span of decades treated in this study, there does not appear to have been a radical alteration in the relative positions of the five occupational strata that have been distinguished in the analysis. The job shifts that represented significant social mobility in the late nineteenth century, it seems, also represented significant social mobility in the middle of the twentieth century. A more refined study based upon much larger samples could, of course, employ a much more finely grained occupational classification system, and such a study might need to take into account subtle shifts in the status of particular callings that cannot be discerned through the rather low-powered lenses utilized here. But there are reasonable grounds for believing that the scheme used in the present investigation was adequate for the purposes at hand.

notes

CHAPTER 1. INTRODUCTION

1. Mary Antin, *The Promised Land* (Boston: Houghton Mifflin, 1912), p. 88.

2. The inadequacies of local newspapers as a source for understanding popular behavior are glaringly revealed in a careful comparison of all names printed in the Hamilton, Ontario, paper for 1851–52 with the full population as recorded in the 1851 manuscript census schedules and the 1852 tax lists of the city. Ninety-four percent of the inhabitants of Hamilton at that time were never mentioned in the press; only 1 percent, the highly visible elite, were mentioned five or more times; Michael B. Katz, "The People of a Canadian City: 1851–52," *Canadian Historical Review,* 53 (1972), pp. 402–426.

3. Eugene J. Webb *et al., Unobtrusive Measures: Nonreactive Research in the Social Sciences* (Chicago: Rand McNally, 1966) offers a detailed and persuasive critique of survey research.

4. Robert and Helen Lynd, *Middletown in Transition: A Study in Cultural Conflict* (New York: Harcourt Brace, 1937), pp. 67–72, 471; Percy Davidson and H. Dewey Anderson, *Occupational Mobility in an American Community* (Stanford, California: Stanford University Press, 1937); W. Lloyd Warner and J. O. Low, *The Social System of the Modern Factory* (New Haven, Conn.: Yale University Press, 1947), pp. 182–185, 87–89; Elbridge Sibley, "Some Demographic Clues to Stratification," *American Sociological Review,* 2 (1942), 322–330.

5. The words are those of Gerhard Lenski, "Social Stratification," in Joseph S. Roucek, ed., *Contemporary Sociology* (New York: Philosophical

Library, 1958), pp. 521–538, but the opinion was widespread; see the citations in John Pease *et al.,* "Ideological Currents in American Stratification Literature," *American Sociologist,* 5 (1970), pp. 127–137.

6. Two partial exceptions to this generalization are Natalie S. Rogoff, *Recent Trends in Occupational Mobility* (Glencoe, Ill.: Free Press, 1953), and August B. Hollingshead, "Trends in Social Stratification: A Case Study," *American Sociological Review,* 17 (1952), 679–686. The former compares rates of intergenerational mobility for samples of men married in Indianapolis in 1910 and 1940 and finds no significant differences between the two samples; it does not, however, extend back into the nineteenth century, nor does it analyze possible changes in patterns of career mobility. The latter essay treats the class structure of New Haven between 1910 and 1950 and asserts that social lines were hardening. Since the analysis takes no account of differential migration into and out of New Haven (see Chapter 3) or of background differences in arriving immigrant groups (see Chapter 6), it is not at all persuasive.

7. Cambridge, Mass.: Harvard University Press, 1964.

8. "Additional Memoranda," in Justin Winsor, ed., *Memorial History of Boston, Including Suffolk County, Massachusetts, 1630–1880* (4 vols.; Boston, 1880–81), IV, 549.

9. S. M. Miller, "Comparative Social Mobility: A Trend Report and Bibliography," *Current Sociology,* 9 (1960), 9.

10. For one promising recent attempt to treat these issues, see Virginia Yans McLaughlin, "Like the Fingers of the Hand: The Family and Community Life of First-Generation Italian-Americans in Buffalo, New York," unpublished doctoral dissertation, State University of New York at Buffalo, 1970, summarized in part in McLaughlin's paper, "Patterns of Work and Family Organization: Buffalo's Italians," *Journal of Interdisciplinary History,* 2 (Autumn 1971), 299–314. See also Peter Y. DeJong, Milton J. Brawer, and Stanely S. Rubin, "Patterns of Female Inter-generational Occupational Mobility: A Comparison with Male Patterns of Inter-generational Occupational Mobility," *American Sociological Review,* 36 (December 1971), 1033–1042.

11. Arthur M. Schlesinger, Jr., "The Humanist Looks at Empirical Social Research," *American Sociological Review,* 27 (1962), 770.

CHAPTER 2. POPULATION GROWTH, MIGRATION, AND TURNOVER

1. Leo F. Schnore, *The Urban Scene: Human Ecology and Demography* (New York: Free Press, 1965), 79–113; Amos H. Hawley, *The Changing Shape of Metropolitan America: Deconcentration Since 1920* (Glencoe, Ill.: Free Press, 1956).

2. Donald J. Bogue, *Population Growth in Standard Metropolitan Areas, 1900–1950* (Washington, D.C.: U.S. Government Printing Office, 1953), pp. 61–71.

3. It follows, that is, if the residual method of estimating net migration is correct. In fact it can produce quite misleading results, as is further indicated in the text and in note 5 below. The method yields net-migration estimates that are too low, because it credits all vital events occurring during the interval under consideration to the population resident there at the start of the interval. It should also be noted that the residual method of estimating net migration tends to load all errors into the migration term—enumeration errors for total population, registration errors for births and deaths, changes of definition, and so on.

4. Ann Ratner Miller, *Net Intercensal Migration to Large Urban Areas of the United States, 1930–1940, 1940–1950, 1950–1960* (Philadelphia: Population Studies Center, University of Pennsylvania, 1964), p. 79.

5. This estimate of residual net migration is actually substantially in error, because it erroneously assumes that all of the births and deaths in the city during the decade are attributable to the initial population. All births and deaths in the 1880's in Boston are removed from the 1890 population total, and only the remaining surplus is attributed to net migration. This ignores the fact that some of these births and deaths were the result of in-migration during the decade. Families who entered the city after the Census of 1880 produced children; in-migration also brought in persons who died before 1890. But these two influences were not of the same magnitude, for newcomers were disproportionately concentrated in the procreative age brackets, in which death rates were low. My coworker, Peter Knights, worked out a means of estimating the share of births and deaths in the city in the 1880's attributable to post-1880 migrants. Via complex procedures unnecessary to describe here he concluded that a minimum of 28 percent of the births in Boston between 1880 and 1890 were due to new migrants arriving during the decade, but only 7 percent of the deaths, and that the true net-migration figure was thus a minimum of 26,000 higher than the simple residual estimate of 65,179.

6. The practice of computing total listings dropped and added from year to year was regrettably not followed by the compilers of the city directories published in most cities. A hasty search of the directories of 21 major nineteenth-century communities turned up no other cases in which this was done. The estimating method developed here therefore will likely not prove directly applicable to a wide range of other cities, but the logic of the analysis should be.

7. The city directories upon which this analysis rests were not, of course, completely free of error; see the discussion of their reliability in Appendix A. The main bias in the enumerations conducted by city-directory canvassers, it is argued there, was not against groups of low status per se, as is often believed, but against very recent migrants. To the extent that this bias prevailed, however, it strengthens rather than weakens the findings of this chapter concerning the exceptionally rapid turnover of the Boston population. A fully accurate enumeration of every individual living in the community, including drifting casual laborers just passing

through, would disclose an even more fluid population. In addition, it should be noted that even a perfectly accurate and comprehensive set of city directories would underestimate the actual fluidity of the population, for canvasses in May 1880 and May 1881 would miss individuals who migrated into the city after May 1880 and left before the May 1881 canvass. A not inconsiderable fraction of the population may have fallen into this category. All in all, it seems likely that the estimates given here err in the conservative direction.

8. This assumes that rates of business and individual turnover were roughly similar. That may not be entirely correct, but analysis of the characteristics of a sample of Boston males drawn from the 1880 manuscript census schedules and traced in the city directory of 1890 reveals that self-employed businessmen remained in the community for 10 years more frequently than the average citizen, which suggests that business turnover probably does not inflate the estimates given here. In his research in progress on the populations of Worcester, Massachusetts, and Boston in the nineteenth century, Professor Sune Akerman of the University of Uppsala has been able to treat the turnover of business enterprises separately, and, he informs me that it is of negligible significance for the problem at hand here.

9. Michael B. Katz, "The People of a Canadian City: 1851–52," *Canadian Historical Review,* 53 (1972), pp. 402–426.

10. In an earlier version of this analysis, Stephen Thernstrom and Peter R. Knights, "Men in Motion: Some Data and Speculations about Urban Population Mobility in Nineteenth-Century America," *Journal of Interdisciplinary History,* 1 (Autumn, 1970), 7–35, I now feel, Knights and I were too confident that the household migration estimates could be translated into individual migration estimates by using a multiplier of five. The present more cautious formulation seems more accurate.

11. The 1890 population of Boston may be divided into three components: persons who had been living in the city since 1880 or earlier; individuals born in Boston since 1880 and still residing there in 1890; and migrants who had entered the community from elsewhere during the decade and remained there (the net total of in-migrants). The first of these components was estimated, through a persistence trace of a census sample of 1880 residents in the 1890 local directory, as 64 percent of the 1880 population. The third could be gauged accurately if the second were known (1890 population minus the sum of 1880 persisters and surviving newborn children = net in-migration). Much depends, therefore, upon obtaining a valid estimate of the number of children born in Boston during the 1880's and remaining there in 1890; they are the key to a reasonably accurate estimate of net decadal in-migration to the city.

The unwary might conclude that the total number of births in Boston in the 1880's, 115,974, would be a satisfactory approximation of the size of this component of the population in 1890, but the true figure, 47,059, was a mere 40 percent of that. Many of the newborns died before 1890; many others moved away along with their parents. To estimate the magnitude of these two influences, several assumptions were made. One was that the City Registrar's annual reports of births and deaths were accurate enough for use. Second, it was assumed that 50 percent of all deaths of children designated as "U.S.-born" were of children born in Boston. The state censuses of 1885 and 1895 show that of all U.S.-born persons residing in Boston, between 50 and 60 percent were born in Boston. The lower figure was used as a conservative estimate of the corresponding proportion of children's deaths to assign to the category "born in Boston." Finally, from an analysis of changes in city-directory listings during 1880–81, 1885–86, and 1890–91 it was discovered that approximately 16 percent of the city's families migrated out of the city annually; for details see Thernstrom and Knights, "Men in Motion." For want of a better figure, this rate was applied to the cohorts of children.

The method of producing the estimates was simple but tedious. For children born in Boston in 1880, we know the number of deaths of U.S.-born aged 1 year and under. For the years 1881–1884, we know the number of deaths of U.S.-born children aged 1 to 5, and for the years 1885–1889 we have the analogous figures for children aged 5 to 10. The mortality among the 1880 cohort through the decade would then be the sum of all deaths of Boston-born (equal to half the native-born) in the following groups: for 1880, all aged under 1; for 1881, one-fifth of those aged 1 to 5, and so on until 1885, when we shift to taking one-fifth of the deaths of children aged 5 to 10 years, continuing to and including 1889. This produces for each year of the decade an estimate of the number of deaths of children born in Boston in 1880. The initial size of the cohort born in 1880 was 10,654; we then subtract 333, the estimated number of deaths of Boston-born children in that year, and 1,776, the estimated out-migration of one-sixth of the children. This leaves 8,545 as the size of the 1880 cohort at the start of 1881. Continuing the estimation process through to 1890 produces a residual for the 1880 cohort of 1,571. The procedure is then carried out for the 1881 cohort, starting with 1881 and going to 1890. When the residuals of all ten cohorts, 1880–1889, are summed, the total is 47,059.

12. Massachusetts Bureau of Statistics of Labor, *Census of the Commonwealth of Massachusetts, 1895. Volume II, Population and Social Statistics* (Boston, 1897), pp. 333, 672, 790–791.

13. For a general discussion of migration "effectiveness," see Henry S. Shyrock, *Population Mobility within the United States* (Chicago: Community and Family Study Center, University of Chicago, 1964), pp. 287 ff.

14. For reasons explained in Appendix A, there were unavoidable differences in the precise populations sampled in 1880, 1910, 1930, and 1958. The 1880 persistence figure given in the text is for males aged 20–39 who were listed as Boston residents in the manuscript schedules of the U. S. Census of 1880. The 1910 sample was composed of men marrying in Boston that year. Married men characteristically are more settled than single

men—the 1880–1890 persistence rate was 67 percent for married men and only 45 percent for single men—but this sample nonetheless had a very low persistence rate of 41 percent. I suspect, however, that many of these men were not normal residents of Boston but had come there only to marry, a suspicion that finds some support in the fact that a much lower proportion of them were included in the Boston city directory for the sample year than was the case with the other samples. The 1930–1940 figure of 59 percent is for a sample of men whose wives gave birth to male children in Boston in 1930; it is not far below the 1880–1890 persistence rate for married men (67 percent) and is probably fairly accurate. The 1958–1968 figure (46 percent) is from a sample of males listed in the 1958 Boston city directory, and is doubtless somewhat too low. By this time the decentralization of Boston had transferred a large proportion of the population of the entire metropolitan area to the suburbs, and the city directories employed to trace sample members provided incomplete coverage of suburbanites who did not work in the city proper. The problem that some fraction of the heavy out-migration from Boston was short-distance movement to suburbs within the metropolitan area affects all of the samples to some extent; see Appendix A for further discussion. But it became increasingly important over the period, and is particularly significant to bear in mind in interpreting the 1958–1968 persistence figures.

It should be noted that persistence estimates cannot be directly translated into true out-migration rates. A 25-percent persistence rate for a decade does not mean that 75 percent of the resident population moved out of the community in the interim; some individuals disappeared because of death. A careful effort to separate these two components of population change in Boston for the years 1880, 1885, and 1890 revealed that about 20 percent of the population disappeared from the city annually (20, 19, and 21 percent respectively), and that deaths accounted for a little less than one-fifth of these disappearances; the true out-migration rate was 16 percent for 1880, 16 percent for 1885, and 17 percent for 1890. See Thernstrom and Knights, "Men in Motion." Increases in longevity since the 1880's should mean that subtracting persistence rates from 100 percent would approximate the true out-migration rate even more closely; for documentation of these changes, see Paul H. Jacobson, "Cohort Survival for Generations Since 1840," *Milbank Memorial Fund Quarterly*, 42 (July 1964), 36–53.

15. On the tendency of recent newcomers to a community to be overrepresented in the out-migration stream see Sidney Goldstein, *Patterns of Mobility, 1910–1950: The Norristown Study* (Philadelphia: University of Pennsylvania Press, 1958), pp. 207 ff.

16. Recent demographic studies that emphasize the same general point are Ira S. Lowry, *Migration and Metropolitan Growth: Two Analytical Models* (San Francisco: Chandler, 1966) and Peter A. Morrison, "Urban Growth, New Cities, and 'the Population Problem,'" Rand Corporation Paper No. P-4515-1, (Santa Monica, California: Rand Corporation, 1970.)

CHAPTER 3. DIFFERENTIAL MIGRATION AND ECONOMIC OPPORTUNITY

1. For an excellent synthesis of the sociological literature supporting this view, see S. M. Lipset and Reinhard Bendix, *Social Mobility in Industrial Society* (Berkeley: University of California Press, 1959), pp. 104–107, 204–226. Representative studies in this vein, in addition to those cited in Lipset and Bendix, are Howard W. Beers and Catherine Heflin, "The Urban Status of Rural Migrants," *Social Forces,* 23 (1944), 32–37; Grace G. Leybourne, "Urban Adjustments of Migrants from the Southern Appalachian Plateaus," *Social Forces,* 16 (1937), 238–246.

2. See, for instance, Oscar Handlin, *The Newcomers: Negroes and Puerto Ricans in a Changing Metropolis* (Cambridge, Mass.: Harvard University Press, 1959); Philip M. Hauser, "Demographic Factors in the Integration of the Negro," *Daedalus,* 94 (Fall 1965), 847–877.

3. Charles Tilly, "Race and Migration to the American City," in James Q. Wilson, ed., *The Metropolitan Enigma* (Cambridge, Mass.: Harvard University Press, 1968), pp. 135–157; Peter M. Blau and Otis Dudley Duncan, *The American Occupational Structure* (New York: Wiley 1967), chap. 7.

4. This means of reconciling the two views is suggested by a study of migrants to St. Paul, Minnesota, in the 1940's, which revealed that migrants from rural and small-town backgrounds clustered at the bottom of the occupational structure, but that newcomers from cities outranked the settled population occupationally; Maurice C. Benewitz, "Migrant and Nonmigrant Occupational Patterns," *Industrial and Labor Relations Review,* 9 (1956), 235–240.

5. A similar study of Yankee rural migrants living in Boston in 1870 yielded much the same results; newcomers from New England farming states did not move into the urban occupational structure in the same manner as European immigrants or the Southern poor-white migrants to Southern cities treated in the Beers and Leybourne articles cited in note 1 above. Some rural settings, it appears, produced migrants who were exceedingly well prepared for the challenges of urban life; Lester Lenoff, "Occupational Mobility Among Yankee Immigrants to Boston," unpublished seminar paper, Brandeis University, 1969.

6. U. S. Bureau of the Census, 1969, Final Report PC(2)-2C, *Mobility for Metropolitan Areas* (Washington, D. C.: U. S. Government Printing Office, 1962), Table 4.

7. In an earlier publication I exaggerated somewhat when I declared that "there is . . . no feasible method of tracing individuals once they disappear from the universe of the community under consideration"; Stephan Thernstrom, "Urbanization, Migration and Social Mobility in Late-Nineteenth Century America," in Barton J. Bernstein, ed., *Towards a New Past: Dissenting Essays in American History* (New York : Pantheon,

1968), p. 167. Through an arduous combing of Massachusetts vital records, cemetery records, and the manuscript census schedules for some 128 cities and towns within Massachusetts, Peter R. Knights successfully tracked down 134 persons who migrated from Boston between 1830 and 1860 and settled elsewhere within the state. The attempt, however, was extremely time consuming and the results were disappointing. The out-migrants who could be identified constituted only 27 percent of all the members of Knights's samples who disappeared from Boston during the period. Worse yet, ordinary workers in general and immigrant workers in particular were drastically underrepresented in the group of traced migrants and correspondingly overrepresented among untraceable out-migrants. It would be most unwise, therefore, to draw any general conclusions about the subsequent fate of out-migrants from Boston on the basis of this evidence. A brief summary of the findings is to be found in Thernstrom and Knights, "Men in Motion: Some Data and Speculations on Urban Population Mobility in Nineteenth-Century America," *Journal of Interdisciplinary History,* 1 (Autumn 1970), 27–31; for the details, see Knights, *The Plain People of Boston, 1830–1860: A Study in City Growth* (New York: Oxford University Press, 1971), chap. 6.

8. For further discussion, see Thernstrom and Knights, "Men in Motion"; for a critique of the ghetto hypothesis from a somewhat different angle, see Sam B. Warner and Colin B. Burke, "Cultural Change and the Ghetto," *Journal of Contemporary History,* 4 (October 1969), 173–187.

9. Francis A. Walker, *The Wages Question: A Treatise on Wages and the Wages Class* (New York, 1876), 188. I am indebted to Daniel Horowitz for this reference.

10. Russell Sage Foundation, *West Side Studies* (New York, 1914), I, 8.

11. See, for instance, Ira S. Lowry, *Migration and Metropolitan Growth: Two Analytical Models* (San Francisco: Chandler, 1966), which is based largely on migration data for 1955–1960. Harvey S. Perloff *et al., Regions, Resources and Economic Growth* (Baltimore: Johns Hopkins University Press, 1960) makes similar assumptions in dealing with regional population change since 1870. The associations between regional wage levels and net migration reported there, however, do not convincingly rule out the possibility suggested here—that migrants who left Boston may not have typically improved their economic position as a consequence of migration. It is likely that most of them continued to circulate within the New England labor market, and quite possible that their movement improved their economic situation little or not at all.

12. For a discussion of the likely political consequences if this was indeed the case, see Stephan Thernstrom, "Working Class Social Mobility in Industrial America," in Melvin Richter, ed., *Essays in Theory and History: An approach to the Social Sciences* (Cambridge, Mass.: Harvard University Press, 1970), 221–238.

13. For an analysis of the social structure of New Haven between 1910 and 1950 which ignores selective in- and out-migration entirely and hence

draws highly doubtful conclusions about changes in the opportunity structure, see August B. Hollingshead, "Trends in Social Stratification: A Case Study," *American Sociological Review,* 17 (1952), 679–686.

CHAPTER 4. OCCUPATIONAL CAREER PATTERNS

1. Frank K. Foster, testimony in U. S. Senate, *Report of the Committee Upon the Relations Between Capital and Labor* (Washington, D. C., 1885), I, 49.

2. Reverend Newman Smyth, *Social Problems: Sermons to Workingmen* (Boston, 1885), pp. 12–13.

3. This term has not been used before, to my knowledge, but Sidney Goldstein discusses the same phenomenon in *Patterns of Mobility: The Norristown Study, 1910–1950* (Philadelphia: University of Pennsylvania Press, 1958), chap. 8. It is analogous to the concept of the "demographic vacuum" created by class differentials in fertility, which has often been utilized in studies of intergenerational social mobility; see, for instance, Elbridge Sibley, "Some Demographic Clues to Stratification," *American Sociological Review,* 7 (1942), 322–330; Joseph A. Kahl, *The American Class Structure* (New York: Rinehart, 1962), 257–58.

4. This formulation neglects the possibility that many of the men identified as out-migrants from Boston moved only as far as the city's suburbs, and that these men were disproportionately clustered in high-status occupations. If so, the apparent migration vacuum created by their departure would be spurious, for they would not have vacated desirable posts and thus increased the range of opportunities for others. I was in fact able to trace substantial numbers of suburban movers (see Appendix A), particularly those who continued to work within the city of Boston proper, but the imperfections of the tracing method makes it impossible to assess the extent of this bias accurately.

5. See, for example, Nelson N. Foote and Paul K. Hatt, "Social Mobility and Economic Advancement," *American Economic Review,* 43 (1958), 364–378.

6. Table 4.3, strictly speaking, measures continuity within a stratum, not within a craft. It was possible for a skilled worker to shift stratum without changing his craft, by becoming a foreman or a self-employed artisan (both considered "low white-collar" employment here.) But there were virtually no self-employed artisans in Boston during the period, and the number of craftsmen in the samples who later became foremen was negligible. Virtually all skilled workers who moved to another stratum left their craft in doing so.

7. Lewis Ferman *et al., Poverty in America* (Ann Arbor: University of Michigan Press, 1965), pp. xv–xvi.

8. In addition, a number of other investigators have used a similar age cutoff point; see, for example, S. M. Lipset and F. T. Malm, "First Jobs

and Career Patterns," *American Journal of Economics and Sociology,* 14 (1954), 247–261.

9. Mobility matrices that disclose occupational shifts over periods of 20 and 30 years reveal very similar patterns; it seemed unnecessary to burden the text with them as well.

10. Note, however, that the measure of the impact of the depression employed here is crude. That few white-collar workers suffered long-term downward occupational mobility is significant, but it could well be that substantial numbers of them experienced severe loss of income and property. The extremely limited information available about the wealth of sample members made it impossible to check this possibility. Clyde Griffen's forthcoming study of nineteenth-century Poughkeepsie, however, will show that small proprietors there were very hard hit by the collapse of 1873. Many managed to continue in business but in much reduced circumstances.

11. Wilbur R. Thompson, *A Preface to Urban Economics* (Baltimore: Johns Hopkins University Press, 1965), p. 19.

12. A. J. Jaffe and R. O. Carlton, *Occupational Mobility in the United States, 1930–1960* (New York: Kings Crown Press, Columbia University, 1954), p. 3.

13. Recall, though, that this conclusion, like all others about occupational mobility, is based upon the experience of men who remained in Boston. It is possible that those high white-collar men most in danger of skidding departed from Boston as a result. Whether a move to a new destination was usually beneficial on this count cannot be determined from the evidence at hand. The whole problem of disappearing out-migrants is crucially important and exceptionally difficult to deal with; cf. Chapter 3, n. 7.

CHAPTER 5. SOCIAL-CLASS ORIGINS AND OCCUPATIONAL ACHIEVEMENT

1. John Boyle O'Reilly, "The City Streets," *The Pilot* [Boston], January 20, 1883.

2. Francis A. Walker, *The Wages Question: A Treatise on Wages and the Wages Class* (New York, 1876), pp. 198–199.

3. Edward R. Laumann, *Prestige and Association in an Urban Community: An Analysis of an Urban Stratification System* (Indianapolis: Bobbs-Merrill, 1966).

4. Some historical records, but none pertaining to Boston, allow one to examine the relation between the occupations of fathers and sons even when the fathers do not live in the community. Marriage-license applications for the state of Indiana, for instance—exploited by Natalie S. Rogoff in an important book, *Recent Trends in Occupational Mobility* (Glencoe, Ill.: Free Press, 1953)—supply the necessary information. Rogoff unfortunately did not seize the opportunity, as she might have, to ex-

plore the connection between migration and intergenerational occupational mobility. For further discussion of this problem, see Chapter 9, note 17.

5. In a pilot attempt to check respondents' recollection of their fathers' occupation when they themselves were 16 against earlier census records giving this information, there was a discrepancy between the two in 30 percent of the cases; Peter M. Blau and Otis Dudley Duncan, *The American Occupational Structure* (New York: Wiley, 1967). This is not quite as dismaying as it may seem, for reasons discussed by Blau and Duncan, but it does indicate the desirability of employing direct data rather than recall evidence whenever possible. Cf. Eugene J. Webb *et al., Unobtrusive Measures: Nonreactive Research in the Social Sciences* (Chicago: Rand McNally, 1966).

6. John Allingham, "Class Regression: An Aspect of the Social Stratification Process," *American Sociological Review,* 32 (1967), 443–449.

7. This assumes that with increasing age the net shift in the distribution of sons is away from their fathers' occupational level. In fact, as will be shown below, the net shift of working-class sons was of this character, whereas middle-class sons displayed the opposite pattern. Since there were more of the former, the generalization in the text is correct.

8. The words are those of Robert McNamara, in a public address in August 1966, quoted by Otis Dudley Duncan, "Inheritance of Poverty or Inheritance of Race?" in Daniel P. Moynihan, ed., *On Understanding Poverty: Perspectives from the Social Sciences* (New York: Basic Books, 1969), pp. 85–110. This view was a cliché in discussions of the poverty problem in the 1960's, and in fact has a long history in the United States. In the 1840's, William Ellery Channing worried about "the fatal inheritance of beggary"; "Discourse on Tuckerman," *Works,* VI (Boston, 1849), p. 101. See also the specimens cited in notes 1 and 2 above.

9. The most important use of the "culture-of-poverty" theory is in the various studies of Oscar Lewis; for a brief exposition, see Lewis's paper, "The Culture of Poverty," in Moynihan, *On Understanding Poverty,* pp. 187–200. For a somewhat overdrawn but stimulating attack on the notion, see Charles A. Valentine, *Culture and Poverty: Critique and Counter-Proposals* (Chicago: University of Chicago Press, 1968), chap. 3. Edward Banfield, *The Unheavenly City: The Nature and Future of Our Urban Crisis* (Boston: Little Brown, 1970), attributes "most" of the problems of the contemporary city to the presence of a "lower class." The "defining characteristic" of the lower-class subculture is a "distinctive psychological orientation toward providing for the future," the "inability to imagine a future and to discipline the self to sacrifice present for future satisfaction," an orientation "learned in childhood and passed on as a kind of collective heritage" (pp. 46–47). Banfield presents no empirical evidence in support of his claim that there is a high degree of intergenerational continuity within the lower-class culture, nor any data indicating what proportion of the tens of millions of Americans who can be classified as "poor" by in-

come level are "lower class" in this sense of the term. For all of its brilliant insights into specific urban policy issues, the book thus rests on an unsubstantiated and extremely shaky premise—that the core of urban difficulties is the existence of an unknown but presumably very large number of people "incapable of looking ahead for more than a day or two or of controlling their impulses" because of their early socialization in a lower-class family. This extremely fatalistic conclusion follows from the premise, but the evidence to establish the premise has yet to be provided. For more optimistic discussions of the same issue, see Herbert J. Gans, "Culture and Class in the Study of Poverty: An Approach to Anti-Poverty Research," and Lee Rainwater, "The Problem of Lower-Class Culture and Poverty War Strategy," in Moynihan, *On Understanding Poverty.*

10. Part of the explanation of this somewhat surprising finding may lie in the fact that although low white-collar jobs were superior to skilled jobs *on the average* (see Appendix B), there was some overlap, particularly in earning levels. Some of the highest-ranked jobs in the skilled categories were doubtless more desirable than some of the least attractive within the low white-collar category. Sons of skilled workers who entered these callings may have preferred them to white-collar jobs they might have obtained. It would take much larger samples and more refined information about the nature of particular occupations to test this possibility. It remains striking, though, that men from low manual households entered white-collar jobs in such large numbers.

11. Nineteenth-century assessment rolls for Canadian cities provide rich detail about individual income and wealth; see Michael B. Katz, "Social Structure in Hamilton, Ontario," in Stephan Thernstrom and Richard Sennett, ed., *Nineteenth-Century Cities: Essays in the New Urban History* (New Haven, Conn.: Yale University Press, 1969), pp. 209–244, and Peter G. Goheen, *Victorian Toronto, 1850–1900: Pattern and Process of Growth* (University of Chicago, Department of Geography Research Paper 127, 1970). Nothing comparable, regrettably, exists for those studying American communities. Manuscript schedules of the U. S. Census of 1850 include information about the ownership of real property; the 1860 and 1870 Censuses inquired into holdings of personal property as well. No property question, unfortunately, appeared in any subsequent U. S. Census. The prime source of information one must turn to for the period since 1870 is local tax records. For the early nineteenth century these typically yield some information about personal-property holdings as well as real estate. But by the late nineteenth century, at least in Boston, the effort to assess personal holdings was so halfhearted that the information was of dubious value. In 1822, 45 percent of the property assessed in Boston was in the form of personal estates. Despite the dramatic rise in income and consumption levels that came in the intervening decades, in 1880 personal estates accounted for only 32 percent of the total, and by 1908 the figure had fallen to only 18 percent; C. H. Huse, *The Financial History of Boston, From May 1, 1822 to January 31, 1909* (Cambridge,

Mass.: Harvard University Press, 1916), pp. 376–377. The Boston tax records for the period dealt with here thus register largely real-estate holdings, and provide only a limited clue to the total wealth of sample members.

12. I initially anticipated that the property evidence, even though confined to real-estate holdings, would be rich enough to provide the basis for a full chapter. It did not because of the two distinctive features of Boston mentioned in the text: (1) the unusually low proportion of single-family dwellings in the city's housing stock, which made home ownership uncommon there; (2) the flight of a large proportion of sample members to suburban communities not covered by Boston tax records, an especially large group in Boston because historically the city proper has contained a much smaller fraction of the total population of the entire metropolitan area than the national norm.

13. Russell H. Conwell, *Acres of Diamonds: His Life and Work,* by Robert Shackleton (New York: Harper, 1915), pp. 19–20.

14. Stephan Thernstrom, *Poverty and Progress: Social Mobility in a Nineteenth-Century City* (Cambridge, Mass.: Harvard University Press, 1964), pp. 154–155.

15. The prosperity of fathers in high white-collar positions is by no means surprising, since wealth was one major criterion employed in assigning men to this category. The category is made up of professionals, plus substantial businessmen, and the means of distinguishing the latter from petty proprietors was to see if they held as much as $5000 in real or $1000 in personal property.

16. These figures, it will be seen, are calculated from the marginals of Table 5.6.

17. It might be thought that perhaps the inverse relation between family property and intergenerational occupational mobility found in Newburyport applied only to the sons of unskilled workers in Boston, and that combining the unskilled and semiskilled categories obscures this. But separate tabulations for unskilled fathers fail to display the Newburyport pattern.

18. For uses of the maximum-stability model, see Elton F. Jackson and Harry J. Crockett, Jr., "Occupational Mobility in the United States: A Point Estimate and Trend Comparison," *American Sociological Review,* 29 (February 1964), 5–15; Blau and Duncan, *The American Occupational Structure,* chap. 3.

19. The pioneering applications were Rogoff, *Recent Trends in Occupational Mobility,* and David V. Glass, ed., *Social Mobility in Britain* (London: Routledge and Kegan Paul, 1954). There are, however, serious questions whether this technique achieves the ends for which it was designed. See the thorough, and highly technical, critique by Duncan, "Methodological Issues in the Analysis of Social Mobility," in Neil J. Smelser and S. M. Lipset, *Social Structure and Mobility in Economic Development* (Chicago: Aldine, 1966), pp. 51–97, some of the chief conclu-

sions of which are summarized in Blau and Duncan, *The American Occupational Structure,* chap. 3. In the latter volume Duncan concludes flatly that the method "is evidently unsuited to the problem of comparisons between time periods," and that "a direct comparison" of mobility tables like those presented earlier "may well be the best strategy for measuring trends in mobility" (p. 97). I must frankly admit that I lack sufficient expertise to be fully certain of my own position on this very complex issue. The results of the analysis that follows, however, are fully consistent with the conclusion ventured earlier about mobility trends on the basis of direct comparison of straightforward mobility tables, and the full-equality model does supply another standard for gauging the significance of the data, so I feel that its use is justified here.

CHAPTER 6. YANKEES AND IMMIGRANTS

1. For a vivid account of this migration, see Oscar Handlin, *Boston's Immigrants, 1790–1880: A Study in Acculturation* (rev. ed., Cambridge, Mass.: Harvard University Press, 1959).

2. E. P. Hutchinson, *Immigrants and Their Children, 1850–1950* (New York: Wiley, 1956), analyzes the occupational achievements of first- and second-generation newcomers on the basis of distributional evidence for the entire United States. A similar attempt, dealing with the relative positions of immigrants and natives, is Joseph Schachter, "Net Immigration of Gainful Workers into the United States, 1870–1930," *Demography,* 9 (1972), 87–105. Local studies in the same vein and subject to the same limitations include W. Lloyd Warner and Leo Srole, *The Social Systems of American Ethnic Groups* (New Haven, Conn.: Yale University Press, 1945); Jerome K. Myers, "Assimilation to the Ecological and Social Systems of a Community," *American Sociological Review,* 15 (1950), 367–372; Francis A. J. Ianni, "Residential and Occupational Mobility as Indices of the Acculturation of an Ethnic Group," *Social Forces,* 36 (1957), 67–72; and much of the literature cited in Fred L. Strodtbeck, "Jewish and Italian Immigration and Subsequent Status Mobility," in David McClelland *et al., Talent and Society* (Princeton, N. J.: Van Nostrand, 1958), pp. 259–268.

3. The differences in climbing and skidding rates in the 1880–1889 and 1900–1909 cohorts are not large enough to be significant, because of the limited sample size, but three of the four comparisons display differences in the direction of the 1850–1859 pattern, which was statistically significant.

4. Calculated from published census data.

5. Calculated from 25-cell tables, classifying fathers' and sons' occupations into five strata.

6. A still finer control for fathers' occupations, not possible here because of limited size of the samples, might shrink or eliminate these differences. Immigrant fathers in low white-collar occupations may have

been disproportionately concentrated in marginal white-collar posts, as small grocers, saloon-keepers, small builders, and the like. Being marginal to the middle-class world, they would be less well placed to assist their sons to enter it. That this may well have been the case is suggested by the unusually high rates of downward career mobility from the middle class by first-generation immigrants in Boston (Table 6.4). Clyde Griffen's study in progress on nineteenth-century Poughkeepsie, which treats the total population rather than samples and thus is not plagued by the problem of small numbers, finds this an important part of the handicap of second-generation youths from white-collar families.

7. Only two of the comparisons yield statistically significant differences, but the others are at least suggestive.

8. For a useful summary of the thinking of many Boston intellectuals on this point, see Barbara M. Solomon, *Ancestors and Immigrants, A Changing New England Tradition* (Cambridge, Mass.: Harvard University Press, 1956). For a valuable critique of the old-new dichotomy, see Oscar Handlin, *Race and Nationality in American Life* (Boston: Little, Brown, 1957), chap. 5.

9. It is difficult to avoid the term "share" in discussing the over- and underrepresentation of groups in different occupations, but it would be a serious mistake to assume that "share" means "*fair* share." The index measures how far the actual distribution of a group deviates from the distribution of the entire labor force of the city, but deviations from a value of 100 are by no means direct evidence of occupational discrimination. Most of the more desirable jobs in an advanced industrial society are held by persons with attributes that are unevenly distributed in the population—education, skills, in some instances capital—and the distribution of those attributes must be taken into account in interpreting indexes of representation. That a group of immigrants with 4 years of schooling on the average does not have its "share" of physicians and lawyers, for instance, is hardly evidence of job discrimination. For further discussion of the differential occupational performance of ethnic groups and an attempt to assess the extent of job discrimination, see Chapters 7 and 8.

10. The question of whether Yankees actually "stood on the shoulders" of immigrants and their children is difficult to resolve empirically, though the evidence given here certainly points to that conclusion. Yankees would indeed have benefited from the presence of masses of immigrants if two conditions prevailed: (1) if Yankees were better qualified for high-status jobs than newcomers, or at least were assumed to be so by employers, and (2) if the demand for labor at a particular status level was largely independent of the supply of labor qualified for such positions. If many immigrants, however, were equipped with education, skills, or capital, and if they were treated fairly by employers, competition from them might be harmful to Yankees. Similarly, if the influx of relatively unskilled newcomers stimulated industrial expansion of a kind that could capitalize upon this cheap labor pool, the position of the Yankee group would not

be improved by the inflow and might indeed be harmed. The main streams of European immigration to Boston did not include large numbers of men who could compete successfully for jobs in the upper echelons, so in this respect immigrant competition posed little threat. It is possible, however, that the existence of an immigrant labor pool induced some expansion of low-skilled jobs, as Oscar Handlin argues with respect to immigration in the 1850–1880 period; see *Boston's Immigrants,* pp. 72–87. This cannot have happened on a large scale later, however, for the overall shape of the Boston occupational structure was changing consistently in the opposite direction. The interpretation given in the text is therefore valid, I think.

CHAPTER 7. PROTESTANTS, CATHOLICS, AND JEWS

1. Max Weber, *The Protestant Ethic and the Spirit of Capitalism,* trans. Talcott Parsons (New York: Scribners, 1958).

2. On this issue the most thorough critique of Weber is Kurt Samuelson, *Religion and Economic Action,* trans. E. G. French (New York: Basic Books, 1961). For a fascinating neo-Weberian analysis of Puritanism as a modernizing influence, see Michael Walzer, "Puritanism as a Revolutionary Ideology," *History and Theory,* 3 (1963), 59–90, and *The Revolution of the Saints: A Study in the Origin of Radical Politics* (Cambridge, Mass.: Harvard University Press, 1965).

3. S. M. Lipset and Reinhard Bendix, *Social Mobility in Industrial Society* (Berkeley: University of California Press, 1959), pp. 48–56; Gerhard Lenski, *The Religious Factor: A Sociologist's Inquiry* (paperback edition, New York: Anchor, 1963), p. 84.

4. Lenski, *The Religious Factor,* chap. 3; Albert J. Mayer and Harry Sharp, "Religious Preference and Worldly Success," *American Journal of Sociology,* 27 (1962), 218–227. Mayer and Sharp's conclusions about the low level of Catholic achievement in Detroit, however, rest upon a highly doubtful scheme designed to measure the importance of various background advantages, a scheme which, astonishingly, ranked Detroit Catholics as high as Episcopalians and Jews in background characteristics. The indices employed and the weights attached to them are open to serious question, and there was a highly curious failure to control for a manifestly significant background characteristic—father's occupation. My belief that the patterns Lenski found in Detroit in the 1950's continued to operate there rests not upon the Mayer and Sharp paper but upon scrutiny of unpublished intergenerational mobility tables from the 1966 Detroit Area Study, which were generously provided me by Professor Edward Laumann of the University of Michigan.

5. Bernard C. Rosen, review of *The Religious Factor, American Sociological Review,* 27 (February 1962), 111–13.

6. Andrew M. Greeley and Peter H. Rossi, *The Education of Catholic*

Americans (New York: Aldine, 1966); Andrew M. Greeley, *Religion and Careers* (New York: Sheed and Ward, 1963).

7. See, for example, Mariam K. Slater, "My Son the Doctor: Aspects of Mobility Among American Jews," *American Sociological Review*, 34 (1969), 359–373; Nathan Glazer, "The American Jew and the Attainment of Middle-Class Rank: Some Trends and Explanations," in Marshall Sklare, ed., *The Jews: Social Patterns of an American Group* (Glencoe, Ill.: Free Press, 1960), pp. 138–146.

8. Clyde Griffen finds that German Catholics fared as well in the occupational competition as German Protestants in nineteenth-century Poughkeepsie; Griffen, "Making It in America: Social Mobility in Mid-Nineteenth Century Poughkeepsie," *New York History*, 51 (October 1970), 479–499.

9. Barbara M. Solomon, *Ancestors and Immigrants, A Changing New England Tradition* (Cambridge, Mass.: Harvard University Press, 1956), p. 93.

10. J. J. Huthmacher, *Massachusetts People and Politics, 1919–1932* (Cambridge, Mass.: Harvard University Press, 1956), p. 235. The Irish themselves frequently complained about what they took to be discriminatory treatment by employers; see, for example, *The Pilot* [Boston], January 3, 1880.

11. Solomon, *Ancestors and Immigrants, passim.*

12. Rina Davis, "The Immigrant and the Boston Public Schools, 1870–1920," unpublished seminar paper, Brandeis University, 1969.

13. Leon Mayhew, *Law and Equal Opportunity: A Study of the Massachusetts Commission Against Discrimination* (Cambridge, Mass.: Harvard University Press, 1968), pp. 67–71; Theodore Malm, "Recruiting Patterns and the Functioning of Labor Markets," *Industrial and Labor Relations Review*, 7 (1954), 508–525.

14. Orvis Collins, "Ethnic Behavior in Industry: Sponsorship and Rejection in a New England Factory," *American Journal of Sociology*, 52 (1946), 293–298.

15. Brinley Thomas, *Migration and Economic Growth: A Study of Great Britain and the Atlantic Economy* (Cambridge, England: Cambridge University Press, 1954), Tables 80–84.

16. U. S. Immigration Commission, *Report*, Vol. 26 (Washington, D.C.: U.S. Government Printing Office, 1911), p. 473.

17. S. Joseph, *Jewish Immigration to the United States from 1881 to 1910* (New York: Columbia University Press, 1914); J. Lestschinsky, "Jewish Migrations, 1840–1946," in L. Finkelstein, ed., *The Jews: Their History, Culture and Religion*, Vol. II (New York: Harper, 1949).

18. Immigration Commission, *Report*, Vol. 26, p. 496. Similar patterns appear in the national data from the 1900–1901 report of the U. S. Commissioner-General of Immigration, as compiled by Frederick A. Bushee in "Ethnic Factors in the Population of Boston," *Publications of the American Economic Association*, Third Series, 4 (May 1903), 19.

19. Bushee, "Ethnic Factors," 14. There is serious doubt, however, that immigrants accurately reported their means upon entering the country; see Frederick Kapp, "Immigration," *Journal of Social Science,* 2 (1870), pp. 1–30. I owe this reference to Patrick Blessing.

20. Stanley Lieberson, *Ethnic Patterns in American Cities* (Glencoe, Ill.: Free Press, 1963), p. 6.

21. Lieberson, *Ethnic Patterns,* p. 209.

22. These data pertain to persistence anywhere within Boston, not to persistence in particular subareas within the city. It is possible that, although the Irish and Italians were little more likely than members of other groups to remain in Boston over a given lapse of time, those who did persist were less mobile residentially *within* the city, which might indicate less responsiveness to alternative employment opportunities elsewhere in the metropolitan area. Flaws in the procedure for coding the addresses of sample members prevent a check of this hypothesis. My hunch, however, is that it is quite unlikely for the Irish, who were so widely scattered throughout the city according to the indexes of dissimilarity computed by Lieberson. There may be more to the argument with respect to the Italians.

23. The rank correlation was performed for the groups for which data were available: English, German, Irish, and Swedish immigrants in 1880, and these four plus Polish, Russian, and Italian newcomers in 1950. Occupational distribution data were taken from published censuses; indexes of residential dissimilarity are from Lieberson, *Ethnic Patterns,* p. 209. Lieberson suggests that Boston may be a special case on this count. He performed a somewhat similar analysis for Boston, Chicago, Cleveland, Philadelphia, and Pittsburgh in 1950 and found that Boston was the only city in which the residential and occupational segregations of immigrant groups were not positively correlated (p. 183.) Lieberson, however, examined the relation between residential segregation and occupational *segregation,* not occupational *status.* A group could have a quite different occupational distribution from the native white population of a city—it could be much more highly concentrated in high-status occupations—and still be considered well assimilated occupationally. The Jews are a case in point. The question posed in the text here—the relation between residential segregation and occupational *status*—would seem to be the pertinent one to explore in studies of ethnic adjustment to the American scene.

24. Birth and death rates by group from reports of the Boston City Registrar, as compiled in Bushee, "Ethnic Factors," pp. 44–51.

25. Immigration Commission, *Report* Vol. 26, p. 448. Though this item refers to a Canadian rather than an American city, and to a somewhat earlier time—the mid-nineteenth century—it is relevant to note that research in progress by Michael B. Katz and a team of investigators at the Ontario Institute for Studies in Education reveals that Irish Catholics in Hamilton, Ontario, tended to have unusually *small* families and that fam-

ily size was positively rather than inversely related to social-class status; Working Papers Nos. 6–10, 12, and 20 of the Hamilton Project, available from the Institute.

26. Marlou Belyea, "Who Has Children and Who Does Not," unpublished seminar paper, University of California, Los Angeles, 1972.

27. Samuel A. Stouffer, "Trends in the Fertility of Catholics and Non-Catholics," *American Journal of Sociology,* 41 (September 1935), 143–166; Frank W. Notestein, "Class Differences in Fertility," *Annals of the American Academy of Political and Social Science,* 188 (November 1936), 33; P. K. Whelpton and C. V. Kiser, "Social and Psychological Factors Affecting Fertility," *Milbank Memorial Fund Quarterly,* 21 (July 1943), 221–280. Some post-World War II studies fail to find clear Protestant-Catholic differences in fertility: R. Freedman, P. K. Whelpton, and A. A. Campbell, *Family Planning, Sterility and Population Growth* (New York: McGraw-Hill, 1959); *Statistical Abstract of the United States: 1958* (Washington, D.C.: Government Printing Office, 1959), Table 40. See Lenski, *The Religious Factor,* pp. 235–243, for a dissenting view.

28. Raymond Breton, "Institutional Completeness of Ethnic Communities and the Personal Relations of Immigrants," *American Journal of Sociology,* 70 (1964), 193–205. For a similar view, see Leo Grebler, Joan W. Moore, and Ralph Guzman, *The Mexican-American People: The Nation's Second Largest Minority* (Glencoe, Ill.: Free Press, 1970): "Interaction and involvement with institutions of the host society are important steps towards assimilation and acculturation. To the extent that the receiving ethnic community provides new members with a prepared institutional structure, furnishing both protection and isolation, a significant opportunity for assimilation becomes relatively weak or ineffective" (p. 48).

29. Oscar Handlin, *Boston's Immigrants, 1790–1880: A Study in Acculturation* (rev. ed., Cambridge, Mass.: Harvard University Press, 1959), pp. 158–163.

30. In addition to Handlin's *Boston's Immigrants,* see particularly Robert A. Woods, *The City Wilderness* (Boston, 1898); Woods, *Americans in Process* (Boston: Houghton Mifflin, 1902); Woods and A. J. Kennedy, *The Zone of Emergence* (Cambridge, Mass.: Joint Center for Urban Studies, 1962); Frank A. Sanborn, *Meg McIntyre's Raffle and Other Stories* (Boston, 1896); Joseph F. Dinneen, *Ward Eight* (New York: Harper, 1936). The Handlin interpretation of the culture of the famine Irish in Boston has been challenged by Francis R. Walsh, in "The Boston *Pilot* and the Boston Irish, 1835–1865," unpublished paper for the 1969 annual meetings of the American Historical Association. Walsh sees less fatalism and greater aspirations for mobility than Handlin in the early *Pilot;* his evidence seems to me to qualify rather than to overturn the Handlin argument. By the late 1870's *The Pilot* had imbibed a hearty dose of the Alger ethic—see, for example, the issues of June 23, 1877, May 8, 1880, September 28, 1880, February 5, 1881, March 5, 1881, and October 8, 1887—but this probably tells us more about the evolving views of John

Boyle O'Reilly, its editor in that period, than about the opinions of the Irish masses.

31. William F. Whyte, *Streetcorner Society: The Social Structure of an Italian Slum* (Chicago: University of Chicago Press, 1943); Walter Firey, *Land Use in Central Boston* (Cambridge, Mass.: Harvard University Press, 1947), chap. 5; Herbert J. Gans, *The Urban Villagers: Group and Class in the Life of Italian Americans* (New York: Free Press, 1962); Marc Fried, *The World of the Urban Working Class* (Cambridge, Mass.: Harvard University Press, 1973).

32. Gans, *The Urban Villagers,* 124.

33. Humbert S. Nelli's study, *Italians in Chicago, 1880–1930: A Study in Ethnic Mobility* (New York: Oxford University Press, 1970) is a regrettably impressionistic treatment of a question that seems to demand systematic quantitative analysis, but it does convincingly establish that Chicago Italians moved very rapidly out of their areas of initial settlement, and it is plain that much the same was true in Boston.

34. Edward R. Laumann, *Prestige and Association in an Urban Community: An Analysis of an Urban Stratification System* (Indianapolis: Bobbs-Merrill, 1966), p. 110. Unlike other Catholics, however, men of Italian descent tended to rank high on the index of status discrimination, a finding that does not square with my argument. One's impression from the works cited in note 31 above is that the Italians of the North and West End would have scored very low on this measure; possibly those who escaped to Cambridge and Belmont were reacting strongly against that cultural pattern.

35. Stephan Thernstrom, *Poverty and Progress: Social Mobility in a Nineteenth-Century City* (Cambridge, Mass.: Harvard University Press, 1964), pp. 155–157.

36. A study in progress of "Intrametropolitan Migration, Public Finance, and Property Values: A Socioeconometric Study," by Matthew Edel, Department of Economics, Massachusetts Institute of Technology, and Elliot D. Sclar, Florence Heller School, Brandeis University, should clarify this issue.

37. Robert K. Merton and Bryce Ryan, "Paternal Status and the Economic Adjustment of High School Graduates," *Social Forces,* 22 (1943), 302–306.

38. The data are not presented in a form to permit definite conclusions, but there are strong indications of the Jewish commitment to education in the Immigration Commission's repsrt on the children of immigrants in Boston schools in 1909; *Report,* Vol. 30, pp. 175–292.

39. Greeley, *Religion and Careers,* 29–30.

CHAPTER 8. BLACKS AND WHITES

1. W. E. B. DuBois, *The Philadelphia Negro: A Social Study* (New York, 1899; Schocken paperback edition, New York, 1967), p. 73. For a

similar analysis of the black community of late-nineteenth- and early-twentieth-century Boston, see John Daniel, *In Freedom's Birthplace: A Study of Boston Negroes* (Boston, 1914), esp. pp. 113–114, 166–173, 327–329.

2. DuBois, *The Philadelphia Negro,* p. 80. Given DuBois' emphasis on this point, it is disappointing that he failed to control for urban-rural background systematically in his subsequent analysis. It is likely that he did not include a question about this variable in the survey questionnaire upon which the book rests, and developed the idea after the data were collected.

3. Irving Kristol, "The Negro Today Is Like the Immigrant of Yesterday," *New York Times Magazine,* September 11, 1966.

4. Oscar Handlin, *The Newcomers: Negroes and Puerto Ricans in a Changing Metropolis* (Cambridge, Mass.: Harvard University Press, 1959); Oscar Handlin, "The Goals of Integration," *Daedalus,* 95 (1966), 268–286; Philip M. Hauser, "Demographic Factors in the Integration of the Negro," *Daedalus,* 94 (1965), 847–877; Nathan Glazer and Daniel P. Moynihan, *Beyond the Melting Pot: The Negroes, Puerto Ricans, Jews, Italians and Irish of New York City* (Cambridge, Mass.: MIT Press, 1959). For an explication of this view by the present author that requires some modification in the light of the evidence in this chapter, see "Up From Slavery," *Perspectives in American History,* 1 (1967), 434–440.

5. The absence of such comparative analyses until now is partly due to the absence of pertinent published evidence. The Bureau of the Census and other data-collecting bodies have not tabulated information about blacks by region of birth, so that the data have to be laboriously gleaned from primary sources. Cf. Karl and Alma Taeuber, "The Negro as an Immigrant Group: Recent Trends in Racial and Ethnic Segregation in Chicago," *American Journal of Sociology,* 69 (January, 1964), 374–382: "We have been unable to locate any data permitting a comparison between Negroes long resident in Chicago, or born and raised in the North, and Negroes with lesser periods of residence in the city. Thus we are not able to make even the crude intergenerational comparisons for Negroes that are possible for the immigrant groups."

6. Oscar Handlin, *Boston's Immigrants, 1790–1880: A Study in Acculturation* (rev. ed., Cambridge, Mass.: Harvard University Press, 1959), p. 70. For supporting detail, see Daniels, *In Freedom's Birthplace,* chaps. 2 and 3.

7. Daniels, *In Freedom's Birthplace,* p. 472; City Registrar's Report, *Boston City Document No. 68 (1884)* (Boston, 1885), pp. 7–8, as cited in Elizabeth H. Pleck, "The Two-Parent Household: Black Family Structure in Late-Nineteenth Century Boston," *Journal of Social History,* 5 (1972), pp. 3–31; 1960 and 1970 Census data.

8. Adelaid Hill (Cromwell), "The Negro Upper Class in Boston: Its Development and Present Status," unpublished doctoral dissertation, Radcliffe College, 1952.

9. The 1870 data were tabulated from the manuscript schedules of the U. S. Census by Isabella MacDougall, for "Negro Wage-Earners in Boston, 1870–1880," unpublished seminar paper, Brandeis University, 1969. The 1880 figures were gleaned from the manuscript census schedules by Elizabeth H. Pleck of Brandeis University, for Thernstrom and Pleck, "The Last of the Immigrants? A comparative Analysis of Immigrant and Black Social Mobility in Late-Nineteenth-Century Boston," unpublished paper for the 1970 meetings of the Organization of American Historians.

10. This estimate was derived by assuming that the ratio of Southern blacks in the labor force to those in the total population that prevailed in 1870 still held in 1900.

11. Massachusetts Bureau of Statistics of Labor, *34th Annual Report* (Boston, 1904), pp. 255–257. The survey covered Negroes living in Boston and seven other Massachusetts cities; Boston's Negroes accounted for 83 percent of the black population of the eight cities combined, so it seems reasonable to take these figures as indicative of the situation of Negroes working in Boston. The actual date of the survey is unknown, but it was made shortly after 1900.

12. Morton Rubin, "The Negro Wish to Move: The Boston Case," *Journal of Social Issues,* 15 (1959), 4–13.

13. It is reasonable to assume that the bulk of these Southern migrants were relatively ill prepared for urban life, but it must be noted that the use of region of birth as an index is imperfect. Some of these Southerners were not from rural backgrounds but from Richmond, Baltimore, and other Southern cities. Some of the Northern-born blacks with whom they are compared may, like W. E. B. DuBois, have been born in rural communities like Great Barrington, Massachusetts, or on farms, though there cannot have been many of these. This issue will be illuminated further in Elizabeth Pleck's forthcoming dissertation on "The Black Community of Boston, 1870–1900," which will include some analysis of blacks marrying in Boston during the period. The marriage records for those years usually indicate city as well as state of birth, allowing a more precise urban-rural control. There is a further difficulty with using place-of-birth data for migration analysis, in that some of the Southern-born blacks who appear in the Boston figures may have come to the city as very young children and thus have spent their formative years in a Northern urban setting. One can only hope that this does not distort the findings significantly.

The question of how many of the Southern black migrants to late-nineteenth-century Boston had been slaves can be answered with only the crude generalization that most of them probably had been. If we could assume that the ratio of ex-slaves to free blacks among the Southern-born Negro residents of Boston in 1880 was equal to the ratio of slaves to free blacks in 1860 in the states in which they were born, 40 percent of all Negroes in Boston in 1880, 51 percent of blacks in the labor force, and 84 percent of the Southern-born Negroes had once been slaves. There were, for example, 1753 blacks who had been born in Virginia living in Boston in 1880; since 89.4 percent of the Virginia Negro population in 1860 was enslaved, we assume there were 1567 ex-slaves and 186 free blacks among the Virginia-born blacks in Boston in 1880. This estimate, however, neglects the fact that some of the Southern blacks residing in Boston in 1880, namely, those under the age of 15, had been born since Emancipation. A more serious flaw is that it assumes there were no selective influences in migration that made free blacks more prone than ex-slaves to move northward, and this was very likely not the case. There is a hint of strong selectivity in black migration in the fact that fully 70 percent of the Southern-born Negro heads of households in Boston in 1880 were literate; Pleck, "The Two-Parent Household." We cannot assume that all slaves were illiterate, of course, and it is likely that some who had been, learned to read and write after being freed. But the predominance of literate persons among Southern-born blacks in the city in 1880 does suggest that more than the estimated 16 percent had been free before the Civil War.

In any event, whatever the balance between ex-slaves and free blacks among Southern migrants to Boston, there is little doubt that the group in general must have been ill prepared for urban life in comparison with Northern-born Negroes. One student of black migration, Carter G. Woodson, denies this, and maintains that Southern black newcomers to Northern cities in this era represented the "Talented Tenth"; Woodson, *A Century of Negro Migration* (Washington, D.C.: Association for the Study of Negro Life and History, 1918), 163. The Boston evidence, however, seems to lend little support to this notion, which Woodson advanced on the basis of a few examples rather than a study of large numbers of representative individuals. Though there were individual exceptions, it appears that on the whole there were sharp differences between Northern-born and Southern-born black residents of Boston in the degree to which they had been "in long, close contact with modern culture." For a thoughtful discussion of these problems see Theodore Hershberg, "Slavery and the Northern City; Ante-bellum Black Philadelphia: An Urban Perspective," unpublished paper delivered to the Association for the Study of Negro Life and History, October 1970.

14. Handlin, *Boston's Immigrants,* pp. 70–84.

15. Quoted in Francis R. Walsh, "The Boston *Pilot* and the Boston Irish, 1835–1865," unpublished paper for the 1969 annual meetings of the American Historical Association.

16. The Census Bureau's definition of "mulatto" was reasonably clear. The enumerators' instructions for 1880 specified: "Be particularly careful in reporting the class *Mulatto.* The word is here generic, and includes quadroons, octoroons, and all persons having any perceptible trace of African blood"; Carroll D. Wright, *The History and Growth of the United States Census* (Washington, D. C.: U.S. Government Printing Office, 1900), p. 171. Just how enumerators obtained this information, and with what degree of reliability, is uncertain, however.

17. If more detailed data were available as to the precise nature of

these unskilled laboring jobs, even this point of similarity between the Irish and the Negroes would probably be less impressive. The position of laborers regularly employed by the city or by large corporations was distinctly superior to that of casual laborers, who were never certain from day to day where they would be employed, if at all. It is probable that by 1890 the Irish held the lion's share of laboring jobs with the city and the large corporations. The earliest evidence is the material on employment patterns of immigrants and blacks in the 1910 Census. The black index for "general laborers" was 220, as opposed to 166 for immigrants; the black score for "laborers, porters and helpers in stores" was 654, against 107 for immigrants. Among presumably more regular laboring posts the situation was reversed. The black index for "laborers, road and street building and repair" was only 29, vs. 183 for immigrants; the black score for "laborers, public service" was 33, vs. 145 for immigrants; the black score for "laborers, steam railroad" was 42, vs. 186 for immigrants.

18. The caution offered in note 9 to Chapter 6—that "expected share" cannot be equated with "fair share"—is pertinent here as well. The occupational qualifications of the group in question must be taken into account in interpreting indexes such as these. The Irish immigrant is used as a point of comparison with blacks for just this reason, in that the Irish too had a heavy burden of background handicaps in late-nineteenth-century America.

19. The absolute number of black professionals, however, was so small —16 out of a total employed of 3614—that the slightly higher index is of little significance.

20. The census figures on median earnings are not precisely comparable, in that the 1960 data pertain to nonwhites rather than to Negroes alone. Blacks earned 0.722 of the city median in 1950 and 0.720 in 1970; nonwhites in 1960 earned 0.650 of the city median.

21. The earnings gap, however, cannot be taken as a simple measure of the extent of discrimination; it could be attributable to differences in job qualifications that led to disproportionate concentration of Negroes in the least well-paid jobs within these broad categories. The average black professional in 1970, for instance, had substantially less schooling than the average white professional, and was for that reason more likely to be a medical technician than a surgeon, a social worker than an attorney. For an effort to assess the relative importance of discrimination and other factors influencing the economic position of blacks, see below.

22. The census supplies such figures for only a few occupational groupings. No information is available concerning racial differences in the median earnings of clerical and sales workers or service workers, and I have had to make some assumptions. It is reasonable to guess that black service employees earned 90 percent of the city median for such work, since in the categories immediately above and below service—operatives and unskilled laborers—they earned 85 percent and 95 percent respectively. For

the calculation I assumed that black clerical and sales workers earned 80 percent of the city median, a generous estimate in the light of the 66-percent figure that prevailed among professionals, proprietors, managers, and officials. An even more generous assumption—of racial parity in median earnings at this level—would only raise the estimated overall black median from 0.770 to 0.806 of the city median.

23. It may be, however, as suggested by Daniel P. Moynihan, Andrew Brimmer, and others on the basis of national data, that the relative constancy of the income gap between blacks and whites in these years conceals two very significant changes within the black community—a sharp improvement in the relative income position of Negro households with both husband and wife present, and a substantial decline in the relative earnings of blacks living in broken family units. The published censuses for Boston unfortunately do not permit a test of this hypothesis. Some consideration is given below, however, to the supposed distinctiveness of black family patterns as a source of economic inequality.

24. No data are available on the relative occupational positions of immigrants and blacks in 1940, but a decade later 30 percent of foreign-born males were in white-collar occupations vs. 15 percent of Negroes, and 28 percent of the immigrants were skilled workers vs. 13 percent of blacks (Tables 6.3 and 8.10.)

25. Stanley Lieberson, *Ethnic Patterns in American Cities* (Glencoe, Ill.: Free Press, 1963), p. 6.

26. Thus in 1960 the median gross monthly rental paid by Negroes living in substandard housing units in Boston was $65, as compared with $59 for white families, even though the substandard housing occupied by Negroes was in substantially worse condition than substandard white housing; Leon Mayhew, *Law and Equal Opportunity: A Study of the Massachusetts Commission Against Discrimination* (Cambridge, Mass.: Harvard University Press, 1968), pp. 52–53. I know of no evidence that any of the European white immigrant groups were forced to pay a comparable premium for housing.

27. Pleck, "The Two-Parent Household."

28. From the respective *Population* volumes of the U. S. Census.

29. This view is, of course, associated with the well-known Moynihan Report: Office of Policy Planning and Research, U. S. Department of Labor, *The Negro Family: The Case for National Action* (Washington, D. C.: U. S. Government Printing Office, 1965). As I interpret it, the report attempts to demonstrate not that the disorganization of the black family is responsible for the low economic status of Negroes but vice versa. But it is ambiguous at some key points, and many readers have understood it to claim that the causal relation runs the other way. The latter, in any event, is the hypothesis I evaluate here.

30. Peter M. Blau and Otis Dudley Duncan, *The American Occupational Structure* (New York: Wiley, 1967), p. 336.

31. Andrew M. Billingsley, *Black Families in White America* (Englewood Cliffs, N. J., Prentice-Hall, 1968), pp. 14–15.

32. E. Franklin Frazier, *The Negro Family in the United States* (Chicago: University of Chicago Press, 1939.)

33. Herbert G. Gutman, *The Invisible Fact: The Black Family in American History, 1850–1930* (New York: Pantheon, forthcoming, 1974).

34. Pleck, "The Two-Parent Household." It is possible that some abandoned wives were reluctant to admit the fact to the census-taker, and that these figures give an exaggerated impression of stability. But it is difficult to see why black wives would be more likely to misreport this information than those from other groups. The comparisons made here should therefore be accurate.

35. Unpublished tables from Hareven's research in progress on the American family.

36. Despite their caution in n. 13, p. 218, Blau and Duncan follow this line in *The American Occupational Structure,* chap. 6. A less cautious example is Paul Siegel, "On the Cost of Being a Negro," *Sociological Inquiry,* 35 (1965), 41–57.

37. Gutman, *The Invisible Fact.*

38. Mayhew, *Law and Equal Opportunity,* 47.

CHAPTER 9. THE BOSTON CASE AND THE AMERICAN PATTERN

1. Asa Briggs, *Victorian Cities* (London: Odhams, 1963), p. 32.

2. Justin Winsor, ed., *Memorial History of Boston, Including Suffolk County, Massachusetts, 1630–1880,* 4 vols. (Boston, 1880–81), IV, 549.

3. Peter R. Knights, "Population Turnover, Persistence, and Residential Mobility in Boston, 1830–60," in Stephan Thernstrom and Richard Sennett, eds., *Nineteenth-Century Cities: Essays in the New Urban History* (New Haven, Conn.: Yale University Press, 1969), 262.

4. Evidence on the stability of the population of American communities prior to 1800 is much sketchier, but there appears to have been much less transiency in early American history. Virtually all of the first generation of residents of Andover, Massachusetts (men who were adults in the 1640's) died there; 78 percent of the second generation died in the community; 61 percent of the third; and 44 percent of the fourth (male adults in the 1750's and 1760's); Philip J. Greven, *Four Generations: Population, Land and Family in Colonial Andover, Massachusetts* (Ithaca, N. Y.: Cornell University Press, 1970), p. 212. Approximately 80 percent of the men included in the 1764 tax list of Lunenburg County, Virginia, were still to be found there 18 years later; 70 percent of the artisans and 77 percent of the nonartisans in Philadelphia in 1769 remained there as of 1782; Jackson Turner Main, *The Social Structure of Revolutionary America* (Princeton, N. J.: Princeton University Press, 1965), pp. 169–170, 195. Main suggests (p. 193) that an average of about 85 percent of the

population of rural communities of late-colonial America persisted at least a decade.

5. Stephan Thernstrom and Peter R. Knights, "Men in Motion: Some Data and Speculations on Urban Population Mobility in Nineteenth-Century America," *Journal of Interdisciplinary History,* 1 (1970), 12.

6. Precise evidence about the volume of in-migration into the two communities is lacking, but this is quite clear from state-of-birth data. As of 1910, 52 percent of the Boston population was Massachusetts-born, whereas only 20 percent of the Los Angeles population was California-born.

7. A similar conclusion has been drawn in contemporary studies of the relation between migration patterns at the community level and rates of local economic growth. Rates of in-migration have been shown to be highly sensitive to local economic conditions—cities that are booming economically draw many more outsiders than depressed communities—but rates of out-migration are not. "Contrary to intuition, people leave prosperous areas as readily as depressed ones . . . The prosperous area successfully replaces its spontaneous outflow by managing to attract an even heavier influx of migrants from elsewhere. But the depressed community typically is unable to replace its population loss. The weakness of its 'pull; not the strength of its 'push' is responsible for an overall net migratory loss'; Peter A. Morrison, "Urban Growth, New Cities, and 'The Population Problem,'" Rand Corporation Paper No. P–4515–1 (1970), p. 15. See also Ira S. Lowry, *Migration and Metropolitan Growth: Two Analytical Models* (San Francisco: Chandler, 1966). Although I have no direct evidence on rates of economic growth in the communities in which historical studies of persistence have been made, rates of population growth are probably a fair proxy for that. If so, the evidence here suggests that Morrison's generalization applies not only to the present but to the United States during the past two centuries.

8. Robert Wiebe, *The Search for Order, 1877–1920* (New York: Hill and Wang, 1967).

9. Michael B. Katz, "The People of a Canadian City: 1851–52," *Canadian Historical Review,* 53 (1972), pp. 402–426.

10. Strong positive correlations between persistence and property ownership appear in unpublished tabulations for the present study, and in the studies of Northampton, Poughkeepsie, antebellum Boston, Trempealeau County, Wapello County, and Roseburg cited in the notes to Tables 9.1 and 9.2.

11. Harvey S. Perloff *et al., Regions, Resources and Economic Growth* (Baltimore: Johns Hopkins University Press, 1960).

12. For further speculation along these lines, see my essay, "Working Class Social Mobility in Industrial America," in Melvin Richter, ed., *Essays in Theory and History: An Approach to the Social Sciences* (Cambridge, Mass.: Harvard University Press, 1970).

13. This evidence is not, of course, precisely comparable. I recognize

the force of Angela Lane's attack upon such efforts to piece together the findings of "research not comparable in study design, sample composition, site, date, etc." to arrive at a "total picture of social stratification" in a whole society; Lane, "Occupational Mobility in Six Cities," *American Sociological Review,* 33 (1968), 740–749. But data that are not perfectly comparable seem to me better than no data at all, and I believe that the uniformities apparent in the evidence reviewed here are strongly suggestive of a national pattern.

Lane's paper, it might be noted, analyzes strictly comparable mobility data from the Six City Survey of Labor Mobility conducted in 1951 and stresses how divergent the patterns visible in the six cities were, which runs counter to the emphasis of the present argument. I would concede that her data reveal some differences, but the crucial question is how much of a difference makes a difference. From my vantage point the divergences between these six cities are quite slight, and I remain impressed with how much uniformity they display. It should also be noted that Lane's data are inadequate for establishing differences in the occupational structures of these various communities, for the sole link of sample members to the city with which they are identified is that they lived there in 1951. Their mobility is measured, however, by comparing their occupational status in 1950 with the level of their fathers' longest jobs. Many, perhaps most, of the fathers in question did not live in the city in which the sons resided in 1951, and it is not even clear how long the sons had done so. Any city differences disclosed by the data, therefore, may merely reflect differentials in the kinds of persons who migrated to different communities rather than true differences in the level of opportunities within each. The same problem appears in other studies of intergenerational mobility in particular communities, such as the Indianapolis, San Jose, and Norristown studies cited in the note to Table 9.7; see note 17 below for further discussion. None of these investigations truly measure intergenerational mobility *within* the community.

14. O. D. Duncan and A. J. Reiss, Jr., *Social Characteristics of Urban and Rural Communities* (New York: Wiley, 1956), p. 96.

15. For an analysis of local variations in occupational structure from 1940 Census data, see Paul B. Gillen, *The Distribution of Occupations as a City Yardstick* (New York: Kings Crown Press, Columbia University, 1951). This reveals that deviations from the norm tend to be lowest in large cities, and largest in those of less than 25,000. This suggests that mobility studies conducted in small cities are more likely to reveal distinctive local patterns than those conducted in major urban centers.

16. That in-migration, but not out-migration, is sensitive to variations in local economic opportunity is indicated in the contemporary studies cited in note 7 above, and in Perloff's analysis of interregional migration in the United States since 1870; Perloff, *Regions, Resources and Economic Growth,* pp. 590–592.

17. How another principal methodological variation between these various studies limits their comparability, if at all, is more difficult to judge. Four of the Boston samples (excepting only Laumann's 1962 sample) and the Poughkeepsie study measure intergenerational occupational change for only those men whose fathers also lived in that community; the historical sources provided no information about the occupations of fathers residing elsewhere or deceased. The remaining studies, based upon surveys of living men, could ascertain the occupation of a respondent's father even if he were not then living in the same city as his son. If there are career advantages that come with growing up in a large city, as suggested by Lipset and Bendix in *Social Mobility in Industrial Society* (Berkeley: University of California Press, 1960), pp. 219–225, these might help to explain the relatively high rates of upward mobility found in Boston. Blau and Duncan, however, have recently presented a mass of evidence that suggests not only that growing up in a big city promotes occupational achievement, as Lipset and Bendix argue, but that migration is also strongly and positively associated with success; *The American Occupational Structure* (New York: Wiley, 1967), chap. 7. Men who move from their place of origin to a different community tend to fare better than those who remain behind. Studying the intergenerational mobility only of those men who lived in the same city as their fathers thus might underestimate total mobility. Whether this pattern held in the past as well, however—whether the son of a Boston carpenter who moved to Chicago in 1920, or of a Chicago carpenter who moved to Boston (neither of whom would be included in the Boston intergenerational mobility calculations) were more successful than they would have been had they stayed at home—is unknown. It is interesting that Blau and Duncan find some hint in their data that "migration has become increasingly selective of high potential achievers in recent decades," a proposition that calls for further historical investigation.

18. Both Lipset and Bendix, *Social Mobility,* pp. 219–225, and Blau and Duncan, *American Occupational Structure,* pp. 262–265, present evidence on the career advantages of growing up in large cities. Blau and Duncan qualify the point only by adding that men who continue to live in the *same* large city in which they grew up—that is, nonmigrants—are less successful than men of comparable origins who migrated to another city.

19. Thernstrom, *Poverty and Progress: Social Mobility in a Nineteenth-Century City* (Cambridge, Mass.: Harvard University Press, 1964), chap. 8. The comparative data presented there in Table 16, p. 218, are also somewhat misleading in that the two mobility estimates most closely resembling those for Newburyport—for San Jose, *c.* 1900, and for New Haven, 1931—are, I have come to conclude, of dubious reliability and should be discarded. The San Jose figures depend upon respondents' recall of the occupations of their fathers and grandfathers; the latter may

well have been deficient. The New Haven estimates were for youths only 16 years old and living at home, and must have been seriously biased downward for that reason.

20. Howard Chudacoff, *Mobile Americans: Residential and Social Mobility in Omaha, 1880–1920* (New York: Oxford University Press, 1972); Dean R. Esslinger, "The Urbanization of South Bend's Immigrants, 1950–1880," unpublished doctoral dissertation, University of Notre Dame, 1972.

21. Richard Hopkins, "Occupational and Geographic Mobility in Atlanta, 1870–1890," *Journal of Southern History,* 34 (1968), 200–213; Alwyn Barr, "Occupational and Geographic Mobility in San Antonio, 1870–1900," *Social Science Quarterly,* 51 (1970), 396–403. Hopkins has since gathered substantially larger samples, and advance tabulations of the results confirm the original findings.

22. Natalie S. Rogoff, *Recent Trends in Occupational Mobility* (Glencoe, Ill.: Free Press, 1953), chap. 6.

23. Esslinger, "Urbanization of South Bend's Immigrants."

24. Thernstrom, *Poverty and Progress;* Charles Buell, dissertation in progress on the workers of Worcester, New York University; Robert Wheeler, "The Fifth-Ward Irish: Mobility at Mid-Century," unpublished seminar paper, Brown University, 1967; advance tabulations from the Poughkeepsie Mobility Study.

25. Niles Carpenter, *Immigrants and Their Children, 1920* (Washington, D. C.: U.S. Government Printing Office, 1927); E. P. Hutchinson, *Immigrants and Their Children, 1850–1950* (New York: Wiley, 1956); Nathan Glazer and Daniel P. Moynihan, *Beyond the Melting Pot: The Negroes, Puerto Ricans, Jews, Italians and Irish of New York City* (Cambridge, Mass.: MIT Press, 1963).

26. See, for example, the papers by Beers and Heflin and by Leybourne cited in Chapter, 3, note 1.

27. Hopkins, "Occupational Mobility in Atlanta"; Barr, "Occupational Mobility in San Antonio."

28. For abundant examples of this reaction on the part of workers living in Boston today, see the fascinating and subtle study by Richard Sennett and Jonathan Cobb, *The Hidden Injuries of Class* (New York, Knopf, 1972), a work based on in-depth interviews with 150 ordinary families.

29. For a stimulating statement of the view that rates of social mobility are much the same in all industrial societies, based largely upon survey data gathered since World War II, see Lipset and Bendix, *Social Mobility in Industrial Society.* S. M. Miller's "Comparative Social Mobility: A Trend Report and Bibliography," *Current Sociology,* 9 (1960), 1–89, draws on the same type of evidence to qualify but not to basically reject the Lipset-Bendix argument. For a debate on the issue of whether these findings are correct and whether they can be safely extrapolated back into the past, see my paper, "Working Class Social Mobility in Industrial

America," Seymour Martin Lipset's critical essay on it, and my brief rejoinder in John H. M. Laslett and S. M. Lipset, ed., *Failure of a Dream? Essays on the History of American Socialism* (New York: Doubleday and Anchor, 1973).

30. William H. Sewell, Jr., "Social Mobility in a Nineteenth Century European City: Some Findings and Implications," unpublished paper for the Mathematical Social Science Board Conference on International Comparisons of Social Mobility in Past Societies, June, 1972, and "The Structure of the Working Class of Marseille in the Middle of the Nineteenth Century," unpublished doctoral dissertation, University of California, Berkeley, 1971; tables from a study in progress of Frankfurt, Rotterdam, and San Francisco by Allen Emrich, Jr. An item of evidence pointing in the other direction, heavily relied upon by Lipset in his comments in the Laslett-Lipset *Failure of a Dream?*, is Tom Rishoj, "Metropolitan Social Mobility, 1850–1950: The Case of Copenhagen, *Quality and Quantity*, 5 (June 1971), 131–140. However, my attempt to verify the key conclusions of this paper by recomputing the raw data given in Tables 1–4 discloses a different pattern than the author believes he has found. A more detailed report on this study will be needed before it can be given much weight in comparative historical analysis in America and Europe.

31. For a brilliant recent philosophical statement of the case for greater equalization of command over resources, see John Rawls, *A Theory of Justice* (Cambridge, Mass.: Harvard University Press, 1971.) My chief quarrel with Rawls's formulation is that I am not sure how his difference principle can be given empirical application; clearly he intends it as an equalizing device, but on certain assumptions about the distribution of skills and incentives it could be used to justify drastic economic inequality. Rawls conducts his argument at a high level of abstraction and neglects such questions of interpretation and application.

APPENDIX A. THE SOURCES AND THE SAMPLES

1. Quoted in *Report of the Massachusetts State Commission on the Cost of Living* (Boston: Commonwealth of Massachusetts, 1910), pp. 572–573.

2. The bulk of the manuscript schedules for the Census of 1890 were destroyed by a fire in Washington. The schedules for all subsequent Censuses are presently classified confidential and are closed to investigators. There is, however, some prospect that the 1900 schedules will soon be opened.

3. The leading contemporary study of occupational mobility in the United States, Peter M. Blau and Otis D. Duncan, *The American Occupational Structure* (New York: Wiley, 1967), pp. 337–340, finds that married men rank somewhat higher in occupational achievement than bachelors, but the difference is a very modest one. The restriction of the 1910 and

1930 samples to married men probably thus imparted a slight upward bias to the results.

4. No attempt was made to trace persistence rates and career patterns for members of Laumann's sample. The survey included information about the occupations of both respondents and their fathers, which was used in the analysis of intergenerational mobility.

5. For a valuable review of the method, see Ian Winchester, "The Linkage of Historical Records by Man and Computer," *Journal of Interdisciplinary History,* 1 (Autumn 1970), 107–124. Advanced discussions of the difficulties may be found in the unpublished papers prepared for a Mathematical Social Science Board conference on Nominal Record Linkage held at the Institute for Advanced Study in Princeton, May 24–27, 1971.

6. See, for instance, those suggested in Sidney Goldstein, *Patterns of Mobility, 1910–1950: The Norristown Study* (Philadelphia: University of Pennsylvania Press, 1958), pp. 76–78.

7. E. R. Mowrer, "Family Disorganization and Mobility," *American Sociological Review,* 23 (1929), 134–145, follows a similar method. The author selected a sample of 1000 names from the Chicago telephone directory, discarding those not sufficiently distinctive to be traced and taking the following name instead.

8. I use the term "random" here to refer to a sample in which all members of a population have an equal chance of being included. In the narrower technical sense the samples were not random but systematic samples of lists of persons. The ordering of the list sampled for 1880 was residential; the census takers went from door to door, street to street, ward to ward. In the other samples the records were ordered alphabetically. A further technicality is that the 1880 sample was partly of individuals, partly of family clusters; all male members of a family were included when the name that appeared on the selected line of the census pages was that of a person who lived in a family rather than alone. The 1930 birth-certificate sample likewise was of clusters, in this case father-son pairs. This is not the purest possible sampling procedure. Biases may creep in, as Frederick Stephan and Philip McCarthy demonstrate in *Sampling Opinions: An Analysis of Survey Procedures* (New York: Wiley 1958), pp. 33–34. But it is close enough to a simple random sample for practical purposes, as the subsequent discussion of check factors should make plain, and was better suited to answering the questions I sought to explore than purer methods devised for contemporary survey research.

9. On errors in recent censuses, see the critical papers by J. S. Siegel, Leon Pritzker and N. D. Rothwell, and by Siegel and Melvin Zelnik in David M. Heer, ed., *Social Statistics and the City* (Cambridge, Mass.: Joint Center for Urban Studies, 1968). On the accuracy of nineteenth-century censuses, see Peter R. Knights, *The Plain People of Boston, 1830–1860: A Study in City Growth* (New York: Oxford University Press, 1971), Appendices B and C.

10. Note, in comparison, that in perhaps the most widely cited and im-

portant study yet made of occupational mobility in an American community, Natalie Rogoff's *Recent Trends in Occupational Mobility* (Glencoe, Ill.: Free Press, 1953), one of the two samples upon which the book rests had 8 percent more white-collar employees aged less than 24 than it should have had according to census check data.

11. F. A. Bushee, "Ethnic Factors in the Population of Boston," *Publications of the American Economic Association,* Third Series, 4 (May 1903), 44–51; Donald J. Bogue, *The Population of the United States* (Glencoe, Ill.: Free Press, 1950), p. 367.

12. S. M. Miller, "Comparative Social Mobility: A Trend Report and Bibliography," *Current Sociology,* 9 (1960); S. M. Lipset and Reinhard Bendix, *Social Mobility in Industrial Society* (Berkeley: University of California Press, 1959); Goldstein, *Patterns of Mobility;* Gerhard Lenski, *The Religious Factor: A Sociologist's Inquiry* (New York: Anchor, 1963).

13. For elaboration of this point, see the Appendix to Lenski, *The Religious Factor.*

14. Further information about the nature of the directories is provided in Peter R. Knights, "City Directories as Aids to Ante-Bellum Urban Studies," *Historical Methods Newsletter,* 2 (September 1969), 1–10, reprinted as Appendix A of *The Plain People of Boston.*

15. The sampling, tracing, and coding for the project were done by Harvard, Radcliffe, and Brandeis undergraduates. David Handlin drew the 1880, 1910, and 1930 samples and traced them through the directories. Michael Foley searched these samples through the Boston's Assessor's Valuation Books. The 1958 sample was gathered and traced by Norman Abrams. Some of the directory tracing was double checked and the original data cards were coded for punching by Donald Acklund, Margaret Beal, Suzanne Keaney, and Glenn Padnick. I checked the coding process for accuracy closely at the outset, and made further spot checks every few days thereafter.

16. Goldstein, *Patterns of Mobility,* 76–77.

17. The use of city directories by historians will doubtless be further stimulated by the massive project now being undertaken by Research Publications, Inc., of New Haven, in which all extant American directories published before 1860 and those for a large number of cities since 1860 are being reprinted on microfiche.

18. Michael B. Katz, "The People of a Canadian City: 1851–52," *Canadian Historical Review,* 52 (1972), pp. 402–426.

19. E. A. Wrigley, ed., *An Introduction to English Historical Demography* (London: Weidenfeld and Nicolson, 1966), pp. 160–161.

APPENDIX B. ON THE SOCIOECONOMIC RANKING OF OCCUPATIONS

1. Alba M. Edwards, "A Social Economic Grouping of the Gainful Workers of the United States," *Journal of the American Statistical Association,* 27 (1933), 377–387. For a valuable discussion of earlier attempts

in this direction and a critique of the scheme, see James Scoville, "The Development and Relevance of U. S. Occupational Data," *Industrial and Labor Relations Review,* 19 (1965), 71–79.

2. Thoughtful consideration has been given these issues in two recent essays: Michael B. Katz, "Occupational Classification in History," *Journal of Interdisciplinary History,* 3 (1972), 63–88, and Clyde Griffen, "The Study of Occupational Mobility in Nineteenth-century America: Problems and Possibilites," *Journal of Social History,* 5 (1972), 310–330. Also relevant is Stuart Blumin, "The Historical Study of Vertical Mobility," *Historical Methods Newsletter,* 1 (September 1968), 1–13, although I find the classification system recommended by Blumin highly unsatisfactory; see note 7 below.

3. See, in addition to the papers cited above, A. J. Reiss, Jr., *Occupations and Social Status* (Glencoe, Ill.: Free Press, 1961); Genevieve Knupfer, *Indices of Socio-Economic Status: A Study of Some Problems of Measurement* (New York: Columbia University Press, 1946); Peter M. Blau and Otis Dudley Duncan, *The American Occupational Structure* (New York: Wiley, 1967), chap. 4.

4. Alba M. Edwards, *Comparative Occupational Statistics for the United States, 1870 to 1940* (Washington, D. C.: U. S. Government Printing Office, 1943), p. 180.

5. It is reassuring that Duncan computed scores on a socioeconomic index (that employed in Table B.2, based on income and educational levels) for some 446 detailed occupational titles as well as for broad occupational groupings like those used in the present study, and found that although there was, of course, heterogeneity of rankings within the broad categories, "the major occupational group classification accounts for three-fourths of the variation in scores among detailed occupations"; see Blau and Duncan, *The American Occupational Structure,* p. 121, and the fuller discussion in Reiss, *Occupations and Social Status.*

6. The principal supports for the "convergence" thesis are to be found in C. Wright Mills, *White Collar: The American Middle Classes* (New York: Oxford University Press, 1951), and a key article by Robert K. Burns, "the Comparative Economic Position of Manual and White-Collar Employees," *Journal of Business,* 27 (1954), 257–267. There are two distinct issues here: (1) whether skilled workers are currently on about the same economic level as low white-collar employees; and (2) whether this represents a major shift from an earlier historical pattern. Mills is largely concerned with the first, although he makes assumptions about the historical question on the basis of impressionistic evidence; Burns deals directly with the second. My judgment on the first issue, which has been strongly influenced by Richard Hamilton's excellent paper, "The Income Difference Between Skilled and White Collar Workers," *British Journal of Sociology,* 14 (1963), 363–373, is advanced at this point in the text. I address the latter question and offer a critique of Burns below (note 11).

7. This is a serious objection to the occupational ranking scheme em-

ployed by Stuart Blumin in his study of Philadelphia, 1820–1860; "The Historical Study of Vertical Mobility," and "Mobility and Change in Ante-Bellum Philadelphia," in Stephan Thernstrom and Richard Sennett, eds., *Nineteenth-Century Cities: Essays in the New Urban History* (New Haven, Conn.: Yale University Press, 1969), pp. 165–208. Blumin put the occupations of his sample members in a rank order according to the mean wealth held by persons in that occupation reported in local tax records for 1820 and the federal census for 1860. Clerks and salesmen ranked very low by this measure—standing 39th and 41st, respectively on the list of 51 occupations—only a shade above domestic servants and far under most skilled artisans. But if Philadelphia's clerks and salesmen in this period were largely young men in the early stages of their careers, and if the city's artisans, after long years as apprentices and journeymen, were at the peak of their careers, this ranking system is of dubious validity. Even if one accepted wealth as the sole criterion of occupational status, and dismissed other dimensions of status—education, security of employment, social prestige, and the like—the appropriate measure of wealth must be a dynamic one that estimates probabilities of accumulating property over a full working life. Blumin does not, regrettably, supply age data from which such dynamic estimates could be made.

8. S. M. Miller and Pamela Roby, *The Future of Inequality* (New York: Basic Books, 1970), p. 56. For supporting data on occupational differentials in unemployment rates, see Donald J. Bogue, *The Population of the United States* (Glencoe, Ill.: Free Press, 1959), p. 642; U. S. Department of Labor, *Manpower Report of the President and a Report on Manpower Requirements, Resources, Utilization and Training* (Washington, D. C.: U. S. Government Printing Office, 1966); U. S. Department of Labor, *Employment and Earnings* (Washington, D. C.: U. S. Government Printing Office, 1967).

9. Blau and Duncan, *The American Occupational Structure,* p. 62.

10. As analyzed in Massachusetts Bureau of Statistics of Labor, *Fourteenth Annual Report* (Boston, 1883). The only distinction reported in the study was between "skilled mechanics" and "ordinary laborers," but the latter were mostly men who would be classified as semiskilled in the categories employed in the present study.

11. The best case that has been made for this view is in the Burns article cited in note 6, which argues that there has been "a long-term trend of decline in white-collar earnings relative to those of the manual group." In 1890, according to Burns, white-collar workers earned nearly twice as much as their blue-collar counterparts; by 1952, manual laborers were actually earning more, on the average, than nonmanual workers.

The evidence Burns presents in support of this dramatic conclusion, however, reveals no such profound shift. The article first presents a time series of annual earnings for blue-collar and white-collar workers, chiefly in *manufacturing,* from 1890 to 1928, a series that reveals almost no change at all; white-collar employees averaged 188 percent of the earnings of blue-collar workers in 1890, and 174 percent in 1928. Closely comparable figures for earnings in Boston manufacturing from 1900 to 1940, computed from mean annual wage and salary payments as reported in the census, reveal a similar pattern, with the ratio of white-collar to blue-collar earnings standing at 190 in 1900, 219 in 1910, 186 in 1920, 209 in 1930, and 223 in 1940. Both sets of data indicate no sharp long-term trend toward convergence during this half-century, but rather modest temporal fluctuations that seem closely related to the business cycle, with the relative position of blue-collar workers improving during prosperity and deteriorating in hard times.

Burns then presents another series for the period 1929 to 1952, a series that seems to indicate convergence but, regrettably, is not closely comparable with the preceding one. It includes a much wider range of white-collar and blue-collar occupations outside of manufacturing, which is of course desirable, but the shift makes comparison with the earlier manufacturing series difficult. The blue-collar–white-collar earnings differential seems to be much sharper in manufacturing than in other spheres of the economy, as may be seen by comparing the data in Table B.5 here with the time series on differentials in Boston manufacturing given above in this note. Second, the post-1928 data offered by Burns refer to weekly earnings rather than annual earnings, and hence are not adjusted for differential unemployment; Burns himself presents evidence demonstrating the continued greater vulnerability of manual workmen to unemployment in the period. A third problem is that figures include women, whose proportion in the labor force rose steadily in the period and who were disproportionately concentrated in low-paying clerical jobs. By 1950 nearly half of all the white-collar employees included in Burns's figures were women, whose generally lower earnings pulled the white-collar average down considerably. Any effort to assess the relative economic status of male white-collar and blue-collar workers would have to separate out women workers, which Burns fails to do.

The resultant lack of comparability between the two series offered by Burns is glaringly evident from the fact that the ratio of white-collar to blue-collar earnings in the last observation from the first series, for 1928, was 174, whereas the ratio according to the first observation in the new series, for just a year later, was only 128. If, therefore, the first series had been constructed with precisely comparable evidence going back to 1890, the estimated ratio of white-collar to blue-collar earnings in the late nineteenth century would have been far lower than that given in Burns's first series.

The post-1928 data offered by Burns do indeed suggest that some convergence in differentials may have taken place between 1929 and 1952, but the change was far less dramatic than hasty comparison with the 1890–1928 series would indicate. Furthermore, it is not clear how much of the modest convergence that did take place in the weekly earnings of males and females lumped together and uncorrected for differential unemployment reflected actual shifts in the *annual* earnings of *male* blue-collar and white-collar workers. A final difficulty is that the only years from the entire 1929–1952 period that saw dramatically greater gains for manual than for nonmanual employees were 1939 to 1944, the war years, with remarkably tight labor-market conditions, and it seems unwise to draw sweeping conclusions about the long-term blurring of class lines in the United States on the basis of that special historical experience.

It is possible, in sum, that there has been some shrinking of "traditional" white-collar–blue-collar wage differentials in the United States in recent decades, but it is far from clear from the evidence that has been brought to bear upon the question so far. What has been assumed to have been the "traditional" differential was probably not nearly so wide as has been thought, and the available data on recent differentials have not been properly controlled for age and sex differences.

index

Index

Index

HARVARD STUDIES IN URBAN HISTORY

The City in the Ancient World, by Mason Hammond, assisted by Lester J. Bartson, 1972

Town into City: Springfield, Massachusetts, and the Meaning of Community, 1840–1880, by Michael H. Frisch, 1972

The Other Bostonians: Poverty and Progress in the American Metropolis, 1880–1970, by Stephan Thernstrom, 1973

Urban Growth and the Circulation of Information: The United States System of Cities, 1790–1840, by Allan R. Pred, 1973

PUBLICATIONS OF THE JOINT CENTER FOR URBAN STUDIES

The Joint Center for Urban Studies, a cooperative venture of the Massachusetts Institute of Technology and Harvard University, was founded in 1959 to organize and encourage research on urban and regional problems. Participants have included scholars from the fields of anthropology, architecture, business, city planning, economics, education, engineering, history, law, philosophy, political science, and sociology.

The findings and conclusions of this book are, as with all Joint Center publications, solely the responsibility of the author.

Published by Harvard University Press

The Intellectual versus the City: From Thomas Jefferson to Frank Lloyd Wright, by Morton and Lucia White, 1962.

Streetcar Suburbs: The Process of Growth in Boston, 1870–1900, by Sam B. Warner, Jr., 1962

City Politics, by Edward C. Banfield and James Q. Wilson, 1963

Law and Land: Anglo-American Planning Practice, edited by Charles M. Haar, 1964

Location and Land Use: Toward a General Theory of Land Rent, by William Alonso, 1964

Poverty and Progress: Social Mobility in a Nineteenth Century City, by Stephan Thernstrom, 1964

Boston: The Job Ahead, by Martin Meyerson and Edward C. Banfield, 1966

The Myth and Reality of Our Urban Problems, by Raymond Vernon, 1966

Muslim Cities in the Later Middle Ages, by Ira Marvin Lapidus, 1967

The Fragmented Metropolis: Los Angeles, 1850–1930, by Robert M. Fogelson, 1967

Law and Equal Opportunity: A Study of the Massachusetts Commission against Discrimination, by Leon H. Mayhew, 1968

Varieties of Police Behavior: The Management of Law and Order in Eight Communities, by James Q. Wilson, 1968

The Metropolitan Enigma: Inquiries into the Nature and Dimensions of America's "Urban Crisis," edited by James Q. Wilson, revised edition, 1968

Traffic and the Police: Variations in Law-Enforcement Policy, by John A. Gardiner, 1969

The Influence of Federal Grants: Public Assistance in Massachusetts, by Martha Derthick, 1970

The Arts in Boston, by Bernard Taper, 1970

Families against the City: Middle Class Homes of Industrial Chicago, 1872–1890, by Richard Sennett, 1970

The Political Economy of Urban Schools, by Martin T. Katzman, 1971

Origins of the Urban School: Public Education in Massachusetts, 1870–1915, by Marvin Lazerson, 1971

The Other Bostonians: Poverty and Progress in the American Metropolis, 1880–1970, by Stephan Thernstrom, 1973

Published by The M.I.T. Press

The Image of the City, by Kevin Lynch, 1960

Housing and Economic Progress: A Study of the Housing Experiences of Boston's Middle-Income Families, by Lloyd Rodwin, 1971

The Historian and the City, edited by Oscar Handlin and John Burchard, 1963

The Federal Bulldozer: A Critical Analysis of Urban Renewal, 1949–1962, by Martin Anderson, 1964

The Future of Old Neighborhoods: Rebuilding for a Changing Population, by Bernard J. Frieden, 1964

Man's Struggle for Shelter in an Urbanizing World, by Charles Abrams, 1964

The View from the Road, by Donald Appleyard, Kevin Lynch, and John R. Myer, 1964

The Public Library and the City, edited by Ralph W. Conant, 1965

Regional Development Policy: A Case Study of Venezuela, by John Friedmann, 1966

Urban Renewal: The Record and the Controversy, edited by James Q. Wilson, 1966

Transport Technology for Developing Regions, by Richard M. Soberman, 1966

Computer Methods in the Analysis of Large-Scale Social Systems, edited by James M. Beshers, revised edition, 1968

Planning Urban Growth and Regional Development: The Experience of the Guayana Program of Venezuela, by Lloyd Rodwin and Associates, 1969

Build a Mill, Build a City, Build a School: Industrialization, Urbaniza-

tion, and Education in Ciudad Guayana, by Noel F. McGinn and Russell G. Davis, 1969

Land-Use Controls in the United States, by John Delafons, second edition, 1969

Beyond the Melting Pot: The Negroes, Puerto Ricans, Jews, Italians, and Irish of New York City, by Nathan Glazer and Daniel Patrick Moynihan, second edition, 1970

Bargaining: Monopoly Power versus Union Power, by George de Menil, 1971

The Joint Center also publishes monographs and reports.